Religions of Atlanta

AAR

American Academy of Religion

The Religions

Editor

Paul B. Courtright

Number 1

RELIGIONS OF ATLANTA

Religious Diversity in the Centennial Olympic City

edited by

Gary Laderman

Religions of Atlanta

Religious Diversity in the Centennial Olympic City

edited by
Gary Laderman

Scholars Press
Atlanta, Georgia

Religions of Atlanta

Religious Diversity in the Centennial Olympic City

edited by
Gary Laderman

Library of Congress Cataloging in Publication Data
Religions of Atlanta : religious diversity in the centennial Olympic city / [edited] by Gary Laderman.
p. cm. — (The religions ; no. 1)
Includes bibliographical references.
ISBN 0-7885-0250-6 (pbk. : alk. paper)
1. Christianity—Georgia—Atlanta Metropolitan Area. 2. Religious pluralism—Georgia—Atlanta Metropolitan Area. 3. Atlanta Metropolitan Area (Ga.)—Religion. I. Laderman, Gary, 1962– . II. Series.
BR560.A84R45 1996
277.58'231—dc20 96-10809
CIP

Printed in the United States of America
on acid-free paper

In Memory of John Fenton

TABLE OF CONTENTS

PART II: VARIETIES OF CHRISTIAN BELIEF AND PRACTICE

PART III: RELIGIOUS DIVERSITY IN THE NEW METROPOLIS

ACKNOWLEDGMENTS

This book could not have been produced without the support, advice, and assistance of a number of people. Elizabeth Hardcastle, Louis A. Ruprecht, Jr., Nancy Eiesland, and Joyce Flueckiger were instrumental to the process, though each contributed in distinctive ways and at different stages of the project. All of my colleagues in the Department of Religion helped along the way, either by providing much appreciated encouragement or by reading some of the essays. I am genuinely grateful to Michael Berger, Leila Berner, Gene Bianchi, David Blumenthal, Martin Buss, Paul Courtright, Barbara DeConcini, Wendy Farley, Joyce Flueckiger, Deborah Lipstadt, Bobbi Patterson, Vernon Robbins, and Thee Smith. The book is dedicated to John Fenton, our colleague who died in January, 1996. As a pioneer scholar in the study of local religious communities, his guidance and confidence were especially important to me.

There are many other individuals in the Emory community who I would like to thank. Most importantly, Toni Avery, Brook Eberline, Yolanda Manora, Pescha Penso, and Lyn Schechtel, all staff members in the Department of Religion office, provided crucial assistance (and comic relief) during the production of this book. I am also grateful to Tom Frank, E. Brooks Holifield, Steve Tipton, Dana White, Gordon Newby, Rudolph Byrd, and Steve Hochman. Sue Thompson helped with editing, and Amy Allman did research for the introduction and the Islam essay. Thanks also to Nancy Ammerman, Janice Morrill of the Atlanta History Center, Gayle White of the *Atlanta Journal and Constitution*, Debra Duchon of the Center for Applied Research in Anthropology, Georgia State University, and Jane Levy of the Jewish Federation. Special thanks go to Charles Barton, whose encouragement and support made this book possible.

SERIES EDITOR'S PREFACE

The **Religions** series was inaugurated in 1994 by the American Academy of Religion to make significant research on the religious traditions of the world available to the scholarly community and general readers. Scholarly monographs, symposia on themes and interpretative issues that enable comparative analysis, and books especially designed to include readers beyond the community of scholars in academia will bring the impact of religion in the modern world to light. The religious traditions now practiced in the United States, Canada, Western Europe, and Australia include many of the religious practices that were once thought to exist only in distant parts of the world. Contemporary migrations of people from societies that a generation ago would have been perceived in the West as "primitive," or "uncivilized" or "third world" are now neighbors, business associates, clients, customers, and parents of children in public schools.

Religions of Atlanta is the first of what we hope will be many studies that can help inform people of the complexity of the religious landscape within their communities. It is our further hope that studies like the present one, written for a wide variety of readers, will both teach us more about who we are becoming as a society and culture, and serve as an invitation to pursue conversation and understanding within and between religious communities.

We wish to thank all the good and hospitable people of Atlanta who opened their doors to our researchers and authors, whose challenge it was to describe, explain, and help us better appreciate the distinctiveness of the many religious traditions that are being practiced in Atlanta on the eve of the centennial Olympic Games. While the Olympics are an opportunity to demonstrate international unity and global awareness, the growing diversity of religions from around the world on our streets and in our neighborhoods requires us to accept a significant characteristic of society at the end of the twentieth century: the global scene is a part of the local scene, and religions that exist around the world also exist in our own backyard. This book, and others like it, can help us to get to know our neighbors better.

Paul B. Courtright, Editor
Atlanta, March, 1996

FOREWORD

Jimmy Carter

During my boyhood in Sumter County, Georgia, nearly everyone I knew was either a Baptist or a Methodist. If I had lived in Atlanta, I would have been exposed to more religious variety, but the state capital was not much different from my part of the state. Protestants predominated. Only small Jewish and Catholic communities existed.

Unlike other parts of the country, the South had not been a major destination for recent immigrants. Therefore, almost everyone followed American religious traditions. To be sure, African Americans had founded their own separate churches after the Civil War, but Christian beliefs drew blacks and whites together across the color line.

Today, the face of religious Atlanta has changed remarkably. I am grateful to the Department of Religion of Emory University for initiating this study of the diverse religious communities that make up what now is a very cosmopolitan city. Atlanta's growth and prosperity have attracted people of ethnic and religious backgrounds that are new to this region. Immigrants from Latin America, Asia, and Africa have contributed to the religious mix. This has created new challenges for us, because even shared religious beliefs sometimes can be overwhelmed by prejudice.

I believe, however, that difference is a strength. Atlanta's commitment to religious freedom and religious pluralism has helped create a climate in which the city has become a leader for global communications, health, sports, business, and humanitarian nonprofit organizations. We must continue to foster understanding within our own community so that we may build better harmony in the global community.

INTRODUCTION

Gary Laderman

Atlanta in 1864. Courtesy of the Atlanta History Center.

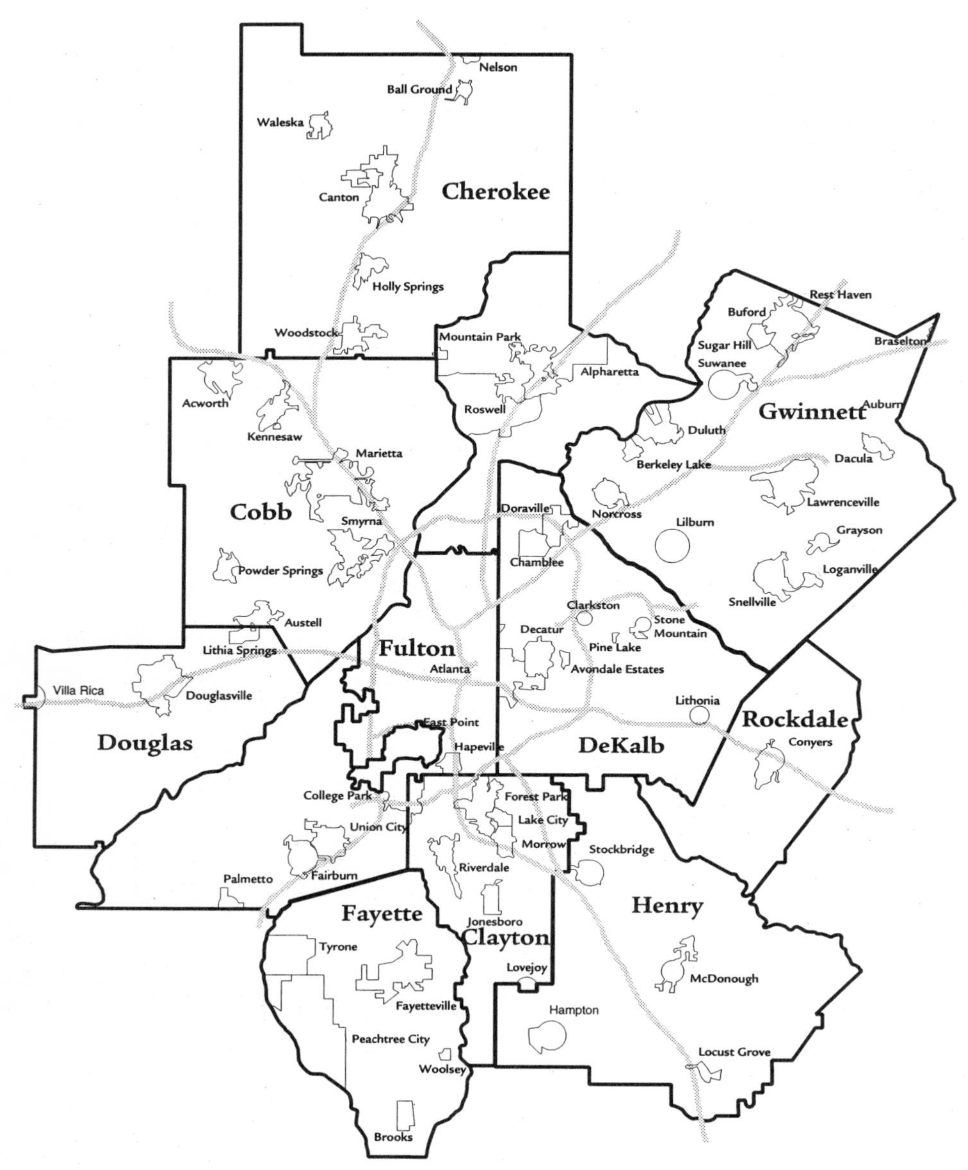

Atlanta Region map. Source: Atlanta Regional Commission.

Soon after Atlanta first came into existence in the 1830s as a railroad terminus, one building served as the meeting space for different Protestant congregations in the area. Now, over a century and a half later, travel north, south, east, or west through metropolitan Atlanta and you will find multiple forms of religious life on almost every street. Homes, churches, synagogues, mosques, community centers, strip malls, office parks, sports arenas, and other venues are used as locations for religious instruction and an assortment of religious practices. In addition, advertisements informing Atlantans of opportunities for religious insight and discovery can be found on bumper stickers, billboards, bulletin boards, business cards, marquees, posters, cable television, the internet, and in local newspapers.

The number of choices available to religious consumers and the range of interests driving Atlanta's spiritual marketplace reflect a new social reality that has not traditionally been associated with this southern city's history: religious diversity. From its early years as a transportation hub in the heart of Dixie before the Civil War, to "the city too busy to hate" in the turbulent 1960s, public declarations of religious faith were generally limited to members of Protestant congregations; the religious pluralism that characterized many urban areas in other parts of the country during these years simply did not develop here. Catholics and Jews were able to establish small religious communities over the course of this history, but not many others. Atlanta's religious culture, like most of the South's, was dominated by various Protestant forms of expression.

Unfortunately, it was also dominated by religious and racial hatreds for much of its early history. The very ground on which city development spread in the mid-nineteenth century had been taken from Native Americans who lived in the region, and who were considered to be less-than-human savages and dangerous heathen by Christian settlers. Cherokees, Creeks, and other indigenous groups in the area were perceived as a serious threat by these early settlers, who did not understand the cultural practices and spiritual principles motivating their behavior. The settlers' voracious appetite for land, and their willingness to take whatever measures were necessary to acquire more of it, gradually led in 1835 to the forced relocation of most Indians in the southeast beyond the Mississippi River. European Protestants from such places as England, Scotland, and Ireland—who came to the "New World" to escape religious persecution—would not tolerate people who looked and acted differently, and who did not appreciate such sacred notions as private property, written laws, and the divinity of Jesus Christ.

For black slaves who came through Atlanta and the surrounding area before the Civil War, conversion to Christianity might have mitigated their circumstances, but it was not enough to ensure just and humane treatment. While many slaves retained vestiges and fragments of African religious systems, whites made sure that Christianity was the only viable religious option available to them. Indeed, one of the consequences of slavery was, in the words of historian Jon Butler, an "African spiritual holocaust." The instances of violence directed toward blacks, in the form of whippings, lynchings, and even murder, reflected the virulent racism prevalent throughout the South that was based on economic interests, political power, and religious attitudes. As long as the institution of slavery continued in the southern states, and as long as racist attitudes permeated a significant portion of the white population, Atlanta would remain inhospitable to blacks, whether they professed Christianity or not.

Evangelical Baptists, Methodists, and Presbyterians played a crucial role in shaping Atlanta's religious culture from its early years in the mid-1800s. But while congregants were preoccupied with social order, racial boundaries, and personal salvation, many in the young city had other concerns as well, primarily related to economic growth. After the railroad terminus became "Marthasville" in 1843, named in honor of Georgia governor Wilson Lumpkin's daughter, and then "Atlanta" in 1847, signaling the city's position as a gateway to the Atlantic, it soon became an important financial and transportation center in the South. More than anything else, the businesses that grew around the railroad depot fueled the city's expansion. As urban historian Dana White remarks, "Commerce is the city's sole reason for being."

During the Civil War, the population of Atlanta swelled to 20,000—close to doubling its prewar numbers. It served as a vital resource and supply center for the Confederacy throughout the conflict, and many realized that if Union forces captured the city, a terrible blow would be struck to the southern war effort. Union General William T. Sherman understood the city's strategic and economic importance, and during the summer of 1864 he set out not only to capture it, but to destroy it as well. The campaign for Atlanta ended September 1, 1864, with Confederate General John B. Hood and his men demolishing anything of military value before evacuating the city. After Sherman took control of Atlanta, he made two ruthless, but militarily crucial decisions: all the civilians were ordered to leave, and all the buildings were to be burned to the ground. (This event later became immortalized as the historical backdrop for Margaret Mitchell's famous novel, *Gone with the Wind*.)

But before Sherman and his men torched the buildings, federal authorities were convinced by a local Catholic leader to spare some of the city's religious houses of worship. Father Thomas O'Reilly, pastor of the Church of the Immaculate Conception, ministered to southern and northern soldiers in Atlanta and commanded a great deal of respect from both sides. His arguments ultimately saved his church and other structures in the immediate vicinity from destruction, including Central Presbyterian, Second Baptist, Trinity Methodist, and St. Philip's Episcopal. In a report to the governor after Sherman and his men left, General Howard described how many Catholics in the Union army made sure no one threatened O'Reilly's church or the surrounding buildings. The report reads, in part: "As a proof of their attachment to their Church and love for Father O'Reilly, a soldier who attempted to fire Col. Calhoun's house . . . , the burning of which would have endangered the whole block, was shot and killed, and his grave now marked. So to Father O'Reilly the country is indebted for the protection of the City Hall, Churches, etc."

Despite the conflagration that left Atlanta in ruins after Sherman's departure, when people began returning to the city they immediately had numerous opportunities for religious worship in the churches that were still standing. Within a decade those churches that had been damaged were restored, and new ones were built to accommodate the growing Protestant congregations in the area. As the city began to rebuild itself during Reconstruction, with northern politics and business interests playing a significant role in this process, many religious leaders advocated a system of values that would contribute to moral uplift, communal regeneration, and perhaps most importantly for the future, economic prosperity. These values, so familiar to Protestants throughout the nation, included self-discipline, hard work, charity, education, and frugality.

Atlanta soon came to represent the progressive and enterprising spirit of the New South. The image that best conveyed this spirit, and captured the hopes and dreams of boosters intent on transforming what was once a desolate southern landscape into a thriving urban center, was the Phoenix rising from the ashes. In fact, the image received formal sanction from local leaders who placed it on the official seal of Atlanta. As Atlanta historian Franklin M. Garrett writes, "Just 23 years after the city was conquered and burned . . . the seal tells, with a single emblem, the story of a resurrected city, rebuilt by dauntless citizens who refused to accept defeat and determined to make their city greater and more beautiful than before."

By the turn of the twentieth century, Atlanta's population had grown to over 70,000. Its position as a major commercial and industrial city in the South was secured partially because of the success of the International Cotton Exposition of 1881, which inspired confidence in local and northern business leaders and encouraged investors to seize the financial opportunities Atlanta's boosters promoted so vigorously. While a number of Atlanta's leading businessmen either were from the North or had ties to northern capital, the majority of people migrating into the city were from surrounding rural areas. This migration not only provided capitalists with a necessary labor force, but it also ensured that conservative Protestantism would remain the dominant religious ethos well into the twentieth century.

Conservative Protestants did not, however, constitute the only religious community in Atlanta at the turn of the century. Liberal Protestant, Catholic, Orthodox, and other non-Christian groups were establishing a presence here or expanding communities that already existed during the first half of the century. One of the more prominent examples of expansion by a non-Christian religious population was in the Jewish community. This community had been in the area from before the Civil War and, in the early part of the twentieth century, initiated a number of new organizations, including the Federation of Jewish Charities, the Jewish Educational Alliance, and the Jewish Welfare Fund. In spite of the horrors associated with the vicious lynching of Leo Frank, who was accused of murdering a young factory girl, and widespread evidence of anti-Semitism, Jews in Atlanta not only persevered, they triumphed as a minority culture with social, economic, and political successes.

In addition to the Jews and the increasingly diverse white Christian groups, blacks who had migrated in large numbers after the war began to build their own distinctive Protestant communities in Atlanta. This was not an easy task, however, because although they were now free, racial prejudice and the threat of violence continued to plague them. Segregationist policies that legitimated unequal treatment and persistent discrimination ensured that most African Americans would have only limited economic opportunities; hateful whites who resorted to acts of brutality—during four days of rioting in 1906, for example, or, more commonly throughout the first half of the century, while hidden beneath white robes—reminded blacks of the lengths some white Southerners would go to maintain the existing power structure. Yet, over time, the African-American community solidified, leading to the creation of their own commercial district east of downtown on Auburn Avenue. "Sweet Auburn," as it was called by the early decades of the century, became the social and cultural heart of black Atlanta.

While economic self-sufficiency and educational advancement were two motivating factors driving many in the community, religion was also a critical source of inspiration and vitality. Wheat Street Baptist, Big Bethel AME, Ebenezer Baptist—all on Auburn Avenue—provided political, economic and spiritual leadership during both good and bad times. (There were, of course, other important churches in the surrounding area as well, such as First Congregational and Friendship Baptist.) It was in this environment of strong black leadership that the young Martin Luther King, Jr. grew up and matured. Calls for justice, equality, and deliverance rang out from pulpits in these churches, but most of Atlanta's non-black residents paid little attention. Although there were attempts made by portions of the white community to improve relations with African Americans, it would take the Civil Rights movement of the 1960s—led by Atlanta's own Dr. King—to bring different religious groups together in a significant way. In this decade Atlanta was fortunate to have progressive leadership in the white political and religious power structures—Jews and Christians worked effectively with emerging black leaders in ways that spared Atlanta much of the racial hatred and bitterness that characterized many other southern urban areas.

From the 1960s on, religious communities in Atlanta became more and more diverse. The reasons for this diversification are numerous, but include increased attention to, and experimentation with, alternative religious systems outside of Judaism and Christianity; substantial economic growth that attracted job-seekers from around the nation; and a surge in the number of immigrants from other countries who made Atlanta their new home. Many leaders in the Atlanta area also projected an image of the city as being "too busy to hate," which contributed to the promotion of such civic values as goodwill and toleration among the various religious communities in the city. These values, along with others that encouraged religious freedom, would serve as an important source of cohesion in metropolitan Atlanta—a region that grew in population from over 1 million in 1960 to close to 3 million in 1990.

In its current incarnation as the centennial Olympic city, and with the reputation it has garnered for itself recently, the conservatism associated with the homogeneity of Atlanta's religious culture in the past has been supplanted by the celebration of the multiple, and increasingly public, religious identities of the present. The religious life of a community, however, is not completely represented by its identifiable public demonstrations and announcements; religious sensibilities are expressed through all kinds of actions, thoughts, and feelings, seen and unseen, that are at work throughout the Atlanta area. Witchcraft in the suburbs, food distribution on urban city streets, periodic visitations from the Virgin, massage therapy in a business office, a personal altar in the home—like most cosmopolitan regions of the United States since the 1960s, the religious landscape in Atlanta has become populated with a wide assortment of traditions, movements, and teachings. Indeed, Atlanta, in many respects, has emerged as a microcosm of the religious transformations taking place across the entire United States.

One of the slogans used to advertise the 1996 Olympics exclaimed: "The world is coming to Atlanta!" In many ways, the "world" has already arrived; the growing number of religious assemblies in Atlanta constitute our own global community. Roman Catholic parishes with Hispanic, Filipino, and Vietnamese leadership and laity are thriving. Mosques and Islamic centers with Pakistani, Arab, Persian, Turkish, African, and Malaysian members are becoming a significant presence. Reform, Conservative, and Orthodox synagogues continue to support the diverse Jewish population. Orthodox Christians from Eastern Europe have built churches to meet the needs of their growing congregations. Caribbean traditions are finding a place in the metro area for communal activities. Additionally, Buddhist, Hindu, and other eastern religions represent integral facets of the religious and cultural pluralism that is transforming Atlanta.

Each of the religious communities in the metro area provides its members with a sense of orientation, identity, meaning, and history. Each attends to the spiritual, as well as practical, needs of citizens and contributes to the rich texture of Atlanta's social tapestry. Perhaps most importantly for the entire region, many of these communities also provide their adherents with a way to act on their faith and work to improve the one characteristic they all share: their local context. While some religious groups administer programs that rely on members' involvement, others operate in a spirit of cooperation with various religious bodies outside their own tradition. Like Miami, Dallas, and other metropolitan regions in the southern United States, Atlanta's multicultural, multiethnic composition requires that people with different religions live and work together with toleration, understanding, and respect.

The following chapters capture the broadening and diversifying religious landscape of the Atlanta region. Although it is certainly not an exhaustive survey, this collection does contain profiles of some of the major religious communities that inhabit this landscape. Many of them bring to light religious traditions and forms of religious expression not discussed in this short historical overview, while others expand on stories that were only briefly mentioned. Some authors who contributed essays went out into various communities and talked to leaders and lay people, asking questions, recording anecdotes, and making observations; others relied on textual materials that illuminate distinctive traits and experiences which bear on a given community. Instead of providing readers with authoritative accounts of each community, the contributors explore some of the concerns, commitments, and motivations operating in segments of these religious groups. Each profile also highlights various dimensions of religious life, focusing on such topics as local history, organizational development, theology, social ethics, and personal spirituality.

Religion is a critical dimension of social life in the United States, and maybe one of the most understudied. Although there are numerous scholarly works that explore the history and teachings of the world's religions, only recently attention has shifted to the "lived" experiences of believers in particular cultural contexts. In the American context, where religious liberty is supposed to be a fundamental right for all citizens, the plurality of religions and the multiplicity of spiritual paths contribute to a vast range of expressions and practices that constitute religious life. In addition, the cultural and social characteristics of various regions in the United States have an impact on many of these expressions and practices—religious communities in California may look and act differently from those in New Hampshire; the kinds of religions available in Ohio may be slightly different from those in Georgia. The goals of this book are to give the reader a glimpse into the religious life of various communities in Atlanta and inspire her or him to learn more about the topography of America's religious landscape.

FOR FURTHER INFORMATION

AIA Guide to the Architecture of Atlanta. Foreword by Dana White. Athens, University of Georgia Press, 1993

W. Fitzhugh Brundage. *Lynching in the New South: Georgia and Virginia, 1880-1930.* Urbana, University of Illinois Press, 1993

Jon Butler. *Awash in a Sea of Faith: Christianizing the American People.* Cambridge, Harvard University Press, 1990

Don H. Doyle. *New Men, New Cities, New South: Atlanta, Charleston, Mobile, 1860-1910.* Chapel Hill, University of North Carolina Press, 1990

Franklin M. Garrett. *Atlanta and Environs: A Chronicle of Its People and Events.* 3 vols. Athens, University of Georgia Press, 1969

Webb Garrison. *The Legacy of Atlanta.* Atlanta, Peachtree, 1987

Clifford M. Kuhn, Harlon E. Joyce, and E. Bernard West. *Living Atlanta: An Oral History of the City, 1914-1948.* Athens, University of Georgia Press, 1990

Charles Reagan Wilson, ed. *Religion in the South.* Athens, University of Georgia Press, 1985

PART I:

RELIGIOUS COMMUNITIES WITH DEEP ROOTS IN THE ATLANTA METROPOLITAN AREA

CHAPTER ONE

MAINLINE PROTESTANTISM IN ATLANTA

Barbara A. B. Patterson and Nancy L. Eiesland

Cathedral of St. Philip. Photograph by Elizabeth Hardcastle.

As Marthasville became the young city of Atlanta, mainline Protestant traditions of Christianity positioned themselves to be important players in the cultural and moral formation of the region. Methodist, Presbyterian, Episcopalian, United Church of Christ, and Lutheran churches were founded in Atlanta in the mid-1800s. These predominantly white denominations expected to have a formative role to play in the life of the New South.

While the congregations of each denomination proclaimed their specific theologies, distinguishing rituals, and particular traditions, they, in fact, held significant points in common. Some of these early similarities no longer exist, but others related to the changing economic, cultural, and political contexts of metro Atlanta continue to unite them. Even today, for example, the Peachtree Corridor Association and the Midtown Assistance Center, two socially active groups that bring together religious congregations and businesses, reflect these shared interests and interdependencies.

These bonds began as white Methodists, Presbyterians, Episcopalians, and Baptists—among others—shared their first worship spaces. Beginning with ecumenical gatherings in a small wooden house near the center of the city, these groups moved toward independent congregations as their denominational support and the interests of city dwellers increased. Many of the initial members of these congregations were business, political, and educational leaders of the city. Even as young, independent congregations, these churches drew some of the finest preachers and pastors in the nation. Members continue to consider their pastors as significant players in the economic and political leadership of Atlanta. These churches conceived their missions with civic determination and moral concern. They have also contributed to the arts not only through their famed architecture and stained glass windows, but also through their choirs, theaters, and dance groups.

With large fellowship halls, many mainline Protestant congregations have been able to provide social activities for all ages as well as centers for feeding and sheltering the homeless, sick, and mentally ill. Even when their memberships moved farther from the city, these churches often continued their ministry, adjusting to the changing times, ethnic shifts, and economic transitions that had an impact on the area. They began specialized ministries of education, advocacy, training, and justice often in partnership with that segment of the business community concerned with maintaining the vitality of the city. They emerged and continue to function as an ecumenical Christian and interfaith source of Atlanta's development, rising ever anew like the Phoenix, symbol of the city of Atlanta and of the seal of downtown's All Saints Episcopal Church.

METHODISTS

Georgia has a special place in American Methodist history. In 1735, John Wesley came to Georgia as an Anglican missionary. On the ship to Savannah he met some German Moravians, whose simple evangelical piety greatly impressed him. He continued to associate with them while in Georgia and translated some of their hymns into English. This association was what eventually led to Wesley's renewal movement, called Methodism.

As the South's second-largest denomination, Methodists have played a major role in the region's self-definition. One example of their influence relates to the dividing line of race in the South that created a schism within Methodism. In 1844, the Methodist Episcopal Church, South, was formed by supporters of slavery when the General Conference became deadlocked over the issue. After the Civil War, two black Methodist denominations and the Methodist Episcopal Church (both northern institutions) tried to proselytize the black congregations within the Methodist Episcopal Church, South, which in response encouraged and authorized its black members to form the Colored Methodist Episcopal Church, now known as the Christian Methodist Episcopal Church. Although there has been fragmentation within the Methodist Church, three of the major Methodist bodies in the United States, namely, the Methodist Episcopal Church, the Methodist Protestant Church, and the Methodist Episcopal Church, South, united in 1939 to form the Methodist Church. In 1968, other mergers created the United Methodist Church.

The strong prohibitionist stand of the Methodists has also shaped the region's culture. While opposition to the consumption of alcohol was especially dominant in the past, there are still several "teetotally" dry Georgia counties and numerous others that prohibit distilled spirits. This demonstrates the continuing role many Methodists play in prohibiting the consumption of alcoholic beverages. Even DeKalb County proscribed the sale of liquor until the 1970s. In 1983, Georgia Governor Joe Frank Harris, an active lay Methodist, received strong support for his decision to have a "dry" inaugural ball.

Methodists have also been instrumental in establishing important cultural, educational, and social institutions in Atlanta. A Methodist bishop, Asa G. Candler, founded Emory University, one of the southeast's, and increasingly one of the nation's, leading educational institutions. Methodists also established two theological institutions in Atlanta, Candler School of Theology and Gammon Theological Seminary (now part of the Interdenominational Theological Center). Methodist organizations and churches dot Atlanta's landscape; this religious community provided early leadership to the nascent city and adapted to the city's changes both in the center city and on its suburban periphery. Today, the Methodist church continues to play a significant role in the religious and civic life of metro Atlanta.

FIRST UNITED METHODIST CHURCH

Methodists were the first to erect a sanctuary in Atlanta. The forerunner to First United Methodist Church (UMC), Wesley Chapel, was founded in 1847. The membership rolls of Wesley Chapel contain many of the young city's early leaders and builders. An early account of this congregation's history celebrates those beginnings:

> Methodists were astir in the little railroad village of Marthasville, terminus for four rail lines then under construction. Small groups met in private homes, in warehouses on Peachtree Street and Auburn Avenue, and even in the Georgia railroad offices where worship services were conducted and future plans discussed by dedicated, visionary citizens.

The congregation's frame building, constructed on Peachtree, had many of the typical architectural features of southern churches, including separate entrances for men and women and a rear gallery for slaves. Members were particularly proud of the bell tower and bell, which have survived to this day. With the onset of the Civil War, many congregations donated their bells to be melted down for cannons. However, Atlanta citizens believed that one bell should be retained. Since Wesley Chapel's bell was located in the geographic center of the city and could be heard throughout the one-mile radius of the city limits, it was saved and used to call people of all denominations to worship and for civic gatherings, to call slaves from the fields, to summon soldiers to attention, to warn of fire, riot, and eventually the approach of the Union army. The bell, which congregants identify as one of Atlanta's most important relics, has relocated with the congregation through several temporary sites to its present location at 360 Peachtree Street.

First United Methodist Church of Atlanta. Photograph by Elizabeth Hardcastle.

The church survived the Civil War intact, despite receiving regular battering from cannon fire that was directed toward the Union Depot but which often fell short, seriously damaging the church building. One commentator spoke about the church's situation at war's end, noting that it looked "more like a pig sty than a place of worship." In addition to the devastation during the Civil War, the congregation has experienced several other periods of dramatic decline. The first period of decline coincided with the Great Depression of the 1930s when the congregation's leadership suffered extensive economic losses.

The church is currently in another decline, with difficult times beginning in the 1980s as the aging congregation became increasingly troubled by the inner-city crime in the church's area. The congregation was especially broken-hearted when several stained glass windows were smashed one Christmas Day. For First UMC congregants, the windows were a tangible reminder of their history in Atlanta. Given as memorials to former clergymen and lay leaders, the windows spoke of the congregation's rich legacy of community service. One set of windows was dedicated to Henry W. Grady, who was editor of the *Atlanta Constitution* and a champion of the South during Reconstruction after the Civil War. Following the destruction of the windows, the congregation placed plexiglass over the outside of the stained glass. Now one must enter the church to appreciate their beauty.

Increasingly, First UMC leaders speak about leaving the downtown area to relocate nearer church members. As one congregational leader said, "One time this was a terrific location, but now nobody lives in the community. People don't want to come down here at night. They are uneasy about parking. But we feel a real ambivalence when we talk about leaving." While the congregation debates the pros and cons of relocation, members continue to support mission activities in downtown Atlanta. The congregation cooperates with the Salvation Army, Atlanta Union Mission, and other agencies assisting the homeless. They have recently begun to provide space for Sheltering Arms, one of the oldest social service programs in Atlanta, which provides affordable child care and a support system for low-income families. Members at First UMC are justifiably proud of their status as the "Mother Church of Atlanta Methodism." It is the history, however, and not the future of the congregation that sustains them now.

CANDLER SCHOOL OF THEOLOGY

Wesley Chapel, and later First UMC, also provided the first temporary housing for the theological school that would become known as Candler School of Theology. In 1914, as Methodist leaders debated about a location for a theological school in the southeast, the Atlanta Chamber of Commerce pledged $500,000 to establish a university in Atlanta. Additionally, Asa G. Candler wrote to his brother, Bishop Warren A. Candler, about extending his full support for an Atlanta location:

> In my opinion, . . . the education which sharpens and strengthens the mental faculties without at the same time invigorating the moral powers and inspiring the religious life is a curse rather than a blessing to men. . . . To this end, as far as education can accomplish it, I offer to the Educational Commission of the Methodist Episcopal Church, South, charged by the General Conference with the duty of establishing an institution of university grade east of the Mississippi River the sum of one million dollars ($1,000,000) for the endowment of such an institu-

tion, the plans and methods of which are to be definitely directed to the advancement of sound learning and pure religion.

Half of Candler's million dollars was given for the endowment of the Candler School of Theology, founded by the Methodist Episcopal Church, South, in 1914, and later incorporated into Emory University when the university was chartered in 1915. The School of Theology occupied the first building on Emory's Atlanta campus.

Through the years, Candler School of Theology has trained generations of Methodist ministers who have served congregations throughout the southeast, the nation, and the world. The theology school offers programs leading to master of divinity, master of theological studies, and master of theology degrees. Its numerous faculty and students sponsor religious activities centered both at the school and in the community.

ST. MARK'S UNITED METHODIST CHURCH

The St. Mark's congregation was established as a mission outpost by First Methodist. It changed locations and names several times before settling into its current location at Peachtree and 5th Streets in 1902. St. Mark's motto as the "Methodist Church in the Heart of Midtown" reveals the congregation's intent to be a neighborhood church. As Midtown's fortunes have changed, so too have those of St. Mark's.

When St. Mark's UMC settled in on Peachtree, it took its place among many of the city's most fashionable residences, enjoying a time of prosperity and enthusiastic ministry. In 1924, when the Atlanta Biltmore Hotel opened at the corner of West Peachtree and 5th Streets, its owners—the Candler family—formed a close relationship with St. Mark's. By the 1950s, however, the change along the Peachtree corridor had dramatically affected the church. Many of the historic old homes were demolished and business establishments and high-rise apartment buildings took their place. As the congregation's members moved to the suburbs, St. Mark's entered a period of steady decline, losing members and falling into disrepair.

During the 1960s, the area around Peachtree and 10th became the hub of hippie activity in Atlanta. St. Mark's members recall with dismay the presence of long-haired young people who hung out in their vicinity. The congregation responded by establishing a ministry to "night people," focused on providing support for those individuals whose principle activities took place in the late night or early morning. Not surprisingly, many of the "night people" who were drawn to the ministry were prostitutes. Eventually, St. Mark's began a ministry directed explicitly toward young pregnant women and homeless mothers and children.

By the early 1980s, Midtown was undergoing another transformation as many of the old Victorian mansions that had become boarding houses were restored to their earlier glory. The restoration efforts were often led by young, professional, community-minded gay men and lesbians. In the late 80s, with a growing awareness of the AIDS crisis, gay and lesbian community organizing and Gay Pride efforts were often centered in Midtown. For St. Mark's, the city's first Gay Pride parade was a turning point. The congregation's pastor, Reverend Michael Cordle, and several congregants stood in front of the church, cheering those marching and providing drinks for them. Slowly gay and lesbian residents of Midtown found their way to St. Mark's. Now on a typical Sunday morning, the pews are filled with a mix of gay and lesbian couples, young families, and long-time members. The choir, which had dwindled, is now a treasured ministry of the congregation, traveling to numerous other Methodist churches for concerts. The finances of the congregation have also improved enough that restoration of the facility has begun. The pastor jokes that the congregation has a myriad of talented architects and interior designers. He quips, "sometimes I wish for a few members who had no opinion about aesthetics."

In addition, the church sponsors numerous AIDS ministries, including Care Teams that provide in-home care to people with AIDS who have become sick, an AIDS Awareness Group that provides support to persons living with AIDS, their partners, and extended families, and Common Ground, a day program for people living with AIDS. The congregation also sponsors Genesis, a support group for married and divorced men dealing with questions about their sexual orientation. As its neighborhood has changed, St. Mark's UMC has altered its mission and outreach to remain a genuine neighborhood church in the heart of Midtown.

FIRST METHODIST CHURCH-DACULA

Neighborhood and community change has also altered the missions of many Methodist congregations on the outskirts of Atlanta. One such congregation is located in Dacula, a former small-town in suburban Gwinnett County. Founded in 1837, Hinton Memorial (as it was known until 1995) was long recognized as the establishment church in Dacula. The congregation evolved from a single-family dominion during the 1960s to become a steadily growing congregation in the late 1980s. In 1990, however, the congregation experienced a schism when their pastor of six years and more than half of the members left the Methodist church to found an independent charismatic congregation. Prior to the split, the congregation had tripled in size in five years, growing from a weekly attendance of 40 to 120.

From 1990 to 1993, the congregation stayed in a "holding pattern" under the pastoral leadership of a traditional Methodist minister. The congregation, hampered by the financial strain of a heavily mortgaged parsonage and sapped of programmatic incentive, allowed youth and children's programs to die slowly. Although some efforts were made to attract the area's retirees, this population represented only a handful of potential congregants compared with the rapid inflow of young suburban families. The congregation gained new members mostly by relying on families who actively sought religious fellowship, who retained denominational brand loyalty (an increasingly uncommon circumstance among unchurched suburbanites), or who were contacted personally and informally by long-time First UMC-Dacula members.

Congregational members have been active in preserving the unique history of Dacula and in promoting a local boosterism. First UMC trustees have begun selling plates and Christmas ornaments with etchings of the area's historic buildings; one member, an Ohio native and suburban newcomer, spearheaded the town's first Dacula Days and Memorial Day parade; and several other area newcomers planned storytelling events at the church, in which congregational oldtimers tell mostly suburban youngsters what the area was like before it became a suburb of Atlanta.

The congregation's newsletter also provides a forum for the dissemination of local history. First UMC-Dacula has used its newsletter to inform the area residents of its commitment to "traditional" small-town values. The "All Around Town" goes to everyone in the Dacula zip code and has become the equivalent of a community crier and historical journal. The monthly newsletter publishes biographies of deceased local dignitaries and Civil War heroes, histories of abandoned local settlements, a "Roots" column detailing the fictitious reminiscences of two young boys named Bogan and Grunt, family recipes, and old photos of Dacula High School sports teams. This newsletter has reinforced and publicized the congregation's self-identity as a traditional, small-town church, despite the rapid change in the area. The "All Around Town" has provided a means for getting out its particular story and culture. Not coincidentally, getting this message out has drawn newcomers to the area who want exactly that type of atmosphere.

In early 1993, however, as it sought new pastoral leadership, the congregation was urged by its district superintendent to become a "redevelopment congregation." This program of the North Georgia Conference of the UMC was designed to enable congregations in the midst of changing communities to gain financial resources, programming, and training in order to engage in active outreach. Under the leadership of an energetic young pastor, a slightly growing number of committed white middle-class young couples with children and a preponderance of elderly oldtimers are reckoning with the changes in their environment. But instead of aggressively pursuing growth as denominational officials have hoped, the congregation, hampered by continued financial instability, is slowly developing programs that exploit their historical identity and call upon newcomers' nostalgia for a simpler past.

PRESBYTERIANS

Presbyterianism has also played an important role in the history of the South in general and Atlanta in particular. Like the Methodist church, the Presbyterian church was deeply affected by slavery and race relations. A division among Presbyterians that occurred during the Civil War produced the United Presbyterian Church in the United States of America, popularly known as the northern Presbyterian church, and the Presbyterian Church in the United States, commonly called the southern Presbyterians. It was not until 1983 that these two bodies were formally reunited as the Presbyterian Church (U.S.A.).

The oldest Presbyterian church in the Atlanta area is Fairview Presbyterian, founded in the 1820s near Lawrenceville, Georgia, about 20 miles from the center of Atlanta. Currently, there are 112 Presbyterian churches in the greater Atlanta metro region, including the largest Presbyterian church in the United States, Peachtree Presbyterian, with 11,000 members. There is a wide range of ethnic groups associated with the Presbyterian church in Atlanta, including African-American, Korean, Taiwanese, Mandarin, and Hispanic communities. This church has maintained its commitment to inclusivity and justice, a commitment exemplified by their significant role in writing the "Atlanta Manifesto" in 1960 against segregation. The denomination is also planting numerous congregations in the city's rapidly growing suburban and exurban periphery. In Cobb County alone there are more than 20 Presbyterian congregations.

CENTRAL PRESBYTERIAN CHURCH

Many members of Central Presbyterian (founded 1858) will quickly tell you that they are "the church that stayed." They are very proud to be part of a community of faith that did not follow its membership to the suburbs; they maintained a strong commitment to urban life, remaining at the original site near City Hall and the State Capitol. Organized after a split with Atlanta's original Presbyterian congregation, Central Presbyterian actually met in City Hall in what was then a very fashionable neighborhood. Even today, members will talk about their church's presence as a "watch guard of justice" in the midst of government—literally and metaphorically. As one member related, "the urban commitment, feeling responsibility for communities other than our own, is what is attractive about Central. If you're a member here, you feel a vital part of the city's future. Our buildings are right here in the center—kind of like the old city green."

While at first having a predominantly white and educated membership, today the congregation's Sunday worship is becoming more integrated, especially with African-American and Hispanic participants. This transition reflects the history of a church that, only a year after it opened its doors, supported the southern cause in the Civil War. The church was used by Sherman's army as a slaughterhouse, and though it suffered extensive damage, like other churches the building was saved when the northern military leader burned the city.

Central Presbyterian's architecture is conservative and traditional, but the ethic of working in the local community is in many ways open and nontraditional. In the early twentieth century, the "Brotherhood of Central," a men's Bible study and prayer group, founded the Atlanta Union Mission. This was the first citywide shelter for men who were out of work, homeless, and/or suffering from addiction. Central's congregation also began a program for women workers in Atlanta, providing them inexpensive room and board in what they called "boarding clubs." These facilities provided women safe and respectable communities during their single working years. Surprisingly, particularly to some of its business membership, in 1913 and 1914 the church was also an early supporter of trade unions. In 1915, under the leadership of an elder, John Eagen, who still remains a presence in the congregation, Central brought Booker T. Washington to Atlanta to help him "enlist the power structures of the city to help achieve better education and increased income for Negroes."

In 1922, Central organized a baby clinic for local poor children. That clinic continues today, staffed partially by church volunteers. Now reconfigured as the Central Health Center, it offers primary medical and dental care, education about health and disease prevention, pastoral counseling, family planning, immunizations, and pharmacy services. The center's approach is holistic, integrating the physical, mental, emotional, and spiritual dimensions of health. Additionally, the church is an active partner in the Capitol Area Ministries, a broad-based ministry to the homeless and poor that includes the Parish House, a program for children and youth. Located near a housing project, this ministry offers after-school programming, tutoring, and a summer program. Many church members volunteer at the Parish House, in the church's night shelter that houses 65 men each night during the winter season, or in the Outreach Office which provides job counseling, food, and occasional financial assistance. As concern for urban children deepened at Central, it opened a Child Development Center that provides comprehensive year-round day care for children of various ethnic and socioeconomic backgrounds. Many children stay at the center 40 to 50 hours a week participating in developmental skills, artistic programs, and educational activities.

Providing shelter for those in need has been an important part of Central Presbyterian's work in Atlanta. During the turbulent 1960s, Central provided shelter for Civil Rights workers, trade unionists, war protesters, and farmers who had come to downtown Atlanta to present grievances at the State Capitol. In 1968, when Atlanta was flooded with grieving supporters of the slain Dr. Martin Luther King, Jr., Central was the first mainline church to offer housing, setting a precedent that other downtown, predominantly white churches followed. During that time one visiting African-American Northerner said that she had been wonderfully surprised to find such warm and caring Southerners at Central, considering the South's history of brutalities towards blacks. Today Central continues to offer urban hospitality not only to those in its immediate neighborhood, but also to visitors from all kinds of places and situations.

FIRST PRESBYTERIAN CHURCH

After the schism that led to the formation of Central Presbyterian, First Presbyterian—from which Central split—continued to develop into a major church in Atlanta. First Presbyterian was founded in 1852 with 19 members who met in a small, simple building near Marietta and Spring Streets. The church remained at that site until March 1922, when it relocated to the corner of Peachtree and 16th Street. At that point, the church was following its membership, who were moving to the prestigious (now, in-town) suburb of Ansley Park. The church was appropriately proud of its stone Gothic architecture and famous Pilcher organ. With beautiful Tiffany and D'Ascenza windows, ten exquisite mosaics, and a baptismal font made from a cornice stone of St. Mary's Church of Ephesus, Turkey (site of the famous ecumenical council of 431 CE), the sanctuary today still reflects a stately beauty amid its long-standing tradition of fine music and preaching.

Members comment that the commitment to the arts at First Presbyterian has always provided "solace and direction in the transitions of the city and culture around them." Located next to the High Museum of Art, First Presbyterian embraced the art of creative communication early on as the first congregation in Atlanta and the United States to have a weekly broadcast of its services. Responding to the schedules of its members and neighboring communities and offices, the church was a pioneer in providing midday lectures, meals, and services during the liturgical seasons of the Christian year (Advent, Lent, and Easter). The church maintains the only ecumenical contemplative prayer group in the city, drawing Atlantans interested in contemporary styles of meditation that connect with ancient Christian roots.

By responding to the changing constituencies of Atlanta, First Presbyterian was drawn to a major ministry that included people who came to the city from all over the world. That ministry continues today as an ecumenical movement for international business people, scholars, students, and visitors, including Villa International, which provides temporary housing, meals, services, and programs. First Presbyterian also is part of the citywide Hispanic Ministry of the Presbyterian Church.

THE OPEN DOOR COMMUNITY

Two Presbyterian ministers, Murphy Davis and Ed Loring, founded a shelter for the homeless called the Open Door, which has become a community of advocacy, resourcing, and worship based on the Catholic Worker model developed by Dorothy Day. Residents and volunteers at the Open Door feed 60 to 80 men, women, and children three meals a day while supporting a live-in community of 30 members transitioning from their life on the streets. A volunteer site for hundreds of Atlantans every year, the Open Door is an alternative urban ministry that has stimulated an interfaith and holistic response to the plight of the poor by addressing issues of health, economics, justice, and spirituality. As one volunteer remarked, "Working in the Open Door, I feel that I touch a reality I don't know how to touch, or help—and sometimes don't want to touch. But working all together here—we keep finding ways to touch and help—and we see changes in our city."

COLUMBIA THEOLOGICAL SEMINARY

Founded in 1828, the Columbia Theological Seminary in Decatur has served as a formative institution for Presbyterian pastors throughout the southeast. Currently enrolling approximately 600 students, Columbia has become a distinguished scholastic center for the study of Christian theology, biblical texts, and pastoral care. The school has also gradually evolved from a regional to a national and international theological center by participating in debates within various branches of the Presbyterian church in the United States and the world.

EPISCOPALIANS

Originally founded in the South as the Church of England, the Episcopal church initially did not have a strong presence in much of Georgia. It was not until the middle of the nineteenth century that the Episcopal church began to experience growth here. Today, however, the Episcopal church is thoroughly rooted in Georgia's soil. There are more than 155 Episcopal congregations in the state, with nearly two-thirds of them located in the Atlanta metro region. Atlanta also boasts the denomination's largest congregation—the Cathedral of St. Philip.

CATHEDRAL OF ST. PHILIP

St. Philip's Church was officially established by five men in 1847, though meetings originally took place in a wooden frame house with other Christian denominations of Atlanta. From 1848 until 1882, its membership met in the center of the city across from the capitol. The congregation's facility was used as a hospital, stable, and bowling alley by the Union Army during the Civil War. As with other churches in the area near the Roman Catholic Shrine of the Immaculate Conception, St. Philip's was spared from Sherman's fires. By 1875, it was the largest Episcopal church in Georgia and had one of the first large pipe organs in the city—a gift of member General George Meade, the regional military commander during Reconstruction.

In 1904, the Cathedral of St. Philip was officially recognized by the national Episcopal church. As a cathedral, it became the home of the bishop of the diocese and of the diocesan staff, thereby becoming the headquarters for establishing priorities, creating programs, and maintaining resources for the Episcopal church in the northern half of Georgia. Currently located in a massive stone structure in Buckhead, in northwest Atlanta, the cathedral hosts diocesan-wide services of baptism, ordination, and healing, particularly for persons living with AIDS. Additionally, the diocesan offices serve as the educational resource for the Diocese, providing national workshops, clergy continuing education, and citywide networks for social justice and advocacy. As the city has changed, the diocese has at times maintained a traditional posture that reflects its southern aristocratic heritage. At other times, however, it has responded to the changing culture of the New South, evidenced, for example, by the 1995 appointment of Assistant Bishop Onell Soto, a South American. Bishop Soto will help coordinate diocesan outreach to Hispanic and other minority groups, whose numbers are rapidly increasing in the city.

In addition to housing the diocesan offices, the Cathedral of St. Philip is also a congregation with a solid base of members whose ministries reflect many of the concerns of Atlanta's middle- and upper-class professionals and business people. The congregation offers a variety of support groups as well as traditional Episcopal guilds and brotherhoods. Among these ministries is the HOPE program, which provides education, referrals, support, and advocacy for addicts and their families, and the Employment Transition Ministry, which includes weekly small group meetings led by two trained volunteers. Both groups involve many lay volunteers from the congregation who have personal experience with these issues.

Worship services in the cathedral reflect a classical, liturgical tradition. The worship scene is set by large and complex stained glass windows, numerous paraments, elaborate vestments for the clergy and robes for the choir, regular use of incense, and a massive pipe organ. Evensong, a sung service relatively rare in Atlanta, occurs twice a week in the cathedral. The dress and demeanor of the congregation is still quite formal. Yet in the last eight years, St. Philip's has become increasingly involved in direct service to the city's poor and ill. Participating in building houses for low income families, volunteering for shelters, and serving in soup kitchens has led the membership to expand their activities from traditional concerns to broader needs of the city. Like other large Christian congregations, St. Philip's has emphasized interreligious and ecumenical dialogue around these needs as well as shared theological convictions.

ST. LUKE'S EPISCOPAL CHURCH

The Reverend Charles Quintard, a physician and chaplain in the Army of Tennessee, founded St. Luke's in 1864. Confederate soldiers erected the frame building that housed the new church, but during the war it was soon completely destroyed. The rebuilt St. Luke's grew in membership and influence rather quickly. In the early 1880s, it was considered an interim co-cathedral candidate with the parish of St. Philip's. But by 1894, all parties were clear that St. Luke's would remain a parish, so in 1896 it moved to a better location to accommodate what was then considered its suburban membership. Finally settling in 1906 at its current location on Peachtree Street near the Civic Center, St. Luke's is considered one of the central players in the urban landscape of Atlanta.

As early as 1912, St. Luke's was identified as a progressive church, frequently taking strong stands on moral issues of the day. In those days, questions about closing the red light districts of Atlanta and defending the rights of striking workers were primary concerns; many of these issues directly affected St. Luke's members. Despite the efforts of members who stood to benefit financially by defending the red light districts, the St. Luke's congregation took its stand and mobilized its members to close them. Throughout the church's history, members have demonstrated a strong resolve to get involved in pressing social and moral questions.

Most recently, the church struggled to decide whether it would continue its daily feeding of hundreds of homeless men. Some of Atlanta's political and business leaders suggested that the daily public display of so many poor on Atlanta's streets would detract from its new Olympic image. Nonetheless, the church decided to continue the daily soup kitchen; but it is in the process of reevaluating ministry to the homeless and hungry by asking deeper questions about systemic poverty and practical responses to the poor. As the city and its influential citizens struggle with these questions, so too do its large downtown churches, like St. Luke's.

Relations between African Americans and whites was another crucial issue for the city and the church. In the early 1900s, St. Luke's was actively involved in the Commission on Interracial Harmony and Peace. When racial riots occurred in 1906, the clergy of St. Luke's helped to conceive "The Atlanta Plan," which called for regular and ongoing consultations between the races about injustices and strategies for correcting them. Several current members of St. Luke's describe how the racial mix of the congregation and clergy positively influences the church's ability to participate in resolving current problems facing Atlanta. As one member noted, "Within house, we can discuss the future of our city from a Christian perspective inclusive of various racial and ethnic communities. We don't have to import those involved and being affected. We are all here." Although the congregation is comprised of older upper-middle, and upper-class Atlantans and younger professional and business people, it continues strong ministries to the homeless, poor, and recent immigrants.

UNITED CHURCH OF CHRIST

The United Church of Christ (UCC), formed in 1957, was the result of a merger between the Congregational Christian Churches and the Evangelical and Reformed Church. Most congregations affiliated with the UCC are known as Congregational churches. In Georgia, there are 23 congregations associated with the UCC; nearly half of that number are located in the Atlanta metro area.

CENTRAL CONGREGATIONAL CHURCH AND FIRST CONGREGATIONAL CHURCH

The Central Congregational Church of Atlanta has roots in the missionary movements of the Congregational church in the South. Begun in 1882 with the arrival of a staff member from the American Missionary Society, the church, from its inception, was racially defined. From the beginning the church declared itself non-segregationist, saying, "We hold ourselves ready to receive any worthy colored applicant." It was not until 1971, however, that the first black member was received.

First Congregational Church, on the other hand, began as an interracial congregation led by the Reverend C. W. Francis, a professor at Atlanta University. Founded fifteen years before Central, the congregation sought to work with Atlanta's freedmen. By the time Central was established, First Congregational already had 200 members. Today First Congregation is rapidly becoming a strongly identified African-American church. The early racial divide shaped the histories and final reconciliations of the two congregations, somewhat mirroring the shapings and reshapings of relations among whites and African Americans in Atlanta.

The first meeting of the congregation was composed of a group of northern émigrés to Atlanta. Like other religious groups, these Congregationalists perceived their church not only as a familiar denominational home, but also as a moral pillar for the post-Civil War South. The church officially began with 14 members. Meeting initially at the YMCA, also affiliated with Congregationalism, the church moved several times before settling in a former volunteer fire company hall—the Tallulah Fire Company. After one year the church had 61 members, who for the most part included regional representatives and agents of national businesses and other professionals. There were also a few local prominent business, real estate, and elected political leaders.

Early on, the Central Congregational Church established ministries for the city, focusing especially on rural Georgians who had come to work in the cotton mills of Atlanta. These mission efforts were theologically grounded in the Social Gospel movements of the northeast and midwest in the early twentieth century. Clergy and staff people were brought to Atlanta to strengthen these missions with support from denominational offices. In 1885, the church was legally chartered in Fulton County and had shed its Yankee stigma. Using money raised from all over the country, the church bought land and built its first building in the same year it was chartered. Although all the major clergy, business leaders, and politicians of the day were present at inaugural ceremonies, the pastor of the church was blatantly mission-oriented.

Believing that the church's work would not be defined by the racial and economic dynamics of the South, members of Central Congregational could not avoid being identified in terms of their relationship with First Congregational, whose work among southern blacks had dated from the Civil War. Central was recognized as the center of the white Congregational church in Atlanta. Embracing Henry Grady's vision of the new, industrial South, Central was not as committed to the struggle for racial equality as it was to the economic success of the South, but it supported a form of the accommodationist doctrine. Although their position was hotly debated on the national level, the local congregation prevailed.

The church grew during the early twentieth century and built another new building on its present property at Ellis Street. The church's pastor was instrumental in establishing Piedmont College as a Congregationalist-sponsored school. Still embracing a Social Gospel ministry, the congregation dedicated the new church in 1905 and the service included Washington

Gladden, the famous Social Gospel advocate. But these days of success were marred by the brutal race riots of Atlanta in 1906. Black men were shot and beaten to death near the church, and the church's response was to endorse the white political power structures calling for a separate but equal policy. Some in the church assessed this response as the only realistic option at the time. By the late 1920s, however, Central began to question its position with intentional discussion groups, such as the Sunday evening program for young people called "The Open Door." While well attended, these were viewed by many in the city as "not in the mainstream."

Although reviving in its social commitments, the church's financial situation was deteriorating. Many other downtown churches had moved out of the city proper, following their members and leaving the problems of the urban scene. Struggling with continuing financial difficulties, the church's new pastor, Dr. Thomas Anderson, set a new course in 1943. He publicly claimed Central as a theologically liberal alternative in Atlanta that would meet the needs of northern Congregationalists while attracting southerners dissatisfied with certain southern forms of religious conservatism. Again claiming a Social Gospel stand, with overtones of progressivism that were welcomed by Atlanta's civic leadership at that time, the church struggled between members who advocated participatory, liberal theology and those who preferred being an inspirational community. Offering up-to-date ministries, such as the Business and Professional Women's Club, the church still floundered in racial relations. It welcomed African-American worshipers, but did not allow them to become members.

The church did not change its membership rules even though individuals during the 1950s actively supported integrationist programs and policies. During the cultural changes of the 1960s, Central experimented in folk liturgies and Christian seasonal liturgies. Many of its members became involved in the Civil Rights movement of Atlanta and had more interactions on a local, and national, denominational level with members of First Congregational Church. In 1967, the church relocated to suburban DeKalb County, and at the dedication in 1968, a representative of First Congregational was present. In 1971, Central accepted its first black member. The church has continued to evolve, reflecting its more suburban setting with special programs for mothers and children, softball teams, gardening groups, etc. Since the 1960s, it has sponsored a once-a-month folk music coffee house that has become a landmark of Central's surrounding neighborhood. Continuing to serve Congregationalists newly arrived in Atlanta,

Central Congregational is now considered one of the mainstream churches that has shaped Atlanta's religious landscape.

LUTHERANS

The Lutheran presence in Atlanta began in 1846 when the Reverend Levi Bedenbaugh was sent by the South Carolina synod to "missionate" in the region. Despite considerable effort, the early attempts by Bedenbaugh and others to establish a Lutheran congregation in Atlanta failed. The first Lutheran congregation in Atlanta was established after the Civil War. This congregation of German-speaking Lutherans organized *Die Deutsche Lutherische Gemeinde*, later known as St. John's Lutheran Church of Atlanta.

A prominent experience in the history of Lutheranism in the United States, and in Georgia, has been the assimilation of immigrant groups. For many immigrants, Lutheran heritage was closely linked with their ethnic background. As Lutherans became acculturated into American society, however, the need for ethnically-specific denominations decreased. By the early 1980s mergers consolidated most Lutherans in the country into five major bodies: the Lutheran Church in America (LCA), Lutheran Church-Missouri Synod (LCMS), the American Lutheran Church (ALC), the Wisconsin Evangelical Lutheran Synod (WELS), and the Association of Evangelical Lutheran Churches (AELC). In 1982, the LCA, ALC, and AELC voted to merge into a single denomination—the Evangelical Lutheran Church in America (ELCA). Today the majority of Lutheran congregations in Atlanta are ELCA, though a significant minority belong to LCMS—a more conservative denominational body.

LUTHERAN CHURCH OF THE REDEEMER

Founded in 1903, the Lutheran Church of the Redeemer was established as an English-language Lutheran congregation. Initially holding meetings in the third-floor hall of the Junior Order, United American Mechanics, the congregation was largely composed of Swedish, Danish, Dutch, German, and Norwegian immigrants. Seeking to establish itself as a player in Atlanta civic life, the young congregation quickly acquired property a block from the state capitol grounds, within sight of prominent Baptist, Presbyterian, and Episcopal congregations. The homes of congregants were located in the white middle-income neighborhoods that then surrounded the capitol building.

When the church leaders broke ground in 1904, the *Atlanta Constitution* noted its arrival on the religious scene: "The English Lutherans, after a hard fight, are at last prepared to erect a church edifice." The church, known affectionately in the community as the Little Stone Church, was built with gifts from Lutherans throughout the southeast. During construction the congregation suffered significant financial hardship as members sacrificed to build the church at the same time as they worked to build their own businesses in the city. The congregation was particularly proud of its first stained glass window—the Good Shepherd Window. The window was presented to the church as a gift from the Sunday School of Grace Church in Prosperity, South Carolina. Grace Church was the home church of nearly one-third of the Atlanta congregation's founding members.

Another stained glass window was given by the Atlanta Police Force in memory of Hans Christian Drasbach, a native Danish policeman who was stabbed to death in the line of duty. From its earliest years in Atlanta, the church has maintained a close relationship with the police force. The pastor's wife, Mrs. Katherine Scherer Cronk, organized and taught a Bible class at police headquarters for policemen whose work kept them from services. The congregation's service to the police was especially valued in the aftermath of the four-day race riot in 1906, when many police officers were injured.

In 1910 the congregation, which was no longer reliant on the Georgia Synod for its ongoing survival, celebrated a Jubilee week and announced a membership total of 281. The antipathy that surrounded German-speaking organizations during World War I accelerated assimilation among many Lutheran immigrants, including some at the newly renamed Church of the Redeemer. Women in the congregation knitted for men in service, the choir participated in flag services at the capitol, and families entertained military personnel in their homes.

By the 1950s, as the residential area around the capitol deteriorated, the congregation could see that it had to move or begin an inexorable decline. Congregants undertook to build what they anticipated would be one of Atlanta's most beautiful churches. The sanctuary of limestone and crab orchard stone included exquisite furnishings of marble, oak, wrought iron, hand carvings, and stained glass. The building was dedicated "To the Worship and Glory of the Living God." But it bore witness as well to the success and determination of a small, largely immigrant Lutheran community that had made Atlanta its home.

Today, the Lutheran Church of the Redeemer continues to grow and expand. Although not a neighborhood church, the congregation offers numerous well-attended weekday ministries, including MOMS, an informal gathering of mothers designed to offer emotional and spiritual support, as well as educational, community service, and fellowship opportunities. The church also sponsors Wednesdays at Redeemer, which includes a common evening meal followed by activities for the entire family, such as adventure land for children, choirs, and a range of classes addressing such topics as astronomy, herb gardening, communicating with medical professionals, genealogy, and dream analysis. As one active lay member of the congregation said, "This ministry is helping people see that the church is about continuing education and not just about religion. Our worship is great, but that is only part of the story. We're here to expand the mind as well."

CONCLUSION

Mainline congregations in Atlanta have helped to shape the region's cultural and moral life. From the prohibitionist stance of Atlanta Methodists to the work among the homeless at the Open Door, mainline ministries have made efforts to place their moral values at the center of the city's self-definition. Increasingly, however, the power of mainline congregations to shape the religious culture of Atlanta is declining as membership in these churches dwindles here as elsewhere in the United States. As a result, many mainline congregations have undergone significant alteration in recent decades. Some congregations have relocated from central city to suburban sites, following their membership; others have sought to attract new inner-city constituencies such as gays and lesbians; and some have established themselves as community and religious centers for a membership that is scattered across the Atlanta landscape. Despite the somewhat shrinking influence of mainline Protestant congregations, they continue to be a lively and vital presence in Atlanta and its environs.

FOR FURTHER INFORMATION

Articles:

Camille J. Kankle, "Atlanta's Churches in 1896," *Atlanta History,* Vol. 33, 1967

Books:

Boone M. Bowen. *The Candler School of Theology: Sixty Years of Service.* Atlanta, Emory University, 1974

The Church of the Lighted Window: Redeemer History, 1903-1993. Atlanta, Lutheran Church of the Redeemer, 1993

Milton Coalter, John Mulder, and Louis Weeks. *The Presbyterian Predicament: Six Perspectives.* Louisville, Westminster/John Knox Press, 1990

Committee on Church History. *A History of St. Mark: St. Mark United Methodist Church,* n.d.

Peachtree and Fifth Streets, Atlanta, Georgia, 1872-1986. Atlanta, St. Mark Methodist Church, 1987

William Henry Forsyth. *The First Methodist Church, Atlanta, Georgia.* Atlanta, Baker Printing, 1989

Nellie Jane Gaertner. *A History of First Presbyterian Church, Atlanta, Georgia.* Atlanta, First Presbyterian Church, 1979

Interfaith Outreach Resource Guide. Atlanta, Midtown Assistance Center, Inc., 1995

Susan Elisabeth Leas. *Alive In Atlanta: A History of St. Luke's Church.* Atlanta, Tucker-Castleberry, 1976

Robert C. McMath, ed. *A Southern Pilgrimage: Central Congregational Church of Atlanta, Georgia, 1882-1982.* Atlanta, R & R Printing, 1982

The Open Door Community. Atlanta, The Open Door Community, 1988

J. McDowell Richards, *As I Remember it: Columbia Theological Seminary, 1932-1971.* Decatur, Columbia Theological Seminary Press, 1985

Russell Richey. *Early American Methodism.* Bloomington, Indiana University Press, 1991

St. Luke's Church: 1864-1964, the First One Hundred Years. Atlanta, St. Luke's Church, 1964

John Robert Smith, *The Church that Stayed: The Life and Times of Central Presbyterian Church in the Heart of Atlanta, 1858-1978.* Atlanta, Historical Society, 1979

CHAPTER TWO

SOUTHERN BAPTISTS AT HOME IN ATLANTA

F. Douglas Alexander

First Baptist Church of Atlanta. Photograph by Elizabeth Hardcastle.

At the corner of Fence and Hebron Church Roads near Highway 316 in Gwinnett County stands a weather-worn wooden sign announcing the location of Hebron Baptist Church. The primitive marker belies what seekers will find when they round the bend. Hebron Baptist Church, sprawled on a plaza of pavement, is composed of several mobile classrooms, a small brick chapel that formerly served as the sanctuary, a massive metal gymnasium, a multistoried Christian Living building, and a modern brick auditorium that seats approximately 1,300 worshipers. Across the street sits a crowded old cemetery, the entrance to which doubles as overflow parking space. This architectural pastiche of old and new reflects the congregation's history and practice. It also reflects the experiences of many Southern Baptist congregations in the metropolitan Atlanta area.

Founded in 1842, Hebron Baptist is an historic congregation. Fifteen years ago, it was the smallest of the dozen or so small independent and Southern Baptist churches in and around northeast Gwinnett County. Today, drawing congregants from seven surrounding counties, Hebron is a congregation of nearly 3,400 regular worshipers. In the 1980s, when Gwinnett was the fastest growing county in the United States, Hebron kept pace with the steady population inflow, becoming the primary beneficiary of suburban growth in the area. The church's pastor, the Reverend Larry Wynn, has been very deliberate in addressing the needs of suburbanites by implementing relevant programs and updating the congregation's worship services. Wynn has led the Hebron congregation in aggressive evangelism in the area's burgeoning subdivisions. Congregants canvass each neighborhood once or twice a month inviting families to attend special programs at the church.

The church's success in retaining suburban newcomers has been due, in part, to its innovative and extensive programming, and celebratory and spiritually challenging worship experiences. Balancing conservative Southern Baptist theology with the language of therapy and self-improvement, Hebron has sought to address the specific familial and lifestyle stresses of suburban baby boomers. Some of the programs that have been particularly successful in attracting new members include occupation and special needs support groups, such as one for public safety personnel and their families that provides peer and professional counseling, seminars in stress management, and topical discussions. Other support groups include Divorce Recovery, Christian Alcohol Recovery, Christian Al-Anon, and Adult Children of Confusion. The church also operates the AlphaCare Therapy Services, an on-site professional counseling group that provides free or low-cost "Christ-centered" individual, marital, and family therapy. In addition to ongoing support and service groups, Hebron offers one-night LifeSkill Seminars designed to develop practical skills for real-life issues such as parenting, finances, dating, and Christian sexuality.

With staff members directing ministries for children, singles, senior adults, high school and middle school students, and preschool youngsters, the church offers a sophisticated array of age-specific programs, choirs, Sunday school classes, and support groups. Hebron currently supports a youth program with a membership of more than 500. The youth program incorporates films, special guests, fellowship and discussion groups, summer and winter retreats, discipleship weekends, and numerous impromptu and planned parties. The annual Vacation Bible School, supplied by an extensive bus ministry, draws more than 500 children.

The congregation's single largest event is the Starlight Crusade, which typically occurs the week before Memorial Day and runs Sunday through Friday nights at the local football stadium. The revival under the stars often draws more than 6,000 people to enjoy the 180-voice Hebron choir and nationally known contemporary Christian musicians who perform each evening. The annual cost of over $45,000 for the Starlight Crusade is paid by the congregation, which takes up a special "love offering for the community" during Easter. The congregation's total annual budget of $1.9 million permits a great deal of programming innovation. The church is not, however, spendthrift, since Wynn refuses to go into debt for any projects, including building new facilities—which explains the congregation's architectural pastiche.

The Sunday morning worship service at Hebron is typical of many Southern Baptist congregations throughout the metropolitan Atlanta region. The congregation holds services at 9 and 11 o'clock in an auditorium, decorated with simple brass chandeliers, powder blue carpet, and department store drapes; the facility is crowded with predominately white, middle-class young families, middle-aged couples, and teenagers. (A children's worship is held elsewhere on the grounds.) A typical Sunday service at the church begins with a water baptism, performed by one of the church's eight pastors who are dressed in black clerical robes. Accompanied by the 15-member orchestra and 75-person robeless choir softly singing a chorus, such as "Let's Just Praise the Lord," the individual is immersed as the pastor recites a traditional baptismal formula. The baptized believer rises from the water to the 1,300 congregants' vigorous applause and loud "amening."

Afterward, the pastor of music ministries quickly rises from his blue padded platform chair to lead the congregation in several fast-paced choruses printed in the bulletin. Often between the first and second chorus, the minister instructs congregants to "turn to your neighbor and tell them how good they look—even if they don't." Most neighbors deftly shake hands and return to singing, ignoring the proposed conversation starter. But when Wynn approaches the microphone to encourage members to greet newcomers, worshipers make the rounds.

Leaning nonchalantly against the oak cross-shaped pulpit, Wynn generally begins his sermon with jocular Christian small-talk with the congregation. But when Wynn instructs congregants to "turn with me in your Bibles to . . . " the mood turns serious. With the rustle of turning pages sounding like rain inside the sanctuary, Wynn offers a pastoral prayer for all those who will hear this message, "Father, just let it convict them of their need for You." Wynn's messages press worshipers to be more conscientious employees and merciful employers, to win souls to Christ, to be more devoted parents, to grow in the faith, and to be more playful spouses. Similar in content to his bi-weekly *Gwinnett Post-Tribune* Spiritual Life columns, with titles like "Only with God's help can we learn to love for a lifetime," "No matter what your status, God can use your talents," and "My encounter with personal pain taught me we don't suffer alone," Wynn's sermons go beyond these more general messages to detail for congregants the dire present-day and other-worldly consequences of failing to heed his and the Bible's call to right living. Wynn intends this conservative fire and brimstone theme, as congregants sometimes term it, to cut through the superficiality of contemporary suburban life, convincing Hebron congregants that Christian commitment really matters now and in the hereafter. The sense of gravity that his tone and topic convey is welcomed by many congregants. A young woman involved in the high school ministry, and a member of a Soul Winning Accountability Team, commented, "He's not just another person telling you, `stop and listen to me.' What he's saying really matters."

Wynn concludes each service with an all-eyes-closed-all-heads-bowed altar call. Sometimes as many as 20 people file forward to pray with pastors arrayed across the front of the auditorium. After a brief time of prayer, Wynn announces the names of those who have responded and their reasons for doing so. Applauding, the congregants stand to their feet, and a receiving line assembles at the front of the sanctuary, as converts, new members, and the troubled are hugged and greeted.[1]

DEMOGRAPHIC PATTERNS

As Hebron's rapid growth illustrates, Southern Baptists have been thriving in the United States. Nationally, Southern Baptists boast a membership of over fifteen million, making it the largest Protestant denomination in the country. Southern Baptist congregations are in every state and on every inhabitable continent, but their geographic and historic center remains in the states of the old Confederacy. More than eighty percent of the members in the United States are located there, and in many areas of the southern states more than half the population is affiliated with a Southern Baptist church. The size and scope of the Southern Baptist denomination makes it a powerful force across the globe, but especially so in the South.

Recently released figures for the 1994 calendar year highlight the growth and expansion of the Southern Baptists. The denomination claims a total of 39,910 churches. A research report published by the Home Mission Board notes that between 1970 and 1993, the number of Southern Baptist churches in the United States grew by 12.6 percent, with growth faster in areas outside the South. Still, the backbone of the Southern Baptist denomination remains the small to medium-sized southern churches whose average membership is around 280 individuals. A 1995 study conducted by Charles Chaney, Vice President of the Home Mission Board, sounded both a warning and a challenge for the future of Southern Baptist growth. The Chaney report, like the Home Mission Board report, found that the Southern Baptist denomination was growing faster outside of the South than within its traditional stronghold. But larger growth rates in membership and church building outside of the South are to be expected because areas outside the region are starting from scratch. The Chaney report also noted, however, that Southern Baptists were slowly losing "market share" in the South itself, especially in cities. While in small southern towns Baptists may offer one of only

1 This snapshot of congregational life in one of Atlanta's dynamic Southern Baptist congregations is drawn from the research of Nancy Eiesland, *A Particular Place: Exurbanization and Religious Response in a Southern Town*, Ann Arbor, UMI Dissertation Services, 1995.

two or three religious alternatives, in southern cities Baptists share the religious marketplace with an increasingly diverse array of congregations.

HISTORY OF THE SOUTHERN BAPTIST COMMUNITY

The roots of the Southern Baptist denomination go back to the first Baptist church in America, which was founded in Providence, Rhode Island, in 1639 by a Boston minister named Roger Williams. Williams was expelled from the colony of Massachusetts because of his beliefs, particularly his conviction that the civil power of the colony should not be used to control the religious beliefs of its citizens. Williams invited fellow dissenters, of all religious backgrounds, to join him in the new Rhode Island colony. From its inception as a religious denomination, personal and religious freedom have been hallmarks of the Baptist community.

The rise of a distinctly southern brand of religion within the Baptist community, and the subsequent founding of the Southern Baptist Convention (SBC), were also centered on issues of personal freedom. However, in this context the personal freedoms at issue were those of African slaves versus their masters. By the 1830s, a majority of Baptists in the North had embraced the anti-slavery movement and were active in abolitionist organizations. In contrast, Baptists in the South were equally zealous in their defense of the institution of slavery, which had become the central organizing force for the prevailing economic and social order in the region.[2]

A turning point in the battle over slavery within the nationally organized Baptist community occurred with the appointment of missionaries by the Home and Foreign Mission Societies. In the fall of 1844, the Georgia Baptist Convention sent James Reeves, a slave-holding preacher, as one of its appointments for missionary work. The members of the Foreign Mission Society, who were predominately anti-slavery, voted against Reeves' appointment. The rejection of Reeves solidified the southern perception that slave-holders would never be allowed appointments as missionaries. As a result, the division of Baptists along geographical lines accelerated. In the spring of 1845 the Home Mission Society decided to carry on its work in separate northern and southern divisions. In May, 328 delegates from nine southern states gathered in Augusta, Georgia, and organized the SBC. The territory of the newly created SBC soon stretched from Florida to Virginia in the east and extended from Texas to Missouri in the west—the territory

2 This historical and theoretical perspective is abbreviated. For a more detailed discussion see Nancy Ammerman, *Baptist Battles: Social Change and Religious Conflict in the Southern Baptist Convention*, New Brunswick, Rutgers University Press, 1990.

that eventually became the Confederacy. Over time, the SBC detached completely from the northern Baptists, creating a completely autonomous religious organization.

SOUTHERN BAPTIST ORGANIZATION, ETHOS, AND THEOLOGY

The SBC was influenced by numerous, and distinctly southern traditions. Among the self-consciously southern attributes of Southern Baptist churches are the focus on family and community as well as the emphasis on hospitality. One of the vestiges of Southern culture in the SBC is the homogeneity of separate congregations—racially mixed congregations are rare. Nonetheless, being a Southern Baptist can mean something very special and unique to congregants. One member described her feelings by saying: "That name, `Southern Baptist,' is dear to your heart when you're out of the South, it really means something . . . It's not just any kind of Baptist."

In addition to being part of the national SBC, local churches gather into state and local organizations as well. In Atlanta, the Atlanta Association of Baptist Churches (AABC) was formed in November, 1909. Rapid growth in the New South's most advanced and populous city required Atlanta-area churches to form their own organization to cope with the changing religious needs of the community. Thirty-eight churches enrolled as charter members. The general objectives of this new organization were simple. Atlanta Baptists sought to develop a close fellowship that harnessed the energies of the area's Southern Baptist churches. Their aim was to concentrate primarily on the city of Atlanta and the problems that were created by its rapid growth. Atlanta Baptists sought to promote evangelism, church organization, and church building in conjunction with the Georgia Baptist and the Southern Baptist Conventions. T. E. McCutcheon was selected as the first superintendent of the AABC. He and his staff worked out of the downtown offices that were provided by the Atlanta First Baptist Church.

By 1912, the AABC had increased to 52 member churches and by 1923, the AABC had become the largest association of its kind in the SBC. Thirty years later, it had nearly tripled in size, with 133 member churches. The AABC changed its official name to the Atlanta Baptist Association (ABA) in 1958.

By the end of World War II, racial unrest was a dominant element in American society. Atlanta-area Baptists were warned that a Baptist witness relied heavily upon racial harmony and a swift adaptation to the changing social realities. In 1960, Atlanta Baptists passed a resolution they hoped would demonstrate a spirit of Christian love to people of all races. While the ABA did not take an active role in the struggle for civil rights, it continually reminded members of the importance of social stability. The ABA was greatly concerned that un-Christian acts by its members in the name of racial segregation would have a destabilizing effect on the life of the city. Atlanta Baptist churches were not without racial tensions in these years however, as several churches, including downtown's First Baptist, sought to physically bar African-Americans from attending. In the years since, most congregations have made their peace with the possibility of black members, but Southern Baptists in Atlanta still largely attend all-white churches. In recent years Southern Baptists have concentrated efforts on inner-city church development and on cultivating new levels of African American and ethnic leadership in efforts to reach minority urban dwellers.

Given the denomination's history, the Racial Reconciliation Resolution, passed by the Southern Baptist Convention in Atlanta in 1995, was an extraordinary event. It essentially apologized for the Southern Baptist role in perpetuating slavery and acknowledged that the relationship of the church with African Americans had been crippled due to lingering racism. Southern Baptists hope this resolution will go a long way in establishing a positive and productive working relationship between the church, African Americans, and other minority groups.

While familiarity with the history and ethos of the SBC is essential for a better understanding of the Southern Baptist community, their theological positions are perhaps even more fundamental to their religious identity. Southern Baptists place a great deal of emphasis on two cornerstones of evangelicalism: the Bible and personal salvation. They believe that the Bible is the divinely inspired word of God and serves as the written record of God's revelation to humankind. Salvation is the redemption of the whole person through the acceptance of Jesus Christ as Lord and Savior. Like most Protestant denominations, Southern Baptists believe that there is only one true God. In addition, they assert that the eternal God is revealed to believers in one of three different forms, as the Father, the Son, or the Holy Spirit. Southern Baptists believe that God the Father reigns over the universe, God the Son is the eternal son of God whose death on the cross instituted a provision for the redemption of humanity from sin, and God the Holy Spirit not only convicts individuals of sin and judgment, but also enlightens and empowers the believer, and the church, in worship and evangelism.

Southern Baptists also believe in baptism by immersion. The baptismal act symbolizes the believer's faith in a crucified, buried, and risen Lord. Baptism also symbolizes the sinner's death to sin and resurrection into the newness of a life as a believer. Southern Baptists define the church as a voluntarily gathered local body of baptized believers.

In keeping with Baptist tradition, the church is viewed as an autonomous body. But each church is free to determine its own membership and to set its own course. Southern Baptists believe in a spirit of cooperation as well. They freely organize into local, state, and national bodies for doing mission work and collectively supporting the work of the church. The cornerstone of their organizational structure is the SBC Cooperative Program of missions, founded in 1925, through which local churches fund worldwide mission efforts. Southern Baptists field more than 4,500 home missionaries and over 3,900 foreign missionaries in 129 countries. Southern Baptists believe, however, that such organizations and associations have no legitimate authority over one another, or over individual churches. Churches have wide-ranging freedom in planning their own programs, budgets, and choosing their own pastors.

Still, within the SBC, this freedom does have its limits. Individual churches can be, and have been, expelled from their local associations and, less often, from state and national conventions. When these associations determine that a church has strayed outside what the association believes to be acceptable practice, the church is "disfellowshipped." The most visible cases in recent years involved a church that performed a same-sex union and another church that licensed a gay man to the ministry. Since most Southern Baptists believe homosexuality to be wrong, these congregations were expelled. Another issue that is a source of contention for Southern Baptist churches is related to women in the ministry. Nearly 50 Southern Baptist churches have called women as pastors, and more than two hundred others have ordained women on their pastoral staffs. Some of those churches have been expelled by their local associations, while others have not; and none of these churches has been expelled from their state conventions or from the national SBC. On this issue, the autonomy of each Baptist body is apparent.

In addition to the mixture of local autonomy with regional organization and accountability, Southern Baptists are also characterized by their strong advocacy for separation of church and state. As mentioned earlier, Roger Williams founded the Baptist church in Rhode Island based on his opposition to state interference in matters of religious belief and practice.

Later Baptists were instrumental in the inclusion of religious liberty as part of the United States Constitution. According to Southern Baptists, a free church in a free state is the Christian ideal. But this does not preclude a great deal of political activism on the part of individual church members. Southern Baptists are members of political groups as diverse as the Christian Coalition and People for the American Way.

In spite of the recent gains made by fundamentalists in the SBC hierarchy, Southern Baptists throughout the nation, as well as in metro Atlanta, are a heterogeneous community. They may have a powerful and deep-rooted presence here, but they do not all think and act alike. According to most, striving for personal salvation and living according to scriptural teachings are primary concerns. Like congregants at Hebron Baptist in Gwinnett, First Baptist of Atlanta, and various other churches throughout the metro area, Southern Baptists understand that although the world may be changing around them, salvation and scripture must remain firmly at the forefront of their consciousness. Their involvement in family, church, and civic life are linked to these concerns, and regardless of where they fall on the political spectrum, members of this community take pride in their religious identity.

FOR FURTHER INFORMATION

Nancy Ammerman. *Baptist Battles: Social Change and Religious Conflict in the Southern Baptist Convention.* New Brunswick, Rutgers University Press, 1990

Nancy Eiesland. *A Particular Place: Exurbanization and Religious Response in a Southern Town.* Ann Arbor, UMI Dissertation Services, 1995

Arthur Emery Farnsley, II. *Southern Baptist Politics: Authority and Power in the Restructuring of an American Denomination.* University Park, Pennsylvania State University Press, 1994

James Melvin Washington. *Frustrated Fellowship: The Black Baptist Quest for Social Power.* Macon, Mercer University Press, 1986

CHAPTER THREE

AFRICAN-AMERICAN EXPRESSIONS OF PROTESTANT CHRISTIANITY IN ATLANTA

Gregory S. Gray

Ebenezer Baptist Church. Photograph by Louis A. Ruprecht, Jr.

"Metropolitan Atlanta is a kind of Mecca of African American spirituality in the Protestant tradition of the Christian church. It may be viewed as a conservative tradition, but yet one out of which emerged perhaps the best known Christian prophet of the 20th century....the Reverend Doctor Martin Luther King, Jr. In addition, the black churches of this city are indeed the center of a powerful musical tradition that has stamped the region as the vortex of gospel song and the Negro Spiritual."

Dr. Lawrence Edward Carter, Sr.
Dean, Martin L. King, Jr. International Chapel
Professor of Philosophy and Religion
Morehouse College

What is the "essence" of African-American Protestantism in Atlanta, Georgia, one of the South's most progressive and rapidly expanding metropolitan areas? A distinct musical tradition, a qualitatively unique style of worship, a heritage of social activism, a shared ancestral identity, and a concern for personal as well as social transformation represent many of the salient features or identifiable patterns that characterize African-American Protestant life. Given the shared historical and cultural realities of the African-American community in Atlanta, one could identify the existence of unifying experiences, common causes, central foci, dominant themes, enjoining inclinations, and mutuality of governing orientations among African Americans. Indeed, the acknowledgment of affiliations, alliances, associations, connections, and other cooperative ventures among African-American churches would at least imply a shared sensitivity and sensibility among members in this diverse religious community. How does this shared spiritual awareness get expressed?

It is expressed in many ways, including the following examples: the interaction of preacher and congregation during worship/sermon in the (African-derived) tradition of "call and response"; an old Baptist deacon, "lining a hymn" in the "old time way"; youth fund raiser car washes; a landmark neon sign atop the steeple of Big Bethel AME Church that reads, "Jesus Saves"; glossolalia (speaking in tongues) and prayers for divine healing at Fellowship of Faith, International; Coretta Scott King, widow of slain Civil

Rights leader Martin L. King, Jr., delivering the annual "State of the Dream" address from the pulpit of the historic Ebenezer Baptist Church; prayer meetings with spontaneous testimonies, ecstatic shouts, waving of uplifted hands, holiness dances, and exuberant rejoicing; a church theater guild performing James Baldwin's, *The Amen Corner*; a Monday morning meeting of the Concerned Black Clergy of Atlanta; observance of the Lord's Supper, Holy Communion, or the Eucharist.

It is also expressed in a midday Bible study at New Life Presbyterian Church; in the gospel radio voices from the "Wings of Faith" choir of Cathedral of Faith Church of God in Christ; at a meeting in the Southern Christian Leadership Conference national headquarters on Auburn Avenue; during an Annual Morehouse/Spelman College Christmas Concert; during celebrations of pastor anniversaries, church anniversaries, choir anniversaries, and usher board anniversaries; through baptism with water, and Baptism of the Holy Spirit; by seminarians in training for ministry at the historically black Interdenominational Theological Center; in the gathering of children, youth, young adults, and adults for Church School; during the singing of that cherished hymn of the Freedom Movement, "We Shall Overcome"; in small storefront congregations and megacongregations.

Given this vast, perplexing panoply of images, rituals, and activities from the religious landscape, how do we identify the common threads weaving through the Atlanta ebony existence? Where is the organizing "frame of reference" that enables us to discern the center from the circumference? Is there some recognizable point of interpenetration, interrelationship, and therefore, interdependence among the African-American Protestant churches in Atlanta? Or is the only real commonality one of pigment and hue rather than of pulpit and pew? If there is a sense of common origin and destiny in African-American Protestantism, what are its sources and what are its outcomes? Perhaps answers to questions of this nature could emerge only by way of an extensive, in-depth study, if at all. It would, however, be well beyond the scope of this essay to survey all the major groups and subgroups within the Atlanta African-American Protestant community. The following series of profiles will not compare the various beliefs and practices found among these bodies. Instead, the present effort is more impressionistic than analytic, and will suggest only preliminary "answers" to the above questions by turning to some representative expressions shared with this writer by selected African-American clergy in Atlanta.

THE OLDEST AFRICAN-AMERICAN PROTESTANT DENOMINATION

The first separate denomination to be formed by African Americans in the United States was the African Methodist Episcopal Church (AME). The AME Church dates from 1787 when Richard Allen and others withdrew from St. George's Methodist Episcopal Church in Philadelphia. They decided to leave this church after being physically removed (while they were praying) from a gallery they did not know was prohibited to blacks. The AME Church was formally organized in 1816, and Allen was consecrated as its first bishop. From its beginning, the AME denomination has provided ministry oriented toward community service, education, and missions, and today it is the largest of the black Methodist denominations. Atlanta's first African-American congregation, the Union Church, was an arm of the AME denomination. Founded in 1847, it later became Big Bethel African Methodist Episcopal Church. It is located in the denomination's 6th Episcopal District, over which the Reverend George Kenneth Ming is the presiding bishop. Over the years many other AME churches have prospered in metropolitan Atlanta, including Allen Temple, Cosmopolitan, Flipper Temple, Hunter Hills, Mt. Carmel, Mt. Zion in Decatur, St. John in East Point, St. Mark, St. Paul, St. Phillip, and Turner Chapel.

Dr. McCleland Cox is chair of Mass Communications and coordinator of Religious Studies at Atlanta's Morris Brown College (an AME-supported institution). He was the former associate minister of Big Bethel AME, under the leadership of Bishop McKinley Young, and currently serves as pastor of Mt. Zion AME Church. Dr. Cox speaks appreciatively of the diversity of African-American religious life in Atlanta and underlines the openness and hospitable nature that are two of the qualities shared by these churches. He describes the African Methodist Episcopal vision of ministry as one that involves spreading the gospel through service to humanity. According to Professor Cox, the AME Church has maintained a focus on the total person, and the society around her or him, in order to demonstrate the fullness of God's love made manifest in Jesus Christ.

Other African-American Methodist denominations in Atlanta include the African Methodist Episcopal Zion Church, the second largest African American Methodist denomination, and the Christian Methodist Episcopal (CME) Church, the smallest of the three black Methodist denominations. United Methodism is also a very visible and viable religious presence among African-American Atlantans. Although United Methodism is a predomi-

Big Bethel AME Church. Photograph by Elizabeth Hardcastle.

nantly white denomination with some 9 million members and some 38,000 churches, at least 350,000 of those members are African American, and some 2,500 of those churches are committed to the black community.

THE LARGEST AFRICAN-AMERICAN PROTESTANT DENOMINATION

Among African Americans in Atlanta, the Baptist denomination is by far the most popular. African-American Baptist churches have their origins in the

South, and some of the earliest black Baptist churches in America were the Silver Bluff Baptist Church (1750 is the date on the cornerstone), located along the South Carolina bank of the Savannah River near Augusta, Georgia, the African Baptist or "Bluestone" Church (1758) on the William Byrd plantation near the Bluestone River in Mecklenberg, Virginia, and the Springfield Baptist Church (1787) of Augusta, Georgia. One of the hallmarks of Baptist polity is the absolute autonomy of each local church. Local congregations may and do enter voluntarily into various alliances, associations, conventions, and so forth, for purposes of fellowship, consultation, and missionary efforts. Yet each local congregation is a self-governing entity, and by virtue of this independence, is in no way bound to the dictates of a hierarchical structure.

There are eight identifiable African-American Baptist communions in the United States: the National Baptist Convention, USA, Inc.; the National Baptist Convention of America; the Progressive National Baptist Convention; the Lott Carey Baptist Foreign Mission Convention; the National Primitive Baptist Convention, USA; the United Free Will Baptist; the National Baptist Evangelical Life and Soul Saving Assembly of the USA; and the Free for All Missionary Baptist Church, Inc. In addition, some estimated 75,000 African Americans hold membership in the Southern Baptist Convention, while another 150,000 belong to the American Baptist Churches in the USA.

Dr. William V. Guy serves as pastor of the Friendship Baptist Church, the oldest African-American Baptist congregation in Atlanta. Dr. Guy finds his greatest pastoral challenge is to "try to bring the people that I have been privileged to lead to a deeper realization of the Christian faith . . . a heightened sense of what it is to be a follower of Christ in this world." Organized in 1866 by former slaves, the congregation worshiped in a boxcar that had been sent to Atlanta from Chattanooga, Tennessee, to house the first classroom of what later became known as Atlanta University. Friendship's role in African-American education has been unique in that it has associations with some of the major black universities in the Atlanta area. Morehouse College, upon moving to Atlanta from Augusta in 1879, set up classes at the Friendship Church, and Spelman College had its beginning in the basement of Friendship in 1881. To this day, an annual Morehouse/Spelman freshmen worship service is observed at Friendship to acknowledge the special relationship that the colleges have with the church and with each other.

In addition, Friendship is known as the "Mother Church" among Baptists in Atlanta because of its role in harmoniously forming several other congregations throughout the city. From the beginning, Friendship has contributed outstanding leaders to Atlanta's African-American community in the fields of education, business, and politics, including several judges and college/university presidents. Baseball home run king Henry "Hank" Aaron, and former three-term Atlanta mayor, Maynard H. Jackson (son of a former Friendship pastor), are members of the Friendship Church family.

Eighty percent of the Friendship congregation are college graduates, by far the exception rather than the rule in the African-American Baptist context. Pastor Guy describes his congregation as traditional, yet progressive. On the one hand, Friendship remains focused upon the central tenets of the Baptist Covenant and the congregation's mission statement, while on the other hand, it assumes a theologically "liberal" posture in life and work. As a case in point, the congregation has numerous women serving not only in leadership capacities generally, but in the role of deacons in particular (again, more the exception than the rule in black Baptist churches). Furthermore, the large percentage of men active in the life and work of the congregation is not representative of black churches as a whole, Baptist or otherwise.

As part of its concern for community outreach in Atlanta, the Friendship congregation has undertaken an extensive housing ministry, including the E. R. Carter Old Folks Home (now demolished), the Samuel W. Williams/Friendship Center Apartments, and the Friendship Tower Highrise for the Elderly and Handicapped. As a sign of continued life and growth, the congregation has committed itself to the construction of a new annex to the church building that will further programs with a community outreach.

Friendship's affiliations with larger church bodies include the American Baptist Churches, USA, the Progressive National Baptist Convention, the World Baptist Alliance, the Christian Council of Metropolitan Atlanta, the National Council of Churches, and the World Council of Churches. Dr. Guy commented that the congregation gives priority to its participation in ecumenical ministries. At the time of this interview, Dr. Guy was to be part of a delegation, sponsored by the American Jewish Committee and Leadership Atlanta, traveling to South Africa to meet with and offer moral support to Archbishop Desmond Tutu as well as President Nelson Mandela.

THE MOST RAPIDLY GROWING AFRICAN-AMERICAN DENOMINATION

The Church of God in Christ (COGIC) is the largest of the black Pentecostal groups in the nation, and also the fastest growing. It is the second largest of all African-American Protestant Christian bodies, superseded only by the National Baptist Convention, Inc. It was founded at the turn of the century by Charles H. Mason, to whom the name, beliefs, and practices of the denomination were "divinely revealed." (The C. H. Mason Temple in Memphis, Tennessee, became the headquarters of the sanitation strike when Martin Luther King was assassinated in 1968.) Mason emphasized sanctification or holiness as a prerequisite of salvation, and encouraged Baptism of the Holy Spirit and speaking in tongues (glossolalia). COGIC has also stressed repentance, regeneration, and the gift of healing as evidence of the Baptism of the Spirit. The ordinances of the church include baptism by immersion, the Lord's Supper, and foot washing.

Elder Thomas Frazier is administrative assistant to Bishop Chandler David Owens, one of five COGIC Bishops in the state of Georgia. Frazier is also chair of the Board of Superintendents of Central Georgia, and vice president of Central Georgia's Board of Ordination. In addition, he serves as pastor of the Temple of Faith Church of God in Christ. Elder Frazier accounts for the rapidity of church growth within the COGIC by pointing to its emphasis upon evangelism, by which countless numbers have been brought into the fold. For Frazier, reaching souls is paramount to the life and work of the church. In Frazier's own congregation, this evangelistic mandate is expressed through a ministry called "Bridge of Hope" in which homeless persons are bussed in from under the bridges of the city and offered a meal, encouragement, and most importantly, salvation.

Elder Paul L. Fortson, pastor of Paradise Church of God in Christ, presents a vision of ministry in which he and his parishioners offer the world just what the name of the congregation intends, paradise. Elder Fortson's view of ministry has two main foci: to reach the lost for the Lord and to share God's love with the community. Fortson recently conducted an open-air crusade at Atlanta's Lakewood Amphitheater emphasizing the message: "The Lord will give anyone a chance . . . whosoever will, let him come." He also believes that "through preaching, praising, and praying, we may bring hope to those who have no hope. This will, in turn, impact our communities. The influence upon our communities will, in turn, impact our world."

AFRICAN AMERICANS IN PREDOMINANTLY WHITE DENOMINATIONS

There are also, of course, African Americans who are members of predominantly white Protestant denominations. Reference has already been made to the United Methodists. Likewise, we will find African Americans in Episcopal, Lutheran, and Presbyterian churches as well. In this section I will focus exclusively on blacks who are involved in the Presbyterian denomination here in Atlanta. The first African-American Presbyterian church in the country was the First African Presbyterian Church of Philadelphia, founded in1807. Today, there are approximately 70,000 African Americans in the Presbyterian Church, 450 African-American churches in the country, and nine African-American Presbyterian churches in Atlanta.

Dr. David Wallace is the dean of Johnson C. Smith Seminary, the Presbyterian constituent member of the Interdenominational Theological Center (ITC) in Atlanta. Dr. Wallace is also the former pastor of the Church of the Master Presbyterian Church, which was founded by the current president of the ITC, Dr. James Costen. Dr. Wallace describes African-American worship among Presbyterians in Atlanta as culturally sensitive, yet committed to the central principles of the Presbyterian Book of Order. He refers to the inclusion of spirituals and gospel songs in worship, liturgical dance, religious drama, and preaching on contemporary issues as reflections of culture sensitivity coupled with traditional commitment.

Wallace further characterizes African-American Presbyterianism by its insistence upon the highest educational credentials for its pastors, a more structured liturgy, and theological clarity, especially emphasizing the sovereignty of God in all things. Community outreach and evangelism also have a place within the Presbyterian understanding of ministry. Some of the programs associated with Wallace's congregation include a narcotics anonymous program, a day care center, a tutorial program, a counseling and referral service, and a food bank. Community involvement includes an Ecumenical Emergency Assistance Center, consisting of approximately 8 churches that seek to provide outreach services to persons in southwest Atlanta.

The New Life Presbyterian Church is perhaps the most rapidly growing of the nine African-American Presbyterian churches in the metropolitan Atlanta area. Located in College Park, this church displays a clear and present acknowledgment of African heritage and culture. Under the leadership of Dr. Lonnie Oliver, the congregation embodies a significant effort to bring the Presbyterian tradition into meaningful engagement with the lived experience of African Americans in contemporary culture.

AFRICAN-AMERICAN NON-DENOMINATIONAL WITNESSES

There are also those African Americans who do not align themselves with any of the traditional mainline denominations. Wayne C. Thompson serves as senior pastor of the charismatic Fellowship of Faith Church International, which is located in East Point, Georgia, and has a membership of several thousand. The highly exuberant worship service at Fellowship of Faith ranges from the lifting of holy hands in praise to the laying on of hands for healing. Pastor Wayne's vision of ministry is "to educate and prepare the people of God to meet the challenges of the future, with God as the center of all things, while remembering Proverbs 1:16, 'The beginning of all knowledge is the fear of the Lord.'"

Fellowship of Faith was founded in 1977 and has grown from what were originally Bible studies conducted by Pastor Wayne in restaurants, trailers, and homes, to a ministry that reaches several thousand people each week through its three worship services on Sunday, two weekly Bible studies, and various seminars focused on the family. The congregation also has numerous other community-related activities, including a feed-the-hungry ministry, a prison ministry, a teen ministry, an athletics and recreation program, a ministry to the deaf, and a senior citizens ministry. Pastor Wayne is also founder of a local private school, the Southwest Atlanta Christian Academy (SACA). With an enrollment of 289, SACA provides a family environment that is biblically-based and promotes academic excellence with the promise of community leadership. Brother Wayne points to the failure of many public school systems to remain true to the principles upon which they were originally founded, and their significant contribution to what he refers to as the "demoralization" of America.

Fellowship of Faith Associate Pastor, Bill Christian, serves as headmaster of SACA. He explained that the Academy includes an early learning center (infancy to 5 years), an elementary school (grades 1 to 6), and a junior/senior high school (grades 7 to 12). Furthermore, according to Christian, the curriculum meets all state requirements for graduation and college preparation. Explaining the purpose of the SACA, Pastor Wayne remarks: "Since God is the source of all existence, and learning is that process whereby we come to know God through His word, wisdom, will and way, it follows then that true education is Christian education."

AFRICAN-AMERICAN PROTESTANT CLERGY

As one might expect, African-American clergy in Atlanta, as anywhere else, represent a wide range of theological beliefs, denominational affiliations, political persuasions, economic backgrounds, educational levels, leadership styles, preaching proclivities, and social orientations. They are "stationed" not only in pastorates, but also in various chaplaincies at hospitals, colleges, prisons, and other agencies. Many clergy serve in assistant or associate positions to senior pastors while others serve as college and/or university professors and administrators. There are also the "street" ministers who allow their voices to fall upon "any who have ears to hear."

For those who seek higher theological education (beyond the baccalaureate degree) within an African-American frame of reference, Atlanta offers the Interdenominational Theological Center (ITC). The ITC is made up of a unique consortium of six denominational seminaries: Turner Theological Seminary (African Methodist Episcopal), Morehouse School of Religion (Baptist), Charles H. Mason Seminary (Church of God in Christ), Phillips School of Theology (Christian Methodist Episcopal), Johnson C. Smith Seminary (Presbyterian), and Gammon Theological Seminary (United Methodist). In addition to the ITC, many African-American clergy (and prospective clergy) attend either Emory University's Candler School of Theology in Atlanta or Columbia Theological Seminary in Decatur, Georgia.

The organization known as the Concerned Black Clergy of Atlanta is under the current leadership of Dr. Gerald Durley, Pastor of Providence Baptist Church (the church home of the late Dr. Benjamin E. Mays, Morehouse College President and mentor to Dr. Martin L. King, Jr.). Durley is the fourth president of this non-profit organization that was formed in 1983 with an initial concern for helping the homeless. Dr. Durley notes that annual assistance to the homeless has grown from 500 persons in 1983 to 16,000 persons in 1995. Concerned Black Clergy meets every Monday morning in an open forum with some 125 clergy and lay people regularly in attendance. Discussions range from HIV/AIDS to school bonds. Two of the organization's main fundraising activities are programs entitled "Salute to Black Fathers" and "Salute to Black Mothers."

The greatest challenge that Concerned Black Clergy of Atlanta has addressed during Dr. Durley's tenure relates to "demonstrating the impact of a conservative Congress's 'Contract on/with America' upon children, the handicapped, those on Medicaid, etc." Dr. Durley, whose advocacy for the "voiceless" is never absent in his community activities, describes his own pastoral mandate as "attempting to meet the physical, social, psychological, educational, as well as spiritual needs of people whom we are called to serve."

AFRICAN-AMERICAN PROTESTANTISM AND WOMEN

Discussion of the "place and plight" of women with respect to both pulpit and pew is as alive among African Americans in Atlanta as anywhere else nationally. It is refreshing, however, to observe that in Atlanta, not only do we find women in the traditional or customary church roles of Sunday School teacher, musician, deaconess, usher, evangelist, secretary, nurse, "mother of the church," etc., but also serving the metropolitan Atlanta area in some form of diaconal or ordained pastoral ministry as well.

The Reverend Gail Bowman, College Minister at Spelman College, brings a unique background in both law and theology to the historic African-American women's campus. She expresses interest in the variety of worship styles that the African-American religious scene in Atlanta presents. She comments: "From the reserved to the charismatic, it's all here." Reverend Bowman also notes how seriously many African-American Atlantans regard church membership and attendance. She reports that even among her Spelman women undergraduates there is a curiosity about and desire for spiritual exploration beyond the academic context.

On the issue of women as clergy, the Reverend Caroline B. Terry, Chaplain to the Atlanta Police Department (and a deacon at Friendship Baptist Church), observes that there are some religious communities that are far more inclusive of women leadership than others. According to Chaplain Terry, "In Atlanta, as anywhere else, there is a continuum of acceptance/non-acceptance in the movement of women from the periphery to the center of church leadership."

The Reverend Cynthia Hale, Pastor of the Ray of Hope Christian Church, whose congregation has grown from a Bible study of four in 1986 to a thriving community of 1,600, relates her considerable involvement in women's ministries. Her participation has ranged from leadership of women's conferences in churches throughout the country, to being a member of "Sisterhood," a group within her own congregation that seeks to minister to the total woman; from involvement in "Sister to Sister," a group of women from several churches in a consortium of which Ray of Hope is a member, to support of Trinity Shelter for homeless women and children; from rallying others to give aid to imprisoned mothers, to ministering to women with AIDS. Reverend Hale also points to other women within the academic as well as the ecclesiastical community who are providing valuable resources to and for women. Dr. Jacquelyn Grant, Professor of Systematic Theology at the ITC and author of *White Women's Christ, Black Women's Jesus*, has provided an academic context in which to engage "Women in Church and Society." The Reverend Dr. Bernice King, daughter of Dr. Martin L. King, Jr. and Associate Pastor at the Greater Rising Star Baptist Church, has organized many conferences, including "Women, Ordering Their Steps in the Lord."

Although there are many doors yet to be opened and challenges yet to be faced, there is abundant evidence that many strides forward have been taken by Atlanta's African-American Protestant Christian women, strides that serve the good of the church and the community as a whole.

CONCLUDING REMARKS

Now that we have surveyed a sample of the broad range of religious expressions and organizations, we may once again raise the question of identifying the "essence" of African-American Protestant Christianity in Atlanta. Is there some unifying substance among African-American Protestants of which the various denominational/non-denominational groups are but passing forms? Is there that which endures time and space, both moment and place, and serves to ground African-American Protestant existence in Atlanta soil? As the African-American church in America has been referred to as a "Nation within a Nation," does African-American Protestantism in Atlanta constitute a "City within a City"?

The Reverend Amy Hartsfield, Chaplain/Counselor at the ITC, Th.D. candidate under the auspices of the Atlanta Theological Association, and spouse of an Atlanta Baptist pastor, views Atlanta African-American religious life as a rich historical and cultural resource, "an abiding foundation of social coherence." In this comment, Chaplain Hartsfield has given expression to an abiding feature of all religious behavior: social cohesion. Given the manifold ways in which African Americans in Atlanta have appropriated Christian symbol and meaning systems, the religious life of this diverse community must surely function to preserve those cherished values, norms, and standards believed to sustain the life and livelihood of a kindred people.

Certainly in a large, metropolitan city such as Atlanta, one may observe within a radius of a few blocks, and often within the same block, the heterogeneous makeup of African-American Protestant Christianity. From the emotionally cathartic expression of the Pentecostals to the more subdued expression of the Episcopalians, from the characteristic preaching of the Baptists to the confessions of the Methodists, from the charismatic emphases of the evangelicals to the prayers of the Presbyterians, one can find it all in black Atlanta. Even within any given black denominational or non-denominational orientation, the diversity is equally apparent. This chapter can only highlight the plethora of beliefs, the polyphony of sounds, the contrast of practices, the tapestry of traditions all representing, yet not fully capturing, African-American expressions of Protestant Christianity in a southern city called "Atlanta."

FOR FURTHER INFORMATION

Edward R. Carter. *The Black Side.* Atlanta, s.n., 1894

Eric C. Lincoln and Lawrence H. Mamiya. *The Black Church in the African American Experience.* Durham, Duke University Press, 1990

Carlyle F. Stewart. *African American Church Growth.* Nashville, Abingdon Press, 1994

C H A P T E R   F O U R

A "CATHOLIC" CATHOLIC CHURCH: THE ROMAN CATHOLIC COMMUNITY OF ATLANTA

Helen Blier

Shrine of the Immaculate Conception. Photograph by Elizabeth Hardcastle.

The history of the Roman Catholic Archdiocese of Atlanta is rather short by anyone's standards, but Catholic roots run deep in the area, dating all the way back to sixteenth-century Spanish colonization. Following the colonial period, the area's Catholics were under the governance of Maryland's, then Charleston's, bishop. By 1850, the Catholic population in Savannah, Georgia, was large enough for it to become a diocese, covering all of Georgia and part of Florida. Over a hundred years later, in 1956, the 71 northernmost counties of Georgia were set aside as an episcopal entity separate from Savannah's diocese.

By 1962, just six years after establishment of the diocese, the populations of both the region and the diocese had grown sufficiently to merit elevation to the status of archdiocese. Today, Atlanta's episcopal office oversees the dioceses of Savannah, Charleston, South Carolina, and Raleigh, North Carolina. Florida, part of the original episcopacy, is now its own province. According to a 1994 census, there were about 200,000 officially registered Catholics in the state of Georgia—roughly 5% of the total population—with most living in the Atlanta metro area. This number seems paltry when compared to predominantly Catholic regions like Boston and Chicago. However, when one considers the fact that just 20 years ago the population stood at 61,000 Catholics, the change in numbers—a 230% increase—becomes staggering.

Why are so many of these new Catholics coming to the metro area? The most important factor relates to economic opportunity. Most of the new people are transplants from the midwest and northeast who have decided to search for financial success here and who have remained committed to the Catholic faith. Yet it is also true that a large number of people have chosen to convert to Catholicism. At the "Rite of Election" in March 1995, over a thousand catechumens (those preparing for baptism) and candidates (those preparing for full entry into the Catholic church, usually from other Christian denominations) were publicly acknowledged and celebrated. A large number of Catholic immigrants, primarily Hispanic and Vietnamese, have also moved into the area, though for various reasons they are not always represented by the census figures. As a result, the actual number of

Catholics in the area is probably significantly higher than the number given above.

The newness of the archdiocese and many of its members gives Atlanta's community a decidedly "post-Vatican II" atmosphere. The Second Vatican Council, convened by Pope John XXIII and held in four sessions from 1962 to 1965, called upon the world's clergy and laity to "open the windows" to an institution that had remained largely unchanged for more than 400 years. The council succeeded in moving the church from cultural confinement to a more world-oriented stance. Some of the changes include underscoring the importance of the role and participation of the laity, the use of vernacular language in the Mass, and an affirmation of the truth embodied in other religious traditions. Atlanta's Catholic communities reflect many of these changes in their architecture, programming, worship, and lay involvement. In fact, people often contrast the progressive, lay-oriented Atlanta community with, for example, the church of Savannah, where old Irish Catholic roots give the community a much more traditional ethos.

One way the Catholic church has accommodated the recent surge in numbers has been to build new churches throughout the metro region. In the past twenty years, the number of parishes in the archdiocese has grown from 41 to 66. This rate of growth, however, is considerably smaller than that of the population as a whole, and means that individual parishes sometimes find themselves bursting at the seams. It is not unusual to find a parish in the suburbs, where most new residents settle, with over 4,000 families. When the numbers become unwieldy, a parish will often sponsor a mission, a smaller community still attached to its parent church while serving a portion of the parishioners. Eventually the mission attains full parish status and becomes pastorally and financially independent from the original congregation. The comparatively small number of priests, 211 as of mid-1994, means that clergy are spread thinly through the area, with some of the larger parishes having only two priests on staff (three if they are fortunate). As a result, the laity are extremely invested and involved in their communities—partially out of necessity, partially out of a heightened commitment to their religious identity in the midst of a largely non-Catholic region. It is not unusual for the overwhelmed clergy to enlist the help of lay members to handle many of the administrative and programming duties presented by such large communities.

This growth, while an evangelist's dream come true, has not been without its problems. "It is an adolescent archdiocese," said Bill Timme, a permanent deacon at Holy Cross Parish in Chamblee. "And like any adolescent, it's had its growing pains." Until recently, the archdiocese had very few of its own men entering the priesthood; as a result, many parishes were established and staffed by religious orders, a tradition stretching back to the church's early days. By 1995, as many as 60 young men from the area were preparing for priesthood. In order to create room for these ordinandi, however, archdiocesan officials have taken positions previously staffed by religious orders and turned them over to diocesan clergy. One such turnover took place recently at Timme's church, where members of the Dominican order, who had staffed the parish for nearly twenty years, were told they had to leave. The laity were incensed, primarily because the move was made without consulting them at all. One insisted, "*We* are the people! *We* are the parish! They didn't even care about that!" Others could not understand the decision itself. "It didn't make sense," said one distraught parishioner. "All these understaffed parishes around here could use these guys."

Although its members proudly speak of the distinct spirit or "charism" that is unique to Holy Cross, Timme's parish is typical of a large suburban Catholic church in Atlanta. The laity are greatly invested in their community, serving as facilitators for the several dozen ministries sponsored by the community, most of them education- and justice-oriented. They have a higher percentage of regular attendees and donate more per capita than nearly any other church in the diocese. Its members also take their Catholic identity very seriously, defining themselves largely by Vatican II standards. Indeed, their anger at the removal of their pastoral leaders was to be expected, given the emphasis the Council placed on lay empowerment.

The "growing pains" experienced by Holy Cross are not unique. As a whole and in its individual communities, the Catholic church in Atlanta has had to struggle with the contradictions associated with living in the contemporary moment and having some sense of rootedness in the greater Catholic tradition. This tension often takes the form of struggling with what it means to be Catholic in the ever-shifting social and cultural "salad bowl" that is Atlanta. How can people belong to a universal church while allowing for inculturated expressions of that faith, expressions which mean something in a particular place and time? The story of the Catholic Archdiocese of Atlanta may best be told through the stories of some of its remarkable individuals and communities, stories of members who have negotiated this struggle and helped shape the identity of the Atlanta Archdiocese.

PASTORS OF A FLEDGLING FLOCK: ATLANTA'S FIRST BISHOPS

The Diocese of Atlanta was established in 1956, during a particularly turbulent time in the history of both the South and the Catholic church. Its formative years were largely influenced by two major transitions of the late 50s and early 60s, the Civil Rights movement, and Vatican II. The church could not ignore the calls for justice and social transformation that were so compelling in these years, and the ecclesial hierarchy was mandating more openness and responsiveness to the modern world. Throughout this period, the attitudes of the laity covered a broad range of positions; while some were enthusiastic about change, others vehemently opposed it. In this context the community's episcopal leaders were left with the challenge of negotiating a course of both formation and reformation.

The first bishop of the new episcopacy, Francis E. Hyland, took on his creative task enthusiastically, overseeing the construction and renovation of more than fifty churches, as well as three high schools. He also made his presence known on the civic circuit. When a bill to legalize sterilization came before the state legislature, he appeared before the sponsoring committee and asserted, "We cannot and must not attempt to breed children as we do cattle!" The bill never left committee, and the following day's headlines read, "Hyland Kills Sterilization Bill." In 1956, he publicly condemned racism "in all its various shapes and forms." Conscious of the use of diocesan schools as havens of "white flight," he mandated the deliberate integration of the area's Catholic schools and hospitals—a decision that was not always popular with the faithful.

With the diocese's elevation to archdiocesan status in 1962 came the appointment of new Archbishop Paul J. Hallinan. Hyland had been forced to resign for health reasons, but Bishop Hallinan vigorously pursued many of the goals of his predecessor. Having attended the Second Vatican Council in Rome, he was deeply influenced by the Council's call to justice at all levels of society. In 1964, Bishop Hallinan publicly opposed America's involvement in Southeast Asia. His friendship with Dr. Martin Luther King, Jr., planted him firmly on the side of actively supporting racial justice at a time when many of his contemporaries preferred to remain "neutral." When his friend received the Nobel Peace Prize in 1965, city officials planned no festivities to honor their local son. Indignant, Bishop Hallinan called on two other friends, Rabbi Jacob Rothschild and Ralph McGill, the publishing magnate. The three oversaw an enormous dinner party to celebrate Dr. King and his work—the only commemoration of the prize in Atlanta. Although Bishop Hallinan was hospitalized with the hepatitis that would eventually kill him, he defied doctor's orders and was present to congratulate his friend.

Archbishop Thomas Donellen followed Hallinan and had the longest and perhaps most stable episcopal tenure to date, from 1968 to 1987. He is often credited with helping the archdiocese establish some equilibrium after the difficult transitions of the 60s. In the six years following Donellen tenure, however, the archdiocesan reins were passed on to three more leaders in rapid succession. Archbishop Eugene Marino stepped down after it was revealed that he had had an affair with a young woman, and Archbishop James Lyke died from cancer just two years after his appointment. Archbishop John Donoghue now holds the episcopal office, the sixth leader in a job usually characterized by lengthy administrations. Catholics who have been in the city long enough to have experienced the quick turnover of leaders feel as if they have been left reeling by the changes. Some describe the premature loss of Marino and Lyke as having "broken their hearts"; others wonder what the future holds for a diocese born in the midst of progress and change.

THE SPIRIT OF FR. O'REILLY: SHRINE OF THE IMMACULATE CONCEPTION

On Martin Luther King, Jr. Boulevard, an oxblood brick church of Gothic revival design sits in the shadow of the gold dome of the State Capitol. Over 120 years old, it is the oldest intact building in downtown Atlanta. Inside, light filters through a stained glass rendering of Mary in blue, illumining ushers wearing wide smiles and Birkenstocks, who greet with a warm, "Happy Sunday!" The priest, whose only vestments are a simple white robe and stole, laughs and chats amiably with congregants before the elaborately carved marble altar. Under ceiling murals of Anglo-looking apostles, racially diverse members prepare themselves for worship. This is a typical Sunday at the Catholic Shrine of the Immaculate Conception, where surprising and varied elements have come, over time, to worship comfortably with each other.

The shrine is probably best known as the home parish of the infamous Fr. Thomas O'Reilly, the feisty Irish cleric who, near the end of the Civil War, stood down Union troops, saving the shrine and more than 400 other buildings from the fire that destroyed most of the rest of Atlanta. The current building is not the original structure he saved. The original church, built in 1848, although spared the fire, was seriously damaged by shelling and because it was used as an infirmary during the war. In 1869, ground was broken for a new building, solely at the suggestion of parishioners. But many Atlantans argued that the project was too ambitious. Only 21,000 people lived in the city at the time, and then, as today, only a small portion were Catholic. But the community was anxious to start life over after the war, and ultimately their resilience prevailed—the new building was dedicated in 1873. Construction was completed seven years later. The finished church was arguably one of the grandest buildings in the city. The *Atlanta Constitution* called it "an especial tribute to the zeal, energy and large-hearted liberality of the membership in Atlanta." It was rededicated and officially designated a shrine following its renovation in 1954.

Fr. John Adamski pastors the parish today. He arrived in 1987, after the Franciscan order left the parish in order to focus on other ministries. At that time, the church's population had dwindled to about a hundred families, mostly "old timers" whose obligations did not extend much beyond attending Sunday service. Today there are over 300 registered families from various ethnic and socioeconomic backgrounds—a threefold increase in just over eight years—who have a very different understanding of what it means to be a practicing Catholic than their predecessors had.

The shrine is what is called an "intentional community." Its members do not attend because they live within the set geographic boundaries that demarcate most Catholic parishes; rather, they choose purposefully to attend the shrine, sometimes driving significant distances for what they identify as the church's unique spirit or "charism." And although the congregation has grown dramatically in recent years, it is still quite small by most standards, nurturing an atmosphere of intimacy and familiarity that many find attractive.

Fr. Adamski credits the church's social outreach programs with drawing most of the new members. Many who belong have found a niche for themselves at the shrine that they could not find elsewhere. The identity of the community is so closely tied to its outreach that at a Mass following Easter, newly baptized and confirmed members were given the opportunity to publicly "covenant" themselves to the social ministry programs of their choice. All of these programs have emerged from the church's response to needs presented by people in the area. In addition to sponsoring a Saturday night meal for Atlanta's homeless, church members currently support one of the largest and most comprehensive AIDS ministries in the city. "We did it before many people did, before it was a popular thing to do," says Fr. Adamski. It began with the "Tuesday Night Dinner" for People With AIDS (PWAs), established shortly after his arrival; at its peak, over 200 meals a week were served. When numbers dwindled, the congregation ended the dinners and focused attention elsewhere. One result of this refocused attention was the establishment of a single-room occupancy house for PWAs near Grady Hospital.

Some of the ministries supported by the shrine have been controversial. In 1992, at the urging of some parishioners, Fr. Adamski challenged the congregation to sponsor a gay and lesbian support group. The subsequent controversy split the congregation, with those against sponsorship citing the Catholic church's opposition to homosexuality. One outraged member brought the story to a local news station, hoping that the negative publicity would quash the ministry. "We were the top 6 o'clock news story," chuckled Fr. Adamski. Undeterred, the community decided to weather the storm and do the ministry—those who could not tolerate the decision went elsewhere to worship.

Asked if he had any regrets about the tension caused by the outreach program, Adamski answered with a firm but thoughtful "No." "I think we're a better community as a result of it," he added. "We've dealt with an issue that is part of the life of the church these days and have managed to get to a place of some peace and some comfort about this issue within our community. To me that's a lot better and healthier than saying, `Oh, no, we can't talk about that!'" He speculated that doing social ministry and responding to the needs of the community would probably always cause fights, but the important thing was having enough peace to get down to the business of doing the ministry.

The shrine's location in downtown Atlanta leads to greater interaction with other religious communities compared to what takes place in the sprawling suburban parishes that comprise most of the metro area's Catholic churches. As a result of being situated close to other Protestant denominations, the church has learned to coexist ecumenically with its neighbors, particularly Central Presbyterian. When Central Presbyterian's overnight shelter for homeless men had to be closed for renovations, the displaced men slept in the shrine's church hall. And each Palm Sunday, the two churches, along with Trinity Methodist down the street, share in a procession with music and banners around downtown. The church also sends representatives to civic meetings concerned with issues of violence, poverty, illness, and so forth.

Adamski says that it is difficult to imagine where the shrine specifically, and the church in general, will be in the next few years. His community is, in many ways, a microcosm of metro Atlanta's Catholic church at large; it has undergone tremendous flux and growth in recent years and has experienced plenty of growing pains as it negotiates its place and identity in the region. The church, he observed, has grown largely through displacement. While it is good to have a variety of perspectives to bring to the table, it also means that people's preexisting relationships are few and far between. Perhaps, he speculated, the role of the church is to offer people a sense of belonging and a place that persists in the midst of so much transition: "If you have been displaced and kind of lost your bearings, then that reasonably strong sense of community can be attractive."

WE'VE COME THIS FAR BY FAITH: THE PARISH OF OUR LADY OF LOURDES

Nestled between the birth home of Dr. Martin Luther King, Jr. and the Baptist church he served is a pair of modest buildings, separated by a bit of asphalt that functions as a playground and parking lot. The buildings are architecturally unremarkable, and visitors to the area's more famous attractions often presume that they are part of the King Center. A sign in front of them tells you, however, that you have arrived at the Catholic Church and School of Our Lady of Lourdes.

The sanctuary of the church is entered through a door in the shape of a large, cut-out cross. It mirrors the wall directly across from it, which separates the altar from a small chapel behind it; in this wall is an identical cut-out in which a crucifix hangs. The wall itself reaches from behind the altar and angles out towards the congregation, appearing to extend from the outstretched arms of the cross. The wall, it is said, has a story. The architect commissioned to do interior renovations attended Mass at the church for several Sundays to get a sense of the parish's spirit before making any changes. He was most profoundly moved by the enthusiastic hospitality of the congregation, best embodied, he felt, in the way they reached across aisles to hold hands while praying the Our Father. The wall was built to symbolize this gesture. But those who know some of the parish's history would agree that the wall symbolizes more than just the gesture; it recalls some of the history of a community that has triumphed over segregation and hostility.

"Lourdes," as its members affectionately call it, has been around since 1912, but its story began about a year prior to that. Fr. Ignatius Lissner, a member of the Society for the African Missions, arrived in Atlanta for a liturgical function. What he saw troubled him deeply; not only were the majority of the city's blacks living in dire poverty, but segregation laws meant that those who were Catholic had nowhere to worship. He immediately submitted a proposal to Bishop Benjamin Kelley of Savannah-Atlanta to establish a mission church and school for black Catholics. Bishop Kelley was supportive but cautious in his reply. He wrote, "Have courage, dear Fr. Lissner. The task before you is a laudable, but a most difficult, one; however, remember the words our Lord addressed to his Apostles, `They will persecute you and drive you out of their city, and think they have performed a good work if they execute and kill you; but I will be with you; I have conquered the world.'"

Fr. Lissner returned to Atlanta to find a site for his new mission, and his experiences confirmed the bishop's concerns. The first one chosen, on Highland Avenue, was successfully blocked by whites from the area. Both anti-black and anti-Catholic sentiments contributed to the vigorous opposition. One evening, not long after the confrontation, one of the men who had led the opposition appeared on Fr. Lissner's doorstep. He was not a Catholic, but he had been impressed by Lissner's fearlessness and refusal to be intimidated. He had come to offer a $25 donation and his support.

In March 1912, the present site on Boulevard was purchased, just a few blocks from the "Sweet Auburn" black business district. Mother Katherine Drexel, a wealthy heiress and founder of the Sisters of the Blessed Sacrament, obtained financing for the project, and by November the building was blessed and dedicated. The three-story, brick complex consisted of a church on the first floor, classrooms on the second, and a social hall on the third. When the parish outgrew its facilities, the entire building was turned over to the school and the present church was built in 1961.

It is extremely difficult for many to understand what life was like for the earliest members of Lourdes. Mrs. Annabella Jones remembers, though. Having attended Lourdes since 1935, she is not only one of the unofficial "mothers" of the church, she is also a living archive of local Catholic lore. She arrived in Atlanta from her native New Orleans in 1934 and, not knowing the city well, chose to attend Sacred Heart first, presuming she would visit the various parishes before settling on one. She recalled her first visit to the church. As she left her pew to join the line when communion time came, a woman pulled her aside and asked, was she new here? Mrs. Jones replied, "Yes." She was black, wasn't she? Yes again. "I'm afraid," said the woman, "you're going to have to wait until everyone else has received to go up." Mrs. Jones drew herself up to her full five foot height and replied that she *would not*: "I go when the bell tells me to go, and I will *not* wait to go last." It became clear, she said, that Lourdes would have to be her home parish.

Mrs. Jones also delights in telling the postscript to the story. She approached the woman after Mass to ask about her reaction and began a conversation that later evolved into a friendship. The woman eventually started a community house near Lourdes to offer basic social and medical services. Mrs. Jones likes to think that her outreach to the woman helped facilitate this change of heart. When asked why she was not angry with the woman, Mrs. Jones replied firmly, "If someone has a problem with me because I'm black, that's *their* problem."

As the history of African Americans shows, however, prejudice and its consequences have indeed been a problem for the black community. Surprisingly, despite its black congregation and location in King's neighborhood, Lourdes played no real institutional role in the Civil Rights movement. Indeed, the Catholic church as a whole has often been criticized for not having played a more active official role in ending racism and segregation in the United States. In reality, however, the situation for Catholics in the South was far more complex than simply deciding whether or not to participate in marches and protests; in some southern areas, for example, white and black sisters of the same religious order could not legally live together until the mid 1950s. Furthermore, given southern anti-Catholic sentiment, the members of Lourdes often found themselves at the edges of the already marginalized black community. Some even recalled the elder Reverend King strongly opposing children from his church attending school at Lourdes.

For people looking back on the movement with the clarity of hindsight, it seems unbelievable that Lourdes could have been in the midst of such social change without being more involved. Janis Griffin, whose family converted to Catholicism while she attended Lourdes' school, recalls being there in the movement's early days. In retrospect, she regrets not having been involved. But people live in the concrete reality of day to day life, and many agreed that it was easy to be insulated from much of the turbulence. Sr. Loretta McCarthy, who was principal of the school in the late 60s, recalls being too caught up in her duties to be all that aware of "what was going on." Furthermore, those who did participate in the marches and protests were often considered "rebels."

Members of Lourdes who reflected on this period of their history had no intention of excusing the church's lack of proactive involvement in the movement's more obvious forms of protest. Nevertheless, all of them wanted to underscore the ongoing role of the parish and school in both providing a sanctuary for blacks and empowering them through education. As Sr. Loretta points out, the church had been responding to the needs of the black community before it was mainstream to do so. Furthermore, in the mid 70s, the Sisters of the Blessed Sacrament turned the leadership of the school over to the laity, recognizing that true empowerment meant directing the means of education as well as being educated. There are also plenty of stories of individuals within the community who marched, intervened, and acted courageously—the nun who protested with sanitation workers, the college students who marched, the pastor who provided sanctuary from the Klan for a black family, and so on.

The best way to understand the unique character of Lourdes today is to attend its weekly worship. After having experienced lean years in the 70s and a rapid turnover of pastors, the parish is experiencing a renaissance. There are currently more than three hundred registered families, and about half attend Mass on a regular basis—well over the standard 35% of most Catholic parishes. In the past decade, the population of the parish has doubled. Most agree that the quality of the Lourdes liturgy is the main attraction. The people of Lourdes have managed to develop a liturgical life that both nurtures and reflects the unique ethnic and spiritual needs of the congregation.

Serious attendance problems precipitated this development. Until the early 1980s, Mass at Lourdes was by and large what one might have found at any European American church; the cultural heritage of the community had yet to find its way into its worship. Membership was down to fewer than 150 families, and many of the youth had stopped attending, preferring to go to communities that acknowledged their ethnic identity. Those who chose to remain felt the need to address the growing malaise of the community. As Mrs. Jones put it, "People never even looked at each other any more."

The situation at Lourdes mirrored problems felt by African-American Catholics at a national level. Black consciousness movements of the 60s and 70s led to a reexamination of what it meant to be both African-American and Catholic, while the changes of the Second Vatican Council opened the door to the possibility of liturgical experimentation. One of the changes Lourdes made was to incorporate music that reflected both the Catholic and African-American elements of their heritage. A Gospel choir was established in the early 80s, and for the past decade they have sung the Mass settings written by Grayson Brown, a black Catholic liturgical musician. His pieces are deeply influenced by Gospel music, black spirituals, and the language of liberation movements. The "Christ has died . . ." sung at Lourdes, for example, shares the melody of "We Shall Overcome."

Janis Griffin was instrumental in establishing the choir and remains an active member of it today. Changes in music, she says, were especially important because young people latch on to music. "[The music] transcends both worlds," she said. "It was Catholic, yet it was ethnic, yet it was acceptable." She credits the music with helping the community establish its unique identity as black and Catholic in not only its membership but also its prayer life. "Finally we realized that as African Americans it was all right to sing our music—we could be black and we could be Catholic and we could do all those things." But it is still comforting, she adds, to know that the basic parts of the ritual are the same and join the worshipers to the universal catholic church.

The changes are working. The church is often full on Sunday mornings, brimming with both older members and young families. There are always a fair number of first-time or repeat visitors as well. Many of the non-African-American attendees are actually registered at other Atlanta parishes, but they attend Mass at Lourdes every few weeks. "It's my 'soul food,'" said one such visitor. Griffin summed up the attraction and her own deep investment this way: "The Catholic church is a church of ritual and not a lot of emotions. And my soul needs a lot of emotions. I find that the way we worship here satisfies me—and I think that's why a lot of people come, because they need more than ritual, too."

Indeed, longtime parishioners have seen the complexion of Lourdes change as more non-black Catholics have been attracted to the parish's liturgy. About 90% of the parish's registered population is African American, but on any given Sunday as many as a fourth of those in attendance are not. Current pastor Fr. Frank Giusta finds this remarkable. "Our population is shifting, the ethnicity is changing—and there is no animosity, no tension. In fact, the people are very welcoming." Mrs. Jones agrees: "There's more love generated now. People are closer together. It's the way it should be."

It is clear that as more of the surrounding neighborhoods are revitalized, the role and membership of Lourdes will continue to change. Few members, though, express deep concern about the church's future. It has managed profound social change both inside and outside its walls, and there is no reason to believe that it will not continue to do so. Sr. Loretta locates the parish's true center of power in the people and not the administration, and this gives her hope. "Lourdes is like a phoenix, rising from the ashes. Despite their woes," she observes, "the people still come together. They can proclaim God's goodness that God will make a way for us. And it can take place in a liturgy that is so alive; it doesn't depend on one person for the charism." Griffin's own testimony to her dedication to Lourdes expresses this spirit well: "Because of blessings I have received through my music ministry, I've seen and visited a lot of churches. They're beautiful, and they have a lot more physical amenities—but," she laughed, "I wouldn't trade my little dinky church for anybody's!"

LOS NIÑOS DE LA VIRGIN MARIA: THE CATHOLIC HISPANIC COMMUNITY

Those with questions about the future of the Catholic church in Atlanta must inevitably look towards the Hispanic community for some of the answers. Of all the communities within the archdiocese, the Hispanics are by far the fastest growing as well as one of the most complex. A 1990 census reported 75,000 Hispanics registered in north Georgia, though the actual figure was probably about double at the time. As of 1995, conservative estimates put the population at nearly a quarter of a million people, representing 21 different nationalities. And worldwide, Hispanics comprise more than 50% of the Roman Catholic church.

The Spanish-speaking Catholic presence is not new to Georgia. In fact, Spanish settlers are credited with bringing Roman Catholicism to the southeast as well as to the rest of the Americas in the sixteenth century. But the new arrivals have greatly different reasons for coming than their predecessors. While their forebears came in search of gold and adventure, today's immigrant often arrives with few material resources in search of hope, a living wage, and freedom from political oppression.

Most are from Mexico, El Salvador, and Guatemala; some, however, are "internal immigrants," driven away from places like California and Texas, where economies are troubled and anti-immigration laws have impacted even naturalized citizens. Attracted by an abundance of low-skill labor opportunities in north Georgia, they usually find work in the poultry or construction industries in Cartersville, Gainesville, or Rome. Those who have already established themselves in the area provide a sophisticated word-of-mouth support network for the new immigrants, helping them negotiate the "system," and find a job and a place to stay. Several full-time employees of the Hispanic Catholic Apostolate assist by offering moral and material support. "It's a sticky situation," says Gonzalo Saldaña, director of the Apostolate. "We cannot do referrals or break the law. But we can act as mediator on behalf of the newly arrived."

The archdiocese established the Hispanic Apostolate to respond to immigrants' needs. What began as a single Spanish-language Mass held outdoors has blossomed into a comprehensive ministry, largely under the stewardship of Archbishop Lyke in the late 1980s. The Apostolate now offers Spanish-language liturgy and religious instruction in nearly 30 missions and parishes throughout the archdiocese. Two women's religious orders, the Missionaries of the Sacred Heart of Jesus and the Handmaids of the Sacred Heart, also provide education, medical attention, and other services at the various missions. Many immigrants have heavy work schedules and most experience strong feelings of dislocation that come with being an immigrant. Most of the immigrant settlements are in semi-rural areas, where there is limited access to public transportation. Saldaña explains that it is important to meet with, and care for, these people where they live. "Besides," he adds, "they are already so overwhelmed."

The particular religious needs of the immigrants are different from mainstream Euro-American parishioners as well, so the missions must be able to "go" where the immigrants are spiritually as well as geographically. While it is hard to characterize "the" Catholic Hispanic faith experience, given the variety of cultural traditions represented, it is safe to say that most share devotion to the Virgin. Many Catholic communities tend to have the weekly liturgy as a central focus of parish life, but the Hispanic communities tend to emphasize festivals in honor of "Our Lady." This is due to several factors. First of all, many of the poorer immigrants come from remote regions where they did not have access to Mass on a regular basis, so weekly worship has never been part of their religious rhythm. Secondly, Mary is seen as an advocate, a gentle and compassionate mediator on behalf of the suffering. She is also revered as patroness of the Americas, and each country celebrates its own incarnation of Mary: the Cubans have Our Lady of Charity, the Puerto Ricans have Our Lady of Divine Providence, and the

Mexicans, of course, have Our Lady of Guadalupe, whose feast day, December 12, is an enormous celebration.

The recent experience of Hispanic immigrants has been complicated by a problem far worse than transportation, excessive demands on time, or even the initial cultural estrangement. The recent surge of anti-immigrant sentiment and legislation has forced many legal as well as undocumented immigrants to go "underground" out of fear. Many refuse to participate in any demographic studies, such as a census, for fear of "exposure," rendering accurate population counts impossible. As a result, the fastest growing community is also the most "invisible," with many members leaving no paper trail of licenses, payroll statements, or registration of any kind to record their presence. According to Saldaña, many Americans seem to find unity in their opposition to immigration, something he cannot understand given the nation's immigrant roots. "Any Catholic—any person of faith—should be sympathetic to what the immigrants experience," he says.

There are probably few people in the archdiocese more familiar with this "invisible" community than Fr. Joseph Fahy, known as "Padre José" to his congregants. As an outreach priest for the Archdiocesan Hispanic Apostolate, Fr. Fahy travels over 200 miles a weekend to minister to the Hispanic communities in the metro-Atlanta area. His ministry includes saying Mass at the missions, leading a Bible study in a trailer park, and visiting with families to offer pastoral care and to ensure that their basic needs are being met. For many, his weekly visits provide a compassionate anchor in an otherwise difficult and troubled world.

Fr. Fahy is no stranger to the Hispanic community. He has been doing Spanish-language ministry in some form for most of his 39 years as a priest. He earned a doctorate in theology at Harvard in 1983, focusing on Latin American theologies of liberation. While finishing his thesis, he received a call requesting that he come to Atlanta, which was tremendously in need of Spanish-speaking priests. Aware of the deep needs in the northeast as well, he was not sure if he should come, but consented to a trial period, asking God to show him what he should do. His first stop was Atlanta's Federal Prison, filled to capacity with "Marielitos," those Cubans arrested after arriving on the controversial Mariel Boat Lift. "When I went to the federal prison and saw five tiers of the men, just shouting, warehoused there, eight to a cell, I knew I had to stay and work with them." He added with a smile, "I guess I got my answer!" While some Marielitos were hard-core criminals, he says, many were serving time for crimes as small as traffic violations. He saw many detainees attempt suicide, homicide, and self-mutilation in their hopelessness; even those close to release saw no future for themselves outside the prison walls.

In June 1995, the Immigration and Naturalization Service arrested and deported more than 2,000 undocumented workers, most of them Hispanic, in Operation South PAW (Protecting America's Workers). "The result was panic," says Saldaña. For people who already lived "on the edge," it was devastating. Those who were not arrested went underground, making an already invisible community even more inaccessible; people were scared even to go shopping or attend church. Hispanic businesses suffered tremendously and those offering basic social services had a difficult time attending to their clients. In light of the operation's fallout, the Hispanic Heritage Festival, sponsored by the Apostolate and held every October in Atlanta, was cancelled in 1995 and replaced by a liturgy for all Catholics to celebrate diversity and pray for unity.

While government officials congratulated themselves on the operation's "success," the leaders of the Catholic community in Atlanta responded with a public outcry against the injustice they saw resulting from the operation. Archbishop John Donoghue wrote a widely circulated pastoral letter calling for a review of immigration laws and compassion for the immigrant. Citing the American heritage rooted in immigration and Jewish and Christian principles, his letter called for a compassionate response to the "aliens in our midst," suggesting that the operation was a result of "excessive and misplaced zeal" and not authentic justice. "Justice," the letter reads, "must be served—but it must be served with compassion." It closes by urging the Justice Department to suspend enforcement of these laws until a full review could be undertaken.

Fr. Fahy contributed his gentle and resolute voice to the movement as well, writing an open letter on behalf of the north Georgia priests "privileged to serve the Hispanic communities" of the area. The letter begins with a quote from the archbishop's statement and asserts that "the acronym Operation South PAW . . . is a blatant misnomer." The operation presumes that American jobs are threatened by the presence of immigrants. Responsible studies, however, indicate that immigration has little effect on native employment. Why? Most of the jobs taken by the newly arrived are service-related. Such jobs are characterized by low wages, few benefits, and less-than-ideal working conditions. The letter states: "Most Americans disdain and deride such positions as dead ends." His piece concluded with

God's injunction to the Israelites in Leviticus 19:33-34: "Have the same love [for the aliens] as for yourselves, for you too were once aliens in the land of Egypt."

If Fr. Fahy is discouraged by anything in his work, it is the stereotypes that he spends so much time dismantling. The immigrants are accused of taking others' jobs and coming to avail themselves of social services and the welfare system. Neither of these stereotypes is true, he asserts. While some places do experience problems because of large immigrant pools, to project some of those problems onto Georgia's situation is false. "[They] have a tremendous work ethic. It is hard for me to comprehend why Americans would believe that a great majority [are lazy]. They come here because they want to work, to get started; many have a family to support back home. [They do not] come here to receive public assistance." The average immigrant is young, healthy, energetic, and of prime working age; instead of seeing them as a problem, he wonders, why haven't we been able to look at them as a blessing and a tremendous resource?

Asked if there was anything he wished people could know about the Hispanic community, he paused thoughtfully and said that we must trust God's providence in bringing them here. We have much to learn from the richness of their cultural and spiritual values. He paused again, and with a twinkle, added a gentle but prophetic challenge: "We pride ourselves on being an international city. I hope we can live up to that. It would be illogical for us not to be as open as we should be to those from other nations at the same time that we convey to the world that we are a cosmopolitan city."

LOOKING AHEAD: THE "CATHOLIC" CHURCH

The word "catholic," according to the Oxford Dictionary, means "universal, of interest or use to all, all-embracing." Indeed, the struggle to be "catholic" appears to be at the heart of many of the individual Catholic communities comprising the archdiocese of Atlanta. The great diversity among the various congregations and missions, rather than indicating a fragmented community, appears to be a sign that Atlanta's Catholics are joined by a common effort. They are struggling to determine what it means to be both historically Catholic—connected to the church at large—as well as embedded in a particular social and cultural context. Much of the identity that emerges from this struggle seems directly linked to being voice and advocate for those on the margins of society as expressed by such organizations as the Shrine's AIDS ministry, the Hispanic Apostolate, the Holy Cross food bank, and Lourdes's history of black education. What emerges is an understanding of the church that operates out of a vision of inclusion—an inclusion that does not deny the unique circumstances of the people in the community but rather addresses them in their specificity.

Trying to live out such a vision in a city that expands and changes at the rate Atlanta does is bound to be fraught with problems. Indeed, the stories above are tales of struggle as much as success. As one parishioner put it, "We've been so busy growing here that we haven't taken time to figure out where we're going." Some interpret the appointment of moderate Archbishop John Donoghue as an attempt to check and stabilize archdiocesan progress. Recent moves toward reinstating the Latin Mass and appointing conservative clergy to various posts have reinforced this popular suspicion.

Nevertheless, it appears that many of Atlanta's Catholics take seriously the Vatican II call to "catholic unity which prefigures and promotes universal peace." It appears as well that much of the impetus for change and social response in the archdiocese has come from the laity and their immediate pastors, people well-acquainted with struggling through difficult times. If so, then the desire to negotiate "catholic" identity should continue to be a hallmark of this community. This vision is perhaps best articulated by the city's favorite native son. In his letter of thanks to Archbishop Hallinan for the Nobel Prize celebration, King wrote: "It was a tribute not only to me but to the greatness of the City of Atlanta, the State, the nation and its ability to rise above the conflict of former generations and really experience that beloved community where all differences are reconciled and all hearts are in harmony with the principles of our great Democracy and the tenants of our Judeo-Christian heritage."

FOR FURTHER INFORMATION

Cyprian Davis. *The History of Black Catholics in the United States*. New York, Crossroad, 1990

James J. Hennesey. *American Catholics: A History of the Roman Catholic Community in the United States*. New York, Oxford University Press, 1982

Brennan Hill. *Exploring Catholic Theology*. Mystic, Twenty-Third Publications, 1995

Richard McBrien. *Catholicism*. San Francisco, HarperSanFrancisco, 1994

Randall M. Miller and Jon L. Wakelyn, eds. *Catholics in the Old South*. Macon, Mercer University Press, 1983

Vincent A. Yzermans, ed. *Days of Hope and Promise: The Writings and Speeches of Paul J. Hallinan, Archbishop of Atlanta*. Collegeville, Liturgical Press, 1973

CHAPTER FIVE

INSIDE/OUTSIDE: THE JEWISH COMMUNITY OF ATLANTA

Doris H. Goldstein

Stained glass depicting two tablets of the Ten Commandments, from former building of Ahavath Achim Synagogue. Ida Pearl and Joseph Cuba Jewish Archives.

The sky darkened late in the afternoon and by early evening the streets glistened in a steady rain. Traffic in the vicinity of Atlanta's Jewish congregations slowed to a crawl as Jews on foot clutched umbrellas in one hand and prayer books in another. It was Kol Nidre (literally meaning "All Vows"), which marks the beginning of Yom Kippur, the Day of Atonement. The rain and increasing wind that were the harbingers of Hurricane Opal did not deter the thousands of worshipers who filled the 23 congregations of Metropolitan Atlanta on Tuesday evening, October 3, 1995.

A GLIMPSE INTO THE TRADITION

All Jewish festivals including the Sabbath are observed from sundown to nightfall on the following day. Yom Kippur is the culmination of a ten day interval of reflection and introspection that begins on Rosh Hashanah (the Jewish New Year). These observances, as is the case with other major festivals, appear in the text of the Torah, which is comprised of the first five books of standard editions of the Hebrew Bible (Genesis, Exodus, Numbers, Leviticus, and Deuteronomy).

Unlike Christmas, New Year's Day, and American Independence Day, which are always celebrated on exactly the same date every year, Jewish festivals and holy days are set by a lunar calendar consisting of 12 months, each containing either 29 or 30 days. Since this measurement does not coincide with the actual rotation of the earth around the sun (there is an eleven-day discrepancy), the Jewish calendar adds an extra month seven times in a 19-year cycle. This adjustment reflects the reality of the physical world and keeps the festivals in their proper seasons as mandated in the Torah.

As a result, Jewish holidays appear at different places on the Gregorian or Western calendar each year. On the sabbath and festivals, traditional Jews participate in synagogue worship, enjoy plentiful, leisurely meals with family and friends, study a particular text, and generally abstain from their normal activities. When the festivals occur during week days, observant Jews miss work, children stay out of school, and the community withdraws from the secular world.

These periodic disruptions in daily life are one of the ways Jews set themselves apart and are naturally separated from the general society in which they live. In traditional Jewish communities, the cycle of observances is a combination of biblical injunctions, commemoration of historical events of the post-Biblical period, and very recent happenings such as the founding of the modern State of Israel (1948). During these observances, Jews who are committed to traditional practices are out of sync with the rest of Atlanta. Keeping the Sabbath has been especially important; this weekly withdrawal has sustained Jews during times when they were subjected to degredation and lived under the most trying circumstances. In today's frenzied society, many see regular Sabbath observance as an island of calm in a world sometimes difficult to manage and understand. Fortunately for Jews living in a pluralistic, multi-cultural America, this self-imposed isolation is accepted and generally respected.

The beginning of Judaism, the mother religion of Christianity and Islam, can be traced to the biblical figure Abraham, who alone in his generation worshiped one God; the belief in a single deity is still the central tenet of Judaism. Many of the traditions and observances that have developed over the centuries focus on how a Jew identifies with this concept and tries to live in an appropriate manner.

Jewish practices are derived from two major sources. The principle fount of religious law is the Torah, which according to tradition was given by God at Mt. Sinai to the Hebrew slaves newly freed from Egypt (12th century BCE). The second source is the Talmud, a compendium of oral traditions that developed from the time of Sinai. These oral traditions were passed from generation to generation by word of mouth until they were organized more formally in the Rabbinic period, which spanned the first five centuries of the common era. Traditional Jews believe that this code of religious jurisprudence was also divinely transmitted at Sinai and that it has equal sanctity with the Torah.

Since Talmudic times, most Jews have observed a system of law and tradition based on the Talmud, which was continually interpreted through the ages. Observing this system of law and tradition is called *halacha,* taken from a Hebrew word meaning "to go" or "to walk." In its broadest sense, the word refers to the path a Jew is to follow. Until the nineteenth century, Jews the world over observed *halacha* with local variation. Since then, as Jews integrated into society, four distinct branches of Judaism developed: Orthodox, Conservative, Reform, and Reconstructionist. The differences among them are based on how each movement views the binding nature of the original covenant between God and the Jewish people, ranging from Orthodox's strict acceptance of the entire *halacha* to Reform's more liberal interpretations that accord with contemporary norms and values. All of these viewpoints are represented in the 23 congregations of the Atlanta area.

BEGINNINGS IN ATLANTA

Jewish life in Atlanta has always reflected a pattern of being *a part of* and *apart from* the community (which is the case wherever Jews live, except in Israel). The first Jews arrived in Atlanta in 1845, not even a decade after the first stake was driven to determine the end of a new railroad line. Two young, ambitious men opened a dry goods store on Whitehall Street, which took its name from a pioneer tavern located nearby. Unlike their neighbors, these men were not farmers from other parts of Georgia or adjoining South Carolina. Jacob Haas and Henry Levi were German immigrants who had been in America only a few years and whose halting English and manner of dress certainly set them apart from frontier Atlanta.

On the eve of the Civil War, there were only 50 Jews in a city of close to 8,000. Either related to or acquaintances of Haas and Levi, they were of German origin and engaged in some form of commerce—a few as shopkeepers, but most as itinerant peddlers. While other religious groups (Baptist, Methodist, Presbyterian, Catholic, and Episcopalian) were organized and had erected their first buildings in the early decades of Atlanta's history, the handful of Jews had done little to establish their presence here. Whether this was due to the difficulty inherent in acculturation, fear of persecution, simple inertia, or a combination of all of these factors, they did not establish Atlanta's first Jewish house of worship until 1867. They did, however, organize a mutual insurance and aid association in 1860 called the Hebrew Benevolent Society, which petitioned the city council for six burial plots in Oakland Cemetery.

During the Civil War, this tiny Jewish community actively supported the Southern war effort. At least five men enlisted in local infantry companies and two established businessmen attained prominent positions: David Mayer was a supply officer for Governor Joseph Brown and S. Solomon organized a foundry that produced supplies for the army. There are also records of others serving as blockade runners, securing much needed commodities for the Confederacy.

In spite of their active participation, there was a certain degree of ambivalence for a cause that sought to forcibly enslave an entire race. Reflecting on their own recent past, and knowledgeable about the subjugation of the ancient Hebrews in Egypt, some Jews were prompted to leave the city and others to doubt their allegiance to their new home. They were both inside and outside Atlanta at the same time.

BOOM YEARS

Both the city of Atlanta in general and the Jewish community in particular experienced phenomenal growth in the decades following the Civil War. By 1880, the Jewish population had soared to 600, and at the turn of the century it was close to 2,000. The Federal Census of 1900 noted a population of 89,872; the Jews, however, were still a tiny minority of 2.25 percent. During these years, several important events marked the emergence of the Jewish community and began the process of growth and development that followed. The first synagogue, the Hebrew Benevolent Congregation, was founded in 1867, an outgrowth of the aid society of the pre-war years. It moved into its first structure on the corner of Garnett and Forsyth Streets in 1877, but is now known as The Temple and occupies a historic building on Peachtree Street. The Concordia Club also came into existence after the war, serving as a social outlet for Jews because they were increasingly refused membership in local private clubs. It later became the Standard Club and is located in suburban Duluth.

The increase in the Jewish population during this era is mainly attributed to the influx of Eastern European Jews fleeing the upsurge of anti-Semitism and violence in Russia and Poland. Generally more pious and lacking specific skills and education, these co-religionists were a concern to those who had recently established a tenuous foothold in an overwhelmingly Christian world. But in spite of their concerns, the Jewish community reached out to help these immigrants begin their odyssey in America. This same pattern has been repeated over and over as each successive immigrant group arrived seeking opportunity, religious freedom, and a better life. In the early 1900s, Jews of Spanish heritage (called Sephardim, from the Hebrew word for Spain) who had lived in Turkey and the Isle of Rhodes arrived in Atlanta; during the late 1930s and again after World War II, victims of Nazi terror came; and in the 1980s and 90s Russian and Iranian Jews escaping totalitarian regimes made their way here.

While most of the community's energy during the post-Civil War era was absorbed with earning a living, raising a family, and adjusting to a completely different life, there were some who ventured out beyond the confines of the Jewish community. David Mayer, active during the war, was one of the most fervent proponents for the establishment of a public school system. Aaron Haas, a relative of the original settler, served as mayor pro tem of the city in 1874 as well as an officer in the Young Men's Library Association, forerunner of the Carnegie Library. Several men joined the Masonic lodge, which was an entry point into the non-Jewish world for many immigrants. These early communal leaders were role models for a legion of civic minded Jewish men and women who have served Atlanta ever since.

IN THE MARKETPLACE

A raw, wide-open boom town like Atlanta was the perfect setting for adventurous individuals. Unfettered by long-established traditions that existed in older cities like Charleston and New Orleans, Atlanta attracted those willing to take advantage of opportunity and try new business ventures. The early Jewish settlers who originally came from other parts of America must have sensed something of what is still called "The Atlanta Spirit." Later immigrants who settled here also soon saw the possibilities for success and were involved in a host of commercial ventures—some prospered beyond their founder's greatest expectations, some floundered and eventually failed, but most provided a modest income for growing families.

Like Haas and Levi, most Jews began their business careers as merchants, either from a fixed location or peddling house to house. One such merchant whose enterprise was to have an enormous impact on the life of the city for over a century was Morris Rich. Arriving from Savannah, Georgia in 1867, perhaps lured by the growth of the railroads after the war, Rich opened a dry goods business on Whitehall Street in a small frame building. As the city prospered, the store became more and more successful, and soon other relatives joined the business. Rich's eventually became the premiere department store of Atlanta, with a reputation for customer service unmatched throughout the entire region. Rich's was also an exemplary corporate citizen, supporting numerous civic and cultural endeavors. A foundation was established in 1943 that still distributes funds to city projects. Rich's passed from family control to the Federated Department Stores in 1976.

Another man who "seized the moment" was Jacob Elsas, a Union soldier whose unit was ordered to stay in Atlanta to guard the supply lines after the fall of the city in 1864. After the war, he invested his army savings in a grocery and supply business. When he experienced difficulty getting the cloth bags he needed to sack flour, sugar, and salt, he decided to manufacture them himself. Thus began his career as one of the most successful mill owners in the state and an exemplar of the New South enterprising spirit.

Most Jewish businessmen, however, did not achieve the success of Rich and Elsas. Many operated profitable wholesale and retail businesses that sold a wide variety of products. "Mom and Pop" grocery stores, often located in lower class neighborhoods, were a common way for newcomers to begin their commercial life. Sometimes these evolved into multilocation enterprises, as was the case with a chain known as Big Apple. This unconnected network of Jewish small businesses enhanced the overall commercial development of the city and offered goods needed by the general population. A small number of semi-professionals founded real estate and insurance firms, and there was also a smattering of small, independent manufacturers. By 1910, there were two Jewish physicians, a pharmacist, a dentist, and a few lawyers. The collection and reselling of scrap metal and other waste required no capital and became another easy beginning for many immigrants. Jewish citizens of metro Atlanta can now be found in every profession, serving in government and academia, working for national and international companies, participating in the arts, and still founding new businesses (Home Depot is the most recent).

An important figure in the development of present-day downtown was Benjamin Massell. Born into a large immigrant family in 1886, Massell began his career as an office boy and progressed to salesman for a grocery company. Saving his meager salary, he bought his first property in 1900 for $5,000. His subsequent purchases amounted to millions as he invested in numerous small to mid-sized commercial buildings in the downtown and Pershing Point areas. A familiar figure in business circles, he was often referred to as "the Builder of Atlanta's Skyline." His most important project was the Merchandise Mart, still an Atlanta landmark.

From its earliest days as a hamlet struggling to become more than a dot on the map, Atlanta has been home to Jews who have been integrally woven into the commercial fabric of the area. Their ambition, foresight, hard work, and belief in Atlanta was and still is a hallmark of their participation in civic life.

TIKUN OLUM ... HEALING THE WORLD

One of the most basic principles of Judaism is the obligation to *Tikun Olum*. This Hebrew phrase can be translated literally as "perfecting or healing the world" and in modern parlance refers to the duty to give back to the community or to leave the world a little better than you found it. The record of civic participation by the Jews of Atlanta, who have always been a tiny minority here, is the fulfillment of that ancient mandate. From their beginnings in the city, when they were approximately 1 percent of the population in 1850, the community's contributions to the betterment of all Atlantans far exceed its numbers. To recognize each and every member of the Jewish community who has worked with other citizens for the common good would be impossible. There have been moments, however, in the city's history when individually or collectively Jews have helped to make a difference.

One such instance previously mentioned was the formation of the public school system and the participation of David Mayer in that effort. Before the Civil War there were a number of short-lived private schools, most of which failed because the tuition was out of reach for many parents. As the city returned to normalcy and began the rebuilding process after the war, many recognized the need for public education. David Mayer had settled in Atlanta with his wife and eight children in 1848. He operated a store on Whitehall Street and was quite successful; by 1862 he had assets of over $59,000, which was quite a fortune for the time. He was active in the Masons and other fraternal groups, as well as Democratic politics. By 1870 his children were beyond school age but he knew that educating the next generation would be vital. Mayer used his numerous connections to promote the founding of the school system and was a pioneer member of the Atlanta Board of Education.

Non-profit organizations and charities were especially vulnerable to the impact of the Great Depression of 1929. For example, the Atlanta Community Chest (forerunner of the United Way), which contributed to the operating budgets of many social service organizations, experienced great difficulty obtaining funds. Knowing of the long history of fund raising within the Jewish community, the leaders called on Louis H. Moss to chair the executive committee of the Community Chest. At the time, Moss was serving as president of the Atlanta Federation of Jewish Charities, the contemporary name of the former Hebrew Benevolent Society of the 1860s. Applying techniques used in the Jewish community, Moss guided the orga-

The Temple. Photograph by Elizabeth Hardcastle

nization through difficult times. By 1935 another member of the Jewish community, Julian Boehm, chaired the first annual campaign drive to exceed its goal in four years. In subsequent years, numerous Jewish men and women have assumed leadership roles in the United Way organization.

The issues of hunger and homelessness are very relevant to every American city in the late twentieth century. While governmental agencies have assumed some responsibility to meet these needs, it is obvious there is much left to do in the private sector. In 1983, two Atlanta synagogues mobilized the Jewish community and founded two shelters, one for women and one for couples. Congregation Shearith Israel, located on University Drive, heard of the need for a women's shelter and created a facility for 16 women. Members solicited and immediately received financial assistance as well as the promise of volunteers from other synagogues. A couples' shelter was likewise created by The Temple in much the same way. The donation of a building by a Temple member made it possible to house 22 couples. The Jewish community, in cooperation with other religious groups, was also instrumental in organizing the Genesis Shelter for mothers and newborns.

To assist in the stocking of the Atlanta Community Food Bank, Congregation Ahavath Achim (Atlanta's second synagogue, founded in 1887) began an annual food drive. It is held on the eve of Yom Kippur, regarded as the holiest night of the year, and called "Operation Isaiah" because part of the liturgy of the day quotes a verse from the Prophet Isaiah:

> Surely you should divide your bread with the hungry
> And bring the moaning poor to your home;
> When you see the naked, cover him;
> And do not ignore your kin.
> Isaiah 58:7

All area synagogues participate in Operation Isaiah, which is the second largest organizational food collection drive in the city, according to the Food Bank.

"RIGHTEOUSNESS, RIGHTEOUSNESS SHALL YOU PURSUE" (DEUTERONOMY 16:20)

These words from the Bible frame the Jewish perspective on what is commonly called "charity." The word charity is unknown in Hebrew; instead, the term used is *tzdakah*, meaning righteousness or justice. *Tzdakah* takes the notion of giving one's material possessions to help others out of the realm of benevolence and links it to the idea that one is only doing that which is right. Therefore, *tzdakah* is an *obligation*, not an *option*. Even one who receives is also obligated to give. Perhaps this accounts for the reputation Jews have acquired for always taking care of their own.

As was previously noted, the first institution formed in this community was a society to help those in need. During the late 1880s, a Hebrew Orphan's Home was established and, throughout the years, numerous other agencies and organizations have been founded to meet whatever needs arose. Until the formation of the non-sectarian Community Chest and subsequent assistance from government, all of these groups were sustained totally by those within the Jewish community. In spite of funds from non-Jewish sources, there is still a need for significant community-wide participation in the support of these agencies. One of the most recent collective efforts is the resettlement program to assist those Jews arriving in Atlanta from the former Soviet Union.

Responsibility for fellow Jews does not end at the outer limits of metro Atlanta. There are beleaguered communities throughout the world that depend on the *tzdakah* of thousands of unseen individuals. The State of Israel, and before 1948, Palestine, has always been a particular concern of the Jewish people. Monies collected in Atlanta as well as in communities everywhere are sent to support a wide range of unmet social needs. An annual campaign has been held since 1936 to raise the necessary funds. Each member of the Jewish community is contacted either personally or by mail and asked to contribute a portion of her or his income. The organization and disbursement of the monies raised are the responsibility of the Atlanta Jewish Federation, which is led and governed by lay leaders from throughout the community. The concept of sharing largesse learned from Jewish values has been carried over to many areas of the general community. In addition to the United Way, Jewish contributors are found on the lists of every major philanthropic endeavor in the city.

ON THE DARK SIDE

Over the course of 150 years, there have been times when Jews did not feel so comfortable among their fellow citizens in Atlanta. Early in the twentieth century, Jewish students were penalized for missing school on religious holidays, and Christian missionary activities to convert Jews were frequently brazen and disrespectful. Sunday closing laws were strictly enforced against Jewish businesses, and sometimes city and county elections were held on important Jewish holidays in spite of protest from the community. In addition, Jews, as well as Catholics and blacks, were excluded from membership in exclusive social clubs.

For Jews, however, the darkest days were experienced from 1913 to 1915 when Leo Frank, the Jewish manager of a pencil factory, was accused of the murder of Mary Phagan, a 13-year-old employee. During a trial marked by crowds inflamed by a vitriolic press shouting "Kill the Jew" in front of the courthouse, the city turned on its Jewish neighbors. Wives and children were sent out of town to family and friends, while those who remained were hesitant to leave their homes. Frank was convicted on flimsy, contradictory evidence and sentenced to death, but eventually Governor John Slaton commuted the sentence to life imprisonment. Vilified and burned in effigy, Slaton and his family had to be protected by the state militia from a mob that marched to his home.

Despite Slaton's decision, Frank was dragged from his prison cell in Milledgeville, brought to Marietta—the birthplace of Mary Phagan—and hanged. The kidnappers proudly posed for a photograph with Frank's lifeless body still on the tree but were never tried for their crime. Fifty years later Alonzo Mann, who had worked in the factory, came forward to reveal that he had seen a janitor carrying Mary's body the night of the murder. Through the efforts of the Jewish community, Frank's case was reopened and he was ultimately granted a posthumous pardon on the grounds that the state of Georgia did not protect him.

The trial and murder of Leo Frank resonated in the entire community. For some Jews, it was a painful reminder of various forms of persecution they had experienced in their former homelands. For those with deep roots in Atlanta, it was a shocking rejection of their citizenship. For Governor Slaton, whose courage to act contrary to the obvious temper of the city, it was the end of a promising political career. For those who continued to hate, the death of Mary Phagan became the impetus for a revived and rejuvenated Ku Klux Klan. And on a national level, the oldest Jewish fraternal organization in America, B'nai Brith, formed the Anti-Defamation League, which is still in existence today fighting anti-Semitism and bigotry against all Americans.

As the civil rights struggle escalated in the late 1950s, the Jewish community was once again the target of acts of hatred. In October 1958, the educational wing of The Temple was bombed, one of a series of bombings in the South directed against those who supported the cause of equal rights and opportunity for the black community. Rabbi Jacob Rothschild of The Temple was an outspoken Jewish advocate and a friend of the Reverend Martin Luther King, Jr. He spoke not only from his own pulpit but also from others in the region, urging his listeners to reject the hatred being preached and to join him and others as they worked for social justice and equality. He was also part of a group of Atlanta clergymen who issued a public statement in support of school desegregation, the first such pronouncement by any group in the South.

When news of the early-morning bombing spread throughout the community, the specter of the Leo Frank case reappeared, along with memories of the alienation and fear that were experienced by Jews in the city. But Atlanta, which liked to call itself "the city too busy to hate," responded to the attack with overwhelming moral and financial support. Local, regional, and national political leaders, as well as other prominent citizens, denounced the bombing, and Atlantans from all walks of life contributed to a fund to repair the building. As a result, the new social hall at The Temple was named "Friendship Hall" in appreciation of all those who helped to rebuild the destruction and to renew the Jewish community's faith in Atlanta. The only smirch on the city's image was that when the perpetrators were brought to justice, the jury failed to convict them.

Since the bombing there have been scattered incidents of anti-Semitism that have usually involved vandalism to communal buildings—but certainly nothing approaching the magnitude of either the Frank case or the temple bombing. Cobb County, where the lynching of Frank took place, was never considered hospitable to Jews. Since 1975, however, when the first synagogue was founded there, the Jewish community has grown to approximately 5,000 residents. It is now home to two other synagogues and a branch of the Jewish Community Center.

COMMUNAL STRUCTURE

For the past 2,000 years, the synagogue has been the focus of Jewish life. "Synagogue" is actually a Greek word meaning assembly, and in the most basic terms a synagogue is a place of Jewish assembly. A more apt term is *kehilla*, a Hebrew word meaning community. It is a place of worship and study, a place to mark life cycle events, a place for fellowship and counsel, and a place to feel connected to the entire Jewish people. Congregations are structured along denominational lines (Orthodox, Conservative, Reform, and Reconstructionist) and have religious leaders called rabbis (Hebrew meaning "my teacher"). Each synagogue is autonomous with the rabbi serving as the authority on Jewish law and practice for the congregation. In the Reform movement, the word temple is commonly used as a way of identifying with the original Temple in Jerusalem.

Originally the synagogue was also the social agency that supervised the dispensing of services and funds to those in need. Since early in the twentieth century, these functions have been taken over by a number of agencies organized for specific purposes, such as care of the elderly, services for families and children, etc. Atlanta's Jewish community has a full range of these professionally run institutions and agencies that are partially supported by voluntary contributions.

Jewish education for the young was also once the exclusive province of the synagogue. Most temples and synagogues maintain an educational program that meets for a limited time after the regular school day and/or on Saturday and Sunday. Children are taught Hebrew prayers and language, Jewish history, and religious practices. Beginning in 1953, a number of private, all day Jewish schools have developed in Atlanta. These schools combine conventional academic studies with a strong grounding in the Hebrew language and in Jewish history, religion, and culture. There are four elementary schools and one high school of this type in Atlanta. These are also identified with one of the four denominations, but enrollment is not restricted by family affiliation.

A vital organization of the local Jewish community is the Atlanta Jewish Federation. Over many years it has become the central planning, fund-raising, and community relations agency serving the diverse elements of Atlanta Jewry. The Federation also founded the Jewish Community Archives, a depository of Atlanta's Jewish history, and has been instrumental in the development of the William Breman Jewish Heritage Museum.

In addition to these major institutions, there is a plethora of social, philanthropic, cultural, fraternal, social service and Israel-related groups usually affiliated with nationwide organizations. These groups provide outlets for socialization, education, and service in a non-religious, but nonetheless Jewish context. They also serve as a meeting and mixing place for those holding differing views of Jewish practice.

POISED FOR THE 21ST CENTURY

Like the entire metropolitan area, the Jewish community is young, growing in numbers, and optimistic about its future. It has benefited from the continuing expansion of opportunity throughout the southeast by attracting singles, young families, professionals, and entrepreneurs to Atlanta. Its dynamism is reflected in the establishment of new congregations in suburban areas, the growth of existing institutions, and the new programs being created.

All of this growth, however, has not been without accompanying difficulties. There has not been a single cohesive Jewish neighborhood since the 1940s, when the entire community was concentrated within the city limits. Now with so many Jews living outside the city in areas like North Fulton, Riverdale, and Snellville, it is difficult to create a sense of belonging and promote involvement. Additionally, so many of the more recent residents have no ties to the community and feel no obligation to participate in communal events. Although there are no current statistics, it is obvious that the rate of affiliation has not equaled the rate of growth.

By far the most pressing problem that will affect the Jewish community now and in the future is the rapidly increasing rate of intermarriage and assimilation on both a local and national level. Stemming partially from greater acceptance by the society at large, the dissolution of communal sanction, and the lack of a strong attachment to Jewish tradition, vast numbers of Jews (most estimates put the number at 50 percent) are creating dual religion or completely secular households. In the overwhelming majority of these families, it is predicted the children will not retain any Jewish identity in adulthood.

As in the past, the Jewish community of Atlanta will continue to meet the internal challenges it faces while its men and women actively participate with their fellow citizens in the continued growth of the area. Its strong infrastructure will enable those who wish to maintain their affiliation remain loyal to their heritage so that they can live both inside and outside the larger community at the same time.

FOR FURTHER INFORMATION

Janice Rothschild Blumberg. *One Voice: Rabbi Jacob M. Rothschild and the Troubled South*. Macon, Mercer University Press, 1985

Leonard Dinnerstein. *The Leo Frank Case*. New York, Columbia University Press, 1968

Eli Evans. *The Provincials: A Personal History of Jews in the South*. New York, Athenaeum, 1973

Doris H. Goldstein. *From Generation to Generation: A Centennial History of Congregation Ahavath Achim, 1887-1987*. Atlanta, Capricorn, 1987

Steven Hertzberg. *Strangers Within the Gate City: The Jews of Atlanta, 1845-1915*. Philadelphia, Jewish Publication Society, 1978

Leigh H. Rogoff. *Congregation Beth Jacob's First Fifty Years, 1943-1993*. Atlanta, Congregation Beth Jacob, 1993

PART II:

VARIETIES OF CHRISTIAN BELIEF AND PRACTICE

CHAPTER SIX

UNITARIAN UNIVERSALISTS: A LIBERAL CHRISTIAN TRADITION IN THE SOUTH

Paige Schneider

Unitarian Universalist Congregation of Atlanta. Photograph by Elizabeth Hardcastle.

American Unitarianism and Universalism emerged out of the liberal and rational reform movements within Protestantism. In their attempt to bridge the chasm between religion and science, religious reformers found inspiration in humanist philosophers associated with the "age of enlightenment," and drew encouragement from the significant advances in scientific knowledge that had occurred over the course of the eighteenth century. Theologians such as Charles Chauncy and William Ellery Channing were influential participants in this reform movement, challenging the core of the more orthodox Calvinist and pietist theologies that had been prevalent in the late-eighteenth and early-nineteenth centuries.

Unitarianism rejected the dogmatic "fire and brimstone" Christianity expressed by conservative theologians associated with the mid-eighteenth-century Great Awakening who, in their revivalistic fervor, preached about original sin, predestination, and a vindictive God who could exact harsh punishment on humankind for earthly transgressions. Liberal Christians wanted little to do with the irrational spiritualism and experiential Christianity of leading evangelicals such as Jonathan Edwards and George Whitefield. Instead, Unitarians offered a more optimistic view of human nature and a more benevolent characterization of the heavenly Father, and placed particular emphasis on humans as "free agents" in the quest for salvation. Unitarianism gained support from former Anglicans and Congregationalists, though their authority remained primarily in the Boston area.

John Murray organized the first Universalist church in Gloucester, Massachusetts in 1779. Asserting that the purpose of Jesus' life on earth was to save every member of the human race rather than a select few, Universalists championed the doctrine of universal salvation and affirmed the potential for moral virtue among humankind. Contrary to the more cultivated and genteel Unitarians, early Universalist leaders demonstrated evangelical tendencies that allowed for greater success in winning adherents from among certain segments in the revivalist camp.

A fundamental principle shared by both Unitarians and Universalists in nineteenth-century America was a belief that all people should be able to practice their religious faith free from persecution by the state or by other religious groups. Puritans, arriving on the coast of North America in the seventeenth century in hopes of securing religious liberty, were often reluctant to extend liberty to others belonging to dissident Christian sects. There were countless instances of threats, and physical violence, visited upon unorthodox Christians by their more traditional brethren, with events such as the notorious Salem witch hunts providing evidence of the potential excesses of religious fundamentalism. Although Unitarians and Universalists often banded together to ward off hostile threats from orthodox Christians, it was not until 1961 that the two denominations officially merged and established the Unitarian Universalist Association.

As a group, Unitarian Universalists (UUs) tend to be socially aware and politically active. In general, their congregations attract older, white, well-educated, relatively affluent individuals—a demographic pattern that holds in the South as well. Theologically, UUs are among the most liberal of all denominations with Protestant roots. UUs tend to interpret the Bible from an historical or literary perspective, rather than as the literal or inspired word of God. For this reason conservative, evangelical Christians have often been antagonistic towards UUs, so much so that from the time of their merger, UU congregations hesitated to include "Unitarian" or "Universalist" in their official church name. Some UUs consider themselves liberal Christians, but most identify themselves as humanists, drawing upon a large body of sacred and philosophical writings for religious inspiration.

In the past fifty years, shifts in population from the northeast and the midwest to the southern region of the United States have increased the presence of UUs here. Atlanta's UUs trace their roots to the founding of the Church of Our Father in 1884, a site that is now the Central Atlanta Public Library. Particularly in the South, UU congregations have offered an alternative to the Christian orthodoxy found in the fundamentalist and evangelical denominations that are so deeply rooted in the area.

THE HISTORY OF UNITARIAN UNIVERSALISTS IN THE SOUTH AND IN ATLANTA

Unitarian congregations were organized in the early 1800s in several southern port cities, including Charleston, South Carolina; New Orleans, Louisiana; Louisville, Kentucky; and Augusta, Georgia. Most of these churches were founded by religious liberals who were first members of Presbyterian or Congregational churches, but who later broke with the more conservative members of their congregations over theological issues, or Unitarian transplants from the North. Universalism, also present in the South during the early 1800s, was frequently regarded as the southern rural counterpart to northeastern, urban Unitarianism. Although southern Universalists tended to be culturally conservative, often sympathetic to segregationist politics, they shared many theological tenets with the northeastern Unitarian transplants. Unitarian and Universalist congregations in the South frequently joined forces and pooled resources to sustain liberal religion in a region hostile to heterodoxy. The most successful southern congregations were those with dynamic, socially active ministers (most often missionaries from Harvard Divinity School) located in cities with a large population of Northeasterners. However, turnover was high among southern Unitarian ministers. Many served for only a few years before returning to the more hospitable environs of Boston.

As mentioned previously, Georgia's liberal Christians first organized into Unitarian and Universalist churches at the beginning of the nineteenth century. Augusta and Savannah had thriving Unitarian churches soon after, and a small number of Universalist congregations were scattered throughout rural Georgia. Atlanta's first Unitarian congregation, formed in 1882, dedicated its first church building, the Church of Our Father, in 1884 under the charismatic leadership of minister George Leonard Chaney. A graduate of Harvard and the Meadville Theological School, Chaney immediately adopted the cause of equality for southern blacks as a personal interest and mission. He helped found the Tuskegee Institute in Alabama and the Artisan's Institute (the predecessor of Georgia Tech), and was a trustee of Atlanta University, an historically black college.

For nine years Chaney guided the spiritual and institutional growth at the Church of Our Father. After his departure, the church went through two decades of financial struggle and a run of short-term ministers before stabilizing. A new 240-seat church was built on West Peachtree Street in 1915, with Chaney returning from Salem, Massachusetts, to address the congregation at the dedication ceremony. Over the next thirty years, however, the church experienced a number of hardships. During a particularly difficult period when the church was impaired by financial turmoil and a string of interim ministers, the congregation approved a merger with the Atlanta Universalists and adopted a new name, the United Liberal Church. But the church continued to struggle because of declining membership and financial instability. The most serious threat to the congregation came in the 1940s, when the church refused membership to the black chairman of the Department of Social Work at Atlanta University. Shortly thereafter, the minister resigned and the American Unitarian Association (AUA) withdrew its financial support.

In 1954 the congregation was reestablished, retaining the name United Liberal Church. One of the first acts of the church was to declare its commitment to civil rights for Atlanta's large African-American population. Under the leadership of minister Ed Cahill, and with the enthusiastic support of the AUA, the church served as a place for grass roots political action. During the 1950s and 1960s, white members of the Atlanta UU congregation worked alongside black religious leaders, and were often subjected to hostile threats and violence from whites desperate to retain their lock on power. By 1965, four years after the establishment of the national Unitarian Universalist Association, the Atlanta UU community was growing stronger, and a new and larger church building was erected at the current Cliff Valley Way location. The church adopted the official Unitarian Universalist denomination title, becoming the Unitarian Universalist Congregation of Atlanta.

UNITARIAN UNIVERSALISM IN ATLANTA TODAY

During the 1970s and continuing into the 1980s, several suburban UU congregations were founded, including the Northwest, Metro Atlanta North, and Gwinnett churches. With over 750 members, the Unitarian Universalist Congregation of Atlanta remains the largest UU church in the Atlanta metropolitan area, and the fifth largest congregation in the country. The church has three full-time ministers, including Edward Frost, a well-known Unitarian writer and speaker. Church membership is comprised of about equal numbers of families, middle-aged couples, singles, senior citizens, and young, unmarried professionals. There are numerous fellowship groups operating within the church that address the needs of the large and diverse membership. A small sample includes the Daylight Focus Group, a social group for senior citizens, Interweave, a network for gay and lesbian UUs, theater social groups for members who like to attend plays, and even a theater company, Underground Theater, for those who would rather perform than be in the audience. In addition, there are a variety of religious education programs for adults and children of all ages.

UUs have historically been known for their commitment to "good works"; this is reflected in the large number of volunteers working for social justice and peace issues. The "social concerns" committees of Unitarian congregations are generally the largest and most active committees in the church. The Atlanta congregation gives both time and money to several local community organizations including Cascade House, a transitional housing shelter for families, Meals on Wheels for the homebound elderly, and the Network for Social Responsibility, a group formed to counter the anti-gay rights initiative passed in Cobb County in 1994. The church is also a "partner" with John Hope Elementary School, sending volunteers to tutor school children who require extra help with their work. Members of the Unitarian Universalist Congregation of Gwinnett have worked closely with, and provided resources to, the Quinn House, a shelter for homeless men. The Gwinett UUs also participate in the Adopt a Highway program, and provide meeting space for Alcoholics Anonymous and Survivors of Childhood Abuse.

A unique UU church in Atlanta is the First Existentialist Congregation, which was formed in 1976 by Reverend Lanier Clance and a handful of other UUs with a mission of providing a place where rationalism, spiritualism, and emotion could be combined to, in the words of Reverend Clance, "inspire, and breathe life into people." As in other UU congregations, there is no official creed, although, as the church name implies, religious and philosophical inspiration is drawn from existentialist philosophy. The social and political philosophy of radical feminism is also very influential in the lives of congregants and in the teachings of the church. The importance that the church places on individualism and the spiritual equality of women has made it an integral and active part of Atlanta's lesbian community. Although the First Existentialist Congregation has a large lesbian population, the congregation eschews labels and points to the many heterosexual singles, couples, and families who are members, thus supporting its claim of welcoming all free-thinking individuals into the church family. With an acceptance of, and respect for, differences of sexual orientation, race, and ethnicity among congregants, the church prides itself in celebrating diversity in word and deed.

Metropolitan Atlanta is home to another distinctive UU congregation, the Thurman Hamer Ellington Congregation (THE) in Decatur, which was organized with the mission of establishing a multiracial congregation. UUs have struggled with the paradox of being a denomination with a strong civil rights record and having members who consider themselves liberal and egalitarian, and yet also being a denomination that attracts few racial minorities. At both the national and local level, church leaders have expressed a desire to institute programs and policies that reach out to ethnic and racial minorities and foster greater diversity among the membership. THE has been successful in achieving an integrated congregation; currently about half of the members are black and half are white. THE is also home to the city's only church drum choir. Using traditional African drums and other percussion instruments, the choir enlivens sermons through performances of traditional African music, poetry, and dance, and occasionally performs for outsiders at community events.

Throughout the 1980s and into the 1990s, Atlanta has experienced rapid population growth. Many of the newcomers were members of liberal religious groups before moving to Atlanta and, once settled, have fueled the expansion of UU congregations in the suburbs. Today there are a total of eight UU congregations in the metro area, four of them located outside the I-285 perimeter. Elena Rigg, the interim minister of the Unitarian Universalist Congregation of Gwinnett, believes that suburban congregations have a special mission, and in large part are viewed by members as "a haven from the conservative political and social climate" of the South. These UU congregations tend to be more family-oriented than their urban counterparts due to the greater number of families with children in the suburbs.

EXPRESSIONS OF FAITH

While Sunday service differs from one church to another, there are some religious principles and beliefs common to all UUs that find expression through the use of various symbols and rituals. The flaming chalice, for example, is an important symbol found in many UU churches, representing religious freedom and toleration. It is often lit at the beginning of the service, frequently by a child from the congregation.

Readings, meditations, and prayers are generally an eclectic mix reflecting the UU belief that wisdom and universal truths exist in the ethical and spiritual teachings of all the world's major religions. On any given Sunday the congregation may sing a traditional Christian hymn in its original German followed by a 1920s labor ballad, both chosen from the newly revised denomination hymnal. Readings are drawn from a variety of sacred texts or even from the inspired words of poets, philosophers, or leading social or political reformers. Because many UUs are committed community and social activists, there is often a rather lengthy period of announcements, where members share information about upcoming events or issues that they feel will be of interest to fellow congregants. As in most church services, an offertory may precede the sermon. Sermon topics run the gamut; a review of recent church newsletters from two Atlanta congregations included sermons entitled: "Patriotism and Faith," "Contours of A Mature Faith," and "International Children's Memorial Day and Peace Service."

UUs have a reputation as independent free-thinkers who thrive in an atmosphere of debate and discussion, a characteristic that is borne out during services at many UU churches. In both the Gwinnett and Atlanta congregations, people attending are encouraged to share their impressions and reflections (officially known as "talk-back") concerning the sermon topic at the end of the service. These free-flowing discussions often continue informally after service when churchgoers gather for coffee and fellowship.

Like other Americans, many UUs appear to be searching for deeper spiritual meaning in their lives. The growth in popularity of "alternative spirituality," which often borrows from eastern religious practices or Native American earth-centered traditions, has also piqued the interest of many UUs. Balancing faith with reason, science with the supernatural, has always been a difficult challenge for UUs. Although the predominant tendency remains a focus on the rational, many UU ministers have recently made an effort to incorporate topics on the transcendent into their sermons. Or, as Reverend Diana Jordan of the Atlanta UU congregation stated, to create a "religion not just of the brain, but of the heart, soul, and spirit."

CONCLUSION

Many of the 200,000 UUs in this country continue to identify themselves as Christian. Thousands of members, however, feel more comfortable identifying themselves as humanists, Jews, Buddhists, deists, agnostics, or even atheists. But regardless of label, all UUs today remain committed to the cornerstones of their faith, expressed in the denomination's Principles and Purposes as the "free and responsible search for truth and meaning, the inherent worth and dignity of every person, and justice, equity and compassion in human relations." Atlanta's UUs are part of a religious community with a rich tradition and long history of producing some of American society's most notable social and political reformers. They take pride in the commitment to act upon their convictions and plan to carry the fundamental principles of their liberal religion into the twenty-first century.

FOR FURTHER INFORMATION

Russell E. Miller. *The Larger Hope: History of the Universalist Church in America.* Volumes I and II, Boston, Unitarian Universalist Historical Society, 1979

Mark D. Morrison-Reed. *Black Pioneers in a White Denomination.* Boston, Beacon Press,1984

David Robinson. *The Unitarians and the Universalists.* Westport, Greenwood Press,1985

Robert B. Tapp. *Religion Among the Unitarian Universalists.* New York, Seminar Press,1973

Conrad Wright. *The Liberal Christians: Essays on American Unitarian History.* Boston, Beacon Press, 1970

CHAPTER SEVEN

CHRISTIAN SCIENCE IN ATLANTA: A RELIGIOUS MESSAGE OF SPIRITUAL HEALING

Kristin Marsh

First Church of Christ Scientist, Atlanta. Photograph by Louis A. Ruprecht, Jr.

Mary Baker Eddy established the Church of Christ, Scientist, in 1879 in Massachusetts. Seven years later, a student by the name of Julia Bartlett arrived in Georgia with Eddy's message. Bartlett began teaching Christian Science herself and one of her students, Sue Harper Mims, became an early leading champion of Christian Science in the Atlanta area. She is also credited with organizing and supporting the church's embryonic Atlanta community. Mims, wife of future Atlanta Mayor Livingston Mims, was an active and prominent local figure in her own right. Sickness had rendered her an invalid, but through her study of Christian Science with Bartlett, Mims experienced complete healing. She then traveled to Boston and studied with Eddy to become a teacher and practitioner, and subsequently became one of the first two women named by Eddy to the Board of Lectureship.

Christian Scientists began meeting regularly in Atlanta in the Mims home (a site that is now occupied by the Georgian Terrace, an historic hotel on the corner of Ponce de Leon Avenue and Peachtree Street that has recently been turned into a condominium). The First Church of Christ Scientist, Atlanta, was officially established in 1893, but did not occupy its own building until 1899. In 1914 it moved to its present location at the corner of Peachtree and 15th Streets. Over the course of the twentieth century, the Christian Science community has exhibited steady growth and now encompasses 23 Christian Science branch churches and societies throughout the state of Georgia.

WHAT IS CHRISTIAN SCIENCE?

In 1875, Eddy published *Science and Health with Key to Scriptures*, a work that serves as the foundational statement for the Christian Science religion. Eddy believed that this book, along with the Bible, could provide individuals with essential teachings about health and spiritual well-being. Christian Scientists emphasize the spiritual tradition linking their beliefs and practices to early Christianity, and argue that their religion is not new, but a rediscovery, or "reinstatement" of spiritual healing into Christianity and a reconfirmation of Jesus' teachings. Indeed, the dominant identifying feature of Christian Science is the focus on spiritual healing as a critical dimension of the teaching and practice of Jesus. Christian Scientists characterize Christianity as a science, and believe that spirituality and health are fundamentally linked in the individual's direct relationship with God.

Two Christian Science publications, *The Christian Science Sentinel* and *The Christian Science Journal*, contain personal testaments to the power of spiritual healing. These include first person accounts about the healing of serious medical conditions that had been diagnosed as untreatable by a variety of health professionals. These testaments also indicate that Christian Scientists are not exclusive in their healing practices; practitioners are available to heal all members of the community, regardless of their particular faith, and often have patients referred to them by physicians.

But the healing of medical ailments is certainly not the only significant component of Christian Science spirituality. Through my several visits to the Christian Science Church and Reading Room in Decatur, I began to recognize a common theme in the conversations I had there. Christian Science offers and supports a specific worldview that allows for a calm acceptance of the events of everyday life, not as a resignation in the face of burdensome obstacles, but as a recognition of certain key principles, such as the futility of over-reaction, the destructiveness of confrontation, and the healthfulness of harmonious interaction. Margie Long, who runs the Christian Science Reading Room, was brought up in the Methodist church and discovered the Church of Christ, Scientist as an adult approximately 40 years ago. Long explained to me that Christian Science is about "reflecting God," and "making God manifest in this world." In an increasingly complex, fast-paced, and stress-inducing society, Christian Scientists choose to "see only the good" and reject discordant elements, such as "evil," "war," and "crime," as false belief rather than as true reflections of God.

ORGANIZATION AND MESSAGE OF THE CHURCH

The Christian Science Church is organized according to a governing structure that Dr. Clifton Irby, from the Christian Science Publications Committee for Georgia, described to me as "two-tiered . . . analogous to our federal system of government." The First Church of Christ, Scientist,

Boston, is the centralizing body—or Mother Church—for 2,500 branch churches in the United States and abroad. The Mother Church contains both a five-person board of directors and the manual of the Mother Church, which defines the system of government. Although there are broad guidelines provided by the Mother Church, the local branches are individually and democratically self-governed.

In spite of the decentralized, representative system of government, this religious institution is unusually consistent, even uniform, among branch churches. Such uniformity is apparent in three respects: the parallel governing structure, the form and content of weekly services, and the coherence in the Christian Science message. These elements were originally implemented by Eddy herself, and the Mother Church oversees their continuation today.

The Christian Science church is a lay organization, meaning every branch church has a democratically elected seven-person board of directors. In place of clergy, a first reader and second reader share responsibilities in leading services. These are also elected positions. Gender equality is institutionalized so that each branch church has a balance between the number of men and women represented in leadership positions. Many churches, but not all, stipulate that three of the board members and one of the readers be women. When I visited Sunday service at First Church, Decatur, I was surprised to see that both readers were women. Dr. Irby confirmed that this is somewhat unusual.

Branch churches also follow a centralized plan in their weekly services. Each branch church offers two weekly meetings. Services are held on Sunday mornings, with separate Sunday school for children and teenagers. The Christian Science service is refreshingly simple. There is no sermon. Instead, weekly readings come from the Bible and Eddy's *Science and Health*. There are 26 subjects of study rotated throughout the year in a centralized lesson plan. In Decatur, a single female singer and an organist lead the congregation from the Christian Science Hymnal.

Wednesday testimonial meetings are somewhat less formal than the Sunday services. The first reader leads the meeting, inviting those in attendance to share their experiences with the congregation. The number of people attending on Wednesday evenings is usually considerably lower than on Sunday. In important ways, however, the Wednesday testimonials reflect the true meaning of Christian Science for the members of this spiritual community. These midweek meetings provide an open forum for the expression of individual experiences and interpretations. I expected to hear accounts of physical healing from participants—success stories after the trial and failure of medical science. Instead, the several testimonials I heard were much more accessible, more relevant to day-to-day experiences. The common message of these separate accounts emphasized the importance of living with God and practicing spiritual thinking. One gentleman simply expressed his gratitude for the message of Christian Science because it gives him strength and carries him through life. Indeed, thankfulness was frequently expressed throughout the testimonials—thankfulness for Christian Science and thankfulness for the presence and protection of God.

CHURCH MEMBERSHIP IN ATLANTA

Because neither the branch churches nor the Mother Church collect demographic data, information on membership is necessarily impressionistic. What exactly is the relationship between church and community? Is community diversity reflected in the membership and activities of parishioners?

Very loosely speaking, the typical Christian Scientist in Atlanta is female, white, middle class, and over forty. Of course, not all Christian Scientists are women, though when I noted attendance at the Decatur church, men seemed underrepresented in comparison with women. There are young adults involved in the church as well, but they seem to represent a shrinking proportion of the larger community. Nevertheless, the Christian Science community is not what one would call diverse. On dimensions of race and class, the disproportion is striking. Most Christian Scientists are either of middle-class or upper-middle-class background, and racial/ethnic diversity is virtually nonexistent.

Does this lack of diversity pose a problem for the church? The larger Atlanta community continues to build its current international reputation on a record of (relative) racial harmony and thriving cultural diversity. Against this backdrop, the homogeneity of the Christian Science community appears oddly out of step. And it seems odder still, when one considers the church's egalitarian tradition, philosophy, and practice, and its emphasis on spiritual over material reality.

The Christian Science community has not achieved visibility based on "community outreach" or recruitment programs. The *Christian Science Sentinel* and *The Christian Science Journal* represent centralized methods of community outreach, and these publications generally reach the whole of the Christian Science community. While the one-person Committee on Publications makes sure that anyone who wants information on the church has access to it, and while the branch churches and reading rooms welcome the public, the church is not overly concerned with attracting potential new members. Nor does the practice of spiritual healing serve as a recruitment platform. Christian Science healing is nonexclusive and available to anyone—Christian Scientist or not. But it would be rash to conclude that Christian Science in Atlanta does not have any religious vitality. While it seems that this is not a period of outstanding growth or visibility, there remains a substantial and dedicated core membership.

FOR FURTHER INFORMATION

Mary Baker Eddy. *Science and Health with Key to the Scriptures.* Boston, The First Church of Christ, Scientist, 1906, 1934

Mary Baker Eddy. *Manual of The Mother Church.* Boston, The First Church of Christ, Scientist, 1908, 1936

Robert Peel. *Spiritual Healing in a Scientific Age.* San Francisco, Harper & Row, 1987

C H A P T E R   E I G H T

FAITH, FAMILY, AND TRADITION AMONG THE LATTER-DAY SAINTS OF ATLANTA

Edward R. Gray

Church of Jesus Christ of Latter–Day Saints, Druid Hills. Photograph by Louis A. Ruprecht, Jr.

The Atlanta Temple of the Church of Jesus Christ of Latter-Day Saints (LDS) sits atop a low hill in the northern suburbs. A broad, well-manicured carpet of rich green lawn, parallel rows of young trees, and bright flower beds lead the eye up to the white building. Soaring several stories above the building, a tower rises from the center. The tower neither houses a bell nor is the perch for a cross. At its apex sits an immense, golden statue of Moroni, trumpet in hand. Inside a paid staff of twenty and a volunteer staff of as many as sixty each shift preside over and help with special "ordinances," rituals available only to "worthy" Mormons. Others can get only as far as the reception desk sitting immediately inside what might be the lobby of a hotel. Those who make it beyond this area hold "Temple recommends," a card bearing the signatures of LDS bishops and presidents. On this day a man altogether white stands at the front desk. He wears white shirt, white necktie, white jacket, white socks, and white shoes. His hair is white. He casually inspects the small, wallet-sized cards presented by well-dressed, temple-worthy Mormons. They come alone and in groups. Some carry garment bags with white uniforms inside. This attire is brought from home or purchased on temple grounds at the Beehive Distribution Center. Participants in "temple work" come to Atlanta to participate in sacred rites for themselves and for their dead. They emerge from private dressing rooms, dressed in white costume, each looking alike.

The business affairs of the Atlanta Temple are supervised by a full-time employee of the church called "The Recorder." In Atlanta, he is a middle-aged man with a Texas accent. He has never lived in Texas, but picked up his twang as a young man working in refineries filled with Texans. One might expect the recorder to have a more winsome South Pacific accent since he has served in the South Pacific long and ably as a full-time financial manager for LDS schools, being moved from one nation in the region to another. Today, he makes sure that the worldly affairs of the Atlanta Temple run smoothly.

ORGANIZATION AND HISTORY

The opening of the Atlanta Temple in 1983 capped the 75th anniversary of sustained Mormon activity in the area, and followed a decade of impressive growth in the metropolitan region. The Latter-Day Saints, also known as Mormons, formed "stakes" in Jonesboro, Tucker, and Sandy Springs in the 1970s, nearly doubling the church's membership in metropolitan Atlanta. In addition, there are 45 LDS wards in six stakes and missions, called "branches," in black, Hispanic, and Vietnamese communities in inner city Atlanta. "Stakes" are ecclesiastical units equivalent to dioceses or districts. The term "stake" reflects the Mormons' conception of themselves as members of a new Zion, a great tabernacle, a tent secured by stakes. Each stake is run by a president and two counselors, and comprises between 2,000 and 6,000 active members in six to eight local congregations called "wards." Wards are headed by bishops who are helped by two counselors. The membership of a ward numbers between 200 and 600 persons. Wards "split" when they become larger, and when they do the two resulting wards are likely to share the same building (two wards per building is the norm in Atlanta). Local wards have gotten larger lately in Atlanta because membership continues to increase. "The problem is assimilating the growth we have," a current bishop said. "We can't provide the leaders and facilities fast enough."

Bishops are volunteers. They receive no compensation for hundreds of hours of service annually. The bishop of a ward in the Roswell stake is a man only days from retirement. He should be glad. He spends upward of 12 hours on ward business each Sunday and conducts member interviews every Thursday night. There are meetings other evenings and special events on weekends. It's a full-time job. He manages the spiritual and financial affairs of a congregation with hundreds of people, interviewing all members at least once a year to recommend them for temple admissions. With his two counselors he also interviews all young men in the congregation between the ages of 12 and 19 every six months. The bishop also interviews children nearing their eighth birthday, those preparing to be baptized. Typically, the child's father, as a priest, baptizes his own children at the ward building. Bishops are appointed by the Quorum of the Twelve Apostles. Based in Salt Lake City, these are the traveling "General Authorities" of the church.

The Mormon presence in the Atlanta region can be traced to the beginning of this century, though their rate of growth in the early years was not as strong as it has been recently. The Mormons started their first mission, or "branch," in Atlanta in 1908 and moved their Southern States Mission Headquarters from Chattanooga, Tennessee to Atlanta in 1919. By 1925, a new meetinghouse was built. In 1937, Mormons organized the Georgia Missionary District—one year after Margaret Mitchell published *Gone with the Wind.* These domestic missionary efforts were not the first attempt to establish a Mormon presence in Georgia. In 1843, Elder John U. Eldredge visited Georgia on a short-lived mission and to campaign for Joseph Smith, a candidate for president of the United States. (Smith enjoyed far greater success as the founder of the Church of Jesus Christ of Latter-Day Saints than as a presidential contender!)

A full understanding of Mormonism must begin with the experiences of its founder. Joseph Smith was born in Sharon, Vermont in 1805 and lived as a boy in a region of New York known later by religious historians as the "Burnt-Over District" because great emotional religious revivals swept through the area like wildfire. It wasn't long before Smith, as a young man, was set afire as well. In a series of fantastic visions, the "Heavenly Father," his Son, Jesus, and a host of other Biblical figures (including John the Baptist, Moses, Elijah, and the Apostles Peter, James, and John) appeared to Smith. These messengers told him to restore the proper authority of the Christian Church through the sacred priesthood. Another celestial messenger, Moroni, revealed to him the location of Gold Plates. Moroni's father, Mormon, had inscribed the sacred texts of an ancient people, the first natives of the Americas, onto plates he made from gold. In a vision their whereabouts were revealed to Smith, who found them and then translated them with the aid of a special spiritual device. In 1829 he published the *Book of Mormon,* a revised Christian scripture about the post-resurrection work of Jesus Christ in America. One historian of American religion has called it "a document of profound social protest." It condemned the wealthy, the powerful, and professional clergy. Mormons consider their book a supplement to the Hebrew Bible and New Testament.

Mormons faced strong condemnation in their early years. The condemnation grew in intensity and finally became violent when the practice of plural marriage (polygamy) became public. Nationwide opposition to this practice and other teachings led to widespread persecution and harassment, eventually leading to the murder of Smith in 1844. In 1890, the First

President, Prophet, Seer, and Revelator of the Church, Wilford Woodruff, announced that the Saints would no longer sanction polygamy. Throughout the twentieth century, Mormons have become an integral component of the American religious landscape. They have also spread their teachings to many parts of the world, though Utah has remained the center of the Mormon universe.

The Atlanta Temple, like all 43 temples throughout the world, is a sacred site. It is a holy place limited to baptized Mormons who keep the dietary laws, tithe 10% of their income, and lead morally clean lives. The Atlanta Temple may be one of the most visited pilgrimage sites in the southeast. On an average day 800 to a thousand people come to the Atlanta Temple from Georgia, Tennessee, Kentucky, Mississippi, Alabama, and elsewhere in the South to perform sacred acts. Others receive the "endowments" that unlock the plan of salvation. Through these ritual activities Mormons—or their ancestors—attain a new, sacred status. The rituals performed at the Atlanta Temple are not discussed with non-Mormons, except in the most oblique way. "It is not because they are secrets," the temple recorder said to me, "but because they are sacred."

THEOLOGY, MISSIONS, AND CONSISTENCY

Most people know something about the keen Mormon interest in family genealogy. The ritual of Baptism for the Dead helps to explain it. Mormons baptize their dead by proxy. A worthy Mormon may baptize an ancestor who did not have the opportunity to hear and accept the restored gospel of Jesus Christ during his or her life. The dead cannot be baptized by their own efforts alone. They need water. The living are baptized for the dead because, while the celestial realm resembles the earth, Jesus commanded that baptism be done with water. So the proxy enters a baptismal pool and is immersed in the water, as Christ commanded. Baptism of the Dead allows the departed to enter the "celestial kingdom." There they too can join the patriarchical line and become like God himself.

The material and the spiritual are not separated in Mormonism. God has a "spiritual body," different from our bodies in this existence, not human, but material in some way. The Heavenly Father is the father of both Jesus' body and soul. According to Mormon theology, the Heavenly Father is the father of one's soul alone. Individuals are the spiritual children of the Heavenly Father, but they also have human mothers and fathers. The belief system is highly complex and based on ongoing revelations, but it plays a critical role in how Mormons live their everyday lives. While the content of their beliefs is of tremendous importance, what Mormons practice reflects their strong and deep commitment to these beliefs.

All young Mormon men are expected to go on a two-year mission, a hallmark of coming of age. Many missionaries also serve domestic fields, like helping with temple work. On the grounds of the Atlanta Temple sits an apartment complex that houses fifty missionaries who serve there. Some of these young male missionaries travel by bicycle around the tree-lined streets of Atlanta bringing the restored gospel of Jesus Christ to the unsaved. Young women may also serve as missionaries, but the church does not require them to do so, nor does it especially encourage them as it does its young men. Female missionaries must wait until they are twenty-one and serve about eighteen months. Men usually start missionary activity when they are nineteen and serve two years.

Missions are expensive and they are not paid for by the church. "The parents or the kids pay for it," said a Mormon manager for a gasoline company who has paid for three missions. Until recently, sending a kid to Japan for two years was the equivalent of taking on a new mortgage. Supporting a mission to some countries in Africa, on the other hand, might cost less than keeping a 19-year-old at home. The bishop of the Alpharetta ward is looking forward to sending his fourth (and last) son off on a mission. The father describes sending his four sons off on missions as a bargain. Where can one find the kind of language education and life experience that comes from two years in a foreign country? Older retired couples also serve as missionaries, and they make up most of the volunteers at the Atlanta Temple.

One retired couple from Druid Hills, a community near Emory University, recently went off to Toronto on a mission. They returned to Atlanta not long ago to attend the high school graduation of their grandson. Both rose to speak during the monthly "testimony" time held during sacrament meeting. Elder Ted spoke about being recently healed. "The hand of the Lord can heal," he assured his former fellow congregants. "I shouldn't be standing here today," he added. He then spoke, with reverence and pleasure, about the number of baptisms, exceeding a thousand a month, at his mission branch in Toronto.

Mormons are required to give 10% of their income to the church—a tithe. All funds are remitted to the General Authorities of the Church, housed at Salt Lake City. The General Authorities then issue funds to the 20,000 wards located throughout the country. Standardization and consistency are hallmarks of Mormon belief and practice. No ward in Atlanta enjoys more luxurious facilities than another. The buildings are paid for by the entire church, so no ward in Atlanta has a financial advantage over another. Whatever the relative affluence of members, ward spending is a function of membership size. A local LDS service center in Atlanta provides all maintenance and grounds-keeping services and pays for utilities at every ward building in all of north Georgia. Even the design of local LDS buildings is chosen from a line of models approved by Salt Lake. These models, currently four, have evocative names like "Heritage" and "Legacy."

Mormon consistency extends beyond blueprints and facilities, a point emphasized by many Atlanta Mormons. "It's exactly the same, the teachings, the same kind of people," said a recent arrival to the Atlanta area. He was comparing his experience at a ward here with wards in California and Utah. A bishop described his own ward members as a "blending and conglomeration" of different backgrounds; the LDS clearly has a "leveling effect." "What is distinctive about Atlanta Mormons compared to Utah Mormons?" I asked. "Nothing," was his answer. "It goes into a blender and comes out smooth."

What comes out clearly in talking to Mormons in Atlanta is just that message. As one southern woman, who serves the church as a volunteer public affairs specialist, put it, "Everything is identical down to what your child is taught in Sunday School." This is because the Mormons are "one people." She, a native Georgian, converted from the Episcopal church. "The consistency is the same anywhere you go," a member told me during a tour of the ward building in Roswell. This observation came from someone who should know. He has lived in Sweden, where he served during his mission, Connecticut, Houston, San Francisco, and Salt Lake City.

The consistency does not begin and end with doctrine and organization either. "You have a network of support the moment you walk in," active LDS members repeated again and again. The support is spiritual, financial, and practical. From a program of home visitation, to annual interviews, to access to food, money, and supplies, Mormons have perfected a social safety net. When they talk about it and the church, they use adjectives like "amazing," "terrific," and "remarkable" liberally. It does not mean, though, that they say it in a boastful way. One detects instead a certain humility that comes from years of service.

MORMONS IN THE SOUTH

If the southern evangelicalism that surrounds them has affected the Mormons of Atlanta, it has been in subtle ways and is linked to the distinctive cultural ethos of the region. Hearing Sister Joy, a missionary in Toronto, speak to the Druid Hills ward you might conclude that you were at a revival meeting. A handsome southern woman in her sixties, she spoke excitedly about her mission service in Canada and about her grandson's high school graduation. "All the graduation speakers spoke of their Lord and Savior Jesus Christ," she noted. Sister Joy found in this a cause for optimism. "The world and the country are in good hands," she said. Her remarks, cheery and optimistic, contrasted with the somber assessment of the state of the world given by the bishop a half-hour earlier.

Sister Joy concluded her testimony by reminding her audience that "Joseph Smith did in fact restore the gospel for this dispensation." Mormons in Atlanta, she exhorted, are "called to bring the church out of obscurity." Atlanta Mormons are moving rapidly out of obscurity. In 1994, the Saints donated over 100,000 pounds of food (worth approximately $300,000) to 26 Atlanta charities. They did this without regard to religious affiliation. More recently, the LDS donated 40,000 pounds of clothing directly to the city of Atlanta. The clothes came from all over the country and were new or freshly laundered at the LDS Sort Center in Salt Lake City. Atlanta was one of 50 cities to receive this kind of assistance, a decision made in Salt Lake City.

Mormons, who eat meat in moderate amounts, fast for two meals each month. The money saved becomes the fast offering. Part of this also supports the nationwide system of storehouses filled with food and emergency provisions. The Bishop's Storehouse in Tucker is a local Mormon Piggly-Wiggly, soup kitchen, and Salvation Army thrift store rolled into one. In the storehouse, members and eligible others can come and receive up to two weeks worth of food with a requisition usually provided by the head of the Women's Relief Society. Different areas of the country produce different goods for the storehouses. The specialty of Atlanta Mormons is beef stew. The food and other emergency relief supplies go to disaster victims like the residents of middle Georgia who suffered during the flooding that occurred in the summer of 1994.

While temple ordinances are unfamiliar, if not strange, to non-Mormons, the regular Sunday meetings should seem rather ordinary. They are simple proceedings taking place in simple buildings. Atlanta Mormons are used to simplicity in their weekly worship. Asking Mormons about the difference between Mormon and evangelical worship, you hear described, as I did, the "pomp and ceremony" of Baptist church services. Only Mormons would find Baptist worship heavy on ceremony.

Mormon worship services are like town meetings. There are no white uniforms, no temple recommends, no rituals for the dead. There are no robes, no crosses, no iconography of any kind at sacrament meetings. When a meeting begins, you might wonder if they have begun early. There were few in attendance when the bishop announced the opening hymn at the service I attended. The congregation sang something from the rich tradition of Mormon hymnology. The young male missionaries scampered in late to the service, wearing engraved plastic name tags on dark jackets. One Sunday at the Druid Hills ward, they distinguished themselves by coming in at the close of the opening hymn, carrying backpacks and bicycle helmets.

People walked in during the first half hour and took their places in the pews without displaying any indication that they had arrived late. There were young families everywhere, with lots of children all neatly dressed and well-behaved. Babies cried and no one tried to intimidate mothers with a disapproving glare. Children fidgeted and expressions dulled when the proceedings grew boring. A woman in her fifties wearing no robe but a severe expression led the singing. She stood and conducted, seemingly ignored by the congregation. The bishop, a medical doctor, also without robes but nattily dressed in a dark suit and bow tie, rose at the conclusion of the hymn to make the announcements. He asked that two women in the congregation be confirmed in positions of service. There was a perfunctory show of hands showing approval. One black woman sat toward the back, though this does not adequately reflect the presence of African Americans in the Mormon religion.

The LDS did not ordain African-American males to the priesthood in its early years. In 1963 however, the LDS addressed the color line in the church. President Hugh B. Brown declared at the General Conference that "There is in this Church no doctrine, belief, or practice that is intended to deny the enjoyment of full civil rights by any person regardless of race, color, or creed." But it was not until a revelation in 1978 that African-American males were admitted to the priesthood. Although church offices at all levels, from the local ward to the international headquarters in Salt Lake City, keep elaborate records of members, one piece of data is not collected. There is no record of the race of active Mormons in the Atlanta area.

A new ward building in Adams Park, a predominantly African-American neighborhood, was dedicated in the summer of 1995. The building is debt-free, like all Mormon property, and has been in use since April 1994. Previously members met in a double-wide mobile trailer, with about 150 attending on a regular Sunday. This mission branch opened in Adams Park in 1989, around the time five other missions opened in predominantly minority sections of Atlanta. Of the six, four remain. The other primarily African-American branch is in East Lake. Branches for Spanish and Vietnamese speakers meet on Ponce de Leon Avenue with the Druid Hills ward. Attendance at the foreign language branches is lower than at the African-American wards, around one hundred weekly. "The language problem is a challenge," a member of the Atlanta Mission District Presidency told me.

This member is an African American, born in Alabama. He began to "investigate" the church while living in Virginia and serving in the Army, before the LDS ordained African-Americans males. "That was a real problem to me," he said. Some of his black friends went further and accused the LDS of being a racist church. Nevertheless, he was receptive when two Mormon missionaries on bicycles rode up to him and asked him to read the *Book of Mormon*. He did and was impressed by the Mormon example of service and the brotherhood he saw between races and the rich and poor. He liked the Mormon concern for a "whole way of life." After investigating for a time, he asked, "What's wrong with this?" "Nothing" was the answer he found in his heart, so he converted. That was almost twenty years ago. The day after I spoke with him he was to dedicate the new ward building at Adams Park. Dedication of a new building is an activity usually reserved for one of the General Authorities of the church. But tomorrow the honor would go to him in recognition of the instrumental role he had played in the life of the developing ward over the last ten years.

Back at Druid Hills, the bishop of the ward presided from the center of a huge high podium of polished wood. The podium dominates a white room with utilitarian dark carpet (ward buildings resemble courtrooms more than sanctuaries). Open a folding room partition and the chapel becomes a gymnasium. Mormons call it the "Cultural Hall." The transformation of the chapel into a basketball court does no violence to the aesthetics or sacrality of the room. If basketball is the national sport of American churches, then the LDS cannot be more American. The game is a weekly affair for Mormon males, with many children of non-members also participating in the tournaments. These tournaments are no longer churchwide, however. Church officials, to their credit, noticed that winning was becoming more important than participating. Getting on the team became harder and more people were feeling left out, so Salt Lake City dropped the highest levels of competition.

To the side of the lectern, two young men presided over the communion table. They are Aaronic priests. The Aaronic is the lower order of the priesthood, open to males between 13 and 18 years of age. Typically, men are ordained as priests at the age of 19. There are no paid clergy in Mormonism, distinguishing it from most American religious groups. Two younger boys, also members of the Aaronic priesthood, helped the others. These boys hold the offices of "teacher" and "deacon," and broke bread during the invocatory prayer led by the two young priests. I was reminded of a comment made by the temple recorder and repeated in one way or another in other interviews. "A man starts training in this church from the time he is born." The priesthood members distributed tiny pieces of bread on small silver serving dishes. Next, they passed trays filled with tiny plastic cups of water. Mormons do not consume alcohol, coffee, or tea and eat meat only in moderation. The young men distributed the sacrament with reverence. The bishop knew these young men well through his regular schedule of interviews with them and remarked on their outstanding service and character at the close of the sacrament.

Things were just getting started for the day when the sacrament meeting ended at Druid Hills. Adult Sunday School followed after a ten-minute break. Then the adults divided: Priests' Quorum for men, Relief Society for women. In their Relief Society meetings the Mormon women of Atlanta learn from each other how to live a life of "compassionate service to everyone." Gender difference, conspicuous in missions, is pervasive throughout Mormon life. As mentioned earlier, only men may be priests. Men and women are socialized into the church differently as well. After 12 years of age, the education of the young takes place along the gender line. Mormons believe that women belong at home if that is financially possible. Nonetheless, in their callings, the various service positions all Mormons hold at the ward or stake level, the expertise and labors of women are worth the same as those of men. Motherhood is considered among the highest of callings because it means the bearing of the "spirit children" of the Heavenly Father.

This is not to say that Mormon women are viewed as child-bearers alone rather than as leaders. "We have different roles, it's not that one is greater than the other or less," said one Mormon woman. Mormon women in Atlanta will give you a strong answer if you suggest that being disqualified from the priesthood makes them second class members. "First, that's wrong! Women do have leadership positions," was one woman's reply. Women run the Relief Society and may serve in any position besides those reserved for the ordained. There are enough opportunities for service to keep nearly everyone happy. Women speak at testimony time and deliver lessons. "We receive revelations for ourselves and for our families. Women aren't made to be less, but we are made more," said the female public affairs director for a suburban stake. "I would never join an organization that thought I was less simply by virtue of my gender," she concluded with conviction.

The global nerve center of Mormon life sits at Temple Square in Salt Lake City. Atlanta Mormons are in close touch with offices there and seem genuinely proud to point to a place where Mormons dominate socially and culturally. In settling the Utah territory in the mid-1800s, the Mormon pioneers had, in effect, left the country. An LDS elder, a man who grew up in Utah and with his wife serves in Decatur as a missionary, described the Mormons to me as "the only group ever forced out of the United States because of religious persecution." Atlanta Mormons, like those in field branches of the corporate world, appreciate the help, advice, and the good intentions of the "Utah Mormons." One local Mormon leader who has lived in Atlanta for less than five years, was once a tenant of the current First President, Prophet, Seer, and Revelator of the Church in Utah. Sometimes, but not too blatantly, he has detected a certain ecclesiastical imperiousness from those "fresh out of Salt Lake." But it quickly settles into a "smooth blending" of their talents and feelings with the Mormons of Atlanta.

Mormons in Atlanta, of course, do not enjoy the dominance that they do in Utah and parts of surrounding states in the West. Mormons in Georgia and elsewhere in the South swim in a sea of evangelical Protestantism. There are around 50,000 Mormons in the entire state, less than 1% of the population; nearly all of them live in the metro-Atlanta region. Mormonism, according to one convert from Methodism, may still strike many people in Atlanta as odd. He had considered the LDS strange before his conversion at the age of 22. To his evangelical mind then, Mormons were "somewhat different, weird in some way. Live out west and have a lot of wives."

In certain evangelical circles in the South, even today, Mormons are considered apostates to Christianity. You can go into a Christian bookstore in Atlanta, for example, and find anti-Mormon literature. In the extreme, some incorrectly consider the LDS Church a cult. Mormons in Atlanta naturally find that accusation a source of pain. Mormons have been theologically innovative, but they *do* believe in the salvific work of Jesus Christ. They set themselves apart from the rest of Christianity, especially the conservative, Bible-based style that dominates the Protestant religious scene of Atlanta, in some remarkable ways. These departures include their adherence to the *Book of Mormon*, their teachings about the nature of God and the afterlife, and their sacred rituals such as marriage for time and eternity.

Living in a new town with a new wife, far from their families, a young Air Force officer who initially shared the southern cultural resistance to Mormonism began to change his opinions. The unique Mormon practice and doctrine of eternal marriage attracted him. "What do you think about being married *forever?*" a Mormon employer asked the newlyweds. Mormon matrimony has no limitation, not by time or death. "Temple marriages," those "sealed" in a temple ordinance, are for "time and all eternity." The sealing ceremony is simple. The eternal partners stand before a "sealer" and a small circle of family and friends to repeat vows making them an eternal couple. These "Temple marriages" continue forever in the celestial realm.

The Mormon family is the basic sacred, that is, earthly and celestial, unit. The family continues in paradise. More than one Mormon has said somberly, quoting a former church president, that "no success in life can compensate for failure in the home." "The LDS is a family church. Everything we do is based on the premise that the family is central to everything," a lifelong Mormon told me. The key to this is that husband and wife remain joined eternally. Eternity has many levels. One is the paradise of which Jesus spoke to the thief with whom he died. There, without our human bodies, we continue to learn and move toward God with spiritual bodies. Mormons strive to do this as part of a patriarchical order that extends throughout eternity. Children, too, may be "sealed" to their parents. The emphasis on family, which is headed by the father, who is literally the family priest, is extraordinary. Families are important in many religions but none make the family the basic unit of eternal life like Mormons do. "We believe that the universe revolves around the family," a high LDS official told me on the 40th anniversary of his marriage. "We want to be with them for all time and the way to do it is one day at a time," an African-American Mormon remarked recently.

It is not surprising that the emphasis on marriage and family finds a friendly reception in the South. Here the extended family is more the center of social life than elsewhere in the nation. Religion is a family affair. Many raised in the South and in Utah are used to going to church with their families, many of which have inter-generational ties to specific congregations. Close family ties and religion are prized in the South for cultural reasons as much as they are in Mormonism for religious ones. You need only ask anyone with southern roots about one of her or his grandparents to find out the importance of the extended family. Religion is also generally more important here than in other parts of the country. Here, newlyweds routinely look for a church home as soon as they start looking for their first house. A young musician who grew up in Idaho, a lifelong Mormon, speaks admirably of the "religious feeling in the South." By that she means the "respect for devotion to God." Since moving to Atlanta she has enjoyed "a common bond with good Christian people of other faiths." Southerners, like Mormons, strongly identify with their dead. Go to Stone Mountain Park for the laser show or to any other ritualistic invocation of the heroic sacrifice of Civil War soldiers if you are looking for one example confirming the southern regard for family and the dead.

The blending of the ties of family, religion, and culture can be ambiguous for Atlanta Mormons. Sometimes it has been a source of tension. "The big struggle that I see," said the bishop of a northern metro ward, is for members of "the immediate family breaking away from close family ties" when they become Latter–Day Saints. "There is a tremendous feeling of abandonment by family and friends," he concluded. He thinks this is especially the case for converts from Southern Baptist and Roman Catholic families. He has seen them disowned and his sympathy shows. As a bishop he has also seen Mormon children "lost" to other faiths. He recognizes that while "you get a feeling of deep religious commitment in the South," many in evangelical Protestant churches would prefer that any new religious commitments not be to the LDS. This bishop wishes for a better understanding of Mormons by other religions in general and the Southern Baptists, whom he admires, in particular. He describes them as having "an iron fist around the culture here." Atlanta Mormons appear to do better converting Protestants from non-evangelical backgrounds. A woman who converted to Mormonism in Texas as a college student recounted her relationship with her Episcopal family afterwards. "Honestly, I wouldn't say they were thrilled in the beginning. It took some getting used to but I wasn't in hot water." Today, these parents "have seen the fruits" of her dedication to the LDS. For this family, it is a loving marriage of fourteen years and long service to the church. Her mom and dad, lifelong churchgoers, now "respect the discipline" of Mormon practice and its emphasis on close families.

During a visit to Atlanta, some of those whom you may overhear talking about scripture, youth groups, the church basketball game, or the state of the world may be Mormons. They are thriving in the principal city of the South, where their deep respect for family, faith, and tradition finds a reception made friendly by Atlanta's own peculiar regional emphasis on family, religion, and culture. Mormons in Atlanta are more than a religious group. They have become a people, with a shared history, a particular heritage, and a sense of cultural uniqueness. In Atlanta, Mormons remain apart even as they blend in.

FOR FURTHER INFORMATION

Leonard J. Arrington and Davis Bitton. *The Mormon Experience: A History of the Latter-day Saints.* New York, Alfred A. Knopf, 1979

Richard L. Bushman. *Joseph Smith and the Beginnings of Mormonism.* Urbana, University of Illinois Press, 1984

Lawrence Foster. *Religion and Sexuality: Three American Communal Experiments of the Nineteenth Century.* New York, Oxford University Press, 1981

Jan Shipps. *Mormonism: The Story of a New Religious Tradition.* Urbana, University of Illinois Press, 1985

CHAPTER NINE

TONGUES AFLAME: PENTECOSTAL AND CHARISMATIC GEORGIANS ON FIRE FOR JESUS

Keith E. McNeal

Greater Bibleway Miracle Temple Worldwide. Photograph by Elizabeth Hardcastle.

"When Pentecost day came round, they had all met together, when suddenly there came from heaven a sound as of a violent wind which filled the entire house in which they were sitting; and there appeared to them tongues as of fire; these separated and came to rest on the head of each of them. They were all filled with the Holy Spirit and began to speak different languages as the Spirit gave them power to express themselves."

Acts 2:1-4

BEYOND THE TOWER OF BABEL

Most Thursday evenings in Cobb County people are making their way home through the steady flow of evening rush-hour traffic. Alongside one of the county's busiest thoroughfares sits a small Hispanic church called Centro Cristiano. The church building looks a bit worn; it seems to have been converted from a house into a church meeting place in the recent past. The mainly Spanish-speaking congregants of Centro Cristiano are gathered on this particular June night to join forces with the members of a fledgling new church—the Abundant Life Church of Pentecost. Centro Cristiano is a non-denominational, charismatic Hispanic church that is temporarily sharing its space with Abundant Life, a Pentecostal congregation that—in mid-June 1995—is little more than seven months old. The previous Sunday was the day of Pentecost, considered the birthday of the Christian church, and all week long Abundant Life has held nightly tent crusades in celebration of both Pentecost itself and the concurrent 50th anniversary of the United Pentecostal Church International (UPCI). Tonight the crusades continue, yet it is a special night because this is the first time the predominantly Hispanic congregation of Centro Cristiano and the small, but diverse Abundant Life congregation will worship and praise together.

The UPCI resulted from the 1945 merger of the Pentecostal Church, Inc., and the Pentecostal Assemblies of Jesus Christ. It is one prominent denomination within the larger Pentecostal fold. Pentecostals point to the Book of Acts in the New Testament as the only book of the Bible that records the beginning and foundation of the Christian church. They believe that the gifts of the Holy Spirit described in the Book of Acts, such as speaking in tongues and faith healing, are present today in the modern world.

Such gifts are, in fact, an authentic sign of one's infilling with the Holy Spirit.

Tonight, before the main worship service begins, the members of Centro Cristiano sing along to upbeat synthesized music, praising in Spanish the love and mercy of *el Cristo*. Hands clap and feet fervently stomp to the background electronic beat as kids run freely about, seemingly uninterested in the service going on around them. Then Pastor W. Wayne Pugh, his wife, whom most refer to as Sister Pugh, and son Aaron take to the front to begin leading a new round of musical worship. Sister Pugh covers the full range of the organ, and Aaron strikes an upbeat tempo on the drums as Pastor Pugh provides a syncopated keyboard background to his own call to worship over the loudspeaker.

The sanctuary is relatively unadorned (most walls are bare) and one is struck by the absence of any iconographic or religious imagery that might be commonplace in a Catholic church or even some Protestant churches. Such a setting is appropriate for Pentecostals, who strongly believe that Christians should focus primarily upon the Word of God as revealed in the Bible. It would be fair to characterize the evening's activities as an experiential melting pot, an event whose purpose is to worship and praise Jesus Christ—the congregants' risen Lord and Savior. The service is bilingual for pragmatic reasons, yet it is also symbolic of the confluence of two very different congregations. Abundant Life's own internal composition is certainly heterogeneous, including immigrants from Liberia and Sierra Leone alongside American blacks, with a few scattered white folks in addition to the Pughs. The featured speaker for the evening is a United States-born missionary to Guyana; his wife is also present and she plays the acoustic guitar Latin-American style as an accompaniment to her bilingual songs of praise. The service is translated from English to Spanish by a Chicano preacher originally from San Antonio, Texas.

If it is true that Sunday morning is "America's most segregated hour," then this Thursday night breaks many traditional patterns found in Protestant churches across the country. Pastor Pugh commented to me after the service that he is "progressive" in the sense that he ministers to everyone regardless of background or ethnic group. He believes that God brought him to heal wounds and bridge worlds here in the Atlanta area, and to minister morally to Cobb County in particular. In his own words, Pastor Pugh "lives like Jesus is going to come at anytime, but works like He's not coming in my lifetime." Indeed, Pastor Pugh has a city to save and a church to fill up.

RELIGIOUS ENTHUSIASM AND EMOTIONAL AUTHENTICITY

Pentecostals and charismatics, like other evangelical Protestants, believe that Jesus is the risen Lord and Savior and that one must sincerely repent of one's sins in order to be "born again." Yet perhaps their most outstanding characteristic is the emotionally fervent, sometimes ecstatic, modes of worship that take place during church services. Holding and waving one's arms up in the air as a form of enthusiastic praise is extremely common, and worship services for many congregations include extended periods of upbeat, foot-stomping music accompanied by loud tambourines, shouts of "Hallelujah," and dancing in the pews and aisles. Anyone brought up in a mainline Protestant church would surely find Pentecostal and charismatic forms of worship a new and rather intense experience. There is, of course, a significant range of intensities in these forms of worship, but the emotionally-fervent enthusiasm, the spontaneous bursts of worshipful expression, and the strong emphasis on authentic experience constitute a unique mode of Christian knowing that is a defining characteristic of these churches.

The Pentecostal movement can be traced back to the black American religious revivals at the beginning of the twentieth century. As Walter Hollenweger argued in his book *The Pentecostals*, it is important to appreciate that the growth of the Pentecostal movement in this century has been predicated upon the use made of African-American "faculties of understanding and communicating by way of enthusiastic spiritual manifestations to build up community and fellowship." Emotionalism and fervor as a means of experiential knowing are significant factors in the continued spread of Pentecostalism both at home and abroad, even though such enthusiasm may often become deflated and institutionalized. Indeed, these forms of worship—hymns, speaking in tongues, interpretations of tongues, spontaneous outbursts of worship, and even dreams—have proven to be of decisive importance in the spread of Pentecostalism throughout developing parts of the world. Most Pentecostal believers consider their movement a return to the charismatic church of primitive Christianity, especially in connection with the Book of Acts, and view themselves as bringing renewal from within the church. Thus, despite some internal matters of theological contention, these movements understand their "experiential" form of religion as a manifestation of true—literally *inspired*—Christianity.

The primary characteristic of this religious enthusiasm is the working of the Holy Spirit on the believer. Luke, the author of Acts, relates the words Jesus had for his disciples before Pentecost and the subsequent founding of the early church: "John baptized with water but, not many days from now, you are going to be baptized with the Holy Spirit" (Acts 1:5). Pentecostals maintain a general distinction between baptism by water and baptism by the Spirit. The latter is responsible for fervent worship practices, and is believed to be a direct sign of divine presence. Common exclamations that one hears at Pentecostal services include: "It's here!" (meaning the Holy Spirit); "I feel anointed right now!"; and "This house is getting ready to be taken over by the Holy Ghost!" During one evening worship service I attended a significant portion of the congregation took to the aisles and to the front of the tabernacle uttering supernatural "prayer languages" (tongues), and shaking with ecstatic praise. During this extended period of fervor the preacher shouted over and over: "It's happening!! It's happening!! It's happening!!"

The Tabernacle. Photograph by Elizabeth Hardcastle.

Before proceeding to a closer examination of this religious community in metro Atlanta, something should be said concerning the terms Pentecostal and charismatic. Both fall generally under the canopy of American evangelicals, who believe that some form of spiritual rebirth or "born again" experience, in which one acknowledges personal sinfulness and Christ's atonement, is necessary for salvation. Evangelicals have, for the most part, emphasized what they refer to as a literalistic understanding of the Bible (one UPCI preacher stated that the Bible is "the only reliable guide for man today") and strongly favor personal spiritual piety. They have also been characterized by a proselytizing zeal that has erupted into large-scale revivals, particularly in the nineteenth century. As mentioned earlier, Pentecostals believe that the spiritual gifts characteristic of the early church described in the book of Acts—tongues, healing, and so on—are available to modern-day believers. And most Pentecostals insist that the spiritual experience of the Holy Spirit as manifested through speaking in tongues is the mark of the true Christian. Common Pentecostal denominations include the Church of God in Christ, the Assemblies of God, the United Pentecostal Church International, Foursquare Gospel churches, and the churches of Apostolic or Oneness Faith, in addition to those independent, nondenominational congregations.

Charismatics, like Pentecostals, believe in the spiritual gifts characterized by the church of Acts, but have chosen not to be affiliated with classical Pentecostal denominations. These congregational communities likewise consider speaking in tongues an important and authoritative experience for true Christians. However, the charismatic movement is not limited to evangelical Protestants. Since 1959, there have been active charismatics among Episcopalians (even in rural Valdosta, Georgia), and since the 1960s the charismatic movement has found increasing resonance within the Catholic church. In fact, the Atlanta Diocese has a separate office for the Catholic Charismatic Renewal movement, and several Catholic parishes in the metropolitan area have subgroups that meet independently of their larger congregations for their own charismatic forms of worship. Thus one should be aware that charismatics are found not among Protestants alone, though Protestants do form the majority of charismatic Christians.

A prevalent and unifying dimension for Pentecostals and charismatics is personal transformation. The working of the Holy Spirit is most powerful when "life is changed." Examples of transformation can be found widely in both communal and personal forms of expression, including speaking in tongues and public healing, and such "real change" constitutes compelling evidence for the power of the Holy Spirit and of God's mercy. References to personal transformation are often encouraged as soon as a service gets going with loud, boisterous exclamations such as "God wants to do a work in the service this morning!" or "The Holy Ghost is going to deliver us tonight!" or "The least we can do is ACT PENTECOSTAL!" The group experience is cyclical in that congregants come together from different settings outside the church, enter the divine world of worship and enthusiastic praise in the presence of Jesus and the Holy Spirit, and then disperse back out into their very different lives. As one pastor put it to his congregation in Decatur: "Isn't coming into the presence of the Lord rejuvenating?"

The complement, therefore, to communal transformation in the church setting can be seen in what happens in the lives of individuals. Acts of healing are common in Pentecostal and charismatic communities; one never ceases to hear testimonies of how the Holy Spirit has worked in the lives of fellow congregants and members can witness important life changes as they take place. One example of this was related to a small congregation and had to do with a woman "consciously battling problems related to her weight" who had recently discovered the Pentecostal church through a friend. She had attended consistently for a few weeks and then decided to join the church. At her baptism she came up out of the water and was immediately filled with the Holy Spirit, speaking in tongues to those present. She experienced this event as life-changing. In the weeks following this conversion experience she found new happiness and contentment, began to find her place within the Pentecostal church community, and even graduated from a beauty school that promised her new prospects in employment and improved self-esteem. Her story was related twice by the pastor at different services I attended, and each time she sat proudly near the front smiling broadly. Publicly retelling stories of transformation such as hers constitute an important aspect of Pentecostal worship.

Various forms of healing can take place at each and every service, yet church communities vary in the extent to which divinely-mediated healings form the backbone of a typical service. In Atlanta, the smaller churches belonging to UPCI or some of the Apostolic Oneness faiths tend to be highly charged with emotionalism and religious fervor, and these churches have a high incidence of public healing. Occasions for healing and demonstrating the presence of the Holy Spirit are often supported by the "laying on of hands" at the front of the worship hall where the supplicant kneels or stands in prayer as others gather round and place their hands all over the individual's torso, arms, and head. This physical contact is an important form of communication between believers during the service. Another characteristic aspect of healing and transformation, though not as common as the "laying on of hands," is the "anointing" of the heads of believers with oil by the pastor. Such anointing is another form of physical communication, this time between the lay congregant and the pastor who is almost always male.

In addition to some of the smaller UPCI and Apostolic Faith church communities that are characterized by intense, emotional praise and frequent healing experiences, there are larger congregational communities with other denominational affiliations (such as the Assemblies of God, or Church of God) or independent, non-denominational identifications. Although there are certainly exceptions, these larger congregations tend to be less intense in their forms of worship, and have fewer instances of in-the-aisles praising and highly charged, front-of-the-tabernacle healing events. What is shared across the range of Pentecostal and charismatic communities both small and large—at least as a minimum identifying characteristic—is the belief that "speaking in tongues" is a direct manifestation of the infilling of the Holy Spirit and that this experience was present among the first Christians. In one relatively large Sunday morning Church of God service there was no in-the-aisles clapping and dancing nor was there much in the way of episodic, spontaneous bursts of praise. An exception to the morning's low-key, sit-down service was a long moment of tongues from a man sitting in an upper balcony; this utterance was followed by its interpretation from a woman sitting in a pew on the main floor near the front stage. Her interpretation emphasized sitting at the feet of the Lord and especially emphasized the importance of "healing mind, body, and spirit."

For many, the characteristic forms of worship in Pentecostal and charismatic services are what make these religious traditions salient, meaningful, transformative, and real both for the faithful congregant and for the potential convert. In fact, the most common themes heard across these churches in Atlanta—intertwined with themes of healing and transformation—were those emphasizing "realness" and "feeling." As one preacher in Cobb County put it, Pentecostalism is "not a religion, but an experience." Or, as another exclaimed in glory during a revival: "They can argue with our theology, but they can't argue with our emotional feeling!" This same speaker shook with intensity and shouted "PURE FEELING!! IT'S REAL!!" later as those present had begun to swarm forward toward the end of the revival meeting, careening about in rapturous praise and gathering collective momentum.

Many people in the United States find this kind of charged, cathartic emotionalism a compelling force that can have life-changing implications. Such power can be seen in the following narrative of a young black woman who offered her perspective on the impact of Pentecostal worship in her life. She said that she belonged to a Baptist church but that it did not "really feed" her. "When I go to the Baptist church in the mornings," she continued, "it's like having breakfast and needing a full dinner for the day." She therefore attends her Pentecostal church to be "fully fed." There, she said, her pastor is very powerful and is a "truly anointed man of God." She "really likes the way God uses him and anoints him," and is attracted to the power and healing he brings.

Such a narrative as this is quite common among Pentecostal and charismatic churchgoers, especially those who attend the smaller, more intense churches. These churches offer worship experiences that many find particularly authentic and personally meaningful, especially in a fast-paced, pluralistic, urban world such as Atlanta where authenticity and meaning are often hard to find. This emotional worship setting provides a powerful conduit for transcendence and transformation—important experiences that bolster one's sense of purpose and security within the church.

ATLANTA'S PENTECOSTAL AND CHARISMATIC LANDSCAPE

Atlanta's Pentecostal and charismatic Christian communities vary both in relation to each other, and in relation to Atlanta's broader religious topography. Most of the church congregations sampled in the current study fall roughly into three socioeconomic categories: (a) those composed mainly of lower-income persons, (b) those chiefly characterized by middle-class congregants, and (c) a few with congregations made up of lower-income and working-class persons worshiping alongside more middle-class folks. Although these observations are strictly impressionistic, almost without exception one rarely sees members of the very wealthy, upper class in Atlanta's Pentecostal or charismatic churches.

Pastors in the more middle-class churches—such as some of those within the Church of God or Assemblies of God affiliations—deliver sermons that affirm members' social position and career path. In a Sunday morning service, for example, one Church of God pastor asked his audience:

"Is it selfish to do what one wants in life?" This question followed such declarations as "Live with passion, joy, and enthusiasm. . . . Do in life what you enjoy doing! Some of you may be shocked to hear this!" Later he continued with: "I'm not gonna spend my life doing what I don't want to do . . . usually what God wants and what you want are the same!" On the other hand such messages hardly ever appear in the smaller Pentecostal churches attended by mostly lower and working-class persons. Churches with congregants from lower income brackets tend to be smaller, with greater emotionalistic fervor in worship, higher incidence of faith healing, and far greater collective ecstasy at the group experiential level. Sermons on healing and transcendence are also more frequent. In these services more time is spent singing and praising, and clapping and dancing, so these smaller churches tend to have longer services regardless of the time of day. In terms of scriptural orientation, smaller churches seem to be more "literal" in their readings of the Bible and fundamentalist with regard to moral norms. Many Pentecostals in the Atlanta area also strongly favor the King James version of the Bible.

As for perceptions about orientation, future plans, and community involvement in Atlanta, many Pentecostals and charismatics feel that they have an extremely important and urgent message for those not involved in their religious communities. Other Christians, however, are not considered "wrong" with regard to their religious emphases and styles of worship. I was told, first of all, that many people join Pentecostal and charismatic churches simply because the enthusiastic modes of worship and praise fill an empty place within their hearts. Secondly, Pentecostals and charismatics say that they do not seek to convince others of their misguided ways (as one might expect), but that they endeavor to share their way of experiencing the Holy Spirit and the Lord's mercy with them. They prefer to show others simply by pointing out those passages in the Book of Acts that describe the religious experience of the early Christians. By doing this they attempt to clarify the importance of spiritual gifts in the most authentic way possible—through direct consultation with scripture. Thus Pentecostals and charismatics are quite eager to share what they have with others, and this translates into a strong moral sense of mission to Atlanta. Theirs is a community that, for the most part, continually seeks growth and strives to bring new souls into the fold.

Rather than continue with general impressions of these religious communities, let's take a brief look at particular congregations and some of their characteristics. The Abundant Life congregation described at the outset of this chapter is a prime example of a small, ethnically-diverse church within the UPCI community. Located north of the city in Cobb County, Abundant Life is a relatively new church that draws members from various communities, and—as noted above—rents church space from an Hispanic charismatic church called Centro Cristiano. Its pastor, W. Wayne Pugh, has spent a good deal of his life traveling and preaching as a missionary, and it was only recently that he felt a call from God to settle down in the Atlanta area to concentrate his "soul winning" here. The pastor's wife not only leads worship services through her command of the organ but also does much to keep the fledgling church going and growing. Every week she conducts numerous Bible studies at the homes of people interested in God's message and joining the church. Indeed, Abundant Life is a small but energetic church on the move. Pastor Pugh even has a daily spot on a local radio station so that Atlantans can tune in to hear his preaching each and every day.

At the other end of the city in south Atlanta is Calvary United Pentecostal Church. Calvary is also a relatively new church, led by Pastor and Sister Varist, and its composition is predominantly black with a few regular white members. Calvary is an offshoot church that grew out of a larger UPCI church in Stone Mountain, Georgia, east of Atlanta. The Varists felt a calling from God to found and lead this fledgling congregation. Like Abundant Life, Calvary's congregation is composed mostly of working-class folks, and they expend a lot of energy not only to keep the church going but also to make it grow. The congregation is extremely warm and welcoming, and—like Abundant Life—the church supports a radio ministry outreach led by Sister Varist called "Focus on the Word," emphasizing Pentecostal ministry to women. Small UPCI churches like Calvary United and Abundant Life are creating intimate worship communities in Atlanta that function as expanded family networks. This is reflected in their common practice of referring to each other as "Brother" so-and-so and "Sister" so-and-so, fostering a close sense of community and facilitating more open and explicit awareness of life changes as they take place in each other's lives.

At the beginning of July 1995, UPCI had its annual, Georgia statewide camp revival meetings at a location about a half-hour's drive south of Atlanta. Leaders, lay congregants, and youth gathered together for a week of preaching, praising, and fellowship. This was, as I was told by Sister Pugh of Abundant Life, where one can experience "full-blown Pentecostalism." The meetings were held in a very large, open-air, corrugated steel building capable of seating two thousand people. At night Pentecostals from across the state and beyond gathered for upbeat, high-energy nightly worship services lasting more than three hours. Prayers were said, offerings were collected, and many songs were sung as the services moved toward a final climax. After the evening's keynote message was delivered by a respected preacher from Florida, the collective ecstasy that had gathered momentum over the course of the evening reached its final, high-intensity peak. People ran down the aisles and around the worship hall shouting "Hallelujah!" A large portion of those present gathered together at the front of the building where healings took place and where many who were moved by the Spirit began speaking in tongues. Individuals would dance or jump in place rhythmically for long intervals, and kids would run freely about dodging those on their feet or shaking ecstatically on the ground. Gradually over time this communal fervor dissipated and the hall slowly emptied. As one attendee observed after the Tuesday night service, "There is really something happening here. It's very real!" The excitement and enthusiasm generated by the evening's activities were reiterated by the keynote preacher, who shouted out over the congregation: "The world is hungry for what we have in this room!!"

Brother McClure, the keynote speaker, made an important observation after one of the night services. He pointed out that approximately 80% of the UPCI church is made up of persons who have converted to the Pentecostal faith. That is, most current members of the UPCI were born and raised in religious traditions outside the Pentecostal fold, primarily as Baptists, Methodists, etc. According to some observers of the global religious scene, evangelical Protestantism—and Pentecostalism in particular—is the world's fastest growing religion; there are active Pentecostal missionaries in most parts of the world, and there is a significant Pentecostal presence in places as far-flung as Korea, the Philippines, Southeast Asia, a number of African nations, and Latin America (especially Central America, Puerto Rico, Brazil, and Chile). This worldwide outreach plays a role in local Pentecostal consciousness because reports of missionary successes and growth are a common source of pride and inspiration. Thus one's global religious awareness is not always so far from one's local Pentecostal consciousness.

Mount Paran Church of God is a large church that many consider one of the oldest Pentecostal communities in the area. It has two locations, a "Central" church located off I-75 close to downtown and a "North" location farther from the city. The church has a number of leaders, with Dr. Paul Walker as Senior Pastor and Dr. David Cooper as Associate Pastor. Like other Pentecostal leaders in the area, Pastor Walker has a radio ministry. Mount Paran offers an extensive array of ministries and services—available both for the Mount Paran congregation and for the Atlanta community at large. Services include home fellowship groups, independent men's and women's ministries, discipleship groups, life support groups, financial management study groups, intercessory prayer groups, youth, collegiate, singles, and senior adult ministries, and even life-enrichment courses through Mount Paran's Psychological Studies Institute, which is affiliated with Georgia State University.

At a Sunday morning service in mid-July, the central location was packed with a predominantly white congregation, filling pews both on the main floor and in the balcony above. There were large flower arrangements in front, and a large choir dressed in robes and accompanied by piano, organ, horn instruments, harp, and violin. The morning's theological message emphasized enjoying life in addition to renewing one's faith and commitment to the "purpose of God." The worship style was relatively docile compared to the extreme enthusiasm of Abundant Life and Calvary United. No one left their seats for the aisles, and there were no front-of-the-worship-hall healings, although spiritual healing through the Holy Spirit was talked about as a vital aspect of the committed Christian life. It was clear from this service that Mount Paran's middle-class, predominantly white congregation conducts itself in a rather subdued manner.

Another Pentecostal community can be found at the Cathedral of the Holy Spirit (formerly called Chapel Hill Harvester Church), located in southeast Atlanta. The Cathedral of the Holy Spirit is an independent, nondenominational congregation led by its senior minister, Bishop Earl Paulk. After seminary, Paulk came to Atlanta in the 1950s as the pastor of one of the Church of God's largest churches. His affiliation with the Church of God ended in 1960, but after some time away, Paulk returned to Atlanta and began an independent ministry. Over time, the church gained important, influential linkages with the city of Atlanta and espoused strong connections with the symbolism of the "New South." In fact, Paulk optimistically commented in 1985 about both the future of the church and the city: "Atlanta will become the religious center of the world. Atlanta became a symbol of victory over defeat. The phoenix that rises out of the dust of defeat, that lifts its head in pride and says, 'God is not done with Atlanta yet!' It is becoming one of the revival centers of the world" (as quoted in "Rising Out of the Ashes," by Scott Thumma). By 1991, Paulk's church was one of the ten largest Protestant megachurches in the nation. In 1995, the Cathedral of the Holy Spirit was housed in a rather impressive cathedral building. Its ethnic composition is mixed and integrated, with blacks numbering over 50%, a considerable white minority, and a small number from other ethnic groups.

I have mentioned the Cathedral of the Holy Spirit not only because of Bishop Paulk's background and former Pentecostal affiliations. The church was recommended to me by several people as an important place to go to see a large Atlanta Pentecostal community. The church is listed in the phone book both under "charismatic" and "Interdenominational" headings. Furthermore, several members of the church told me at a Wednesday night service that speaking in tongues is practiced by some within the congregation, and that it can be a very important aspect of worshiping God. As one of the music leaders of the service declared to those present: "The Spirit is moving . . . get in on it!!" The Cathedral of the Holy Spirit represents an important non-denominational Atlanta community where Pentecostal/charismatic modes of worship are welcomed but not necessarily encouraged. Perhaps one church member put it best: "This church is holy. There's no running around or anything like that—just do whatever the Spirit leads you to do. I've been to other churches that put a bunch of criteria on you, but God isn't like that—He wants you to be who you are. I like this church because people let you be yourself." One senses an impulse for international awareness inside the worship hall whose walls and balconies are lined with flags from all over the globe. Such a symbolic statement dovetails well with Atlanta's "international upsurge" associated with the 1996 Olympics.

In the southwest part of the city is Greater Bible Way Miracle Temple Worldwide of the Apostolic Faith. This predominantly black church has a worship hall with white walls and blue carpets and pews. A banner at the front of the hall says: "VISION TO VICTORY!" I attended Greater Bible Way on a special Friday night featuring a female evangelist from Dallas, Texas. The congregation was predominantly female, and some women had brought their children. A significant portion of the service was spent in musical worship and praise. For the first fifteen minutes, everyone present congregated at the front of the worship hall, singing enthusiastically along with several women holding microphones and leading the group's rounds of song from the stage. The songleader crooned loudly over the sound system: "In the Pentecostal spirit, Praise Him! With my whole body, thank you Jesus,

He's here right now . . . let him loose!! You can have just what you want! He's here right now! Praise Him. It's already happening. . . . We magnify your greatness!" Later in the service the songleader made an observation with regard to the draw and spread of Pentecostalism: "Jesus is reaching out to everybody—not just Pentecostals. He's reaching out to Baptists, Presbyterians, Lutherans, and everyone else!"

Atlanta is also home to The Tabernacle in Decatur, east of the city. The congregation has more whites than blacks, but blacks are certainly a large presence in the church community. On a July evening in 1995, the worship hall was decorated with flowers, and rising above the back of the choir loft was a large stained-glass window with a dove, a crown, and rays of light superimposed upon a very large cross. Services were accompanied by piano, electric guitar, and drums. An usher mentioned that The Tabernacle actually used to be located down near the Grant Park area just southeast of downtown. As the church grew it needed a larger set of facilities, so it moved out to Decatur where it is currently located. The usher also said that the church does not do too much in the way of outreach to the city. What the church does do, however, is provide a medium-sized Pentecostal congregational community to those who are seeking a church home. The Tabernacle's style of worship falls somewhere in the middle between the extremes of highly charged emotionalism and low-intensity, quiet worship. The service gets going with several rounds of song led by an enthusiastic music minister. "God made us emotional people!" exclaimed one of the songleaders, "aren't you glad you aren't fighting the Battle?" Some of the church members dance around in the aisles during song, shaking tambourines and exclaiming "Yes Lord!" or a simple "Hallelujah!" Yet those less inclined toward energetic, excitable church worship can also feel comfortable and at home here. This is perhaps the church's particular draw, a moderation in worship where various modalities are expressed and none in particular dominates the service.

CONCLUSION: COMMONALITY AND COMMUNITY AMONG DIVERSITY

As this brief cross-section of church communities has attempted to illustrate, the various forms of Pentecostal and charismatic religious organizations in Atlanta are diverse with regard to congregational composition, styles of worship, and social orientation. In addition to these communities, there are a number of other ethnically-derived Pentecostal and charismatic churches that contribute to Atlanta's religious landscape. These include Hispanic,

French Creole, and Nigerian church communities, among others. What is evident within the world of Pentecostal and charismatic Christians, even from such a brief exploration, is that diversity exists not only along separate ethnic and racial lines, but also with regard to the intermingling and "multicultural" interaction that can be seen within these religious communities. The portrait of Abundant Life painted at the outset of this chapter is perhaps a prime example of this pluralistic sort of social interaction.

But what makes such community possible and so effective within the lives of so many different people? The answer that Pentecostals and charismatics themselves give is that it is the work of God, through the Holy Spirit. One should add that there is some degree of common ground shared by all Pentecostal and charismatic Christians. That common ground is not simply theological, but includes fervent, enthusiastic worship and speaking in tongues as particularly important practices within members' religious lives. These practices form a central core for what makes Pentecostal and charismatic forms of religion so compelling to those involved. Many Pentecostals—both leaders and lay congregants alike—would agree with the following statement: "They can argue with our theology, but they can't argue with our emotional feeling. They argued with Christ's message, but they couldn't conceive of his compassion, his weeping, his touch!" It seems that a common belief in an active, caring God, along with a shared conviction that God's activity in the world today transforms through healing and speaking in tongues, ties a large, diverse group of people together in the Pentecostal and charismatic communities. Such practice and belief contributes to the creation and ongoing maintenance of commonality and community among diversity.

FOR FURTHER INFORMATION

Articles:

Scott Thumma. "Rising Out of the Ashes: An Exploration of One Congregation's Use of Southern Symbolism." *Religion in the Contemporary South: Diversity, Community, and Identity.* O. Dendall White, Jr. and Daryl White, eds. Athens, University of Georgia Press, 1995

Books:

Randall Balmer. *Mine Eyes have Seen the Glory: A Journey into the Evangelical Subculture in America.* New York, Oxford University Press, 1993

Harvey Cox. *Fire from Heaven: The Rise of Pentecostal Spirituality and the Reshaping of Religion in the Twenty-first Century.* Reading, Addison-Wesley, 1995

Donald W. Dayton. *The Theological Roots of Pentecostalism.* Grand Rapids, Francis Asbury, 1987

Walter Hollenweger. *The Pentecostals: The Charismatic Movement in Churches.* Minneapolis, Augsburg, 1972

Richard Quebedeaux. *The Worldly Evangelicals.* San Francisco, Harper and Row, 1978

C H A P T E R T E N

THE EASTERN ORTHODOX CHURCHES OF ATLANTA

Louis A. Ruprecht, Jr.

Easter week celebration, 1993. Greek Orthodox Cathedral. Photograph by Lee Wilson. Courtesy of the Atlanta History Center.

The face of Jesus Christ Pantocrator, *"the ruler of all," looms down from a sixty-foot domed ceiling, with glass and tile renditions of some of the most dramatic scenes from the gospels, all set in a sea of blue stone. Candles burn throughout the outer sanctuary, thin white tapers offered by the congregants in veneration before the holy icons, especially to Mary* Theotokos, *"the mother of God." Incense and the dim natural lighting contribute to the atmosphere of sanctity and ceremony. A constant flow of parishioners come and go. This human traffic seems to follow a calendar and a clock of its own, having little to do with the church's schedule for worship. The Divine Liturgy is being celebrated, about half of it in Greek, with short sections in English being chanted and sung, not spoken. This is the Cathedral of the Annunciation, a Greek Orthodox church on Clairmont Road in Decatur. Many Christians, especially* Protestants *might not recognize this as a "church" at all. "This used to make me angry," says the priest, "but now I find it rather funny. After all, this is the oldest continuous church in Christendom."*

HISTORICAL BACKGROUND

Orthodox Christianity originally came to the northeastern region of North America, and thus to a predominantly Protestant country, the way most other religions did—as the native religion of various immigrant communities, primarily Greek and Slavic in the early years of this nation's history, but more recently Middle Eastern and African as well. These churches are known as *"national* churches," and in this way serve as an important vehicle for the maintenance of ethnic identity and ethnic education in the religiously plural North American setting.

Perhaps the best way to understand what we mean by Eastern Orthodox Christianity is to focus upon these two terms: "Eastern," and "Orthodox." Eastern churches are all those Christian churches *east of Rome* that are neither Catholic nor Protestant. In the words of His Holiness the

Ecumenical Patriarch Bartholomew I, "You could be forgiven, after speaking to the average person, for thinking that the history of Christianity starts with Jesus Christ, moves on with St. Paul at Corinth and Ephesus, continues with the Bishop of Rome and ends with the Protestant Reformation." We can be forgiven, he suggested, for thinking of Christianity as a strictly western phenomenon, and for narrating the story of the Christian Church in a seemingly straight (and westward) line: from Jerusalem, to Rome, to northern Europe, and then to North America. Christianity, the Orthodox are quick to remind us, has moved in a great many other directions as well—east into India and the Far East, throughout the Middle East, northward into the Balkans and Russia. It is here, in the eastern Mediterranean, and north of it, that we can locate the Eastern Orthodox churches.

"Orthodox" is a name which comes from a Greek word, *orthê-doxa* or *orthodoxia,* which means "right belief" or "straight-thinking." When they claim that they are the "Orthodox" churches, are they implying that other churches are unorthodox, or heretical? This is a difficult question to answer because matters of doctrine in the early church were so thoroughly bound up in questions of culture, politics, and geography. It is easy to forget how quickly Christianity spread in its first three generations. By the time Paul and the other apostles had died, there were Christian enclaves in many places throughout the eastern Mediterranean. In another generation or two the word had spread to Spain and Gaul, and far deeper into the African interior. It was spreading *eastward* at the time as well—into Syria, Lebanon, Persia, even India.

The churches naturally adopted many of the cultural practices of the lands into which they had come—matters of dress, of cuisine, of language, and certain matters of philosophical and practical belief. Christianity, which had not yet settled upon a single set of doctrinal beliefs, was potentially becoming many things in many different parts of the world. Less than three hundred years after the Romans executed Jesus Christ, and less than fifteen years after the Roman Emperor Constantine converted to Christianity, the first in a series of ecumenical councils was called to establish uniformity in certain matters of essential Christian doctrine. Three areas of contention, related to culture, theology, and politics, were especially important to these councils (there were seven councils in all, the first held in 325 CE, in Nicaea, and the seventh held in 787 CE, also in Nicaea); each highlighted sources of continual dispute between the Christian churches in the east and those in the west.

First, the cultural matter. The eastern churches all came from a part of the world that was speaking Greek, *the* international language of the eastern Mediterranean at that time. That is why the early apostles chose to write and to communicate in Greek, and thus why the New Testament was written in Greek. The western churches, on the other hand, spoke Latin. Since the New Testament was written in Greek, the *western* churches needed the books translated into Latin. The great age of Christian translation began in the fourth century. And the great translators were, naturally enough, Greek-speaking bishops in the east.

Certain theological problems arose out of this linguistic dilemma. When the creeds were written in the fourth and fifth centuries, they were also written in Greek. Thus the eastern churches, for whom Greek was a native tongue, seemed to have an obvious kind of authority in interpreting what they meant. The most important of these creeds attempted to define in a more philosophical way how Jesus Christ was related to God the Father and to the Holy Spirit. The doctrine of the Trinity was not formulated in something like its present form until 451 CE, at the Fourth Ecumenical Council in Chalcedon. In that doctrine of the Trinity, God was said to be one being in three persons. The Son was said to have been "begotten, not made" from God the Father (trying to make the point that there was never a time when Jesus Christ did not exist), and the Holy Spirit was said to have "proceeded" from God the Father. When this creed was translated into Latin, it was made to say that the Holy Spirit "proceeded" from the Father and *from the Son.* The Latin word is *filioque,* and the eastern churches worried that this word made it seem as if the Father and Son were somehow superior to the Holy Spirit, thus destroying the carefully worked out equivalence of the three divine persons. That seemingly minor detail was the source of continuing conflict in the ensuing centuries. The Greek-speaking (eastern) churches objected that the Latin (western) churches were taking an inappropriate kind of authority upon themselves in translating (and interpreting) the creeds this way.

The reason for the conflict had as much to do with politics as with theology. From the Orthodox perspective, this symbolized a failure to honor the equal authority of the eastern, Greek-speaking churches. Very early in Christian history, there had been five recognized centers of the Christian world called patriarchates: Jerusalem, Alexandria, Antioch, Constantinople, and Rome. Constantinople, although it was founded later (in 330 CE), was intended to be the capital of the eastern Roman Empire while Rome was the center of western Christendom.

In the early ecumenical councils, there were repeated attempts to resolve the problem of the *political* relationship among these five early Christian centers. In essence, Rome was claiming to be the *single* head of the Christian world, whereas the so-called "eastern churches" were insisting that the five patriarchates had equal political authority. The Orthodox freely granted a "primacy of honor" to Rome, but they were unwilling to grant a primacy of doctrinal authority to the Pope (whom the Orthodox continue to call "the bishop of Rome"). It was precisely this argument about the comparative centralization of Christian authority that resulted in the "Great Schism," an event that finally divided the eastern and western churches for good in 1054 CE. (A first step toward reconciling these differences was taken in 1965.)

Eastern Orthodoxy came to North America gradually. Russian missionaries first brought Christian Orthodoxy to the New World in 1794, beginning in Alaska. Other Orthodox groups followed during the next century, especially Greeks. The single most difficult and sensitive matter in the North American Orthodox experience relates to the issue of *nationalism*. Building upon the principle of "autocephalous" churches (independent national churches assigned to one of the patriarchates), the Slavic churches became *national* churches under the Ottoman Empire . Farther east, there are also Syrian (Antiochian) and other Orthodox communities—also emerging in their present form out of the Ottoman experience. These churches, transplanted now to North America, have experienced the same cultural tension that all immigrant identities seem to face in the North American "melting pot."

Orthodox churches in America, faced with the task of establishing what were highly nationalistic religious institutions in a new nation, have become one of the foci for ethnic traditions and ethnic identity. It is often unclear, for example, whether the chief function of the Greek Orthodox church here in Atlanta is to celebrate its Orthodoxy or its Greek-ness. The two cannot be so easily separated. The Greek Orthodox Cathedral of the Annunciation celebrates a Greek festival every year in mid-September, just as the St. Elias Antiochian Orthodox Church celebrates a Mideast Festival in late May.

The Orthodox churches have faced many of the same debates about liberalization as the Roman Catholic church, and at roughly the same time.

Like the Catholics, the Orthodox began celebrating their liturgies bilingually in the 1970s, thereby acknowledging that their congregants were assimilated to North American culture. The Orthodox churches will not eliminate the use of traditional liturgical languages, but few, if any, congregations in the New World conduct their worship *solely* in their "native" language. English is one of the glues used to cement North American civil society, and the Orthodox churches want to contribute to the cohesiveness of this society.

GREEK ORTHODOX

The Greek Cathedral of the Annunciation is both the oldest and the largest Orthodox church in Atlanta. It was founded in 1905 and celebrated its 90th anniversary on October 21-22 of last year. It currently has somewhere between 1,200 and 1,500 families on its membership rolls. Everything about the cathedral speaks of its marvelous history and traditions. Most impressive are the mosaics and icons described at the beginning of this chapter.

There is also a fascinating series of images on the walls in the offices of Father Homer Goumenis. To be sure, there are icons, countless icons. And there is a lovely El Greco print in the corner, "The Passion of Christ." But what stands out most dramatically are the *other* images: a stunning pastel portrait of the Parthenon, now in ruins; the famous "Mourning Athena" copied from the marble original in the Acropolis Museum in Athens; the head of the so-called "Blonde Boy," a copy of another famous early Classical sculpture from the Acropolis Museum. Replicas of other famous Classical artworks are tastefully placed throughout the sanctuary building as well—here a famous Hermes by Praxiteles, a copy of a marble original housed in the Delphi Museum, there some Dionysian memorabilia. This combination of images—Classical Greek on the one hand, Orthodox Christian on the other—nicely symbolizes the fascinating community that can be found at the Cathedral of the Annunciation.

Father Homer's personal journey, all of it related in a soft and perfectly inflected voice that has obviously been trained by years of liturgical chanting, also symbolizes something of the Greek diaspora experience, especially in the United States. Born and raised in Lowell, Massachusetts (where there were four Orthodox churches, three of them Greek-speaking and one Antiochian), Father Homer was the second son born to immigrant parents, both hailing from the region around Sparta, Greece. He studied at the Orthodox Seminary in Pomfret, Connecticut. After several years in

Columbia, South Carolina, where he served his first congregation, and with two young children in tow, Father Homer was called by the bishop some thirty-four years ago to take over this church in Atlanta.

The story of the sanctuary reflects a common pattern for non-Protestant religions in North America. The local Greek community in Atlanta originally met for worship on the second floor of a building on Whitehall Street, above a sporting goods store. In the following year (1906) an old Presbyterian church on Garnett Street was purchased for that same purpose. There the congregation remained until 1928, when an impressive Jewish synagogue was purchased. Since this building already boasted a large interior dome and a broadly neo-Classical facade popular at the time, all that needed to be added to this structure were three crosses, one atop the central dome, and two flanking the front pediment. This sanctuary on Pryor Street was eventually abandoned in 1967 in order to move the congregation into the present cathedral. The mosaics in the cathedral, all commissioned by an Italian artist named Sirio Tonelli, include the *Pantocrator,* which at sixty feet in diameter is one of the largest mosaic depictions of Christ in the world.

Just last year, a new building was completed immediately to the north-east of the cathedral to house the diocesan offices. As Atlanta has grown in regional importance, it has become more important in the North American Greek Orthodox hierarchy as well. The political organization of the Orthodox churches has given an interesting texture to North American Orthodoxy. There is an ecclesiastical structure that leads in a direct line from the Diocese of Atlanta, to the Archdiocese of New York, and then on to the Patriarchate of Constantinople (Istanbul). The diocese used to be located in Charlotte, North Carolina, but Atlanta has become the capital of the south-eastern Orthodox community—officially so just this last year, with the completion of the diocesan building and the installation of the bishop in residence there.

My conversation with Father Homer, alternating between Greek and English, turned first to the all-important matter of language. "I cannot read the history of the Church," Father Homer said quietly, "without saying something about the role Greek played—both philosophically and linguistically." Greek, he went on to suggest, was an ideal medium for the presentation of Christian truth—an internationalized and even global language designed for the presentation of a universal message of reconciliation. The Jewish community in North Africa had already translated their scriptures into Greek in the third century before the Common Era—they needed to do so, he noted, since Greek was the only language many of them spoke. "It was not simply an accident," Father Homer smiled gently, "one might almost say that it happened in the fullness of time (as St. John put it)."

Father Homer studied Latin intensively in high school and continued with his classical training in seminary. But for him, despite its own rich poetic traditions, Latin remains the language of practicality, the language of civil administration. "There is an intangible in Greek," he said. "And this is as it should be. After all, we cannot describe God fully in words." "Mystery," I gradually discovered, is an essential word in the Orthodox lexicon.

In the course of his thirty-four-year tenure at the Cathedral of the Annunciation, Father Homer has seen many changes—one of the most dramatic being the introduction of the English language into the celebration of the divine liturgy. There was some resistance on the part of the congregation to this change—much like the Catholic response to the addition of English after the Second Vatican Council. Father Homer, ever the peacemaker, settled upon a workable compromise in his congregation. Members celebrate two liturgies every Sunday morning, one at 8:30, almost entirely in English, and then another at 11:00, which is conducted roughly half in Greek. Occasionally, during a smaller and more intimate celebration, if he knows everyone who is present, Father Homer will celebrate entirely in Greek. "This means a lot to my older members," he smiles.

In the face of these changes, the Cathedral of the Annunciation has taken upon itself some responsibility for educating the laity regarding the Orthodox church's rootedness in Greek culture and the Greek world. It runs a Greek language school that is sanctioned by the archdiocese and serves 70-80 students per year. The school meets for two hours each day, Monday to Friday, and has three teachers, all trained in Greece, who teach six different grade levels. The children put on plays, sing songs, and design a processional each year for March 25th (Greek Independence Day). Father Homer is the principal of this school. They hope to expand these programs in the near future.

In addition to the Sunday School and Greek language school they already have, Father Homer would like to see a day care program that might be expanded to an actual pre-school for children from one to five years of age. The cathedral also owns and operates the Hellenic Center on Cheshire Bridge Road, which they acquired several years ago and utilize as a sort of cultural center. They also administer "the Hellenic Tower" in Roswell, a home for the elderly comprised of 125 individual apartments. Owned by

HUD, the project is administered by the cathedral. Father Homer sits on the Board of Trustees.

The church itself boasts a well-stocked bilingual library, with a collection spanning both Greek history and culture and the mysteries of the Orthodox faith. To the southeast of the present sanctuary, the church owns some ten acres of as-yet undeveloped land. Father Homer brightens when he considers the possibilities—a new library? another home for the elderly? perhaps even an Orthodox seminary, since there is only one in the country now.

And so our conversation comes full circle. At the outset, I had asked Father Homer about "Greek Orthodoxy:" "You notice that I give the primacy to Orthodoxy," he smiled. "Notice that I did not even say `Greek'." What, then, does Orthodoxy have to contribute to the modern world, and to the spiritual consciousness of a major metropolis like Atlanta? Deeply committed to conversing with the entire human family, Father Homer is as expansive in his answer to this last question as he has been to every one of my questions. "The Orthodox church appeals to the whole person: as a body and as a spirit-mind." He continues: "I would not want to split the two—that would be a heresy, wouldn't it? For me, the appeal of Orthodoxy must be its *holism*. There is philosophy there, but there is also an appeal to the physical senses." This brings to my mind images of the incense, the bread and wine, the mosaics and icons, the chanting, the *sensuality* of this kind of worship. "This is a valid act on the part of the church," Father Homer insists, bringing his own passion to bear on one of the central tenets of the church. "Since it speaks to the total man, it becomes a total experience. You pray that, with time, there will be a also a total response."

So, in the end, this is an Orthodox church, not just a Greek one. Yet it is inescapably Greek as well. As I left the cathedral, I was drawn to a miniature bronze model of a statue in the Carlos meeting hall. They hope it will be erected in the vicinity of the new Olympic stadium. It is an arc of a circle, with three figures emerging from the surface of the bronze. One is an ancient athlete, symbol of the original Greek Games. The next is clearly a European runner, meant to commemorate the renewal of the Modern Games in Athens in 1896. Lastly, there is a woman, symbolic of the modern athlete on the hundredth anniversary of the Modern Games. This artistic celebration of embodiment and of antiquity seemed as eloquent a symbol for the cathedral of the Annunciation as the mosaics themselves.

ANTIOCHIAN ORTHODOX

The second-largest Orthodox congregation in Atlanta, numbering some four hundred persons (approximately 225 families), is the St. Elias Antiochian Orthodox Church. From the outside, it is a fairly non-descript building, made of lighter stone than most of the other churches on Ponce de Leon Avenue. But moving to the interior, St. Elias is one of the loveliest Orthodox churches in Atlanta. Its walls are covered in dark wood, arching toward the ceiling in a manner reminiscent of a ship's hull. Since the Christian church was often described as a ship at sea on a journey of faith, the architecture is singularly appropriate. The dark wood makes a stunning effect during the midnight Paschal services each spring. The face of Jesus Christ, *Pantocrator,* is prominently displayed in the center of this sanctuary as it is at the Greek Orthodox Cathedral. Above the altar is Mary, *Theotokos*—the mother of God, and "ever-virgin," as they emphasize in the liturgy—cradling her infant son. Beneath them we see the Last Supper of Jesus and his disciples. And below them, behind the altar screen, is a depiction of the Crucifixion, God's great ascetic and salvific labor.

St. Elias Antiochian Church. Photograph by Louis A. Ruprecht, Jr.

To either side of the screen there are four dramatic and colorfully painted panels. To the left: Mary, again; then St. Elias (known to us as Elijah) ascending into heaven in a chariot; St. Stephen, the church's first martyr; and St. George slaying a dragon. To the right: Jesus, now a grown man; then St. John the Baptist dressed in camel hair, alone in the wilderness; the Archangel Michael, symbolic of the spiritual community in heaven; and finally the twin founders of the Christian church, Peter and Paul, sharing a panel as they shared the work of the early church. The stained glass windows, three on each side, depict the lives of other notable saints of the eastern churches, heroes in the struggle of an emerging faith. A United States flag tightly folded to the left speaks of the spiritual virtue of patriotism, conceived as a willingness to work for the good of the local community—the nation—in which one finds oneself. In this congregation, the priests are especially conscientious in praying for the political leadership of the country—the president, to be sure, but also for a vast array of local officials.

The name "Antiochian" speaks to the complex ecclesiastical developments of the Christian church in its formative centuries. One of the original five patriarchates was Syrian Antioch. The Antiochian churches in the United States are still under the authority of this patriarchate. The majority of this congregation today is thus of Lebanese or Syrian descent, and the liturgy takes place in Arabic, a little Greek, and (mostly) English.

In the summer of 1995, the Antiochian church celebrated its one hundredth anniversary in the Americas. Atlanta served as the host city for this landmark celebration, and St. Elias was the host institution. There was a lovely liturgy celebrated with all the panoply of the archdiocese at the conclusion of the week-long celebration. It was held in the grand ballroom of the Hilton Hotel downtown, into which the entire wood-panelled altar facade from St. Elias had been installed. The assembled hierarchy of the Antiochian church in the Americas numbered some 400 officials. They captured the antiochian presence in North, Central, and South America, including representatives from Brazil, Chile, Panama, most of the fifty United States, and Canada.

Father Michael, who was installed at St. Elias just over one year ago, barely in time for these centennial celebrations, was prominent in the celebration of the Holy Liturgy of St. Basil. The southeast has proven to be remarkably fertile ground for the growth of Antiochian Orthodoxy. There were some seventy churches in the region a decade ago. They now number one hundred and ninety. His Grace the Bishop Antoun (now in Metuchen,

New Jersey) noted this in his convocational homily, saying that no one could have anticipated this even five years ago. He now looks forward to steady and sustained growth for these communities, both among new arrivals to the Atlanta area and also among converts from other Christian (mostly Protestant) communities. The church is unified and one. "We work to worship and honor God," he reminds the flock in the midst of their celebration, "no one else."

RUSSIAN ORTHODOX

When Constantinople succumbed to invading Turkish forces in May 1453, it signalled the symbolic end of the Byzantine Empire. The emperor himself died on the ramparts. The death knell of the Byzantine Empire, however, was also a clarion call for spiritual renewal in another part of the Orthodox world: Russia. The Slavic conversions to Christianity were initiated by the Byzantine brothers, Cyril and Methodius. St. Petersburg eventually became the new capital of Orthodoxy, and so it remained until the Russian Revolution in 1917. Russian monks first brought Orthodoxy to the New World, but Greek Orthodoxy soon supplanted it on the eastern seaboard. It is only recently, in the last thirty years or so—first on the west coast and now even more visibly on the east coast—that Russian Orthodoxy has become a powerful new spiritual force. An important trend in recent Orthodox developments has been the comparatively widespread conversion of entire Protestant congregations to Orthodoxy. One finds ample evidence of this trend in Atlanta.

The story of Eastern European immigration to Atlanta is a story still very much in progress. As events in Eastern Europe continue to unfold, and as people are free to leave if they so desire, many persons from Rumania, Bulgaria, Russia, the Ukraine, and Soviet Georgia (its capital, Tbilisi, is Atlanta's sister-city) have made Atlanta their home in the past six years. A growing number of them are finding a spiritual home in, among other places, the St. Mary of Egypt Orthodox Church. This church makes an interesting comparison to that of the Cathedral of the Annuciation. In a sense, they represent the opposite extremes of Orthodoxy in the South. Father John Townshend founded this Russian Orthodox parish in his apartment in 1976. After worshiping in his living room for nearly a year, Father John arranged to have the use of a community room in a local bank. Bringing with him everything needed to convert a common sitting room into sacred space, Father John built a genuine congregation over the next two years.

The congregation soon purchased six and one-half acres of land, with an eye toward the continued growth of a congregation that has, if anything, exceeded Father John's own grand anticipation. While originally composed mostly of local converts to the faith, the congregation—some 350 strong now—is roughly two-thirds recent immigrants. The church has grown so quickly that a small group—mostly Rumanian, but some Ukrainian and Soviet Georgian as well—split from the church and formed its own community. While that church is still in communion with this parish, Father John has concerns about such churchly divisions. "The celebration of ethnicity has little to do with the celebration of Orthodoxy," he insists. The Orthodox church represents one world-wide koinonia, or community: "It is Christ we celebrate when we come together, not where we come from."

Still, as in the Greek case, congregants *do* all come from somewhere, and their attitudes toward Atlanta are often shaped by the experiences they have left behind. Most of the congregants at St. Mary's love Atlanta. While the free-wheeling capitalist orientation is a bit shocking and the culture of the shopping mall a little overwhelming at times, the comparative freedoms they enjoy here more than outweigh the potential dangers. "Communist regimes tended to pay a great deal of attention to the creation of beautiful public spaces," Father John observes—"flowers, parks, places to sit. Here, businesses seem free to destroy anything and everything." Although most congregants felt an overwhelming sense of despair when they fled their old world, here they find a freedom—not only a freedom to practice religion, but also a freedom to rediscover the moral life in the context of one's family and one's spirituality—that seems to animate all that this congregation does and believes.

When I asked him about the essence of the faith he celebrates, Father John did not hesitate. "Orthodoxy teaches the possibility of human beings being united with our Creator, a union of our person with the persons of the Holy Trinity. That is not only possible, it is actually the fulfilling of our nature." In the words of the great fourth-century Orthodox bishop, Athanasius of Alexandria, "God became man so that we might become divine." The Greek word for that is *theôsis,* an image of "redeemability"—the possibility of moral perfectability through a discipline of ascetic practice and liturgical celebration—that Father John and his congregation celebrate each and every Sunday. "Redemption" is as important a word as "mystery" to the Orthodox community.

That is why Pascha (the Greek name for Easter), not Christmas, is the "feast of feasts" for this church. Christmas has become so commercial that it is not really a Christian holiday at all, Father John explains. Santa Claus is not a part of Christian worship; Christ is. Father John cherishes the subtle differences of the Orthodox calendar, which allow his congregation to celebrate their religious festivals *religiously*. Easter is the best example of this. Because of the differences between the Greek and Latin calendars, Pascha usually takes place anywhere from one to three weeks later than it does in western churches. So it is that this Orthodox church gets to celebrate the crucifixion and resurrection without the distractions of the Easter bunny and the shopping mall. Father John is adamant about this.

He is equally firm in his position on ecumenical dialogue. The Russian churches seem to be, as a rule, far stricter in their approach to interfaith dialogue. This surely has something to do with what these churches have already been through in the former Soviet Union. It would seem a shame to have defended one's spiritual integrity for so long in the face of Soviet persecution only to lose it now in the morass of North American pluralism. In addition, there is a kind of zealousness which often accompanies conversion to a different faith, and there are a great many Protestant converts in these newer Russian congregations. Father John states, "We are the true church, the only church. Period." There is a smile in his voice when he says this—it is a matter of pride to him, a matter of being true to the church's *history*, not a matter of mere exclusivity. "Our greatest North American bishop got us involved in ecumenical dialogue to *witness*, not to be converted. The true church is not divided; it is one."

If anything, Father Hieromonk Nikifor of the Holy Resurrection Orthodox Church is even more adamant about this. "The Orthodox church's mission is to present the truth to all," he insists, "not to dilute, camouflage or confuse it. Those so-called Orthodox Christians, be they clergy or laymen, who are active in the ecumenical movement have reduced Holy Orthodoxy in the eyes of the heterodox to an ethnic restaurant, which albeit offering exotic and spicy foods is no different, essentially, than McDonald's." He does not stop there. "Ecumenism is not merely a heresy; it is the arch-heresy." Clearly, there are serious concerns about maintaining one's religious integrity in the new pressures of a democratic, urban pluralism such as the one embodied in Atlanta and other cities of the New South.

These sentiments were echoed, but muted, by Father Jacob Myer of St. John the Wonderworker Orthodox Church. He observes: "We're just not that ecumenical. Orthodoxy is the oldest form of Christianity, and the one that has changed the least." But Father Jacob is quick to add an important caveat: "Not that we don't enjoy brotherhood with other Christians. We simply don't go outside of the [ritual] forms we have, because we know that they contain real *spirit.* In a sense, we are upholding this for the entire church . . . which *is* an ecumenical thought of a sort, if you think about it."

Father Jacob's story is, in its own way, as dramatic as Father John's, although it touches on a very different spiritual and communal plane. This is emphatically *not* an ethnic church. The church that is now St. John the Wonderworker (named for a newly canonized Russian saint), was, itself, converted to Orthodoxy roughly a decade ago. It had been a Christian Service Community, very active in serving the poor. But there was, in spite of all the activism, something missing at the spiritual heart of this congregation. The leadership of the church, and then the congregation, were catechized by a Russian monk in California (a disciple of Father Seraphim Rose, who became a notable grass-roots crusader for spiritual reform among the Orthodox community in northern California—what he called the church's "catacomb network"—until his untimely death in 1982). They have been Orthodox ever since, under the administrative control of their Greek bishop in Queens, New York.

If one thing were to distinguish this community, it might well be *food.* Their religious calendar is absolutely filled with spiritual practices and preparations, all of which center around the major feasts of the Orthodox church. There are twelve major feasts in the calendar in addition to Pascha. The whole religious cycle of this congregation centers around fasting and feasting, preparing for these feasts, and then celebrating them. Two of the church's fasts are major, forty-day periods in which the congregants eat no meat or dairy products. Another fast lasts for fourteen days. This is, in Father Jacob's words, "a *praying* religious community," and here again the Orthodox calendar facilitates this self-understanding. There is not a day that does not have its appointed saint and its own special prayer or ritual practice. This keeps the faith ever-new. "No two days are alike in our daily calendar of prayer and worship," Father Jacob observes.

It is surely not accidental, then, that this church serves the larger Atlanta community, primarily with food. Receiving food from the Atlanta Food Bank (itself an ecumenical religious organization), they box it and distribute it to individuals and families in need. St. John serves perhaps 45-50 families a month in this way. Father Jacob is already considering how this church may serve the indigent population here in what is sure to be a disruptive one-month period when the Olympic Games will be under way. "Since we are actually in the heart of all the Olympic activity," Father Jacob observes, "there will be a great deal we can do."

One thing they have already done is witness to the existence of Orthodoxy as a credible spiritual option in the modern, urban world. Their ceiling has recently been painted in brilliant colors depicting the lives of the saints, and their sanctuary is filled with all the splendor of the holy icons. "Orthodoxy," Father Jacob notes, "is a *timeless* form of Christianity that has been kept alive by the oldest church. It is tactile. It is beautiful. There is a sense, when you walk into an Orthodox church, that you are walking into the Kingdom of Heaven."

FOR FURTHER INFORMATION

Articles:

Gayle White. "Southern Orthodoxy: Antiochians Discovering Small Towns". *Atlanta Journal Constitution* (July 22, 1995)

Books:

Caroline Walker Bynum. *Holy Feast and Holy Fast: The Religious Significance of Food to Medieval Women*. Berkeley, University of California Press, 1987

Monk Damascene Christensen. *Not of This World: The Life and Teaching of Fr. Seraphim Rose, Pathfinder to the Heart of Ancient Christianity*. Forestville, Fr. Seraphim Rose Foundation, 1993

Timothy Ware. *The Orthodox Church*. New York, Penguin Books, 1983

The Way of a Pilgrim and The Pilgrim Continues His Way. Translated by Helen Bacovin. Garden City, Image Books, 1978

CHAPTER ELEVEN

CHURCHES OF AFRICAN ORIGIN IN ATLANTA

Louis A. Ruprecht, Jr.

Saint John Chrysostum Melkite Catholic Church. Photograph by Louis A. Ruprecht, Jr.

On an unusually cool summer night in late July, in the waning light of a summer evening, Vespers are being celebrated at the St. Mary Coptic Orthodox Church in Roswell. The services are being held in a non-descript building that can no longer be seen from the outside. A stunning new sanctuary is being built around *the old worship space, an impressive cathedral perhaps most reminiscent of the ark-shaped sanctuary of the St. Elias Antiochian Orthodox Church described in the last chapter. The faithful—four men and seven women, seated on opposite sides of the sanctuary—listen attentively to the liturgy being celebrated, primarily in Coptic, but with a healthy dose of English and Arabic.*

The gospel reading for this evening's Vespers service is a well-known scene in which Jesus is asked to heal a Roman centurion's slave, and then does so, albeit at a distance. It is a singular reading, chanted first in Arabic, then again in English. As a young man and a young boy scurry around the priest, bringing him all that he needs for the liturgy to continue, they continually kiss his ring and his hand, then bow deeply before moving aside. They bring incense, the Holy Gospels encased in silver, icons held aloft, and they chant on his command. The men and women then listen just as attentively to a whirlwind one-hour Bible lesson. In that time, the priest touches on all four gospels, two letters of St. Paul, and the mysteries of the Book of Revelation, as well as the lingering doctrinal and liturgical matters separating Protestants from the Orthodox. This is only one of many numerous scenes that occur throughout the city in Christian churches that have links to Orthodoxy, but that have their spiritual origins in Africa.

HISTORICAL BACKGROUND

Africa is no longer as central to the Orthodox story as it once was. In the early Christian period, the north African coast (present-day Egypt and Libya) was important Christian territory, and Christianity penetrated into the African interior with surprising rapidity. Alexandria was arguably the single greatest and most influential cultural center of the early Christian world. Certainly it was *the* premier Christian patriarchate already in the early second century. North African Christianity, so rich and so culturally distinct, enjoyed an influence on subsequent Christian developments out of all proportion to its geography and demographics.

The ascetic tradition was born in the Egyptian desert, under the astonishing influence of St. Anthony early in the third century. The Coptic church was instrumental in the spread of Christianity throughout the African continent, as well as in the creation of a monastic tradition that took root and exerted its influence on subsequent European developments as far away as Ireland. It has been speculated that the chanting and liturgical forms so characteristic of Orthodox Christianity as a whole owe much to far more ancient traditions of Egyptian sacred music.

Suffice it to say that North African Christianity was the *most* influential brand of regional Christianity in the first two to three Christian centuries. African Christianity gradually detached itself from the Eastern Orthodox world beginning in the fifth century when the lines of influence moved decisively north, to Constantinople and to Rome. That detachment and shift are two of the reasons (there are many, of course, both theological and political) African Christianity subsequently developed along the lines it did. Today, the traditions of African Christianity, most notably the Coptic and Ethiopic traditions, are independent traditions. There are three such traditions that are important in a descriptive survey of Atlanta: the Coptic, the Ethiopian, and, in a rather different way, the Melkite.

THE COPTIC CHURCH

The Coptic church takes its name from the Greek word for Egypt and Egyptian, *Aigyptos*. There are venerable ecclesiastical traditions that assign the arrival of Christianity to each of the major geographical areas in the eastern Mediterranean to important figures from the New Testament. So it is that St. Mark, the author of the second gospel, is assigned the honor of having brought Christianity to Alexandria—much as Paul and Peter were assigned to Rome, Thomas was assigned to India, and (as we shall see) an anonymous royal servant was assigned the honor of having brought Christianity to Ethiopia. But Egypt's involvement with this new faith is even older than St. Mark. Matthew's Gospel (2:13-21) describes the flight of the holy family *to* Egypt, just before King Herod massacred all the newborn children in Bethlehem. There they stayed for several years, until Herod's death. And there the faith returned, shortly after the crucifixion and resurrection of Jesus.

The Coptic church formally separated from the Orthodox church after the Council of Chalcedon in 451 CE. The Copts (read: "Egyptians"), however, also consider themselves to be "orthodox." One reason for the separation hinged on whether Jesus Christ had one "nature" or two (divine and/or human) and who had the authority to decide this question. The Copts were considered—perhaps quite wrongly—to be *Monophysite* Christians, "monophysitism" deriving from a Greek word meaning, literally, "one-naturism." The Monophysite Christians in North Africa were unwilling to accept the creed as it had been written, feeling that the Chalcedonian Creed was incompatible with their monophysite beliefs. So the Christian community in northern Africa split in two at this time. The division was between what were known as "monophysite" (and later as "Coptic") Christians on the one hand, and what became known as "Melkite" Christians (those who remained loyal to the emperor and his creed) on the other. The Melkites were Byzantines, fully participant in the broadly international Hellenistic culture of the eastern Roman Empire. The Copts, by contrast, were fiercely nationalistic, interested in maintaining their cultural, as well as their religious, distinctiveness.

Over time, the Coptic church was gradually reintegrated into the broad spectrum of Orthodox Christian identity. As Father Louka Wassif, of the St. Mary Coptic Orthodox Church, put it, "To call us `monophysite' is ambiguous. It might be better to call us miaphysite. We believe that Christ had one nature—he was one person—but that it came out of the blending of two natures, divine and human." The distinction is a fine one, but important nonetheless. The prefix "mono" suggests "one-and-only-ness." *Mono*physitism suggested that Jesus Christ had one, and only one, nature—and that was divine. Basically, monophysitism implicitly denied Jesus' humanity altogether. Father Louka insists that the Copts did not support this narrow view of Jesus. This is an important point because, if true, it means that the original split between the Coptic and Melkite churches was, sadly enough, entirely unnecessary. Father Louka believes that it *was* unnecessary. The Copts have been reconciled to the other Orthodox churches quite recently and even joined the World Council of Churches in 1954.

Most distinctive of the Coptic church is a profound tradition of ascetic spirituality, which grows out of their long experience (and long memory) of persecution and martyrdom. These persecutions lasted much longer than they did for other Christians, since the persecutors of the Copts were largely Christians themselves, not merely Roman governors. Essential to the maintenance of Coptic identity through the millennia has been the idea of racial continuity as well—namely, the belief that the Copts are the true descendants of the ancient Egyptians who taught the "Greeks" everything they knew. This tradition, too, enjoys a much wider scholarly currency today, under the rubric of a movement perhaps best known as "Afrocentric."

The community now known as the St. Mary of Egypt Coptic Orthodox Church began its religious life in the Greek Orthodox Cathedral of the Annunciation, discussed in the last chapter. In 1989, this Egyptian community purchased a parcel of land in Roswell and built a small sanctuary that was consecrated in October of that year. It was a small community, comprised of barely ten families at the time. When Father Louka came to the church three years ago, there were only forty families. Now there are one hundred and twenty. They are currently involved in an exciting task that is a highly symbolic event in the community's history—the building of a gorgeous new sanctuary. It was still under construction when I visited the church for the first time in July, 1995.

Father Louka and I visited together after evening Vespers and Bible study. He had been constantly active for over two hours, and seemed prepared to talk all night if I so desired. I asked him first about the complex question of Egyptian identity in the Coptic church. "Coptic," after all, simply means "Egyptian" in Greek. But history has not stood still since the advent of Christianity in North Africa in the first century. Most emphatically, Islam came to North Africa in the seventh century. Egypt is now a nominally Muslim country, and Arabic is its official language. Father Louka has monitored the ascendence of a more conservative, and more politicized, Muslim identity in that country with some concern. The Coptic identity is being gradually detached from the national, Egyptian identity—even though the administrative and spiritual center of the faith is still the Patriarchate of Alexandria. Indeed, two of the most popular feasts of this particular community are the Coptic New Year (on September 11) and the feast of St. Mary of Egypt (a famous Egyptian nun born in the fourth century) celebrated on August 21. These feasts lend an Egyptian flavor to the standard Orthodox religious calendar of major and minor feasts.

While this community is no longer Egyptian in quite the same way as before, it does not see itself as North American, either. Father Louka was insistent about this. "In western countries . . . where are the Ten Commandments?" he asked. "And where are the Christian practices? 'Christian' is just a name, in this country. I do not see the real, authentic

Christian life here." Father Louka sees the Coptic church's mission in explicitly ancient terms. "We hope to recreate the church of the disciples, the earliest church," he concludes. Father Louka labors consciously against the dominant Protestantism in this country. It is ironic, given the tremendous strides that have been made toward reconciliation among the various Orthodox churches, that no progress is anticipated between the Orthodox and Protestant churches. The matter is largely a practical one. "The Protestants do not believe in sacraments," Father Louka noted. "That is a big problem."

During the Bible study, Father Louka paid special attention to the Eucharist, the church's great sacramental mystery in which bread and wine are taken as the body and blood of Christ's new covenant. Theological matters were discussed, but the balance of the discussion was practical—involving the *practice* of communion as a decidedly Christian virtue. The discussion was surprisingly pragmatic, earthy, concrete. Believers are to prepare to receive communion, and should continue to prepare themselves devotionally after receiving it. "Christ is inside of you," notes the priest, "you should act accordingly." One should not eat or drink for twelve hours before receiving communion (the time-frame varies from one church to another—this is the Coptic way). One should also abstain from all sexual activity for twelve hours before and after receiving communion. This discussion, followed by equally matter-of-fact questions from the congregation—is the host digested like normal food? how often may one take it?—takes place entirely in Arabic. It is an astonishingly frank discussion of *bodily* matters—eating, drinking, and sexuality most of all—that would seem oddly out of place in a Protestant church. The body matters enormously to Coptic Christian practice.

If Protestants lack the sacramental vision of the Orthodox churches, they lack a sense of Christian history even more so in the judgment of this quietly convicted priest. Protestants tend to know very little about early church history, or where, geographically speaking, their faith came from. Churches like the Coptic church are a powerful reminder of where, and when, Christianity developed. "People used to think I was a rabbi when they saw me," Father Louka smiles. "Now they are beginning to recognize me, and perhaps they are beginning to know a little bit about the ancient churches."

What, then, is the essence of the Coptic faith? Father Louka does not hesitate. It is an interesting, and unexpected, answer. "We teach how to apply the Bible in the practical life. This is Egyptian Christianity, this is true Christianity—how to follow the commandments of Jesus Christ in the practical life." Clearly for this community religion is not simply a set of ideas, but a set of practices. "These, and the seven sacraments," Father Louka continues, "which are the foundation, or the pillars, of the church."

Given the ecumenical experience of the Coptic church in recent years, and given the exciting developments of this particular congregation, the future for the Egyptian community in Atlanta looks bright indeed. One should not light a candle and then put it under a bushel, Jesus warned. The light is lit in order to enlighten others. That task too is a Coptic calling. "The church is the body of Christ," Father Louka concluded at the end of our evening together, "and it must be one body."

THE ETHIOPIAN ORTHODOX CHURCH

Perhaps the most "national" of all the national Orthodox churches is the Ethiopian church, which is not only entirely independent of the Orthodox hierarchy, but also separate from the Coptic hierarchy to which it had belonged until 1950 (the first non-Coptic, native Ethiopian was consecrated as patriarch of the church in 1951). Theology and politics mix here just as they do in the other Orthodox communities. The Ethiopian Church also lays claim to the most ancient traditions in Christian belief and Christian practice. It, too, calls itself "the oldest church." There is a famous story in the New Testament (Acts 8:26-39) in which an anonymous man who served in the royal court of Ethiopia is converted to this new faith (he is given the name Qinâqis in local Ethiopian tradition). One of the early apostles, Philip by name, comes to him in the desert of Gaza, where the Ethiopian is making his way slowly through the desert toward home. He happens to be reading from the prophet Isaiah as Philip catches up to him. When the so-called Ethiopian eunuch admits that he cannot understand this scripture without instruction, Philip instructs him. He is then baptized, at which point Philip miraculously disappears. It is this momentous event, in the year 34 CE, that the Ethiopian church marks as its beginning. The royal servant did return directly to Ethiopia, and straightaway spread the word of salvation throughout the land.

In other respects, the Ethiopian experience shares many of the characteristics of Coptic Christianity—the same dubious monophysitism, the same experiences of persecution, the same dilemmas of being a minority religious tradition in a nominally Muslim (and now communist) land. Yet the

Ethiopian church has always managed to maintain its cultural independence. A number of its ritual practices are distinct (recognizing the Sabbath on both Saturday and Sunday, circumcision, certain dietary restrictions), and it has always maintained a vital tradition of literature and liturgy in its native languages (ancient Ethiopic, and present-day Amharic).

It is because of the antiquity of these traditions that the Ethiopian church faces the same pragmatic needs for bilingualism as most other churches that call themselves "Orthodox." Here in Atlanta, the entire service at Kidist Miriam (the word "kidist" being the feminine form of the word for "saint") in Decatur takes place in Amharic, the most prominent native Ethiopian dialect. The Bibles and songbooks are all printed in this language, and most of the celebration uses it as well. But important parts of the liturgy, especially those having to do with the description of the Holy Trinity, are kept in Ge'ez, the medieval form of a liturgical language better known as Ethiopic. That Coptic/Ethiopic liturgy—very much like the Greek liturgy in the Byzantine churches—originated in the fifth century. It acquired its final, and present, form in the fifteenth century.

There is no English in the ritual practice of this church as of yet. In fact, Father Gebre Mariam, who had just come from Ethiopia two months previously when we visited for the first time, spoke no English at all. He had been the leader of an enormous church in Ethiopia, overseeing a church hierarchy of some eighty priests and a congregation of between fifteen and twenty thousand (an estimate—the concept of church "membership" is new to the Ethiopian experience). He now finds himself in a small community with only one other deacon assisting him. His mission, as he sees it, is to educate his people into the meaning of their spiritual traditions, as well as to remind them of the importance of maintaining their cultural identity—which is, in some important ways, their Ethiopian identity—in a new and vastly different world. He does not miss an opportunity to educate in this way. Even the weddings to which I was kindly invited were liberally overlaid with explanatory homilies on the true meaning of Orthodox Christianity. I visited with Father Gebre Mariam and three of his congregants—Eskedar Awlachew, Almaz Akalewold, and Teru Mengistu—each of whom helped me by translating my questions and the Father's answers, and by giving me a better sense of the distinctive flavor of their community and its engaging style.

This religious community was founded in 1988, when it was given permission to use a side chapel in the Central Presbyterian Church, across the street from the State Capitol building. There they remained until August of

1994, when they purchased an old church building in Decatur and made it into their central worship space. From the outside it looks much like all the other brick Baptist churches in this region, all done in the Georgian style. The only clue that this is not what it appears to be is the portrait of Mary and the infant Jesus hanging to the right of the entranceway, with a message written in Amharic above it, announcing it as the Kidist Miriam Ethiopian Church.

Inside the sanctuary there is little doubt about which religious community worships here. Leaving your shoes at the door, you are whisked into a lovely carpeted sanctuary with fresh flowers and several potted trees at the front of the church where the altar once would have been. There are wooden pews still to the sides of the sanctuary. Nearly every window has a narrative picture from the gospels prominently displayed. Most of these depict Mary, the mother of God, with the infant Jesus. There is also a scene from the Last Supper, one of Jesus praying in Gethsemane, and a larger portrait of Jesus as a shepherd among his sheep near the front of the sanctuary. Eventually, the congregation plans to alter the interior of this church to make it resemble more closely the traditional worship spaces of their own country. "Our church is our country, in a sense," said Father Gebre Mariam, when I asked him about their plans for the future. "There is no change whatsoever in our practice or our faith when we bring it from our own country to this one."

In fact, the term "Coptic" does not actually appear in the self-description of this church. "We are the Ethiopian Orthodox Tawâhedo Church," he insisted. The term, "Tawâhedo," proves to be very difficult to translate. It might best be translated as "Unionate," having something to do with the mystery of the Incarnation, and indicating their monophysite (miaphysite?) belief in the union of Christ's divine and human natures. Father Gebre Mariam added that this term speaks to the mystery of God becoming a man, and the human capacity to become divine.

It is here, in the Ethiopian church, that we see most clearly how central the doctrine of the Trinity is to all of the "Orthodox" churches. The doctrine of the Trinity is the core belief that binds the Orthodox churches together, yet it is also the thing that keeps them apart. For each and every time the original creed has been translated from one language into another, nuances have been added, and others have been lost. Those creeds were all originally written in Greek. So long as the Orthodox churches are as regionally and linguistically diverse as they are, such differences will be inescapable. The political differences—matters of church organization and the like—clearly map these differences in language. Here in Atlanta the Trinity is widely confessed every Sunday—in Greek, in Latin, in English, in Russian, in Arabic, in Amharic, and in Ge'ez. It both is and is not the same confession in each of these languages. "`Orthodox' is a simple word which means `by the book,'" Father Gebre Mariam reminded me at the end of our meeting. With elegant deliberateness, he picked up his Bible, turned to Matthew 28:29 and insisted on reading it, in Amharic. It is the last thing Jesus says to his disciples in that gospel, telling them to preach his message of salvation "to the ends of the earth," and to baptize "in the name of the Father, and of the Son, and of the Holy Spirit." "He did not say 'in the name of Jesus' only," Father Gebre Mariam reminded me, "and he did not say to baptize simply in the name of God."

He is smiling when he says that, smiling in a way that makes me think that he has learned something already about the ways in which some Southern Baptists ("in the precious name of Jesus") and Unitarians (where Jesus is often left unnamed) baptize their flocks. The word this ancient church has been commanded to keep and to spread is a mysterious word about God being three persons in one being. That message, they insist, did not change when it made its miraculous way from Jerusalem to North Africa and thence to Ethiopia, some two thousand years ago. It will not change now, they insist, as it is transplanted from Ethiopia to a much newer world, faced with its own unique challenges and opportunities. The Ethiopian community in Atlanta is growing at a tremendous rate. There are already some two hundred members. And this church will surely add its own very distinctive cadence to the remarkable liturgical sounds of Christian Orthodoxy in Atlanta.

MELKITE (BYZANTINE RITE) CHURCHES

Another slice of vintage Americana, St. John Chrysostom's Melkite Church in Atlanta is sandwiched between the Church of Jesus Christ of Latter-Day Saints (Mormons) on its left, and the St. John's Lutheran Church on its right. The Mormon church is built of the solid Georgia brick one tends to associate with the Baptists, and the Lutheran church is done over, appropriately enough, in the grey granite one might expect in Protestant northern Germany. But St. John Chrysostom's Melkite Church is a prominent building. It stands out first for its colors—brilliantly yellow and white, fairly blazing against the hot summer sun. It is, architecturally, a church built for the summertime—light colors, large stained glass windows designed to capture the long summer light, large shaded porticoes on the sides and in front offering a respite from the direct heat of the sun. This church building was dedicated on June 9, 1957, as a marble inscription tells us in English and in Arabic. And it currently boasts an enrollment of some two to three hundred members. The majority of them have emigrated here from a variety of countries in the Middle East, primarily Lebanon and Syria, but this should not be thought of as a regional or ethnic community. Just the opposite. "We are an *international* church," Father William, from St. John Chrysostom, insists. "Anyone from anywhere can join the Melkite church. Anyone can become Melkite."

This church takes us another step in our ecumenical discussion, as well as to the heart of the controversies surrounding the Fourth Ecumenical Council in Chalcedon. It was in north Africa, after all, that the distinction between "monophysite" and "melkite" was introduced after 451 CE. While the original conflict was between Alexandria and Constantinople, between North Africa and the Near East, that conflict has been supplanted by the much more visible split between the east and the west. The Orthodox churches in Africa, as we have seen, have long been permitted to go their own way.

The Melkite church now sees itself very clearly as a mediator and as a bridge between the eastern (Byzantine) and western (Roman) churches. Indeed, there are a large number of Roman Catholics who have been attracted to the Melkite church precisely for its ritual, due to their disaffection with what they perceive as a loss of ritual in light of the reforms of Vatican II. Simply put, the Melkite church follows the liturgical and devotional practices of the eastern Orthodox churches (called the "Byzantine rite"), but it acknowledges the single authority of Rome in terms of ecclesiastical structure. It is, *culturally* speaking, an ancient eastern church, but it is *politically* western. The issue seems to be the age-old question of church unity. "There is no unity in the Orthodox churches such as we have in the Roman Catholic church," Father William cautions. He suggests that the various patriarchs may get together to discuss matters of doctrinal importance but, absent a single recognized authority figure, no ultimate consensus is possible. That authority is the Pope for those churches that see themselves as *Roman* Catholic. The Melkite church is such a church.

"'Melkite' was synonymous with 'Catholic' in the beginning," Father William tells me. In the middle of the fifth century, he goes on to explain (both personally to me, as well as in his sermon on Sunday), the word "melkite" was used as a way of indicating which churches remained faithful to the Roman emperors (and the Roman bishop). "Melkite" is thus a word that derives from the Semitic (Hebrew and Arabic) root for royalty, *m-l-k*.

So, in an important sense, this church also considers itself "orthodox" (although that term does not appear in their name). Given its allegiance to Rome, the name would clearly mean something quite different to them. "'Orthodox' was originally a Greek word," Father William states, "meant to indicate 'the right way.'" The Greek language, he adds, was one of the essential unifying factors for the early church, even in Rome in the first century. Clearly, this church feels that it has preserved the singularly appropriate Christian path—*eastern* in all matters of liturgy and practice, *Roman* in all matters of church hierarchy.

It was in the eleventh century, roughly in the period of the Great Schism between the eastern and western churches (1054 CE), that the Melkites began using other names for themselves: *Roman* Catholic in the west, and *Orthodox* in the east. That is why the name "Melkite" is so important to this congregation—it has become symbolic of an important third path, a way to mediate between the east-west divisions that otherwise seem so inescapable and unresolvable in Christian history. It is a path that first emerged, historically, in Africa.

At St. John Chrysostom's Melkite Church, the use of the vernacular is crucial. It is another element in the fundamental task of bridge building. Most of the service takes place in English, and the sermon always does. Father William will occasionally use Greek when he is chanting the liturgy, just to remind his parishioners of the first unity the early church had, and the language in which that unity was expressed. The gospels are read in Arabic, as well as in English, for those members of the community who do not yet speak English well enough to understand it this way alone.

There is a second Roman Catholic priest, Father Thomas Flynn, who assists at St. John Chrysostom and who has what they call "bi-ritual faculty." He is authorized to perform *both* the Latin Mass *and* the Byzantine rite performed at St. John Chrysostom. He received this authority two years ago, after practicing for some five years, from both the Melkite Exarch in Newtown, Massachusetts and his own Latin bishop. Father Tom is a story unto himself. He is a professor of Philosophy at Emory University who specializes in certain "existentialist" philosophers (primarily Jean-Paul Sartre). He has been a priest for thirty-five years (he was ordained in Rome in 1961) and has been working with Father William at the Melkite Church for the past six years, literally performing a rite of ecumenical healing each and every time he takes over celebration of the liturgy.

"The church is like a garden," Father William tells me at the end of our brief conversation. "There are a great many flowers, but there can only be one gardener." Clearly, according to the Melkite tradition, for all the cultural flowering in their ritual, that gardener lives in Rome. Yet it is the explosion of colors in the garden that captures one's attention in worship—not only in *this* church, but in *every* eastern church that graces Atlanta with its rich liturgical presence.

FOR FURTHER INFORMATION

A. S Atiya. *A History of Eastern Christianity.* London, Methuen, 1968

Roberta Bondi. *To Love As God Loves: Conversations With the Early Church.* Philadelphia, Fortress Press, 1987

Jon Bonk. *An Annotated and Classified Bibliography of English Literature Pertaining to the Ethiopian Orthodox Church.* Metuchen, American Theological Library, 1984

Georg Gerster. *Churches in Rock: Early Christian Art in Ethiopia.* London, Praeger, 1970

Iris Habib el Masri. *The Story of the Copts.* Cairo, American University in Cairo Press, 1978

Otto F. A. Meinardus. *Christian Egypt: Ancient and Modern.* Cairo, American University in Cairo Press, 1965

Edward Ullendorff. *Ethiopia and the Bible.* London, Oxford University Press, 1968

CHAPTER TWELVE

THE SHRINE OF THE BLACK MADONNA OF THE PAN-AFRICAN ORTHODOX CHRISTIAN CHURCH

Louis A. Ruprecht, Jr. and Theophus H. Smith

Shrine of the Black Madonna. Photograph by Elizabeth Hardcastle.

The first Shrine of the Black Madonna emerged in the 1960s in Detroit, Michigan. Its roots were established by a group of African-American church members seeking increased community involvement. After starting their own church in the mid-1950s they launched a local movement that eventually became national—the Black Christian Nationalist (BCN) movement. The chief architect and the most prolific herald of that movement was the Reverend Albert Cleage. Cleage was (and still is) a United Church of Christ minister, but today he is also known as "Jaramogi Abebe Agyeman," and is acknowledged as the Holy Patriarch and founder of nearly a dozen shrines across the United States. His founding role began as pastor of the Central Congregational Church in Detroit when, in 1966, an event occurred that signaled the congregation's transformation into the nation's first Shrine of the Black Madonna. That event was the inaugural display of the church's new identifying icon: a fifteen-foot painting of the Black Madonna and Child.

Black Madonnas originated in medieval European church sculpture and painting. Whether in the form of statues or iconic paintings, they were manifest representations of the Virgin Mary. Some commentators argue, however, that they were also covert representations of pre-Christian earth goddesses. On the one hand, Roman Catholic church officials insist that the dark coloring of approximately 400 statues indicates either the hue of the original materials employed, or changes in the original material due to the process of aging or to environmental influences such as fire and smoke. Such long-standing interpretations of the Madonnas, both popular and official, account for the ethnic neutrality with which the images are venerated by the churches. They are valued without explicit reference to the significance of their color, but rather for their traditional role as sacred objects for conventional Catholic piety. But in the United States, in the midst of the 1960s black consciousness movement, Cleage and his community effected a counter-conventional appropriation of the Black Madonna image. Through the Shrines of the Black Madonna a Euro-Christian oddity became an Afro-Christian emblem.

Another innovation ensued in the early years of this movement: Black *Madonna* iconography was appropriated in concert with a Black *Messiah* theology. Alongside his congregation's Madonna and Child symbolism, the Reverend Cleage began preaching and proclaiming Jesus as the Black Messiah. Moreover, in 1968, he published a series of provocative sermons called *The Black Messiah*. The sermons portrayed New Testament Jews as a black nation resisting oppression by a white Roman empire. In this reconstructive black theology Jesus was proclaimed to be a revolutionary savior—a literal "black messiah." There followed, in 1972, a more programmatic statement of the movement, the founder's second book called *Black Christian Nationalism: New Directions for the Black Church*. A BCN center opened in Atlanta in 1974, with shrine offices and a training center following in 1975. New shrines opened in 1977 in Kalamazoo, Michigan, and in Houston, Texas. When the first Pan-African Synod occurred in Houston, in 1978, a new Christian denomination was born and a more expansive designation, the "Pan-African Orthodox Church," was adopted. As of this writing, two more shrines are planned to open soon in New York City and in northern California.

SITE VISIT

During a site visit, one of us met with Cardinal Aminifu in his office at the community center. In addition to the community center, the Atlanta Shrine now houses one of the best Black Studies bookstores in the southeastern United States. The center itself is located adjacent to a large worship structure, and provides space for educational and training programs for youth and adults. The cardinal administers some of those programs himself. He received his seminary training at the Yale Divinity School, from which he graduated in 1972. He looks back on those years now through the lens of his own life's commitments to social reform and a very social gospel. Seminarians in the 1960s and early 1970s were torn—torn between the radical new possibilities opened up by the new questions that emerged, and the tempting pull of tradition. "What were we to do?" he asked. "To take our training and go back home to preach the same thing all over again? Or to preach something new?" He smiles, dismayed at what he takes to be a very disturbing retreat back into the traditional in this country, what he calls "the new traditionalism." Clearly, he chose the less-travelled path.

While on that path, Cardinal Aminifu, then Woodrow Smith, Jr., discovered the theology and writings of Albert Cleage. As he also discovered, there are no niceties, and still less theological hair-splitting, in those writings and sermons. Instead, one finds a theology rooted in the common reality of black experience. And it is the work of this religious community to transform the reality of that experience—in the words of the Psalmist, to turn oppression into liberation, weeping into laughter, sorrow into joy. Cleage's writings attempt to effect such transformation by identifying black experience with biblical experience, not only in the Psalms but throughout the Hebrew and Christian scriptures. This kind of identification goes back to slave religion in the United States, where African Americans first began to correlate their experience of bondage in the United States with the ancient Hebrews' experience of Egyptian bondage.

However, for Cleage the Jewish people described in the scriptures were a black nation, ethnically and physically. Jesus, who saw himself in full continuity with Jewish identity and the Mosaic revelation, was also a Black Messiah. He intended to carry on the work begun by Moses—namely, the liberation of the black nation from (white) gentile oppression on the one hand, and deliverance from the pagan tendencies toward an excessive individualism (rather than communalism) on the other. Jesus' religion was essentially an "apocalyptic nationalism," grounded in the idea that salvation is a collective, not an individual, experience. As one can well understand, this is at times an angry theology, but it should not be confused with blind rage. Cardinal Aminifu emphasized this point clearly.

The word "programmatic" is never very far from the cardinal's lips and from his thoughts. To rage blindly against injustice is to accomplish nothing of substance and nothing of lasting value, he insists. Worse, it is to condemn oneself to a continuous experience of more of the same oppression. The task of Black Christian Nationalism is to provide a *programmatic alternative* to the oppressive environment in which the peoples of African descent have lived for so long in this country. In the final analysis, this church is founded upon a clear, concise, and knowing theological response to what it knows its problems to be (and who it knows its adversaries are).

At the conclusion of our two-hour conversation, Cardinal Aminifu stated how he thought the essence of the faith he celebrated might best be described. "Black Christian Nationalism celebrates the possibility of communal living," he said, "and this is connected to our belief that this is the will of God—to live unselfishly, and to live in love." "It is a sort of heaven on earth idea," he concluded. He went on to allude to a well-known passage from the first letter of John in the New Testament (I John 4:17-21), a passage which insists that one knows God, as love, in the form of other human beings whom one loves fully and in complete selflessness. Jesus himself was asked much the same question, and he gave pretty much the same answer that Cardinal Aminifu gave. He was asked what the most important commandment was, that is, what the essence of his faith might best be considered to be. He did not hesitate. "To love God with all one's heart, and to love one's neighbor as oneself" (Matthew 22:35-40; Mark 12:28-31). That is an elegant articulation of Cardinal Aminifu's remarks.

THEOLOGICAL HIGHLIGHTS

In this section we offer additional highlights of the shrine's theology and ecclesiology as presented by Cardinal Aminifu. It is useful to begin with the more extensive title that connects the various Shrines of the Black Madonna throughout the United States—and connects them as well to the earliest New Testament churches: "Pan-African *Orthodox* Christian Church." The term "orthodox" bears similar import to what it means for some other communities described in this book. "Orthodoxy" has essentially to do with reclaiming the very *oldest* traditions of Christian history. It means "traditional" only in the strict sense of laying claim to the radicalness of the original Christian message. "Orthodoxy" is all about resurrecting that earliest church experience. It is especially about recreating and reconstituting the radically nationalistic religion of Jesus as found in the gospels (this, and not the semi-pagan sacrificial theology found in the writings of St. Paul).

Finally, the term "orthodox" in this sense is not intended to indicate affiliation with the various Eastern Orthodox church bodies—whether Greek or Russian on the one hand, or Coptic or Ethiopian on the other (for example, the shrines do not endorse the traditional creeds of the older Orthodox churches). Whatever affiliations the shrines seek are best indicated, rather, by the term "Pan-African." For Black Christian Nationalism, Jesus as Black Messiah is the preeminent ancestor among a host of biblical, African, and African American ancestors. Together those ancestors constitute a prophetic heritage and a source of continuing empowerment for contemporary peoples of African descent everywhere. In this connection, *Pan-African* designates both the living and the dead, from the biblical ancients to their modern heirs in the struggle for liberation and social justice.

How was this ancestral religious nationalism, the religion of Jesus, lost? That has been a crucial question in the evolving spiritual life of this community. How was the religious vision of Jesus compromised and eventually forgotten entirely? A variety of factors contributed to this loss. First and foremost, there was the increasing *otherworldliness* of the church. The belief that all would be made well in heaven (Luke 16:19-31) too often contributed to a gospel of quietism and a too-docile acceptance of the (unjust) status quo. Political oppression, economic injustice, poverty, hunger, and homelessness—these crushing social facts lose something of their urgency when their ultimacy is denied. The radical prophetic task of criticizing the contemporary political and social order in the name of God's will gave way finally to Paul's idea that slavery was an acceptable social practice (Philemon), and that the state was to be obeyed in all things (Romans 13). In short, the *radicalism* of Jesus was lost.

The early Christians went one step beyond the prophetic tradition, and this is essential to the task of a constructive Black Christian Nationalism. "We focus more on *Acts* [the New Testament book] than on the [Hebrew] prophets," Cardinal Aminifu told me. "The prophets criticized without having a positive program. The early church was more programmatic." He was thinking particularly of the famous comment made in Acts 4:32, where we are told that these earliest Christian communities lived together and held all things in common. It was communalism of a particularly disciplined and radical sort. It is precisely this communalism that Black Christian Nationalism is designed to recreate.

CONTEMPORARY APPLICATIONS

It is important, in this regard, to understand that "integration" is not the programmatic goal of this community. Black Christian Nationalists see White Supremacist America as the enemy. Positive energy is wasted, they argue, by attempting to find peace and reconciliation with those who do not honestly desire it. In the Civil Rights movements of the 1960s and 1970s, black people wasted some of their best energies in the attempt to make peace with fellow citizens who continued to institutionalize racial prejudices and other, subtler forms of hostility against them. The Shrine of the Black Madonna preaches a different approach, the creation of a *separate* black nation within the larger nation—a larger nation that is only nominally the "United States of America." The energies of this community are devoted to the creation of a positive self-image for black people, the promulgation of the beauty in blackness, and a positive communal environment for them—all of this as a countercultural alternative to the dominant individualism and consumer culture of North America.

The shrines' accomplishments in this essential task of community-building are impressive, to say the least. In particular the Atlanta Shrine of the Black Madonna is not only a church, but a community in every sense of the word. There is a nursery here, as well as a youth center, both designed to foster a positive self-image and a nurturing environment for young people. In the words of the West African proverb, "it takes a community to raise one child." There is a bookstore here, holding many titles not so easily accessible anywhere else in Atlanta or the southeast. There are now two large residential complexes that have been purchased by the community—all of this, again, designed to nurture an awareness of community, and to foster the creation and maintenance of authentic community among those present in it and therefore accountable to one another.

Responsibility implies accountability. That is a difficult idea for some of us to grasp. Printed in the church bulletin each week, among other more expected announcements, are notices indicating which community members have "established a personal relationship," which others have "terminated" relationships, who has been censured for violating some section of the BCN Code, and who has been placed on probation. This is a community that views the maintenance of the common life with the greatest seriousness. Incidentally, that is one reason why there is no simple way to count "church membership" in this community. Church membership is a noble Protestant idea, Cardinal Aminifu suggested, which tells us only that certain people make a point of coming to church for one hour at least once a year. To be a member of this community carries with it a more serious set of obligations and commitments. That is one reason why the numbers are constantly changing.

It is helpful here to review the BCN Creed, which serves the same identity-forming and doctrinal function among the shrines as the Nicene Creed performs among other "orthodox" Christian communities. First and foremost it begins, not with God the Father, but rather with human society: "I believe that human society stands under the judgment of one God, revealed to all, and known by many names." For community members, this is the God who created humanity in His own image—in Africa, some one million or more years ago—and it is the same God who will judge the continued oppression of His chosen people, the Black Nation.

Jesus is not defined as the second person of a cosmic Trinity: "I believe that Jesus, the Black Messiah, was a revolutionary leader, sent by God to rebuild the Black Nation and to liberate Black people from powerlessness and from the oppression, brutality, and exploitation of the white gentile world." Jesus, too, has been brought emphatically down to earth, taken from the heavenly context of the Holy Trinity, and reunited with a political and social world from which he was allegedly alienated by the later church.

So too for the Holy Spirit. Here one finds no debate about whether the Spirit proceeds from the Father and/or the Son. Instead, there is commitment to a spirit of revolutionary praxis. "I believe that the revolutionary spirit of God, embodied in the Black Messiah, is born anew in each generation, and that Black Christian Nationalists constitute the living remnant of God's Chosen People in this day."

To this interesting and radical reappraisal of the traditional, creedal language of the Trinity, the Black Christian Nationalist Creed now adds a fourth—and probably the most important—point: "I believe that both my survival and my salvation depend upon my willingness to reject INDIVIDUALISM and so I commit my life to the Liberation Struggle of Black people." Clearly, this is a community that has carefully constructed itself as a coherent alternative to what it perceives as the rampant and toxic individualism of North American society. It has cast its lot with the principle of solidarity. And it now sees itself as a community of solidarity—a solidarity borne of the millennia-long experience of persecution and oppression, a solidarity borne of the hope that the Nation will indeed ultimately be delivered and redeemed, *through spiritually grounded collective action.*

Indeed, its practices are grounded in devotional disciplines oriented to both adults and youth. These practices are geared toward a recognition of dependence, of the need for God and for one another, as well as a recognition of the power of God, a transformative power perceived as a personal spirit within each human being. The spiritual practices of the church are eclectic, borrowing freely from the North American context and the therapeutic practices that are so pervasive here. Theirs is an interesting seven-step program of devotional channeling and spiritual direction. These devotional sessions, which last for some three and one-half hours and are conducted weekly, are aimed ultimately at the creation of reconciliation as a personal and social reality. "Sin is not smoke or drink," Cardinal Aminifu smiles. "Sin is rather about how and where you have hurt another human being." Such sin must be publicly acknowledged before any reconciliation worthy of the name can occur, he believes. Scriptural insights are combined with Gestalt-therapy to assist in this devotional *practice* of reconciliation.

Mental analysis is then followed by massage techniques that are designed, not to celebrate embodiment *per se,* but rather to release the vast inner resources of personal (divine) energy. In this connection the shrine community has recently become more interested in food and its contribution to the wellness (or illness) of the community. Many congregants are now practicing a macrobiotic diet, and the community has plans (called the "Beulah Land Farm Project") to purchase a 5,000-6,000 acre farm—first in order to feed itself and become self-sustaining, and then to feed others in the indigent community here in the city.

Beyond New York and California, the community also has its eyes set on international expansion. The gospel of Pan-Africanism is scheduled to spread first to Central and South America, and then back to the African homeland. Programmatic and slow, steady growth is the key. This community takes the long view of things—thinking in terms of decades and half-centuries, not months or even years. They have done this consistently since the mid 1950s, and their patient visionary practices promise to bear fruit in the mid 1990s and beyond.

FOR FURTHER INFORMATION

Articles

"Black Messiah: Revising the Color Symbolism of Western Christology." *Journal of the Interdenominational Theological Center,* Fall 1974

Books:

The Black Messiah. Trenton, African World Press, Inc., 1989

John H. Bracey, August Meier, and Elliott M. Rudwick, eds.. *Black Nationalism in America.* Indianapolis, Bobbs-Merrill, 1970

Albert B. Cleage, Jr. *Black Christian Nationalism: New Directions for the Black Church.* Detroit, Luxor Publishers of the Pan-African Orthodox Church, 1972, 1987

James H. Cone. *A Black Theology of Liberation.* Maryknoll, Orbis Books, 1970, 1990

E.U. Essien-Udom. *Black Nationalism: A Search for Identity in America.* Chicago, University of Chicago Press, 1962

Lawrence L. Levine. *Black Culture and Black Consciousness: Afro-American Folk Thought from Slavery to Freedom.* New York, Oxford University Press, 1977

C. Eric Lincoln and Lawrence H. Mamiya. *The Black Church in the African-American Experience.* Durham, Duke University Press, 1990

Wilson Jeremiah Moses. *Black Messiahs and Uncle Toms: Social and Literary Manipulations of a Religious Myth.* University Park, Pennsylvania State University Press, 1982

Albert Raboteau. *Slave Religion: The Invisible Institution in the Antebellum South.* New York Oxford University Press, 1980.

Gayraud S. Wilmore. *Black Religion and Black Radicalism: An Interpretation of the Religious History of Afro-American People.* Maryknoll, Orbis Books, 1983

Josiah Ulysses Young, III. *A Pan-African Theology: Providence and the Legacy of the Ancestors.* Trenton, African World Press, Inc., 1992

CHAPTER THIRTEEN

MEGACHURCHES OF ATLANTA

Scott Lee Thumma

Cathedral of the Holy Spirit. Photograph by Elizabeth Hardcastle.

It is 10:30 on a Sunday morning. You are in your car driving through an unknown town in search of a newspaper and a bagel. Suddenly you find yourself in the middle of rush-hour traffic. Up ahead you see several members of the police force directing cars. Must be an accident, you think, but as you reach the heart of the congestion you notice a huge parking lot to the left, crawling with cars. Smartly dressed people are coming and going. It reminds you of the local mall during Christmas shopping season. In the middle of this activity sits a building that could easily be confused with most office complexes, sports arenas, or even shopping malls. It is however, a new center for religious worship.

Your interest is peaked. Hand gestures from the police motion you toward the parking area. Large directional signs, vested parking lot attendants, and a steady stream of cars move you in the appropriate direction. You park in a special visitors' space, and make a surprisingly short walk to a well-defined entrance. Passing through broad inviting doors, surrounded by expanses of glass and ushers ready to assist, you enter a large fellowship foyer or reception atrium. A few folks who attended the 9 o'clock service are still milling around in small groups, chatting with friends. Several persons cluster around the visitors' information center. You notice that broad hallways radiate from the foyer and lead, according to the signs, to the classroom buildings. Several television monitors describe the weekly events and this semester's educational courses.

Following the sounds of an upbeat, jazzy rendition of a traditional church hymn, you make your way into the worship area. Immediately you are struck by the size of this room, and the thousands upon thousands of people inside. You wander through the huge semi-circular auditorium noticing that the space is well-lit, comfortable, and invitingly decorated with plants and floral arrangements, though there are surprisingly few religious symbols. Finally you find an open seat in one of the curved rows of cushioned theater seats. On the large stage down front, amid the theater spotlights, expansive sound system, and television cameras stands a portable, clear plexiglass podium. Off to the right a 25-piece orchestra is playing. Balancing this on the left, in rows of removable chairs, sit a dozen associate pastors. A professional vocal group, accompanied by a hundred-member choir and a deaf interpreter, begins to sing Sandi Patti's latest top-ten contemporary Christian hit. Around you casually dressed young families and middle-aged Baby Boomers stop chatting with each other. Their attention focuses on the performance—some sing along, others raise their hands in an expression of praise. The music swells and crescendos. On cue, a well-dressed attractive minister walks out radiating warmth and charisma. He exclaims: "First-timers, welcome to our megachurch."

THE MEGACHURCH

A megachurch is any congregation with a consistent weekly worship *attendance* of 2,000 or more persons. There are between 350 and 400 such churches in America, with a cumulative weekly attendance of one and a quarter million persons. In the Atlanta metropolitan area there are at least 23 megachurches, comprising about six percent of all such churches in the country. As several commentators have observed, megachurches represent one of the most significant religious phenomena in the latter half of the twentieth century.

These churches are the everyday gathering places of spiritual seekers who desire a communal and entertaining experience, a relevant religious message, and a place that meets their needs. Megachurches have become popular centers of worship for people who believe that our society is growing more and more secular. These mass gatherings of thousands of Christians represent a potent voice in the Atlanta community and a powerful sacred presence in the United States today. How these churches function varies considerably between individual megachurches, yet as a whole they share many common characteristics.

One characteristic shared by these very large congregations is that they are a *modern phenomenon*. Well over half of the American megachurches did not exist prior to 1965. Of those that have extended histories, the majority reached mega proportions only within the last 25 years. Of the nearly two dozen Atlanta megachurches, only First Baptist Church of Atlanta was this large before the sixties.

A second, and the most obvious, characteristic megachurches share is their *size*. Across the country, these congregations range from 2,000 to approximately 25,000 members (Willow Creek Community Church, located in a suburb of Chicago, is one of the largest). Attendance at Atlanta megachurches varies between those that hover around the 2,000 mark to

Mt. Paran Church of God, which reports attendance figures of 9,500. Size is an attractive feature for many members. One megachurch visitor suggested, "This place is so big, something good must be going on here."

The size of these congregations creates *organizational similarities* as well. A whole host of structural and institutional problems arise once a church becomes this large. The needs of the membership are more diverse. The additional revenue that is generated offers new opportunities for ministries and services smaller churches could not afford, but also demands more careful fiscal management. Increased ministries, in turn, require additional staff and volunteers, all of which need to be supervised. Mega-size, then, demands both new ministerial approaches and new forms of leadership.

Another characteristic megachurches generally have in common is *location*. The majority of megachurches in the United States are in the southern and western regions, with almost 75 percent found in the Sunbelt. California has the greatest number of megachurches (70 congregations), accounting for 20%. Georgia has the fourth largest concentration of megachurches, following Texas and Florida. Almost all megachurches across the country are located in the *suburban* areas of major metropolitan cities rather than in urban downtown or rural areas. The Atlanta churches are generally situated on highly visible tracts of land, often near the intersection of major highways (frequently just off of the I-285 perimeter) for ease of access. The majority of Atlanta's megachurches can be found in the northern, eastern, and southern suburban edges of the city.

A *conservative theological orientation* is another common element of a majority of megachurches. These churches are usually evangelical, charismatic, or of a mild fundamentalist bent in terms of their beliefs about God, the Bible, and the human condition. Nine of Atlanta's megachurches (40%) are affiliated with the Southern Baptist Convention. Approximately a quarter are African-American congregations and are associated with the National Baptist, American Baptist, Church of God in Christ (COGIC), and United Methodist denominations, or they are independent. The Assemblies of God and other conservative denominations account for several more megachurches in the area. Four Atlanta megachurches are non-denominational—that is, affiliated with no traditional denomination. Six congregations have ties to moderate or liberal Protestant groups such as the United Methodist, Episcopal, and Presbyterian denominations. Although these massive religious communities are not solely linked to Protestant Christianity, this is predominantly the case in Atlanta. In most cases the actual denominational affiliation of megachurches is inconsequential. My experience with such churches suggests that the large denominational churches usually function as if they were independent. They downplay denominational ties, seldom broadcasting their denominational affiliation in their television programs or in advertising.

Another feature common among megachurches both in Atlanta and around the country is their *strong central leadership*. Leaders are often personally charismatic, exceptionally gifted men (there are no female megachurch pastors in Atlanta) who function as the dominant influence in the congregation. An associate pastor at one megachurch stated his perspective on megachurch leadership in the following way: "You can't run a church this big by committee." These men are usually visionaries and innovative entrepreneurs. Many are the founding pastors of their churches. They have been their church's senior minister for an extended time period, and were in charge when the church grew so large. The character of these churches is definitely shaped around the personalities of their senior ministers. In many cases it would be difficult to imagine these megachurches functioning without their core leader.

Most members of megachurches share *similar demographic characteristics*. The typical congregation is comprised of young to middle-aged adults (average age around 35 years), with about 70 percent being married and having two children. Members are often college educated, and are solidly in the middle class. Sixty to seventy percent of those who attend megachurches are female. Many of the churches encourage and support participation of persons from diverse ethnic and racial backgrounds. A few of Atlanta's megachurches, such as the Cathedral of the Holy Spirit, World Changers, and the Cathedral of Faith, have sizable populations of members from Africa, Asia, the Caribbean Islands, and Central America.

Megachurch participants attend services very often, though they may not be official members. In fact, many megachurches have done away with the idea of membership. If you attend, participate, and give, then you belong. Participants often drive ten to thirty minutes to come to "their" megachurch. As one person explained, "The drive is worth it. It wasn't a question of where you had to go but what you got once you got there." One megachurch in Atlanta even advertises, "The difference is worth the distance!" Those in attendance generally are very devout in their personal religious practices, such as Bible reading, daily prayer, and involvement in church activities. Many have switched from other churches or have recently returned to religion. Finally, they are usually both theologically and politically conservative—though some may hold socially progressive views on certain issues such as race relations, environmentalism, and economics.

Another characteristic of many megachurches is a *particular style of worship*. Worship is experiential, non-traditional, and innovative, marked by an intensity that can only be generated by thousands of persons gathering together. The service often contains professional, high-quality music and other dramatic arts, presented in a highly-orchestrated but relaxed manner. The congregational atmosphere is defined by openness, acceptance, and friendliness. Yet the size of the worshiping congregation promotes anonymity and a privatized spirituality. Though sermon presentation varies considerably depending upon the minister or the religious tradition, the sermon content almost always reflects a culturally relevant, practical, "down-to-earth" message. Relevance to everyday living is an important feature of megachurches. One megachurch member commented: "It seemed like the pastor preached on the topics that we were discussing during the week . . . He was always right on the money." Sermons encourage members to evangelize, render assistance, and influence their neighbors in positive ways. The underlying message of such sermons is that since the church has an obvious community presence, members must have a corresponding greater responsibility toward their local context, whether spiritually, politically, or socially.

Although the ministries of these megachurches vary quite a bit, they generally adopt a *similar functional ministerial pattern* of what one writer calls "full-service" or "seven-day-a-week" church structuring. These congregations offer throughout the week a plethora of religious, recreational, educational, and self-help ministries, or as one member put it, "everything I need in one package." The facilities are in use every day of the week, not just on Sunday. Another megachurch member suggested: "It's a good feeling to know . . . your tithes and offerings are at work."

Given the common size and functioning of these megachurches, their facilities often share similarities. Megachurch buildings usually are designed to be user-friendly, convenient, and "consumer"-oriented. They hold thousands of persons comfortably in a space that can be adapted to multiple ministries, but above all they are buildings that enhance a communal, public worship experience.

Megachurches almost always organize their *social community* by employing a "cell-group" structure that consists of small, intense fellowship groups intended to promote intimate friendships, create community spirit, and solidify church commitment. Such groups are organized either around vocational interests, hobbies, or geographic placement.

Finally, most megachurches engage in *diverse media expressions,* whether through advertising, selling books, producing television shows, or holding national conferences. Half of the megachurches in Atlanta have television programs, several of which are broadcast nationally.

ATLANTA'S MEGACHURCHES

A quick glimpse at the megachurches of Atlanta might give one the impression that they are all quite similar. Upon closer inspection, however, it is clear that this is not the case, and that these congregations exhibit considerable diversity. The unique character of each megachurch is evident not just in its pastor's sermons and written material, but also symbolically in its worship rituals and even in its architectural forms. The external and internal physical characteristics of a megachurch are often intentionally designed to reflect its distinctive theological message—to symbolize its ideology, identity, and relationship with the city. Within this variety, however, at least three distinct styles can be identified among Atlanta megachurches in relation to their religious tradition as well as in relation to southern religion in general. These three styles can be described as "conventional," "non-traditional," and "composite." To understand these distinct patterns one must examine the multiple ways the congregations represent themselves through their theology, their worship rituals, and the architectural form of each megachurch.

The "conventional" style is seen in those megachurches that hold fast to the traditional image of religion in the South, both theologically and architecturally. The message of the church building as well as the worship experience that takes place within it is one of successful traditionalism. Megachurches of this type replicate traditional theology, ministries, and worship forms, but on a grander scale. First Baptist Church of Atlanta is the foremost example of this "conventional" megachurch style. Located downtown on Peachtree Street, the impressive sanctuary, with its Georgian Colonial architecture, seats 2,300. It was built in 1930 and enlarged in 1950. The church occupies several blocks of prime development land in the heart of the downtown area, though currently it is in the process of selling this land and building an 8,000-seat sanctuary in a northern suburb. The current minister, Charles Stanley, has been a popular pastor, author, and television preacher, and has been a leader in the fundamentalist takeover of the

Southern Baptist denomination. The theology of the congregation is conservative, evangelical, and traditional. The worship is also traditional, but professional and polished.

For over half of the megachurches in Atlanta, the theological and architectural approach epitomized by First Baptist is *the* form to imitate. It is symbolic of traditional religion in the South, and not surprisingly, many of the more recently constructed megachurches, especially those in the distant suburban areas, have chosen this cultural style. Like First Baptist of Atlanta, they have intentionally copied the form of traditional southern religion, but enlarged it to "mega" proportions. In this style every detail of the religious tradition is reproduced at 200 percent or more of its normal size. The message conveyed by the architecture, the worship, and the theology of these churches is that they are *ultra-traditional* in every way except their scale. They portray themselves as "exciting" or "successful" versions of what churchgoers in the South have always known, and they strive to create a nostalgic continuity between old southern traditions and a new suburban reality. Their worship is the least innovative of all megachurches. Likewise, they employ more traditional symbols both on their buildings and in their interior decor than do the other two styles. The best example of this in a suburban megachurch is Rehoboth Baptist Church—"Atlanta's exciting Metrochurch." Although a very new church, it is an exact copy of smaller traditional churches. Its box-shaped interior design, with balconies, straight rows of pews, and poor lighting, seats 1,500 rather uncomfortably. Its current minister, Richard Lee, is a young dynamic speaker, a leader in the fundamentalist wing of the Southern Baptist denomination, and the host of the church's "There's Hope" television show.

A second Atlanta megachurch pattern, the "non-traditional" style, is related to the creation of a religious experience that reflects an unconventional approach to church life. Congregations adopting this approach often express a theological desire to break with traditional forms of religion. Their church buildings are often quite ordinary, modeled after everyday structures such as office buildings or community colleges, though some border on the outrageous and extravagant (such as the Crystal Cathedral in a suburb of Los Angeles). In either case the goal of these churches is to portray their message and spiritual product as "not your ordinary Christianity." They eschew traditional religious rituals and symbols, and strive to reinvent or revitalize worship forms and members' religious experiences. Their theology often exhibits a practical, this-worldly orientation where religion is seen as relevant and a part of ordinary life. In line with this theology, worship services are highly entertaining, casual, non-dogmatic, and often devoid of traditional religious language or an emphasis on giving.

This approach of combining a secularized church design and a non-traditional worship style is perhaps the most common megachurch form nationally. When compared to Los Angeles or Chicago, Atlanta (and the South in general) has fewer megachurches that follow this pattern. Conventional religion, for the most part, is still "socially acceptable" and the cultural norm in southern states. Spiritual seekers in the South generally still want a religion that "looks and feels" like the religion of their parents. Nevertheless, there are still at least five such non-traditional megachurches in the Atlanta area. One example involves First Baptist of Atlanta, in the form of its northern campus. This satellite congregation meets in a converted Avon corporate headquarters building which seats 3,000 and, until recently, was pastored by Charles Stanley's son. Compared with the downtown church, the northern congregation's worship atmosphere, its youthfulness, its lack of traditional church symbols, and even its theological approach display a casual unconventionality.

The presence of multiple congregations with differing styles unified under a single church identity is a very common feature of megachurches. As has been noted, First Baptist of Atlanta is actually two distinct churches. Another successful megachurch in the city, Mt. Paran Church of God, also combines several diverse congregations. Its main church, located in a residential northern area with an attendance of several thousand, exemplifies a traditional approach to theology, worship, and architecture. Its four satellite congregations, all considered a part of the "mother" church, are located in the distant suburbs and draw thousands of worshipers. Several of these "campuses" pattern themselves after the non-traditional style, providing a worship experience for every member's taste or preference. Its Marietta North congregation is situated in a sprawling office park and can be recognized as a church only by the minimal steeple at one end of the building. The senior pastor of thirty-five years, Paul Walker, Jr., guides this multiple-congregational Pentecostal church, which is the largest one in the Church of God, Cleveland, Tennessee, denomination. Walker is also a psychologist, author, and television personality.

One of the most interesting and dynamic megachurches in Atlanta that embodies this nontraditional style is World Changers Ministries Christian Center, located in College Park, a southern suburb of the city. This congregation, pastored by its charismatic minister Creflo A. Dollar, Jr., is predominantly African American and is one of the fastest growing churches in the United States. It began as a non-denominational church in 1986 with eight members and currently claims a membership of over 9,000. The lively, emotional, and entertaining worship services of the church are held in its new "faithdome," which seats 8,000 persons in a round sanctuary resembling the Astrodome in Houston, Texas. Reverend Dollar, in his popular national television program and at the church, preaches that the membership is not "just playing church," but rather attempting to "get understanding and act upon God's Word" in order to become "world changers."

Finally, a third pattern evidenced by some megachurches, the "composite" style, is an attempt to retain some traditional religious symbols, theology, and historic architectural forms yet, at the same time, intentionally adopt an unconventional worship format and use the structural conveniences of a modern building design. Representatives of this type are fewer in number both in Atlanta and throughout the country. These congregations seek to maintain a connection with some past religious tradition while also accepting the necessity of user-friendly building and worship features, such as a casual atmosphere, expressive and entertaining services, spacious seating, and an adaptable performance sanctuary. Many of the members in these composite style megachurches describe their religious orientation as new, original, and "a fresh revelation from God," yet they clearly want to embed their approach in a traditional framework.

One local congregation explicitly employing this style is Chapel Hill Harvester Church, now referred to as the Cathedral of the Holy Spirit. This independent, non-denominational church, led by Earl Paulk, Jr., was once a thriving multiracial congregation of 12,000 members. It currently draws approximately 2,500, with a large number of African Americans. This church demonstrates a common tendency in megachurches, that of employing different styles as they evolve over time. The church became a megachurch while in a hexagonal stone building, espousing at first a traditional Pentecostal theology and worship style. The congregation then spent several years in a circus tent as it attempted to build a glorious state-of-the-art worship center similar to the Crystal Cathedral, while preaching and practicing a vibrant charismatic theology. When this building attempt failed, the church finally settled for a prefab utilitarian structure resembling a television studio which seated 3,000. This period of the church's history reflected the unconventional megachurch style. Non-traditional worship forms were adopted, while traditional church symbols and rituals were downplayed.

When the congregation outgrew this building in 1990, the senior minister had begun to stress the need for reclaiming past traditions, merging them with charismatic spirituality. A new sanctuary, loosely based on the neo-Gothic cathedral form, was built to symbolize this connection with a "High Church" European heritage. This quasi-traditional form houses a user-friendly megachurch interior that is adorned with diverse liturgical implements, tapestries laden with traditional church symbols, and other conventional religious trappings. The church's worship format reflected this change by incorporating more traditional hymns into its musical repertoire of gospel, rap, and charismatic choruses, as well as a greater use of liturgy and high church rituals. The leadership also instituted a separate service in the form of a charismatic Mass. These changes were seen as embodying their explicit theological conviction that all churches should attempt to retain the best of a traditional religious heritage while also embracing contemporary, unconventional worship forms and building structures.

Another local megachurch, Mt. Carmel Christian Church, also exemplifies this composite approach. Unlike the Cathedral of the Holy Spirit, their merging of old and new is not a verbally explicit aspect of their theology. This relatively new megachurch, sitting in the shadow of Stone Mountain, seats about 2,000 in a beautiful, traditional Colonial Palladian structure. The interior of the church, however, is an ultra-modern theater auditorium. The worship of this church, too, reflects a mix of traditional and contemporary music and worship forms in a relaxed atmosphere. Reverend Phil Gambill leads this theologically conservative congregation.

Roswell Baptist Church in Marietta, a northern suburban town, demonstrates how certain megachurches attempt to create a composite style using several buildings at one location. They try to combine the unconventional and traditional in one congregation, though not in one building. This fundamentalist congregation of several thousand, led by Nelson Price, meets in an ultramodern semicircular sanctuary that is nearly devoid of any religious symbols. Attached at one corner of this huge unconventional structure is the seldom used, diminutive traditional sanctuary. Yet the church's brochure and advertisements prominently feature this traditional church in the foreground, overshadowing the newer worship center. In reality this modern worship facility dwarfs the earlier traditional structure. This church, which describes itself as a "big down home church," wants to retain a "traditional" identity and conservative theology. Reverend Price's sermon content and delivery follow a traditionally southern style of preaching. At the same time, however, the church's sanctuary is characteristic of the unconventional approach. Furthermore, its worship format, which includes an orchestra, contemporary music, and an expressive, relaxed style, demonstrates a nontraditional rendering of Southern Baptist Christianity.

THE MESSAGE OF MEGACHURCHES

Taken together, the megachurches of Atlanta tell a story about the city, its religious community, and its cultural and social situation. Located deep in the heart of Dixie, Atlanta has a rich history and heritage. It is steeped in an Old South traditionalism characterized by hospitality, regional pride, localism, and social conservatism. Traditional religion still holds a significant place in this ethos. At the same time Atlanta is a youthful, suburban city, brimming with major international corporations and service industries. It prides itself on being the "gem of the New South" and one of the most progressive metropolitan areas in the region. The city is full of highly mobile, educated, modern people, many of whom grew up outside the South. Compared to residents in the rest of Georgia and the South, the inhabitants of Atlanta are characterized by unconventionality, cosmopolitanism, and pluralism. These cultural realities coexist in some tension in the urban context of Atlanta. City leaders have worked hard over the last few decades to make these cultural currents more compatible by merging reconfigured "Old South" traditions into a "New South" climate. Religious organizations must also respond to this cultural situation, reworking old patterns and striving to be relevant in a changing society. In this setting the megachurch makes sense, in each of its three forms. The modern megachurch is a product of suburbia. It is at home with, in fact may actually be neighbors to, the megamall, the warehouse supermarket, the medical center complex, or the 10-screen multiplex cinema. There is a cultural fit between these phenomena. The same tastes, needs, social pressures, and market forces shape them all.

Like Atlanta itself, the city's megachurches are comprised predominantly of persons born after 1950. Many of these participants were born in some giant hospital complex and educated in massive high schools and universities. Their entertainment tastes were shaped by television, Disney World, rock concerts, and Six Flags. They are now employed as business managers, sales associates, or office workers by Coca-Cola, Turner Enterprises, or one of Atlanta's other large complex corporations and bureaucratic service industries. Megachurch members then are not only familiar with complex institutional contexts, but they have actually been shaped and nurtured by them. They are at home with large-scale organizations. They can find their way through vast spaces and mazes of halls guided by impersonal directional signs. They can balance their own ambitions and interests against the anonymity of mass culture and its nearly infinite number of choices of goods and services. And they know what they want out of a religious experience and are willing to "shop around" until they find the right product.

Megachurches offer what the more than 75,000 Atlanta Christians who attend them each week want—a religion that is alive and successful. These congregations provide passionate, experiential, high-quality worship combined with practical, relevant teachings. They offer a religious experience that is integrated into daily life, not just a sacred hour or two each week. They provide a "home" and a "place" for transplanted souls. Megachurches also offer "one-stop shopping" where members' personal, social, and spiritual needs can be met, all within a "wholesome" Christian context. In addition, these mall-like complexes of ministries provide the opportunity to become involved in the community, to serve others, and to develop one's personal ministry skills. One megachurch member addressed these features in discussing her attraction to her church: "Everything about our church is MEGA—the worship and teachings, the fact that there are blacks and whites here together, our ministries, and our theological unity. Our church is one of the most exciting things that is happening on the face of this earth for God's kingdom."

Megachurches, with their huge crowds of committed active members, occupy a prominent position in Atlanta. With their size, central locations, extensive ministries, and abundant public relations budgets, megachurches are quite visible. The scale and presence of the megachurch is symbolic of the actual social influence many such ministries have in their locales. Religiously, these large churches set the norms and standards by which many smaller congregations judge themselves or establish their goals. They wield a tremendous influence over how things are done in the religious world, whether architecturally, artistically, or in terms of ministry. After all, everyone learns from the success stories, and these congregations have the resources to televise their successes to the nation.

On the other hand, in terms of service to their local communities, Atlanta megachurches have made and continue to make tremendous personal and societal changes through their ministries. They provide tutorial programs, health clinics, food and monetary assistance, job networks, psychological counseling, and self-help services. Economically, they generate and expend enormous amounts of money. An average megachurch might have a yearly budget ranging from two to ten million dollars. These funds are used almost as quickly as they are received. Large congregations also often provide stability to communities in transition and "public space" for local events.

Politically, many of these churches have become the favorite haunts of office-seekers or politicians attempting to rally support for new legislation. Few other social settings present such an opportunity to address thousands of concerned registered voters. With the force of this voting constituency behind him, the megachurch pastor can wield more than just moral persuasion when attempting to influence the decisions of city and county officials. In Atlanta, many of the megachurch pastors are respected members of the power elite in the city. Even if they are not privy to the decision-making process, they are almost always the religious figures called upon to add a spiritual stamp of approval.

The cumulative weight of the actual or perceived social power and influence of Atlanta's megachurches is very attractive to their constituents. In a survey of one megachurch, 95 percent of the congregation agreed that their church contained people who could get things done in Atlanta. As one woman said, "I love going to a church that has a public voice which is listened to." Another member of this congregation summarized the appeal of this social power, saying, "That's what our church is about, influencing government, and the whole world!" Although it is by no means the only thing megachurches are about, the powerful public presence these churches have is essential to understanding the appeal of megachurches. This presence is symbolized in the massive dimensions of megachurch structures and ministries. It is reflected in their theology, and often expressed in such phrases as "changing the world" and "transforming the city." Most importantly, it is written on the hearts and minds of thousands of megachurch members—that they are a part of a church that has a powerful public presence, a church that makes a difference in Atlanta.

FOR FURTHER INFORMATION

Articles:

Gustav Niebuhr. "Megachurches." *New York Times*. Series of 4 articles. (April 16-April 20, 1995)

Richard Ostling. "Superchurches and How They Grew." *Time*. (August 5, 1991): 62-63

Lyle Schaller. "Megachurch!" *Christianity Today*. (March 5, 1990): 20-24

Books:

Lyle Schaller. *The Seven-Day-a-Week Church*. Nashville, Abingdon, 1992

John Vaughan. *Megachurches & America's Cities*. Grand Rapids, Baker, 1993

CHAPTER FOURTEEN

THE MARIAN APPARITION SITE AT CONYERS, GEORGIA

Victor Balaban

Photograph by Victor Balaban

During the month of October, several thousand pilgrims make their way to a large field about 30 miles outside the city of Atlanta at Conyers, a small suburban community that has one of the longest-lived Marian apparition sites in the United States. At this place, from October 13, 1990 to May 13, 1994, the Virgin Mary appeared to Nancy Fowler on the thirteenth of every month and gave her messages for the United States. Since May 13, 1994, however, Mary has given messages only on October 13 of each year. In addition to the apparitions on the thirteenth, Fowler also receives visions of Mary and Jesus almost daily. Messages have ranged from warnings of war to advice on dieting. Mary and Jesus frequently plead for people to return to the church, to stop abortion, and to pray. On the thirteenth Fowler will usually speak for an hour or two and answer questions from the pilgrims before the crowds begin to disperse. Most pilgrims do not spend much time in Conyers after the apparition, although some visit the nearby Monastery of the Holy Spirit.

Pilgrims usually start to arrive the night before the Virgin's appearance. They can pick up religious literature at the small bookstore on the property, or visit two gift shops located nearby. By the morning of the thirteenth several thousand people will have gathered outside the house where Fowler has her visions. Members of Our Loving Mother's Children, the volunteer group that organizes the gatherings, are on hand to give directions and answer questions. Many pilgrims first go to a small hill on the property that the Virgin Mary declared as a holy site. A large crucifix and an altar in the shape of a cross now mark the Holy Hill. The base of the cross is covered with small statuettes, votive candles, flowers, letters, and photographs. Nearby is a well with a sign that reads "Blessed Well Water," which is where the faithful stop to fill bottles and jugs with holy water to take home with them. Pilgrims can then walk down a trail marked "To the Farm & Apparition Room. Walking Time—One Rosary."

The trail leads to the farmhouse, an ordinary house where Fowler will receive the message in the Apparition Room. Pilgrims bring blankets to sit on and umbrellas to protect them from the sun; some have dozens of icons and rosaries laid out on their blankets. Using loudspeakers, members of Our Loving Mother's Children lead the crowds in prayer from the porch. Starting at noon, those gathered begin to pray the Consecrations to the Sacred Heart of Jesus and to the Immaculate Heart of Mary. They then sing the Fatima Song and pray all 15 decades of the Rosary. Individual rosaries are said in the language of the pilgrims' native countries, including English, Spanish, Russian, and Chinese. During this time Fowler is in the Apparition Room receiving a message, which is then broadcast over the loudspeakers. The Virgin has told Fowler that "there are no walls to the Apparition Room," and so as the vision is coming to an end many pilgrims hold up rosaries or icons to be blessed by the presence of Mary.

The crowds come from all over the world, but most are from the southern United States. There are many Hispanic pilgrims from south Florida and elsewhere, so rosaries and Mary's messages are read to the crowds in English and Spanish. People make the pilgrimage for many reasons—because they feel they have been called to come, because they want to reaffirm their faith together with other believers, or because they are simply skeptical and curious. Some pray for a change in their life, others just want to be in the presence of the Virgin. Still others bring petitions and requests for healing, which are left in baskets in the Apparition Room or on the altar on the Holy Hill These are periodically gathered up and burned so that the smoke ascending to heaven can bear the messages to Jesus and Mary. Many pilgrims have seen signs of Mary's presence. Rosaries have turned golden and the scent of rose petals has been in the air when no flowers were nearby—traditional signs of the Virgin. The sun has been seen to spin, to move in the sky, and to change colors. This echoes the "Miracle of the Sun" at Fatima in 1917. Some pilgrims bring Polaroid cameras and video cameras to capture images of the sun in which they see Jesus and Mary in the shapes and flares around it. Pilgrims have also come in all seasons and endured all sorts of weather conditions. On March 13, 1993, for example, 7,000 pilgrims braved a blizzard to hear Mary's message. Those who were there reported that the snowflakes smelled like rose petals.

Many Americans are surprised to learn that there are Marian apparitions occurring in the United States, but these events are not new. There is a long history of Marian apparitions in other parts of the world and many of the customs at Conyers date back to the Marian devotions of the Middle Ages.

A BRIEF HISTORY OF MARIAN APPARITIONS

There is a long tradition in Christianity of belief in the powers of various saints and of miracles associated with particular tombs or relics, but until the early Middle Ages there were no special powers associated with the Virgin. There is very little mention of Mary in the Bible, and images of the Virgin in the first few centuries of the Common Era tend to depict her as an empress holding the child-king Jesus in her lap. It has been speculated that the Great Councils' emphasis on the divinity of Jesus in the second and fifth centuries led to the emergence of a new perspective on Mary, who began to be viewed as a mediator whom ordinary people could approach for intercession in childbirth or at harvest. It was only in the Middle Ages that devotion to the Virgin Mary exclusively became widespread; she began to be depicted as "the Lady," the embodiment of the ideal of courtly love. By the early Renaissance images of Mary had evolved into the more human and compassionate Madonna figure.

Although Marian apparitions are an old phenomenon, the Catholic church's official position on apparitions was not decided until Pope Benedict XIV (1740-1758) wrote the treatise *De servorum Dei beatificatione.* He stated that approved revelations could be publicized "for the instruction and good of the faithful." Approval by the Vatican only means that the apparitions have been judged to be consistent with tradition and scripture and free of error. Devotion to such an apparition can be beneficial to an individual's faith, but belief in any approved apparition is left to the individual's conscience. Individual dioceses can investigate the authenticity of an apparition site at any time, but the Vatican generally will not pronounce a vision credible until the apparitions have stopped. Even then, the visions must be investigated by a formal commission and it can be decades before a final decision is made. In the history of the Catholic church, only 18 sites have been judged authentic by the Vatican, although many more either have been approved by local bishops or are currently under investigation.

Perhaps the most famous pre-modern apparition of Mary occurred on December 9, 1531, in Guadalupe, Mexico. The Virgin appeared to Juan Diego, a native peasant and a recent convert to Christianity. She told him to ask the Spanish bishop to build a shrine on the hillside where she stood. The bishop did not believe Juan, and when the Virgin appeared to Juan again she showed him roses she had caused to bloom in the winter. Juan filled his cloak with the roses and took them to the bishop. When he spilled the roses out of his cloak, they found that the image of the Virgin as an Aztec woman had become imprinted on it. The date of the second apparition, December 12, is now celebrated as Guadalupe Day. Interpretations of this apparition of Mary portrayed her as a mediator for the dispossessed, a voice for those who felt alienated from the church hierarchy. It became a very influential moment for subsequent believers in the later Marian movement.

In the nineteenth century, Marian doctrines were promoted by the Vatican as part of their efforts to reassert the role of the church in a rapidly changing society. This is evident in the two most famous nineteenth-century Marian apparitions, at La Salette and Lourdes. These were the first Marian apparitions in modern times to take place outside of a cloistered church setting, be officially recognized by the Vatican, and gain worldwide attention.

In 1846 in the village of La Salette, two peasant children, Francois-Melanie Mathieu and Pierre-Maximin Giraud, saw the figure of a weeping woman bathed in light. The woman told the children (in their local dialect) that she was suffering for them because she did not want Jesus to abandon them. Soon after this happened, word of the vision spread and the site became known for healings and eventually as a pilgrimage site. It was officially recognized by the Vatican in 1851, and was widely interpreted as a message calling for Catholics to return to the church and do penance.

Twelve years later, in 1858, Bernadette Soubrious experienced a series of 18 apparitions of a beautiful woman in Lourdes, France. When Soubrious asked the woman her name, she replied: "I am the Immaculate Conception." This was seen as an affirmation of the dogma of the Immaculate Conception, which had only been proclaimed by Pius IX four years earlier. Lourdes quickly became an international sensation and an integral part of the church's campaigns against secular trends in Western culture (it was recognized by the Vatican in 1862). Soubrious was canonized in 1933, and Lourdes remains a popular pilgrimage site today.

In the twentieth century, a more political element appeared in Mary's messages, particularly with regard to a vision that took place in Fatima, Portugal in 1917. Three peasant children saw a series of six apparitions beginning on May 13. The final apparition took place on October 13, when thousands witnessed the "Miracle of the Sun" in which the sun spun and moved in the sky when Mary appeared. Fatima is considered the most ideologically important apparition in the modern Marian movement. Although the apparitions occurred in 1917, the more elaborate devotions to Our Lady of Fatima did not develop until after World War II, when the messages from Fatima and from other apparition sites were incorporated into the church's strong anti-communist message.

Fatima continues to have a tremendous influence in the contemporary period. On May 13, 1991, Pope John Paul II celebrated the tenth anniversary of the assassination attempt on his life by placing a crown of diamonds on a statue of Mary in Fatima. The crown included one of the bullets from the attack. Mary has also appeared to Nancy Fowler as Our Lady of Fatima, reportedly saying "Please review my words that I spoke at Fatima. . . . The times are not unlike the times I appeared at Fatima."

There was less emphasis on the cult of Mary within the Catholic church after Vatican II, but since the 1980s reports of Marian apparitions have been increasing. The focus of much of the revived interest in Marian apparitions has been at Medjugorje, in what was formerly Yugoslavia. On June 24, 1981, six young men and women, ranging in ages from ten to seventeen, saw the Virgin Mary appear over a hillside holding the child Jesus in her arms. The community of Medjugorje, guided by the Franciscan clergy of the parish, developed an elaborate program of confessions, masses, and apparitions for the millions of pilgrims who have come to the village since 1981. Attendance at Medjugorje has declined since war broke out in the former Yugoslavia, but many still brave the dangers to make the pilgrimage. Those who remain in Medjugorje still report daily visions of Mary.

Messages from the Virgin Mary in the nineteenth century tended to emphasize humankind's sins against the church. Most contained the common theme that Jesus is offended by these sins and that Mary, in her benevolence, is intervening. Apocalyptic pronouncements were not usually central to Mary's message. Recent apparitions in the twentieth century, however, such as those in Medjugorje and Conyers, have a much stronger apocalyptic content. In many of Fowler's apparitions, Mary has cried tears and shed drops of blood. She has warned of wars and natural disasters that will happen unless people return to the church and pray. Fowler has been shown maps of the world that slowly turn red, while Mary pleads for people to stop offending God.

THE APPARITIONS AT CONYERS

Nancy Fowler was born in Cambridge, Massachusetts. Her mother died when she was 11 years old, so she asked the Blessed Mother to be her mother. She is the wife of a retired Air Force officer and mother of two children. Her mystical experiences began in the early 1980s, and in February 1987, she had an apparition of Jesus. He appeared again in November of the same year, and she recalls that "He was much smaller than the first time I saw Him, and He was smiling broadly." "What do you ask of me?" she inquired. Jesus replied, "To bear witness that I am the living son of God."

The family moved to Norcross, Georgia, in 1988, and there Fowler began to have daily visions of Jesus. She also began to see apparitions of the Virgin Mary, always announced by the chirping of a bird. In July 1990, Fowler and her family moved to Conyers. Starting on October 13, 1990, the Virgin Mary began appearing to her on the 13th of every month to give a message for the United States. The message on that day was the following:

> Pray much because there is too little prayer from the heart. There is too little prayer. Your prayers and sacrifices are needed in order to spare you a great punishment form God. My Son's Heart is heavily burdened. You will only be able to console Him by giving Him your heart. My dear children, please give my Son your hearts in prayer. Pray, pray, pray. I encourage family prayer. When you fail to pray in families you will have greater sufferings and Satan will divide. I have come to represent the Holy Family. You are called to imitate us and stay together. Satan seeks greater division in families and countries and church.

After this first message, several hundred people began gathering in Fowler's backyard in Conyers on the thirteenth of every month to hear the message. By August 1991, the Rockdale County government had decided that such crowds could not congregate on the property. That summer, the 130 acres of land adjacent to the Fowlers' home were purchased by Robert Hughes, a wealthy businessman from Virginia and one of Fowler's main supporters. Mr. Hughes also formed Our Loving Mother's Children, the non-profit organization that plans the apparition gatherings.

In fall 1991, the Archdiocese of Atlanta began to take notice of the events in Conyers. The Archbishop of Atlanta, James P. Lyke, sent a letter to priests in the archdiocese, cautioning that any reported vision or apparition must not be allowed to distract from the essential faith of the church. He also asked that priests not lead groups to Conyers and that Mass not be conducted on the Fowler property. He declined to start a formal investigation, quoting Acts 5:38-39: "Leave them alone, for if this plan and work of theirs is a man-made thing, it will disappear; but if it comes from God you cannot possibly defeat them." In a later statement in March 1992, Archbishop Lyke expressed stronger reservations. In a letter to Catholic bishops in the United States, he wrote: "The authenticity of these apparitions is in grave doubt."

The archbishop's letter did not deter the faithful, and on June 13, 1992, an estimated 12,000 people waited in the rain to hear the next message. The message was more serious this time:

> Dear children of America, please forgive one another. When you fail to forgive, you fail to love. Your sins are many. Please children, you must stop offending God, who is grievously offended. When you remain in serious sin, you risk losing your soul. You allow Satan to guide you. Walk away from the darkness of sin. Come to the light of truth. Satan is deceiving you and you do not recognize him. The darkness over this land will grow darker and you will have more sufferings unless you return to God.

After Archbishop Lyke died in December 1992, the new Archbishop, John F. Donoghue, decided not to investigate the apparitions. He said, "Whether she is appearing at Conyers or not, I don't know. . . . As long as nothing is being taught or said contrary to church teaching, I don't think I have to say anything." Attendance at the apparitions continued to grow, and by January 13, 1993, as many as 40,000 people were coming to Conyers to hear Mary's message. The size of the crowds and the attendant traffic and crowd-control problems reached a turning point; many residents of Conyers began to complain about pilgrims parking in their yards and driveways, and of not being able to leave their houses on the thirteenth of each month because of traffic jams. County officials considered taking legal action, first under public-nuisance laws, then under a little-used state mass-gathering law, in order to regulate the meetings. However, traffic and crowd control problems did not occur during spring 1993, so county officials declined to take legal action at that time, though they continued to monitor events. A County Requirements Fund was set up, soliciting donations to pay for off-duty police, fire, and traffic personnel, but there was still some local resentment against the crowds that continued to gather each month.

By summer 1993, Conyers was one of the largest Marian apparition sites in the world. On June 13, 1993, an estimated 80,000 people came to hear Mary's message, this time suggesting that the apparitions might come to an end: "I am preparing you for the time when you will no longer receive

Photograph by Victor Balaban

a message for the United States." County officials announced that new regulations were being planned that would require gatherings of more than 500 people to have street lighting, running water, paved walkways, and medical facilities. Members of Our Loving Mother's Children complained that the new regulations were targeted at the apparition site, but county officials stated that the ordinance was enacted in preparation for the equestrian events of the 1996 Olympics, to be held in Conyers.

On May 13, 1994, Mary announced that "The purpose of my coming is to bring you my Son. . . . The time has now come for you to live the message and to walk in faith. I love you." Fowler announced to the 50,000 present that formal messages for the United States would cease. Many people understood this to mean that the apparitions were ending altogether, but in fact Fowler still receives a teaching message on the thirteenth of each month, and Mary gives a special message for the United States on October 13 of every year. About 5,000 pilgrims congregate each month now, although there are some events that bring many more people. On October 13, 1994, 25,000 pilgrims waited in the rain and heard Mary's message for the United States. It stated, in part:

> My dear children, in the peace of my Son, Jesus, I greet you. Peace, peace will not come upon the world unless you return to God. . . . Please dear children, you must stop offending God. I have warned you of wars,

> of natural disasters, famines, droughts, floods, epidemics and suffering of every kind and you fail to understand that God wants you to amend your ways. . . . Take to heart these words and return to God.

SPREADING THE WORD

One important task for the faithful who believe in apparitions is to spread Mary's messages. At least since the apparition at La Salette, informal networks of believers who distribute newsletters and devotional literature have sprung up around apparitions sites, and Conyers is no exception. Our Loving Mother's Network distributes the "Journal of Reported Teachings and Messages of Our Lord and Our Loving Mother at Conyers, Ga., USA." An interesting outgrowth of the apparitions at Conyers is the creation of Marian groups on the Internet.

The Conyers-List and Apparition-List Usenet groups are the project of Jim and Rosemary Drzymala. After the Drzymala's second visit to Conyers in May 1993, they decided to see if there was a way to distribute the newsletters via computers. Jim, a programmer and systems analyst, was working at a university that ran listserv software and was given permission to start a new group. The first group was Conyers-List, created in September 1993. The purpose of Conyers-List is to distribute messages and information about Fowler's apparitions, and to give subscribers a forum to discuss the events at Conyers. Very soon it became apparent that many subscribers wanted to talk about other apparitions, so in April 1995, a second group, Apparition-List, was formed. The purpose of this list is to discuss and spread the messages of approved apparitions from around the world. An average listserv group has 150 to 200 subscribers. As of August 1995, there were approximately 400 subscribers on Apparition-List. Most subscribers are American, but there are some from as far away as Thailand and South Africa. While not officially connected, Conyers-List and Apparition-List are now part of a loose network of religious discussion groups on the Internet that range from Bible study groups to theology groups to devotional groups. A World Wide Web page is being constructed that will provide a centralized source of information about Marian apparitions around the world and carry Mary's message into cyberspace.

CONCLUSION

Reports of Marian apparitions continue to increase in the 1990s. In recent years there have been reported apparitions in Falmouth, Kentucky; Denver,

Colorado; Scottsdale, Arizona; Emmittsburg, Maryland; and Belleville, Illinois, as well as abroad in Italy, Japan, Ireland, Rwanda, and Venezuela. Some have speculated that this increase is connected with the approaching millennium, while others point to socioeconomic factors or disaffection with changes in the Catholic church since Vatican II. The majority of reported apparitions, however, are very short-lived. Only a small number become matters of public interest and fewer still become the focus of widespread religious devotion. It is unclear whether Conyers will continue to inspire the same fervor in the future as it has in the past.

Regardless of the question of the vision's authenticity, an important factor in the longevity of an apparition site in the United States is the issue of conflict with local authorities. It is difficult to imagine how any pilgrimage site in the United States could reach the proportions of Lourdes or Fatima or Medjugorje without encountering such difficulties. One recent example can be found in the apparitions of Joseph Januszkiewicz in Marlborough, New Jersey. In spring 1992, Januszkiewicz announced that Mary was appearing to him on the first Sunday of each month. Soon thousands of pilgrims began attending, causing traffic jams and crowds that caused resentment among neighbors and local officials. The Virgin told Januszkiewicz that the crowds and traffic jams were "a sacrifice" for her. In August 1993, Januszkiewicz was forbidden by the bishop of the Diocese of Trenton, John C. Reiss, to speak publicly of any further visions. The bishop declared that no true miracle had occurred at the site; specifically mentioning Mary's statement about the "sacrifice," he wrote: "In view of the hardship that had already been caused to many people in the township, grave doubts arise that such a response would come from the Virgin Mary."

The apparition site at Conyers has avoided the kind of censure that happened in Marlborough. Since Mary stopped giving the message for the United States monthly attendance at Conyers has dropped off. The Archbishop of Atlanta, John F. Donoghue, while ambivalent, has declined to investigate. Through a spokesman, he has said, "We fully acknowledge that people are coming here seeking something they don't seem to be finding elsewhere, including in their own congregations. In the same breath we are concerned about the damage this could do to these believers if it turns out to be false." The believers who make the pilgrimage every month are more certain. As one pilgrim recently put it, "The visions must be true, because I know people who have rediscovered their faith here. The Blessed Mother wouldn't let something good come out of bad."

FOR FURTHER INFORMATION

Books:

Nancy Fowler. *To Bear Witness That I Am The Living Son of God,* Our Loving Mother's Children, n.d.

Sandra L. Zimdars-Swartz. *Encountering Mary: From La Salette to Medjugorje.* Princeton University Press, 1991

Technology:

World Wide Web Page for Catholic Apparitions of Jesus and Mary http://www.frontier.net/~mbd/apparitions.html

PART III:

RELIGIOUS DIVERSITY IN THE NEW METROPOLIS

CHAPTER FIFTEEN

RELIGIOUS LIFE IN THE MUSLIM COMMUNITY

Janice Morrill

Prayer at Al–Farooq Masjid of Atlanta. Photograph by John McWilliams. Courtesy of the Atlanta History Center.

Shelha, a 20-year-old student at Emory University, is the daughter of Pakistani immigrants who grew up in Charleston, West Virginia. Saira, a 21-year old Emory student, is the daughter of Indian immigrants who grew up in Conyers, just outside the city of Atlanta. Shelha and Saira became friends several years ago when they were introduced by their older brothers, both students attending Emory. The two girls began exchanging letters in order to have a female friend who was also Muslim. As they put it, "we wrote pages and pages to each other because we had finally found someone who understood being young and Muslim."

Like many other young Muslim women in the United States, Shelha and Saira wear western-style clothing to school rather than traditional Muslim forms of dress because, they say, the purpose of covering the body in loose-fitting clothing and covering their hair is not to draw attention to themselves. They and their parents feel that women can accomplish this goal by wearing conservative western dress. When they attend the mosque, however, they wear traditional Muslim head covering *(hejab)*. They also fast during the month of *Ramadan*, from sunrise to sunset, as prescribed by the Qur'an. And they intend to marry within the religion, though each would like to choose an appropriate husband on her own rather than have an arranged marriage. While Shelha and Saira's practice of Islam is not typical of Muslim women around the world, it is common for Muslims in the United States. As with other world religions, Muslims do not form a single community, nor are they of a single mind when it comes to issues such as women's wearing of *hejab*. While some point out that the Qur'an—more than once—calls for the wearing of *hejab*, others choose to interpret the practice in new ways.

Like other Muslims living in the United States, Shelha and Saira have grown accustomed to the lack of understanding that many Americans share about Islam. But they still get frustrated when all Muslims are automatically held responsible for the activities of a few. They described how, for example, the media immediately blamed Muslim extremists for the Oklahoma City bombing in 1995 because a brown-skinned man was seen leaving the area. (As evidence developed, suspicion for the bombing shifted to one or more

Americans.) Shelha and Saira were blamed by others at school simply because they are Muslims. One of them recounts: "I remember a Hindu boy coming up to me and saying `Look at what your brothers have done!'" They also recall Muslims in America being spat upon during the Persian Gulf War and the Iranian hostage crisis.

Unfortunately, reports surrounding the 1993 bombing of the World Trade Center and other recent activities of Muslim extremists have perpetuated inaccurate stereotypes about Islam. General perceptions common in the media suggest that it is a violent religion, that it is intolerant of non-Muslims and is anti-western, and that it supports maltreatment of women. Such perceptions, say many Muslims, reflect media sensationalism and are simply not true of the majority of Muslims. One example of this kind of sensationalism can be found in a June 28, 1992, article in the *Atlanta Journal/Constitution* titled "Women of the Veil," which described oppressive practices toward women in various Islamic countries. Even liberal Muslim women in Atlanta—women who work outside the home and wear western clothing—felt the article was more damaging than accurate, full of extreme examples rather than depicting the norms of these communities. "Its approach was the same as a reporter traveling to the most impoverished and backward part of the United States, and describing what they found as `typically American,'" stated one Muslim woman. The imam (spiritual leader) of Al-Farooq Masjid (mosque) of Atlanta described this article as another instance of condemning the religion for what are basically cultural practices not prescribed by the Qur'an.

The Muslim community in Atlanta, which numbers around 30,000, is a diverse one, made up of such groups as black Americans and their children who have converted to Islam, American converts from other races, and immigrants who have came to Atlanta from around the world and practice various forms of the religion. There are Atlanta-area Muslims originally from the Middle East, Afghanistan, Pakistan, India, North Africa, Europe, Russia, and elsewhere. Some have come to the United States for school or work, and some have come as a result of political conflicts. For example, according to statistics from the Center for Applied Research in Anthropology at Georgia State University, there are approximately 2,000 Somalis, approximately 1,400 Afghanis, and at least 1,000 Iranians living in Atlanta, most of whom fled their homelands during times of social and political upheaval.

While African-American mosques in Atlanta were established in the late 1950s, the foreign-born Muslim population in the area has really flourished and become organized during the last 20 years. Tehmina, an Indian woman who came to Atlanta 28 years ago, remembers the days when there were no mosques for Sunni Muslims and no markets where properly prepared meat (*halaal*) was available for purchase. "We used to shop at the kosher markets, since kosher meats are prepared the same as *halaal*." Now there are several markets offering *halaal* food, and there are many formal and informal Muslim associations for groups from all over the world. The Al-Farooq Masjid, where more than 2,500 pray each week, and the Dar Un Noor School, with about 200 students from pre-K through 9th grade, are both located on 14th Street close to downtown. They serve Muslims from every corner of the globe, though most who attend are Sunni Muslims. Several smaller mosques around town are attended by specific communities, such as the Ismali Center, whose members are Muslims from Afghanistan, Iraq, Iran, and elsewhere.

There are two major divisions in Islam, the Sunni and the Shi'ah; in addition, there are different groups within each of these major denominations. Historically the divisions between Sunni and Shi'ah have been based on doctrinal issues as well as political and cultural differences. Iranians, who are Persians and primarily Shi'ah, are historically and culturally distinct from the Arabs in the Middle East, where Sunnis are often in the majority. In general, Iranians in Atlanta do not attend the Al-Farooq Masjid, except perhaps for funerals. A group of Shi'ah Muslims from Iran have recently formed a mosque called the Saheboczaman Islamic Center of Atlanta. Previously, members of this group gathered in each other's homes and at other locations for Friday prayers and to celebrate various religious holidays.

The rituals demanded by the religion can be practiced in the absence of a mosque. To be a faithful Muslim, one must follow the Qur'an and the *sunnah* (a set of established customs and practices), which denote normative behavior and are derived from the Prophet Muhammad's teaching and conduct. The term *islam* itself means "to surrender to God's law and thus be an integral whole," so a Muslim is one who surrenders. Like Christianity and Judaism, Islam recognizes the Prophet Abraham as a messenger of God. Jesus Christ is also recognized as a messenger, but not as the son of God. Muhammad, who was born in 570 CE in Mecca, is considered the final messenger of God, and the Qur'an records Muhammad's recitations and explicates for believers the correct way of life.

Islam is the second-largest religion worldwide, with more than a billion practitioners. It is also the fastest-growing religion in the world. Its appeal to converts throughout the world is certainly related to the social doctrine of

Atlanta Masjid of Al–Islam. Photgraph by Louis A. Ruprecht, Jr.

the Qur'an, which attempts to ameliorate the condition of the weak, and often abused, segments of society. The Qur'an proclaims the basic equality of all people and discounts ethnic differences. For example, it states: "O you people, we have created you from a male and a female, and we have made you into different nations and tribes [only] for the purpose of identification—otherwise, the noblest of you in the sight of God is the one who is the most righteous" (49:13).

The basic constituents of Islamic faith include belief in God, in angels, in revealed books, in God's messengers, and in the Last Day, or Judgment Day. The corresponding fivefold doctrine, or Five Pillars, instructs Muslims to perform specific acts. A Muslim should bear witness in public that "There is no god but Allah and Muhammad is his prophet." This statement is all that is required to become a Muslim. A second Pillar requires prayer five times a day while facing Mecca. Third, Muslims must pay *zakat* (tithes) to help support the needy. Fourth, Muslims are instructed to fast during the month of Ramadan, with no eating, drinking, smoking, or sexual intercourse from dawn until sunset. Finally, if possible, each Muslim should make a pilgrimage to the *ka'bah* in Mecca at least once during her or his lifetime. This pilgrimage should take place during the last ten days of the year, and is required only if one can afford the journey and leave enough provisions for one's family.

While Muslims are not required to pray at a mosque, many generally visit these sites of worship for Friday afternoon prayers (men more frequently than women). Obviously, it can be difficult for Muslims living in the United States to leave work on Friday afternoons, just as it can be a problem on other days of the week to break away from a meeting or leave class in order to pray. "Usually, it's people who work for themselves or schedule their own appointments who are able to attend Friday prayers. For those who work in production it's more difficult to attend," explains Obaid Rasoul, an Atlantan originally from Afghanistan. Muslims experience the basic difficulty that many foreigners encounter in having to adjust to the daily schedules and calendar of western countries.

Two major religious events enjoined by the Qur'an are celebrated in Atlanta as well as throughout the Muslim world. *'Id al-Adha* (Large Feast) takes place during the last lunar month and is a time of much festivity and giving. Every Muslim who can afford to is obliged to donate so that poorer people can also prepare for the celebration. The holiday recalls how, 4,000 years ago, Abraham sacrificed a ram after first offering his own son's life to God. In commemoration, each family sacrifices an animal, such as a goat or a ram, and distributes a portion of the meat to friends and the needy. In the United States, where licenses are needed to engage in this kind of activity, it is not possible to perform the actual sacrifice at home, so people make arrangements for a slaughterhouse to sacrifice an animal on their behalf.

The second major religious ceremony takes place during Ramadan, the month of fasting. Muslims describe the fast not as a chore but as a time of spiritual cleansing, a time to exercise discipline and generate strength to carry out duties for God. Elsewhere in the world, Muslim families celebrate the breaking of the fast each evening with special meals and visits with friends. In the United States, Muslim families try to maintain this tradition; however, with the hectic schedules that many have today, it is difficult to sustain this level of activity and communal solidarity throughout the month. The celebration of the end of Ramadan, called *'Id al-Fitr* (Feast of Fastbreaking), is a special event for all Muslims. Large groups of Sunni Muslims gather in a park or, in the case of rain, a large covered facility, for a day of prayers, feasting, and gift giving.

The beginning of Ramadan, like each month of the Islamic calendar, is reckoned from the appearance of the new moon that must, according to tradition, be reported by at least two trustworthy witnesses. Fasting does not actually begin until the moon has been sighted. For this reason, local weather conditions can cause the beginning of the month to be postponed. On February 20, 1993, for example, a group of men set out from Al-Farooq Masjid to sight the moon for the commencement of Ramadan. Because of cloud cover, they had to return the following night to identify the new moon before the month of fasting could begin. Likewise, the end of the fast does not occur until the sighting of the first moon of Shawwal, the month following Ramadan. Because of potential difficulties in planning for the feast celebrations at the end of Ramadan, some choose to follow the beginning and end of Ramadan as it occurs in such Islamic countries as Saudi Arabia or Pakistan.

Besides the two *'Ids* described above, another significant event in the Islamic calendar is the *hajj* (pilgrimage), which begins on the 10th day of the 12th month, Dhu al-Hijjah. According to dictates in the Qur'an, this is the time that is set aside for pilgrimage to Mecca. While only a small percentage of the world's Muslim population journeys to Mecca each year, all are aware of the occasion, which is one expression of the unity of Muslims everywhere. Often, those who are leaving for the *hajj* are recognized before their departure and after their return with a gathering of family and friends, with Qur'anic recitations, prayers, and special foods. Another significant holiday in the Islamic calendar is *12 Rabi'ah al-Awwal*, the day of the Prophet's birth. Images of the Prophet are not part of Islamic worship, and he is honored as a messenger of God rather than as a divine figure. Special poems in his honor may be recited in people's homes or at the mosque.

In addition, Shi'ah Muslims in Atlanta as well as in other parts of the world recognize a number of birth dates of religious leaders and days of mourning. The 15th of Shaban, which is the birthdate of the Twelfth or "Hidden" imam, is celebrated in Iran with firecrackers and great festivity—in the words of one American Muslim, "just as the fourth of July is celebrated here." The first ten days of the month of Muharram are also especially important to the Shi'ah. The tenth of Muharram, which is called *Ashura,* is associated with the death of Muhammad's grandson, Husayn ibn 'Ali, who was killed in the Battle of Karbala on 10 Muharram 81 AH (After Hejira—Hejira referring to Muhammed's emigration from Medina to Mecca).

Muslims also find other occasions to get together besides religious holidays. For Iranians, the New Year celebration called *No Rooz* is a special time for families. An assemblage of objects symbolizing a new beginning are placed on a table (called the *haft-sin*) in the home along with a copy of the Qur'an. The Persian Community Center also holds a celebration with an elaborately decorated *haft-sin* table. For immigrants from Pakistan, the celebration of their national independence in August is a day to get together with fellow nationals and with other Muslims. Members of the Pakistan Society of Atlanta celebrate the national independence of their homeland with a picnic at Buford Dam Park. Several years ago, they were joined by a handful of Muslims who were not from Pakistan but from India, suggesting that their affiliation as fellow Muslims and friends is a strong one that can transcend national identities.

Like foreign-born Muslims living in the United States who are victims of prejudice perpetuated by the media and the general public, African-American Muslims are frequently misunderstood in American society as well. People often associate all African-American Muslims with the highly politicized Nation of Islam, which in fact represents only a small minority in the black Muslim religious community. The Nation of Islam, founded in the 1930s, was popularized by Elijah Muhammed. A small segment of that original group is now led by Louis Farrakhan. But Elijah Muhammed's son, Warith Deen Muhammad, has led the majority of his father's community into mainstream Islam. A mosque of the Nation of Islam was established in Atlanta in 1957 and became a center of black Muslim activity for the southeast. It was visited frequently by Malcolm X, who served as Elijah Muhammed's chief assistant, and by other black activists during the 1960s.

Many American-born Muslims who have converted to Islam were inspired by Malcolm X and the Civil Rights movement. Like Malcolm X, who eventually rejected the Nation of Islam, the majority of converts have become drawn to Islam in its orthodox form. *American Jihad: Islam after Malcolm X* explores this movement through the stories of a variety of converts. Steven Barboza writes in the introduction:

> Where Islam was once used by some as a platform from which to espouse racist ideology in the United States, it now promotes brotherhood with few exceptions. And where orthodoxy was once limited principally to immigrants, it has opened its ranks to those born in America. Eighty-five to 90 percent of American converts are black, and the vast majority of both blacks and whites now appear to want an Islam of broader scope, an Islam grounded in history or in the capacity to inspire a sense of personal rebirth.

Atlanta's Community Mosque of the West End is led by Jamil Abdullah Al-Amin, formerly known as H. Rap Brown, who worked as a black activist during the 1960s and converted to Islam while in prison. As quoted in *American Jihad*, Al-Amin remarks: "I think everybody who was in the [Civil Rights] movement during that particular time to some degree was upset and perturbed and angry. Islam enables you and it teaches you not to be controlled or to do things out of anger." He describes one of the basic principles of Islam, *jihad*, meaning struggle, in the following way: "The Islamic movement itself is built upon that level of consciousness concerning struggle, so again the difference in my struggling in terms of the movement during [the 1960s] was that it was a struggle that was not based upon sound guidelines and principles." Today, Al-Amin preaches discipline through prayer, fasting, charity, and steadfastness.

The vast majority of African-American Muslims in Atlanta practice Sunni Islam in a manner similar to fellow Muslims throughout the world, and their agenda is not politically charged. Ibrahim Pasha, assistant imam of the Mosque of Al-Islam in southwest Atlanta, explains that his relationship with Atlanta's Temple #15 (of the Nation of Islam) is cordial, but they are not closely aligned. Al-Islam is more closely associated with Sunni organizations in a worldwide network. Founded in 1965, this mosque of 1,300 families (mostly African-American) participates in local clerical and social service organizations and runs a school of 300 students, making it the second-largest Islamic school in the country.

The Muslim population of Atlanta is growing not only as new immigrants make their homes in the area, but also as greater numbers of American-born citizens decide to convert and have children who are raised according to the teachings of the Islamic religion. It is incumbent upon the general public to acquire more balanced perceptions about this faith, which is clearly shaping the lives of many in the Atlanta area, in the United States, and in the world. As Muslims in Atlanta preserve these teachings in a variety of ways, they also contribute to the richness and vitality of the city in their day-to-day lives.

FOR FURTHER INFORMATION

Steven Barboza. *American Jihad: Islam after Malcolm X.* New York, Doubleday, 1993

Norman Daniel. *Islam and the West: The Making of an Image.* Oxford, Oneworld Publications, Ltd., 1960, 1993

Mircea Eliade, ed. *Encyclopedia of World Religions.* New York, MacMillan; see entries under "Ashura," "Islam: An Overview," "Islamic Religious Year," "Sunnah," "Shiism," and others.

John L. Esposito. *Islam: The Straight Path.* New York, Oxford University Press, 1991

Margaret Read MacDonald, ed. *The Folklore of World Holidays.* Detroit, Gale Research, Inc., 1992

Al-Hajj Wali Muhammad. *Muslims in Georgia: A Chronology & Oral History.* Fayetteville, The Brandon Institute, 1994

Adib Rashad. *The History of Islam and Black Nationalism in the Americas.* Beltsville, Writers' Inc., 1985

CHAPTER SIXTEEN

HINDU COMMUNITIES IN ATLANTA

Renee Bhatia
Ajit Bhatia

Tower at the Hindu Riverdale Temple. Photograph by Elizabeth Hardcastle.

There are now approximately 13,000 Indians (sometimes called Asian Indians) living in Atlanta and the surrounding suburbs. As the numbers continue to grow because of increased immigration, the presence of Indian ethnic and religious activities becomes more prominent in the metro area. The most visible aspect of their presence in Atlanta is related to the many Indian restaurants and the several strip malls that contain Indian shops selling imported foods, clothing, and music. Although it is difficult to separate Indian culture from religion, the largest religious group originating in India are the Hindus, who now constitute a thriving community taking care of their own spiritual needs in this city (there are other religious groups from India here as well, including Jains, Sikhs, and Christians).

But what exactly is Hinduism? The Random House dictionary defines Hinduism as "the common religion of India based upon the religion of the original Aryan settlers as expounded and evolved in the Vedas, the Upanishads, the Bhagavad-Gita, etc., having an extremely diversified character with many schools of philosophy and theology, many popular cults, and a large pantheon symbolizing the many attributes of a single god." Other definitions of Hinduism take a negative approach, defining Hinduism by what it is *not*—such as that religion indigenous to India and practiced there that is not otherwise designated as Buddhist, Jain, Sikh, Christian, Muslim, etc. Neither definition seems to make Hinduism any clearer. Instead of attempting to define Hinduism, it is more useful to point to some patterns of practice and belief found in various Hindu communities in Atlanta that will provide a greater understanding of this complex, multifaceted religion.

Hinduism is often described as a polytheistic religion, since there are many gods with different names that are found in a variety of myths. Some of the major deities include Brahma, the creator god, Vishnu, the preserver, Shiva, the destroyer, and the goddess (Devi). Of these, Vishnu and Shiva are the most commonly worshiped. While there are thousands of other gods, Hindus also often assert that there is really only one God; the Hindu worldview argues that we see distinctions in this world in our imperfect state, but in the ultimate reality God, and even our various human souls, are one.

Hindus come together for worship in temples dedicated to particular gods. There is no set day of the week considered sacred by Hindus. Rather there are *pujas*, or worship services, in which the gods are displayed. The gods in Hindu temples take on human forms, so they must be bathed, dressed, and fed, and they even need time to "sleep." When they are sleeping, a curtain generally covers the images and worshipers cannot see them. An important element in Hindu rituals then is *darshan*, or "seeing" the gods. Hindus go to the temple for *darshan*, for catching a glimpse of the divinity when the deities are unveiled. In addition, devotees come to the temple bringing offerings, often of fruit or other food for the gods. In return they receive *prasad*, or a food offering back from God. It is essential to take one's shoes off when entering a Hindu temple because it is considered holy ground and shoes would bring in contamination from the world outside. In fact, many devout Hindu homes also have rooms set aside with little shrines, and shoes must be removed before entering these rooms.

A BRIEF HISTORY OF HINDUS IN ATLANTA

The last thirty years have seen a large increase in the number of immigrants from India, and as a result activities within the Hindu religious community have become more organized and diverse. But in the early years when there was only a small number of Hindus in Atlanta, steps were taken to bring members of this group together. The first gathering of Hindu communities dates back to the 1960s. These gatherings often took place in Atlanta universities. Georgia Tech, for example, had an India Club that became the focus for Hindu cultural life in the late 1960s. This group was primarily made up of male graduate students from India, many of whom were homesick and longed for some form of contact with their culture. Often students would host cultural events, such as *Diwali* (Festival of Lights, the Hindu New Year celebration), and members from the community at large would participate.

In the late 60s and early 70s, with changes in American immigration law that permitted larger numbers of Indians to settle here and bring their families, Indians began to spread out across the city; they tended to gather around the student population and develop close ties because of their small numbers. While many of the new Indian immigrants were successful professionals, there emerged a need to create a well-rounded organization for the growing Hindu community. One such organization was the India American Cultural Association (IACA), which formed in 1975. This group planned events, celebrated festivals, and became a nucleus for Indian cultural and Hindu religious activity. In 1983 the IACA purchased a center that continues to serve as a place for diverse cultural, as well as religious, activities in the Indian community. The IACA has always encouraged religious diversity, and has tried to promote good relations among the numerous cultural and religious communities that have links to India—the Indian community in the metro area reflects the diversity of Indian society.

While Atlanta now has several temples, it is important to remember that Hindu forms of worship do not always take place there. Many religious practices occur in the home. Several Indian families in Atlanta have shrines in their homes, often in the form of pictures and *murtis* (images) of different deities. The construction of temples grew more out of the desire for communal gathering among Atlanta's Hindus than from a sense of religious urgency. As Dr. Venugopal Rao, an Emory University professor of physics and significant contributor to the early gatherings of Hindus in Atlanta, put it: "We were all being good Hindus before the temples were built in this country." But Hindu temples have been, and continue to be built. They serve a critical religious and communal purpose for Atlanta's Hindus and, along with other places for spiritual expression, capture the vibrant and multilayered dimensions of this rapidly growing community.

There are four major communal centers of Hindu activity in Atlanta that will be addressed in this essay: 1) the Hindu temple in Riverdale; 2) the IACA and the India Cultural and Religious Center (ICRC); 3) the Hare Krishna temple; and 4) the center for the Eternal Quest. These centers certainly do not exhaust the range of religious options for Indian immigrants. There are other groups representing different regions of India such as the Gujarati Samaj, the Bengali Association, the Georgia Tamil Sangam, the Sindhi Association, the Maharashtra Mandal, the Telegu Association, and the Malayali Association, to name a few. These groups are both cultural and religious organizations, and there are others such as the Vishwa Hindu Parishad and the Swaminarayans that are primarily religious in nature. The four centers discussed here are just a sampling of Hindu organizations in metropolitan Atlanta.

THE HINDU TEMPLE OF ATLANTA IN RIVERDALE

The seeds for building a new Hindu temple in Riverdale were planted in the minds of five physicians in the 1970s. They began discussions about constructing a Sri Venkateshwara (a form of the god Vishnu) temple in Atlanta to fill a void in the Hindu community. At the time, the only temple for Hindu worship was the International Society for Krishna Consciousness (ISKCON) temple, also known as the Hare Krishna temple, on Ponce de Leon. Dr. B. K. Mohan, a local cardiologist and one of the founding fathers of the Riverdale temple, remembers fondly: "Naive as we were, we thought that we could do it with about $100,000, land, and a small temple." All the money bought was a five acre plot in Riverdale, in Atlanta's south metro area. It became clear that additional funding, somewhere around $450,000, would be required to get started. In 1983 the planning group had expanded to fifteen, who then began a fund-raising drive to obtain additional financial support. The temple construction finally began in 1986 and is occurring in several stages, beginning with the internal temple shell followed by the temple walls, tower, and entrance.

The architectural style of the temple resembles that of the famous temple built to honor Sri Venkateshwara at Tirupti in South India. Situated on Georgia's state highway 316, the temple is an imposing structure, perched high upon a hill. Signs of ongoing construction are ubiquitous, but the temple's majesty is already unmistakable. Amidst the chaos of construction, a concrete staircase leads up to the first floor, which houses the temple's main auditorium. This cavernous room is often used for discussions, *pujas*, general meetings, and as a lecture hall for religious or cultural speakers all year round. Another staircase leads up to the second floor. This is the central sanctuary where the main deities reside. The primary deity in the center is that of Sri Venkateshwara, also known as Balaji (Vishnu). In a room recessed from the main hall the arresting and alluring dark image of Sri Venkateshwara is resplendent in fine clothes and adorned with garlands of flowers. The image is flanked by Sri Padmavathi (a form of Vishnu's consort) on the left and Sri Andel (Mother Earth) on the right. To the left of the main wall is a shrine for Durga Mata (a form of Shiva's consort), and the Navagrihas (the Nine planets, which are worshiped as gods in Indian mythology) to the right. In between Sri Padmavathi and Sri Venkateshwara is a shrine for Sri Ganesha (the elephant-head god). The images of Sri Satyanarayana (another form of Vishnu) and Sri Lakshmi (another form of Vishnu's consort) are in between Sri Venkateshwara and Sri Andel. When construction is finished, the main deities will be surrounded by the ten incarnations of Vishnu carved on pillars that encircle the central sanctuary.

The variety of deities helps to broaden the appeal of the temple and draws worshipers from around the southeastern United States, thus fulfilling the original hope of founders and supporters. The temple serves as a natural magnet for local Hindus on holidays, weekends, and major religious festivals, bringing the community together for worship and social gatherings. On worship, Dr. Mohan commented: "There is a saying that if you pray in your home, you are praying for yourself, it is like lighting a small lamp in your room, making you see [around] your confines; when you pray in the temple, it is like the sun itself lighting the whole place. The difference between prayer at home and in the temple is very simple: at home one is very self-centered and very focal, whereas prayer in the temple is very universal."

The temple has three full-time priests (*pujaris*) who perform all the rituals, *pujas,* and celebrations for the deities on a daily basis and during major religious festivals. *Puja,* as mentioned earlier, is often performed by a trained Hindu priest, reciting texts in Sanskrit for various occasions such as weddings (*Vivah*), the blessing of a new home (*Grihapravesh* or *Grihavastu*), or for good fortune in business in the coming year (*Lakshmi Puja*), and success in a new venture or passing through a crisis (*Satyanarayana Puja*). Some *pujas* are performed in the temple with a large gathering, as in the case of celebrating the Birth of Lord Krishna (*Janamashtami*).

The Riverdale temple is in its final stage of construction. Skilled Indian artisans (*silpis*) have been commissioned to individually carve the hundreds of intricate images that will adorn the external walls and the temple tower. These master sculptors have almost completed carving the ten incarnations of Vishnu (Dasavartar) on pillars that encircle the central sanctuary housing the main deities. The consecration and dedication of the temple (*Kumbhabhishek*) is scheduled for mid-1996.

THE INDIA AMERICAN CULTURAL ASSOCIATION AND THE INDIA CULTURAL AND RELIGIOUS CENTER

The IACA, mentioned earlier in this chapter, was originally incorporated in the 1970s to support the Indian Red Cross in their efforts during the Indo-Pakistan War that created the independent nation of Bangladesh. In 1975, the IACA's mission was broadened and formalized to promote Indian culture and improve relations between Americans and Indians in Atlanta. At that time, there was no center to house the IACA and help it meet its objectives in promoting Indian culture, so a fundraising drive was organized for the establishment of such a center. The pioneers of the IACA wished to purchase a building where a wide mix of Indian cultural programs could be offered to the public. They wanted the center to be located in an easily accessible area in metro Atlanta that could serve as a communal gathering place for all Indians. In 1984, the IACA purchased property situated on Cooper Lake Road in Smyrna, a suburb in northwestern metro Atlanta—property once owned by a Pentecostal church.

The Indian and American flags fly in front of the main entrance of the IACA, a testament to the commitment to promoting Indo-American relations. Entering through its large glass doors, one immediately sees what used to be the Pentecostal church's worship hall or sanctuary, which contained the traditional altar and baptismal font. After the church was purchased in 1984, the altar and the font were replaced by a large stage and a seating area for 200 people. On the walls encircling the hall are pictures and images from India. The auditorium, equipped with a full-featured sound system, hosts many of the center's religious and cultural activities. Events such as popular Hindi plays, regional spelling bee contests, classical music and dance performances, and the annual General Body Meeting are some of the activities held here; annual religious festivals, religious discussions, and sometimes even weddings are some of the more sacred functions that take place in the center.

Some of the IACA's most popular events are the annual *Mela* (festival) celebrating India's independence from British rule, the Beauty Pageant that has sent many of its winners to national and international events, and an annual banquet that features an elaborate dinner, dancing, member recognition, and celebrity speeches. The center's auditorium is also made available to various local Indian organizations for hosting their individual events and functions. Now 500 families strong, the IACA's functions are organized with the aim of fostering community solidarity and cohesion as well as raising cultural awareness among the Indian population in Atlanta. These events broaden support for the center and help it raise revenues needed for day-to-day operations.

The center also has a large hall upstairs that has been renovated to serve as a temple room for Hindu worship, the India Cultural and Religious Center (ICRC). The establishment of the temple on the premises of a secular cultural facility raised important questions for the community about the relation of Indian culture to religion. Some of the original supporters who provided funding for the IACA took the view that even though it was primarily a cultural center, there would be various rooms that would be used as temporary worship sites for various Indian groups, such as Sikhs, Jains, and

Christians. Others were opposed to the idea of having any religious facility at all. Amidst much discussion and argument it was decided that since Indian religion and culture are very much intertwined and non-exclusive, the IACA could have an area set aside for worship. The first proposal was that of a Hindu temple, and the ICRC was born.

The ICRC temple is in a large hall on the second floor of the center. Various images of deities *(murtis)* are enclosed in a large glass area that surrounds them from three sides, with the front remaining open. The glass area is situated away from the walls to allow circumambulation *(parikrama)* of the deities, an important temple ritual. All of the images in the ICRC were imported from India in 1986. The glass case contains images of Ganesha, Shiva-Parvati, Radha-Krishna, Venkateshwara, Rama-Sita-Hanuman, Durga Mata, Bala Krishna, and the Shiva Lingam, all popular deities worshiped throughout India. A Jain image of Sri Mahavira was also added to this sanctuary of Hindu deities. The temple has one priest, Pundit Vishnu Bhatt, who also serves as the IACA's caretaker.

Regular activities conducted at the ICRC temple include *Satyanarayan katha* (a prayer ceremony of thanksgiving) on the second Sunday of the month, *bhajans* (devotional songs or hymns) on the first Sunday, and a lecture or discourse on the Bhagavad Gita (one of the Hindu sacred texts) on the third Sunday of the month. Worship of the images *(puja)* is conducted daily at 7 in the evening and the *arati* (prayer and fire offering) is conducted at 12 noon every Sunday. During the *arati* the deities are worshiped with the chanting of Sanskrit verses *(slokas)* and the singing of *bhajans*. At the end of the *arati* and *puja* ceremonies, the priest distributes food that has been blessed by God *(prasad)* to all present. The temple also celebrates major Hindu festivals such as *Janmashtami* (Krishna's birthday), *Diwali* (Festival of Lights), and *Shivratri* (Shiva's prayer or celebration).

THE HARE KRISHNA TEMPLE

On almost any afternoon, in a large old house on South Ponce de Leon Avenue, one can hear drums, tambourines, and singing from the Hare Krishna Temple. The temple, now located in Decatur, was the first Hindu site of worship to be built in Atlanta. The Hare Krishna movement came to Atlanta in the early 1970s, when an Emory student began having gatherings in his dormitory room. While the first center started on Juniper Street in downtown Atlanta in 1975, the community soon became big enough to purchase the building at its current location.

The Hare Krishna movement, also known as the International Society for Krishna Consciousness (ISKCON), was started in India by Swami Pradhupada Bhaktivedanta, who brought his form of ecstatic Krishna devotion to the United States in 1966. The movement grew rapidly, recruiting mostly American followers who adopted a strict practice of worship, education, communal living, and stringent vegetarian diets. Initially the Hare Krishna community had only modest appeal to South Asian Hindus, many of whom regarded it with ambivalence. Hare Krishnas worship Krishna, an incarnation of Vishnu, and they are characterized by a more charismatic style of worship than other Hindu groups. As in other Hindu temples, the deities in Hare Krishna temples have to be dressed, bathed, and fed seven times a day. When the deities are revealed and the people come to see the image, or have *darshan*, the worship becomes lively and joyous, with the participants singing and dancing in ecstatic delight. This differs greatly from the more formal style one sees in the Hindu Temple in Riverdale.

The Hare Krishna temple in Atlanta now has several resident priests who oversee the daily *pujas* and operation of the temple. According to one priest, while there are only about forty members who have taken formal initiation into the community, there are approximately nine hundred families who visit the temple with some regularity. An initiated member formally places her or himself under the authority and leadership of a spiritual mentor (*guru*), and often receives a new name. When the Hare Krishna temple moved to its present location, there were approximately eighty initiated members living communally in the temple. The Hare Krishna community, however, has encouraged these and other members to live in the secular world if they can support themselves, so today there are only twenty-seven people living in the temple, including four children.

As in other parts of the United States, the Hare Krishna movement in Atlanta began as an idealistic, countercultural phenomenon. Although the movement began in this manner, the ethnic makeup of the community has since diversified. In the early 1970s ninety percent of the devotees in Atlanta were white Americans. Native-born South Asian Hindu participation especially increased in 1975, when the temple brought over the Jagannath *murtis*, a form of Krishna worshiped in Orissa, India. Today sixty-five to seventy percent of the worshipers are from the Indian community, and the temple remains a primary place for Krishna devotees to worship.

In addition to the daily *puja* and the Sunday worship, the Hare Krishna temple resembles traditionally American religious communities in providing

Celebration of Krishna's Birthday at the India Cultural and Religious Center. Photograph by Elizabeth Turk. Courtesy of the Atlanta History Center.

outreach programs such as food distribution, counseling, and interfaith activities. The temple also operates a gift shop and a restaurant on its premises. One of the temple priests suggests that the Hare Krishna temple is a great resource for the Atlanta community. It offers what he calls "authentic Vedic culture" and shows Atlantans another slice of Indian religious life. He says Atlanta has been good to the Hare Krishnas, and they try to give something back with the services they provide.

THE CENTER OF THE ETERNAL QUEST

The Eternal Quest was formed in Atlanta in the late 1960s. At that time it was called the Vedanta Society of Atlanta and was part of a movement that began in India in the late nineteenth century under the spiritual leadership of Swami Vivekananda, who was from Calcutta. Calcutta was a cosmopolitan city, and Vivekananda found himself surrounded by religious diversity. He was a Hindu, but he believed that all religions worship the same god under different names and forms. Vivekananda visited the United States in 1893 and participated in the Parliament of World Religions. He toured the country and spread his message, which led to the formation of many Vedanta societies in major American cities. These societies study the Hindu tradition primarily in terms of its philosophical, theological, and ethical teachings.

The Eternal Quest began in Atlanta as an off-shoot of a Chicago Vedanta Society when a *swami* (holy man or priest) from Chicago came to Atlanta and gave talks and retreats. In 1979 the Atlanta group meeting as the Vedanta Society raised enough money to get a resident *swami*. In 1981 the second resident *swami*, Swami Yogeshananda came to Atlanta and remains the current spiritual leader today.

In 1992 Swami Yogeshananda changed the name from the Vedanta Society of Atlanta to the Eternal Quest. The name was changed because several people did not know what the Vedanta Society was, and many misspelled and mispronounced it. (It was often referred to as the Vendetta Society!) "Eternal Quest" was considered an English equivalent. This also suggests that the primary target audience of Eternal Quest is American rather than Indian. The center now has a total of about forty members, about the same number of people it had in the 1980s. Then it was mostly Indian; now it is mostly American.

Located in Decatur, just east of the downtown Atlanta area, the Eternal Quest resides in an old house that has been converted into a religious center. The center has a room for communal gathering, a library, and a meditation room. The meditation room is treated like a Hindu temple, and devotees are asked to take their shoes off before entering. Inside the meditation room the altar reflects the ecumenical spirit of Vivekananda. On the altar are images of Ganesha and the Shiva Lingam, and there are plans to soon acquire an image of Krishna as well. Above the altar is the sign of the *OM* or *AUM*—the symbol of Hinduism—and pictures of Ganesha, the Buddha, Jesus, Swami Vivekananda, and Ramakrishna and Devi (the Holy Mother, wife of Ramakrishna), Vivekananda's gurus. The Eternal Quest encourages dialogue between faiths, and Swami Yogeshananda speaks frequently to other religious communities. The center also encourages social outreach, and is involved in programs such as AID Atlanta, volunteering at Cafe 458 (a center that feeds and supports homeless recovering addicts), and tutoring at local low-income housing projects. The future of Eternal Quest looks bright as Atlanta continues to grow and develop. Swami Yogeshananda thinks Atlanta is becoming a cosmopolitan city like San Francisco and Washington, DC, and hopes this center in Atlanta will soon be one of the Vedanta Society's permanent centers.

CONCLUSION

While there is diversity within the Hindu communities of Atlanta, there are efforts to bring these communities together with others that have strong ties to the immigrant Indian populations. Organizations such as the Federation of Indian Associations (FIA) are trying to unite the various Indian cultural and religious organizations not only in Atlanta, but nationwide. Their goal is to create one umbrella organization that would serve the social, political, cultural, and religious interests of Indian Americans. There is a strong resistance to this, however, since many organizations see themselves as distinct and would rather remain independent than unite on such a large scale.

A significant factor contributing to the growth of religious institutions and organizations is the strong desire among first-generation Hindus to carry forward a viable Indian identity and instill cultural and religious values among their children, who are growing up in American culture. Indian parents recognize the difficulties associated with teaching Hindu traditions and values to their children, who become steeped in American culture from their earliest years. For example, first-generation Hindus lived in a society that regarded dating and marrying outside the tradition as taboo. Conversely, for second- and third-generation Indian Americans, freedom to choose whom to date and marry is an integral part of courtship in this country, much to the chagrin of their parents. Parents recognize this cultural change as an inevitable yet undesirable part of rearing children in the United States.

Indian-American children are faced with a difficult challenge because they are often torn between wanting to please their parents and feeling a strong attachment to American customs and attitudes. Many Hindu children lament the fact that their parents would like them to marry within their caste, or at the very least another Hindu, and abstain from dating. While some children acquiesce to their parents' wishes, many find ways of getting around these restrictions, even if it means creating domestic friction. Disagreements over such issues as dating and marriage are countered by numerous areas of agreement, including the emphasis placed on close family ties, education, ambition, and financial success. The initial momentum created by the first generation has been passed on to subsequent generations, which seem committed to keeping alive Hindu identity in Atlanta. The longing for a distinctive Hindu identity, along with the inevitable transformation of Atlanta into a major international, social, and cultural hub, will continue to nourish a vital and diverse Hindu presence here.

FOR FURTHER INFORMATION

John Fenton. *Transplanting Religious Traditions: Asian Indians in America*. New York, Praeger, 1988

Thomas J. Hopkins. *The Hindu Religious Tradition*. Belmont, Wadsworth, 1971

E. Burke Rochford, Jr. *Hare Krishna in America*. New Brunswick, Rutgers University Press, 1985

Parmatma Saran and Edwin Eames. *The New Ethnics: Asian Indians in the United States*. New York, Praeger, 1980

Raymond Williams. *Religions of Immigrants from India and Pakistan: New Threads in the American Tapestry*. New York, Cambridge University Press, 1988

C H A P T E R   S E V E N T E E N

A GLOBAL RELIGION: THE RISE OF BUDDHISM AND ITS GROWTH IN ATLANTA

Eric Riles

Vietnamese celebration of the Buddha's Birthday, Grant Park, 1993. Photograph by Elizabeth Turk. Courtesy of the Atlanta History Center.

Buddhism originated in India around 500 BCE with relatively few followers, but in time the religion grew in numbers and eventually spread in influence throughout the world. Despite the fact that several hundred years after its founding the religion had all but disappeared from India, the teachings of the Buddha have reached a worldwide audience. Today, there are over 250 million Buddhists around the globe. They are found primarily in Asia, where Buddhism has attained a solid foothold in such countries as Tibet, Thailand, China, Korea, and Japan.

Another area where Buddhism has found a particularly receptive audience is the United States. Asians have immigrated here in large numbers during this century and, consequently, the Buddhist religion has become one of the fastest-growing religions in America. Although it has become quite popular, Buddhism is still considered to be in its early stages in this country, with a membership of about five million people. It is expected to become more prominent in the decades to come as larger numbers of Americans of European descent turn to Buddhist practices and teachings, and as increasing numbers of immigrants from Asia arrive in the United States. Many of these immigrants are settling in and around major urban centers; in the southeast, metro Atlanta has become one of the most common destinations for newly-arriving Buddhist immigrants. While Buddhist religious communities throughout the country contain a variety of ethnic groups from around the world, a substantial number of individuals who frequent Buddhist temples and centers are American-born and come out of Christian or Jewish traditions.

HISTORICAL BACKGROUND

The history of Buddhism begins with Siddhartha Gautama, a prince who was born in the sixth century BCE in what is now the northern part of India. According to Buddhist tradition, Gautama lived the typical life of a prince; he was married and resided in splendor in his father's kingdom. When he was in his mid-thirties, a radical change in Gautama occurred after he saw four different examples of the human condition—a sick person, an old person, a corpse, and an ascetic, who had renounced the pleasures of everyday life.

The first three sights convinced the prince that the world was full of suffering, so he decided to follow the path of the ascetic. Gautama abandoned his previous existence as a prince and took up the life of a wandering holy man.

After a period of fasting, Gautama was near starvation and realized that the mere denial of pleasures and physical well-being did not grant him the release from suffering that he was seeking. This discovery led him to choose a more balanced discipline called the Middle Path, characterized by neither pain nor pleasure. By following this Middle Path, Gautama still accepted a life of disciplined asceticism, but he avoided extremes of indulgence or of self-denial. Gautama's wanderings finally led him to the Bodhi tree, where he sat meditating for many days, searching for the secret of liberation from the cycle of birth, death, rebirth, and suffering. As he sat in meditation, he finally experienced enlightenment. Gautama realized that he had discovered the meaning of life and a way to live that could bring freedom from suffering. The key to such a life was breaking through the attachments the mind has to pleasure and fear, and instead cultivating the ability to live freely in the immediacy of the moment. He understood that all experience is in constant flux, and that non-attachment brings true freedom.

Once the Buddha had experienced this awakening, he continued to wander, observing the world around him. He decided to spend his time teaching people how to gain release from their attachments to worldly pleasures and anxieties, and how to attain the state of enlightenment he had achieved under the Bodhi tree. For the remainder of his life, the Buddha gathered around himself communities of monks, and taught people from all walks of life. From this point Buddhism began to spread in India and into other areas of Asia through sermons given by the Buddha and through the formation of an order of monks who followed and learned from him. By the seventh century Buddhism was quite strong in India, but a decline occurred in the following centuries because of invading forces and the different religions of those groups. Because of the patronage of merchant communities, the work of the Buddha's followers continued, spreading his teachings to people throughout Southeast Asia, Tibet, China, and Japan.

BASIC TENETS AND BELIEFS OF BUDDHIST TEACHINGS

There has always been a fair amount of regional variation in the Buddhist religion as a result of its global expansion. There are, however, three major branches of the religion that have been identified by Buddhist scholars. Theravada Buddhism, also called the Path of the Elders, is the most conservative in nature. It emphasizes monasticism and is most prevalent in Sri Lanka and Southeast Asia. The scriptures of Theravada Buddhism have been preserved in Pali texts, the original language of the Buddha. The second branch, Mahayana Buddhism, spread primarily to East Asia, particularly China, Korea, and Japan. Its scriptures were recorded first in Sanskrit, and then translated into Chinese, and include the *Lotus Sutra* and the *Perfection of Wisdom Sutra*. The Zen school, which focuses on clearing the mind through meditation, is also part of Mahayana Buddhism. The third branch is Vajrayana Buddhism, which is found primarily in Tibet. This school focuses on the concept of compassion and emphasizes meditation. Its influence has been especially profound in the United States because it has attracted an intellectual group of American believers and because the Dalai Lama (the spiritual leader of Tibet) has participated in many religious seminars in America over the past 40 years.

The three branches of Buddhism interpret many of the Buddha's teachings in different ways, but they all share a common commitment to the doctrine of the Four Noble Truths, the cornerstone of Buddhist thought and practice. The truths are associated with the Buddha's awakening experience under the Bodhi tree. The first truth is that suffering exists. Suffering, or *dukkha,* is an existential condition, and a broader meaning for the word must be explained in order to understand how the Buddha defined it. Essentially, life itself—birth, aging, sorrow, pain, despair—is suffering. The happiness that we may experience is only transitory, but pain and sorrow are constantly around us. However, *dukkha* is translated in other ways as well—sometimes referring to the discomfort and irritation that characterizes life. Suffering in this complete definition is wholly integrated into the human experience. If suffering is indeed at the foundation of the human experience, what could be its cause? How did it arise?

The second truth explains the cause of suffering. The Buddha taught that suffering arose out of people's desires and cravings. Desires are often considered to be associated with sensual pleasure, but the Buddha also included in his definition a desire for escape from what is unpleasant. Thus, according to Buddhist philosophy, people are constantly craving things—sensory pleasures, material items, and escape from pain and unpleasant situations.

The third truth posits that suffering can be transcended. A person can achieve freedom and release from suffering through the voluntary alteration of attitudes and behaviors, which is a twofold process. First, one must recognize the existence of suffering, as it is explained in the Four Noble Truths. Second, cravings can be controlled and transformed through a disciplinary process explained by the Buddha in the fourth truth.

The fourth truth describes how suffering may be overcome. There are three primary components of this process: morality, meditation, and wisdom. Morality includes a truthful and disciplined method of living life. It could also be described as simply treating others with dignity, respect, and kindness, as you yourself would want to be treated. Through meditation, one is able to focus on overcoming desires, refraining from harming others, and trying to live a moral, compassionate life. Meditation also allows one to achieve clarity of mind and awareness of actions and their consequences, thus enabling one to do good and to live life according to Buddhist morality.

The third part of the process to end suffering is the acquisition of wisdom, which is essential because it allows one to see the world as it truly is and to live in accordance with the Four Noble Truths. A new frame of mind develops and, combined with the power of meditation, one can stand apart from the experiences of the world. Observation is a critical component of this process; through wisdom, one is able to observe desires and pleasures yet resist the temptation to pursue them.

BUDDHISM IN ATLANTA

The history of Buddhism in the Atlanta area, as in the United States as a whole, is difficult to trace. Many Buddhists in North America cite Chicago's 1893 World's Parliament of Religions, a major gathering of clergy and laity from religions across the globe, as a critical turning point in the history of Buddhism on this continent. At this conference, a group of Theravada monks spoke of the historical significance of the Buddha. In addition to introducing the philosophical principles of the religion to Americans, this conference marked the first time that a group of Buddhists had been popularly received in the United States. While Buddhism has been present on the religious landscape since then, it was not until the 1970s that Buddhism became much stronger as an organized religious tradition in American society.

Until fairly recently, Buddhism was relatively unknown in Atlanta to people outside of the small Asian communities in the area. In the past fifteen to twenty years, however, Buddhism has become more visible in metropolitan Atlanta. There are two main reasons for this growing visibility. First,

Atlanta has become an attractive location for Buddhist immigrants arriving in the country from Southeast Asia and China because of the economic opportunities that are available here. Many Buddhists arrived as refugees beginning in the late 1970s from Vietnam, Laos, and Cambodia following the war in Indochina. Second, a growing number of non-Asian Americans in Atlanta view Buddhism as an attractive alternative to the more mainstream and well-established religions in this country. It is clear that the number of Buddhists in metro Atlanta will grow as the city's international connections expand and as more people embark on spiritual paths that just a few decades ago were practically unknown in the southern United States.

In 1993, the Center for Applied Research in Anthropology at Georgia State University estimated that there were approximately 10,000 Buddhists in the Atlanta metropolitan area. In 1995, estimated immigrant populations from Southeast and East Asia include the following: Thai, 1,400; Cambodian, 6,200; Lao, 8,200; Vietnamese, 10,200; Chinese, 10,500; and Korean, 13,100. Given the fact that a significant percentage of Thai, Cambodian, Laotian, and Vietnamese refugees practice Buddhism, the estimate for the total number of practicing Buddhists in Atlanta is probably on the conservative side. On the other hand, some of the immigrant groups also have ties to Christian churches. For example, a large number of Koreans and Chinese are Christians, and some of the Laotian, Cambodian, and Vietnamese refugees were sponsored by Christian churches, leading many of them to join the church that sponsored them either before leaving their country of origin or after their arrival in America. Because many of the refugees and immigrants attend both Christian churches and Buddhist temples, there may be a much larger number of Buddhists here than show up in quantitative studies.

Jose Morelli is a member of Losel Shedrup Ling, a Tibetan monastery in Mineral Bluff, Georgia, which has a local membership in Atlanta that consists largely of Buddhist converts. He explains that there are generally two types of people to be found at Atlanta temples. The first group, which is larger in number, is simply curious about the Buddhist tradition. They want to learn more about the religion and are often on an "intellectual and internal search" for peace. The second, smaller group tends to be composed of those people who have a more complete existential interest in Buddhism. They are people who practice Buddhist teachings and beliefs on a daily basis. Likewise, Mei Liang, a spokesperson for the Atlanta Buddhist Association, says that the actual number of Americans who convert is difficult to estimate because attendance at a temple is not a requirement for one to be a Buddhist. Many Buddhists worship in their homes and by themselves, often reading and practicing the teachings of the Buddha without attending meditations or services at a house of worship.

Another reason it is difficult to estimate the number of Buddhists in Atlanta is that many of the people who attend meetings actually consider themselves to be believers of another religious tradition. At Losel Shedrup Ling, for example, one finds Buddhists, Christians, Jews, and others all meditating together. One need not be a Buddhist to practice meditation and participate in other Buddhist rituals. Morelli explains that many of the non-Buddhists in attendance tend to use meditation as a calming and relaxing mechanism.

Services at many temples often include discussions about Buddhism in general. At the Atlanta Buddhist Association, for example, a monk comes in one Sunday each month to speak about Buddhism. Other services may include specific readings from a Dharma text and a conversation about the teachings of the Buddha. Losel Shedrup Ling has a monk who speaks every week about the basic tenets and foundations of Buddhism, touching on such topics as meditation, various formal Buddhist teachings, and *Lamrim,* which are more detailed teachings about the stages on the path to enlightenment.

Temples and worship places are open to everyone for teaching, instruction, and meditation. Typically, the majority of Buddhist temples in metro Atlanta serve a specific ethnic population. They often serve a dual purpose—as temples for Buddhist readings and meditation and as meeting places to retain cultural traditions. Most of the worshipers at Wat Buddha Bucha, for example, are Thai, while most members at the Atlanta Buddhist Association are Chinese. The Zen centers are an exception because they often attract Americans of European descent who are interested in learning more about Buddhism.

While there is a variety of reasons that explain why certain sites appeal to certain groups of people, one of the more significant elements at work in the religious community of a particular temple or center relates to maintaining extended family networks. Other opportunities to maintain extended family relationships occur at cultural fairs and at international festivals focusing on Buddhism. Retreats are another way of strengthening community ties among members of a temple. The temple at Wat Buddha Bucha is itself essentially organized as a retreat center. With spacious grounds at its Decatur location, this temple often hosts several students, who come and stay for periods of time and study with the monks. Losel Shedrup Ling often organizes retreats to Mineral Bluff, where individuals can meditate and use the location to rest and relax.

Symbolic offerings to monks are an important aspect of religious life at Buddhist temples. Monks do not receive any official salary or income from their temples, so these offerings serve a dual purpose. First, the offerings typically consist of food, flowers, and necessities, and serve as gestures of thanks to the monk. Second, they are also meaningful offerings to ancestors. Buddhists ensure that ancestors are cared for in the afterlife, so these offerings are understood as a vital duty for descendants who want to maintain good relations between the spirits and the living community. One of the ways that offerings are made to the monk is through the use of a wishing tree (money tree). These "trees" are often small plants decorated with dollar bills and flowers. They are used to raise money for special projects and to offer useful items to the monk.

Buddhist traditions and celebrations generally coincide with the religious year, the founding of Buddhism, major events within its early history, and its most significant turning points. Important observances during the Buddhist year include the life of Buddha, proclamation of the Buddha's teachings, and saints' anniversaries. Buddha's Day, also known as *Visakha Puja* ("worship during the month of Visakha"), is considered to be the most holy day in the Buddhist year. It occurs on the day of the full moon in late May or early June. The holiday commemorates the Buddha's birth and death (for Theravada Buddhists, the anniversary of these events is on the same day, while for Mahayana Buddhists, they are on different days), and the day is marked by a candlelit procession around the temple and other ceremonies and festivities. The New Year is another important religious and social event. It is celebrated in early to mid-April, and is characterized by offerings of food, money, and flowers before the Buddha statues, and by rituals that clear the old year and bring good luck to the new one.

Buddhists in metro Atlanta are enthusiastic about the future of their religion here. The international flavor of metro Atlanta is continuing to expand, and as the presence of immigrants from various parts of Asia and their descendants increases, the influence of Buddhism will become more prevalent as well. In addition, a growing number of Americans of European descent are looking for alternatives to the traditional mainstream religions, and many of these individuals are interested in Buddhist teachings. Many who are actively exploring differing religious paths are curious about the faith. A large number of Christians and Jews frequent Buddhist temples with no intention of converting—they are primarily interested in applying meditative techniques to enrich their own lives. The growing openness to eastern religious and spiritual interests among Atlantans is expected to flourish, which means more and more people will look to Buddhism as a viable alternative path to greater personal understanding and fulfillment.

FOR FURTHER INFORMATION

Rick Fields. *How the Swans Came to the Lake: A Narrative History of Buddhism in America.* Boulder, Shambhala, 1981

Tetsuden Kashima. *Buddhism in America: The Social Organization of an Ethnic Religious Institution.* Westport, Greenwood Press, 1977

Emma McCloy Layman. *Buddhism in America.* Chicago, Nelson-Hall, 1976

Charles S. Prebish. *American Buddhism.* North Scituate, Duxbury Press, 1979

Richard H. Robinson and Willard L. Johnson. *The Buddhist Religion: A Historical Introduction.* Belmont, Wadsworth, 1982

CHAPTER EIGHTEEN

THE ATLANTA BAHÁ'Í COMMUNITY

Mike McMullen

Atlanta Bahá'í Center. Photograph by Louis A. Ruprecht, Jr.

The Bahá'í faith is one of the fastest growing independent religious systems in the world today. According to the World Christian Encyclopedia, *during the years 1970 to 1985, the Bahá'í faith's growth outpaced that of Islam, Christianity, Hinduism, Buddhism, and Judaism. The 1992* Encyclopedia Britannica Book of the Year *reported that the Bahá'ís were second only to Christianity in geographical expansion, establishing "significant communities" in 205 countries. Currently, there are over 5 million Bahá'ís worldwide, represented by more than 2,100 of the world's racial and ethnic groups. In addition, their scripture has been translated into 800 languages. Despite this global diversity, the Bahá'ís have managed to avoid denominational schism or sectarian divisions throughout their 152-year history.*

Although the Bahá'í faith has emerged from its nineteenth-century Islamic roots as an independent world religion, most of its growth in the past 40 years has been in the developing world (especially India), thus limiting the recognition of this unique religious movement in the United States. However, one of the largest Bahá'í communities in the South is in Atlanta. In describing the life of this small yet active religious community, I will examine how Atlanta Bahá'ís are a particular local expression of the Bahá'í faith's globally-embracing social structure and worldview. I will also explore how this community has effectively borne witness to their faith in the context of the Deep South for the past 85 years.

BAHÁ'Í ORIGINS

The Bahá'í faith was historically preceded by the Bábí religion, which began in 1844 when a Persian merchant named Siyyid `Alí-Muhammad revealed himself to be the Qá'im, or the Twelfth or Hidden Imam sought by Shi'ite Muslims. He took on the title of "the Báb," which in Arabic means "the Gate," and began to reveal new religious teachings. The thrust of his message heralded the coming of "One Whom God Will Make Manifest," a prophet of greater importance who would lead humankind into a new era of peace. The Báb attracted a substantial following from his fellow Iranians, arousing the suspicions and distrust of Islamic authorities. In an effort to crush the movement, the government of Persia executed the Báb in 1850, which almost destroyed the new religion. The Báb had not revealed when the "One Whom God Shall Make Manifest" would come, but had indicated the time would be soon.

Upon hearing of the religious teachings of the Báb, Mírzá Husayn `Alí, a Persian whose family was part of the governing class of the country, quickly converted and began spreading its message. His growing leadership role within the Bábí movement revitalized and invigorated the new religion. `Alí's social position protected him at first from the persecutions of the Persian authorities, but as fervor increased, he too was imprisoned. While held captive in Tehran in 1852-53, Bahá'ís believe God revealed to `Alí that he was the prophesied "One Whom God Will Make Manifest." When released from prison he, along with his family and fellow Bábís, were banished to Baghdad, thus beginning a lifetime of exile and incarceration at various sites throughout the Middle East. While in Baghdad, he took the title Bahá'u'lláh (which means "The Glory of God" in Arabic), and announced that he was the one promised by the Báb. The vast majority of Bábís pledged allegiance to Bahá'u'lláh as their new religious leader.

In 1863 the group of Bahá'ís (the new name given to the followers of Bahá'u'lláh) was expelled from Baghdad and sent to Constantinople (now known as Istanbul) and then to Adrianople (now Edirne) in Turkey. Finally, in 1868, the group was exiled permanently to `Akká, the prison city in Palestine where the worst criminals of the Turkish empire were sent to die. Here, as in the other cities of his banishment, Bahá'u'lláh carried on his ministry, wrote nearly one hundred volumes that became part of Bahá'í scripture, and met with pilgrims who traveled to `Akká to see the man whose message was spreading throughout Persia and the Middle East.

When Bahá'u'lláh died in 1892, he left behind a growing movement and a will and testament that named his eldest son, `Abdu'l-Bahá ("Servant of God" in Arabic) his successor and the authoritative interpreter of Bahá'í writings. After the Young Turk Revolution in 1908, all political and religious prisoners of the Ottoman Empire were released, thus freeing `Abdu'l-Bahá to begin establishing his father's covenant: the organization of the Bahá'í World Order as communicated through Bahá'u'lláh's writings. Before `Abdu'l-Bahá's death in 1921, Shoghi Effendi (Bahá'u'lláh's great-grandson) was named to continue this work and led the Bahá'í faith until his death in 1957. Shortly thereafter, in 1963, the Bahá'ís of the world elected the first Universal House of Justice, headquartered in Haifa, Israel, near `Akká, which remains the permanent head of the world's 5 million Bahá'ís.

STRUCTURE AND PRINCIPAL TEACHINGS OF THE BAHÁ'Í FAITH

The Bahá'í structural organization has three main levels, which together comprise the authority of its "Administrative Order." At the top of the hierarchy is the Universal House of Justice, a nine-man authoritative body elected every five years which carries out administrative functions and the translation and interpretation of hundreds of volumes of Bahá'í writings left behind by the Báb, Bahá'u'lláh, `Abdu'l-Bahá, and Shoghi Effendi. At the next level down are the 165 National Spiritual Assemblies located throughout the world. These are nine-person, elected bodies that coordinate Bahá'í activity on a national (or regional) level and are responsible to the World Center in Haifa. Below this level are the approximately 20,000 Local Spiritual Assemblies around the globe. A Local Spiritual Assembly (LSA) consists of nine adult Bahá'ís who are elected among the local Bahá'í community. The LSA coordinates grassroots activities and is the foundation for local Bahá'í life. The faith has no organized clergy and depends upon the commitment of individual Bahá'ís and the authority in the three-tiered assembly structure for vitality and direction. Decisions within the faith are arrived at through a process of consultation, wherein a consensus is sought to govern policy at all three levels of administration.

The religion's teachings rest upon three major tenets: the oneness of God, the oneness of religion, and the oneness of humankind. Bahá'ís assert that there is only one God, who has revealed all of the world's religious systems through individual religious messengers called "Manifestations of God." Thus, Bahá'ís recognize the divine mission of all the world's religious founders, including (but not limited to) Abraham, Krishna, Zoroaster, Buddha, Moses, Christ, Muhammad, the Báb, and Bahá'u'lláh. A central tenet of the Bahá'í's philosophy of religion is "progressive revelation." Bahá'ís believe that religious truth is revealed by God incrementally in an evolutionary process, with each major manifestation of faith adding to the spiritual guidance given to humanity throughout history. According to Bahá'í theology, God reveals a renewed version of the one true faith whenever humanity's moral and social life are no longer served by the previous manifestation, therefore building upon the spiritual truths provided by all the religions, and abrogating or legislating new social laws that humanity requires for that age in order to mature individually and collectively. Bahá'ís claim that contradictions between successive religious systems are due to humanity's misinterpretation of previous religious law or to the corruption of the clergy who seek their own power. It is this doctrine of progressive revelation that allows Bahá'ís to view their religion not as the only path to truth, nor the last perfect guidance from God, but merely the latest in a series of revelations that will continue indefinitely into the future.

Bahá'u'lláh said this to his followers concerning the purpose of religion for humanity: "The fundamental purpose animating the Faith of God and His Religion is to safeguard the interests and promote the unity of the human race, and foster the spirit of love and fellowship amongst men." Although each manifestation of God reveals a comprehensive set of teachings, there is a special message emphasized by each of them. Bahá'ís believe that Bahá'u'lláh's unique mission has the universal goal of uniting all of humankind under one religious banner, which then leads to the elimination of all forms of prejudice. Bahá'ís believe that Bahá'u'lláh fulfills all the prophesies of the world's religions, thus inaugurating a new era in humanity's religious history.

The bulk of the Administrative Order also functions to promote basic Bahá'í principles: the abandonment of all forms of superstition and prejudice, the recognition of the unity of religion and science, the promotion of the equality of women and men, the advancement of universal education and economic justice, the need for a spiritual foundation for society, and the development of an auxiliary international language and script, as well as a single international code of law upheld by global courts and international collective security. For Bahá'ís, this would lead to the establishment of the "Most Great Peace"—the Kingdom of God on earth.

A DEMOGRAPHIC PICTURE OF ATLANTA BAHÁ'ÍS

There are over 500 Bahá'ís who live in the Atlanta metropolitan area, comprising 17 LSAs. Each assembly jurisdiction maps out a geographical boundary, much like a Catholic parish. A recent survey done by this author found that on average, metro-Atlanta Bahá'ís are middle-class college graduates, with the majority employed in white-collar or professional jobs. However, the community as a whole displays a remarkable amount of racial and ethnic diversity. Nearly one-half of survey respondents describe themselves as white or of European background, another 25% define themselves as black or African American, and over 13% are of Persian background, or trace their heritage back to Iran, the birthplace of the Bahá'í faith. The remainder of survey respondents characterized themselves as having "other" or "mixed" ethnic heritage.

Atlanta's Bahá'í community ranges in age from the very young to the elderly, with the mean age at 42 years old. The average Bahá'í has been a member of the faith for over 20 years, with less than one-third of those responding having been raised as a Bahá'í. Of the 70% who converted to the Bahá'í faith, nearly three-fourths come from Protestant denominations (over 14 different denominations represented), almost 17% from Catholic or Orthodox denominations, and the remaining 11% from non-Christian traditions (either Islamic, Jewish, or Buddhist). Finally, of the Bahá'ís who indicated that they were married, over three-fourths are married to a Bahá'í spouse.

Thus, although members of Atlanta's Bahá'í community tend to be middle-class professionals, they evince wide racial and religious diversity. This is important for Bahá'ís because it reflects two of the guiding principles that underlie adherence to the faith of Bahá'u'lláh: the oneness of humanity (not divided by racial strife), and the oneness of religion (recognizing that all religions are part of God's plan of progressive revelation).

THE ATLANTA BAHÁ'Í CENTER

When Bahá'ís gather for study or worship, they open their homes to all of the community's diverse members in a particular local assembly jurisdiction. However, the LSA of the city of Atlanta has its own Bahá'í Center on Edgewood Avenue. It is located one block off historic Auburn Avenue, in the heart of the once-thriving "Sweet Auburn" district of African-American entrepreneurship, and adjacent to the Martin Luther King, Jr. Center for Nonviolent Social Change. Over the past 30 years this area has suffered the same plight as many urban areas, resulting in numerous closed businesses and abandoned buildings.

Despite this, the Atlanta Bahá'í Center remains the symbolic heart of the metro Bahá'í community, a source of pride and solidarity as it stands in the shadows of renowned Ebenezer Baptist and Wheat Street Baptist churches. Bahá'ís gather here for administrative meetings, worship services, children's classes, "deepenings" (intensive study of Bahá'í scripture), to commemorate special festivals and holidays, and to socialize. The first thing one notices upon approaching the building is the dedication sign to the right of the doorway, which reads: "Atlanta Bahá'í Center, 1950, Built by Leroy

Burns, Sr. as a place for all races to come together and worship." Bahá'ís welcome persons off the street searching for spiritual as well as physical nourishment, and embrace Bahá'ís traveling through the city from across the country or another part of the world.

Upon entering the meeting area, one might first notice the simple chairs arranged in a semicircle, or perhaps the picture of `Abdu'l-Bahá respectfully displayed on the wall. The shelves at one end of the room are replete with a selection of not only Bahá'í scripture, but also an assortment of all the world's religious literature, from the Bible to the Qur'an to the Bhagavad Gita. But eventually, one notices arguably the most striking characteristic of the Bahá'í community: the wide diversity of humanity that inevitably populates Bahá'í gatherings. Bahá'ís seek "unity in diversity," viewing their religion as the means to bridge all of humanity's cultural and ethnic divisions, but without imposing uniformity. Many Bahá'ís cite this unity in diversity as a powerful force attracting them to their new faith. One man spoke of how his perspective expanded upon becoming a Bahá'í: "You become global in the sense that your family is scattered around the globe. That was one of the things that I remember when I first came into the faith, realizing that no matter what city I was in anywhere, that if there is a Bahá'í community there, I've got family. And I think that contributes to a closeness in the Bahá'í community." Another man, a Bahá'í of 30 years, echoed these sentiments, saying that upon converting in the mid-1960s, "the world had grown. I had embraced the world. The world was my home. Wherever I was, it was home, wherever I laid my head, was home."

Other symbols in the room speak of the global character of this religion. Several pictures of the shrines located at the World Center in Haifa, Israel, adorn the walls, as well as pictures of Bahá'í houses of worship built around the world. One of the most prominent symbols of the Bahá'í religion in the room is a nine-pointed star (oftentimes depicted with a globe in the middle of it). Nine has special religious significance for Bahá'ís. The word "Bahá" in Arabic (which means "glory") has, when each of its Arabic letters is converted into its corresponding number, a combined numerical value of nine.

The Atlanta Bahá'í Center is located in the central city, so urban noises often intrude upon the "sacred space" created by the center. To counter the "profane" and cultivate a more serene atmosphere, candles are often lit, or music is played softly on the stereo. It is not uncommon to hear "Bahá'í Gospel" songs during worship with congregants enthusiastically joining in, intermingled with the more hushed sounds of a Persian believer chanting one of Bahá'u'lláh's prayers in Arabic. All in all, the Atlanta Bahá'í Center creates in urban Atlanta a little pocket of religious symbols and worship that reinforces for Bahá'ís the global character of their faith and its goal to unite all of humanity.

But there is more to the Atlanta Bahá'í Center than being a place of worship and evocative symbolism. The history of the building is itself symbolic of the Bahá'í commitment to racial equality and overcoming prejudice. Back in the 1940s, the small Bahá'í community in Atlanta met in members' homes as an integrated group for worship. However, in the Jim Crow culture of the Deep South, Bahá'ís living out their religious beliefs often provoked the resentment of neighbors. One incident, more than any other, prompted early Bahá'ís in Atlanta to build their own center, dedicated to religious worship and the peaceful coexistence of the races.

On April 28, 1947, the Bahá'í community was worshiping in one of the believer's homes in a section of southwest Atlanta known as West End. Before the meeting concluded, it was interrupted by the scuffle of feet and muted voices on the front porch. When some of the Bahá'ís investigated, they found an agitated band of white men demanding to know if there was "race-mixing" going on in that home. While some of the Bahá'ís tried to explain to the men that they were conducting a religious meeting, others moved to the rear of the house and called the police. After the authorities arrived, the growing crowd reluctantly dispersed, and the officers escorted the black believers to their homes, asking that the Bahá'í community no longer hold interracial meetings at that location. Although the troublemakers had identified themselves as the Ku Klux Klan, the police later determined they were part of the West End Cooperative Corporation, a supremacist group intent on keeping the West End segregated.

The Bahá'ís decided it was time to find a place where they could worship according to their beliefs. After renting space in downtown Atlanta, they made use of the property on Edgewood Avenue donated by Leroy Burns, Sr., a devoted African-American believer. The bricks for the building were made by Mr. Burns and his son, Onslow, and the center itself was constructed with the help of both blacks and whites in the Bahá'í community. Since its dedication in 1950, the Atlanta Bahá'í Center has been a monument to the commitment of the Atlanta Bahá'í community; this commitment toward racial unity is part of their obedience to Bahá'u'lláh. One woman talked about how being a Bahá'í has compelled her to change her behavior regarding interracial friendships: "The best thing that I like is I like to make friends with people and love people that I would never under any other circumstances have anything to do with. It [the Bahá'í faith] has jerked me out of my narrow, white, upper middle-class educational station, and having to come to terms with [diverse people] is just wonderful."

THE BAHÁ'Í CALENDAR

A Bahá'í's personal life is divided up into daily devotional requirements, as well as monthly and yearly festivals that conform to specific laws of Bahá'u'lláh and the dictates of the Bahá'í calendar. In the Kitáb-i-Aqdas (the central scriptural text of the Bahá'í faith), Bahá'u'lláh prescribed for his followers a daily regimen of prayer and scripture reading, periodic contributions to Bahá'í funds, and, if financially possible during one's lifetime, a pilgrimage to the world center in Haifa. In addition to the numerous prayers authored by Bahá'u'lláh for a Bahá'í's personal devotion, he ordained that all followers recite one of three specially revealed "obligatory prayers" each day, and read from Bahá'í scripture every morning and evening. The whole canon of Bahá'í scripture (regarded as the writings of the Báb, Bahá'u'lláh, `Abdu'l-Bahá, and Shoghi Effendi) covers various topics, such as religious philosophy, the nature of the soul, life after death, legal and social issues, administrative procedure, ethics, world history, and global order.

While a Bahá'í's daily life is governed by the personal laws given to the Bahá'í community by Bahá'u'lláh, collective life is dictated by the rituals of the Bahá'í calendar. Bahá'ís point out that whenever new manifestations of God appear to humanity, they bring with them a new calendar to institutionalize new patterns of worship, social festivals, and holidays. The Bahá'í year is divided into 19 months with 19 days each (totaling 361 days), with the insertion of "Intercalary Days" (four in an ordinary year, five in a leap year) between the 18th and 19th months to adjust the calendar to the solar year. The Báb named each month after an "attribute of God"—virtues that Bahá'ís are to strive for throughout their lives (such as mercy, perfection, knowledge, speech, honor, and grandeur). The Bahá'í New Year (the festival of *Naw-Rúz*), like the ancient Persian New Year, begins on the spring equinox (March 21). In addition, the last month of the Bahá'í year is a prescribed month of fasting. Similar to Muslims during Ramadan, Bahá'ís abstain from food and water for 19 days from sunup to sundown, reserving extra time for prayer and study.

On the first day of each Bahá'í month, Bahá'ís in Atlanta (as well as all around the world) gather for the Nineteen Day Feast, which is the central worship experience in the Bahá'í faith. The Nineteen Day Feast consists of three loosely structured parts. The first is a devotional period, where the writings and prayers of the Báb, Bahá'u'lláh, and/or `Abdu'l-Bahá are read, as well as passages from other holy scripture. The Atlanta community rotates responsibility for planning devotions among its members since there are no clergy in the Bahá'í faith. In that way, each Bahá'í has a chance to tailor the community's worship experience to personal interests and strengths. The second part of the feast is an administrative period, where the chair of the LSA leads community-wide consultation on important issues facing the community. Finally, the feast includes a social portion, involving fellowship and refreshments. Sometimes, several LSAs will all meet together for what is known as a "Unity Feast."

The administrative portion is in some ways the most important aspect of a feast. Each nineteen days, participants brainstorm about new local "teaching" (evangelizing) or service projects. A treasurer's report updates members on the financial health of the community. Someone usually informs the community of future activities, teaching trips, study classes, or social events. Sometimes, individuals will give reports on trips they recently took to teach non-Bahá'ís about their faith. Recommendations for community action that require official approval are referred to the LSA for consideration. In a sense, each feast represents a mini-town hall meeting, where Bahá'ís can give input into community governance and exchange information, as well as worship together as followers of Bahá'u'lláh. The feast is therefore given high priority among Atlanta Bahá'ís as a chance for the whole community to participate in spiritual fellowship and democratic administration. Bahá'ís frequently allude to its importance by quoting `Abdu'l-Bahá, who said this about the feast: "If this feast be held in the proper fashion, the friends will, once in nineteen days, find themselves spiritually restored, and endued with a power that is not of this world."

Most feasts are accompanied by a letter from the National Spiritual Assembly, informing local communities of decisions made by that body or those of the Universal House of Justice. Several times a year, the national assembly distributes a videocassette called the "Bahá'í Newsreel," which describes activity going on around the world and new developments at the World Center in Haifa. The feast letter and the "Bahá'í Newsreel" serve as sources of communication that link the local Bahá'í community with the national and international levels of Bahá'í social life, helping to fortify an individual Bahá'í's identity as a member of a globally encompassing movement. It also links the Bahá'í community in Atlanta to her sister communities throughout the United States and around the world.

The diversity in the Atlanta Bahá'í community is reflected in the various styles that are incorporated into the flexible Nineteen Day Feast format. At times, feasts have the feel of a church revival, comprising Gospel-style singing with appropriate Bahá'í words and themes inserted, hand clapping, and believers "testifying" to the power of Bahá'u'lláh to change their hearts and change the world. At other times, the feast is a more solemn experience. A Persian believer might chant a prayer in Arabic or Persian, or impart the most recent news from the persecuted Bahá'í community in Iran. Many of the Persian Bahá'ís in Atlanta escaped from their native country during the 1978-79 Iranian revolution, after which a renewed wave of oppression swept through the Bahá'í community there. The feast, then, is in part a ritual for incorporating the cultural diversity of the community into the fabric of its own collective identity. In addition, individuals are encouraged to incorporate their own talents into devotions. Some Bahá'ís have put Bahá'í scripture to music; others, who are members of the Atlanta Bahá'í Arts Institute, have performed interpretive poetry or dance to communicate the message of Bahá'u'lláh. Bahá'ís definitely live out their diversity in their worship experience, reinforcing the idea that there is no one right way to express their Bahá'í identity.

The other main collective rituals of the Bahá'í calendar are the holy days and special event days that commemorate specific occasions in Bahá'í history or celebrate the global vision of the faith. Holy days tend to take on two distinct moods, one festive and celebratory, the other reverent and somber. The festivals of *Ayyám-i-Há* (or Intercalary Days, right before the month of fasting) and *Naw-Rúz* (the Bahá'í New Year) are bright, joyful occasions, with many Bahá'ís bringing non-Bahá'í friends to introduce them to the community's hospitality at its best. The Atlanta Bahá'í Center is decorated with balloons and banners, and festive music is played. *Ayyám-i-Há* is also a period of exchanging gifts and doing charitable work, and the local community gathers at the Bahá'í center for a group gift-exchange and party. On the other hand, the Ascension of Bahá'u'lláh, commemorating his death on May 29, 1892, has a more subdued feel, evoking reverence and veneration among Bahá'ís for the founder of their faith. It is held at 3 a.m.—the recorded time of Bahá'u'lláh's death—and the quiet stillness of downtown

Atlanta surrounding the Bahá'í center adds to the sense of the sacred. Lit candles, soft music, and the recitation of specifically prescribed verses enhance the hallowed atmosphere.

Work is suspended on the more important of the holy days; Bahá'ís themselves talk about the importance of properly commemorating holy days by taking the day off from work or school to establish more clearly a sense of Bahá'í identity. One Bahá'í focused on the global solidarity produced by the worldwide Bahá'í community observing certain holy days: "I guess it strikes me on the holy days, you know, like the noon celebration of the Martyrdom of the Báb, moving around the globe, or the 3 a.m. Ascension of Bahá'u'lláh. . . . Yea, there is a neat concept to that wave moving around the planet."

CONNECTION TO ATLANTA INSTITUTIONS

There are approximately 20,000 Bahá'í LSAs around the world. Like the rituals of the Atlanta LSA described above, feasts and holy day celebrations follow the same flexible format in every corner of the globe. However, the distinction of the Bahá'ís in Atlanta involves the deep ties they have fostered with some of Atlanta's best-known institutions. The first Bahá'í to settle in Atlanta was Dr. James C. Oakshette, a professor of physiotherapy who arrived in 1909 from Chicago. Within a few years he began "teaching the cause"—or spreading the Bahá'í message—to both blacks and whites in Atlanta. Over the next two decades, the small but growing Bahá'í community established contacts with esteemed African-American institutions such as Morehouse College, Morris Brown University, Spelman Seminary, Gammon Theological Seminary, Clark College, and the First Congregational Church. (Years later, Bahá'í would also initiate ties with the Hungry Club of Butler YMCA and Paschal's Motor Restaurant—important settings for 1960s Civil Rights strategizing, and frequent meeting sites for Bahá'ís).

These ties were of both symbolic and practical importance. First, they began a track record among Atlanta Bahá'ís as supporters of African-American civil rights and equality during a time when race relations were strained. Second, these institutions in black Atlanta generously opened their doors as forums for presenting the Bahá'í message. Many of the large meeting halls in Atlanta hotels were strictly segregated, and would not allow mixed audiences, let alone African-American speakers (as were some of the Bahá'í lecturers who traveled throughout the South in the 1910s and 1920s). Black Atlanta's institutions were at times the only available public arenas to present a talk on Bahá'í ideals of the "oneness of humanity" to an *integrated* audience.

Many of these ties continue today. Bahá'í activities are still welcome at the Atlanta University Center—the name for the consortium of African-American educational institutions in Atlanta. In addition, new relationships have been developed and strengthened. Since 1986, the Bahá'ís have established a growing presence at the Martin Luther King, Jr. Center for Nonviolent Social Change, the non-profit institute run by Mrs. Coretta Scott King to promote her husband's vision of the "Beloved Community." Beginning as mere entrants in the King Day Parade a decade ago, Bahá'ís have been asked to co-marshal the annual event for the past four years in recognition of Bahá'í efforts to promote racial unity. Moreover, two Bahá'ís now sit on the King Federal Holiday Commission, which oversees the national observance commemorating King's birthday.

Bahá'ís have also branched out to become active in other Atlanta institutions. Bahá'í scripture forbids Bahá'ís from becoming involved in partisan political activity (since partisanship breeds disunity, contrary to Bahá'í goals of unity amid diversity). However, this does not prevent Bahá'ís from addressing political leaders with their concerns about social problems. Atlanta Bahá'ís teamed up with the Carter Presidential Center in bringing Atlanta's political, religious, and civic leaders together to address the problem of racism in American society—a problem Bahá'ís consider to be America's "most vital and challenging issue." On April 4, 1992, 200 participants gathered at the Carter Center for the "Vision of Race Unity Conference" to hear keynote addresses from U.S. Representative Ben Jones of Georgia and Dr. Joy Berry, executive director of the Georgia Human Relations Commission, as well as presentations from Bahá'í speakers.

CONCLUSION

I hope I have done three things in this short essay: first, familiarized the reader with some of the beliefs and rituals of the Atlanta Bahá'í community; second, shown that the LSA of Atlanta is connected to a network of Bahá'í organizations throughout the world through their worship and through their Administrative Order; and third, demonstrated that while any one local Bahá'í community is connected to others in a hierarchy of democratically elected institutions, each is also active in addressing the concerns of its particular location. In the case of Atlanta's Bahá'í community, this concern has historically been focused on efforts to promote racial unity and the oneness of humanity. Despite the pressures of the Jim Crow South, Atlanta Bahá'ís established ties to African-American institutions throughout the city early on—ties that continue to develop today.

FOR FURTHER INFORMATION

Abdu'l-Bahá. *The Promulgation of Universal Peace: Talks Delivered by `Abdu'l-Bahá during His Visit to the United States and Canada in 1912*. Comp. Howard MacNutt, 2nd ed., Wilmette, Bahá'í Publishing Trust, 1982

Bahá'u'lláh. *Gleanings from the Writings of Bahá'u'lláh*. Trans. Shoghi Effendi, Wilmette, Bahá'í Publishing Trust, 1985

J. E. Esslemont. *Bahá'u'lláh and the New Era: An Introduction to the Bahá'í Faith*. Wilmette, Bahá'í Books, 1970

William S. Hatcher and J. Douglas Martin. *The Bahá'í Faith: The Emerging Global Religion*. New York Harper & Row, 1985

Gayle Morrison. *To Move the World: Louis G. Gregory and the Advancement of Racial Unity in America*. Wilmette, Bahá'í Publishing Trust, 1982

Shoghi Effendi. *The Advent of Divine Justice*. Wilmette, Bahá'í Publishing Trust, IL, 1990

Robert H. Stockman. *The Bahá'í Faith in America: Origins 1982-1900*. Wilmette, Bahá'í Publishing Trust, 1985

CHAPTER NINETEEN

ON THE ROAD TO CLEAR: THE SCIENTOLOGY COMMUNITY OF ATLANTA

Mark Padilla

Hubbard Dianetics Center. Photograph by Louis A. Ruprecht, Jr.

It is early afternoon on Sunday and the streets of downtown Atlanta are bustling with churchgoers headed for home. On West Peachtree Street, the last of the parishioners at First Baptist Church make their way down the sidewalks and to the waiting cars outside. As they pass the brick office building at the corner of 13th Street, they do not seem to notice the imposing banner above the door that reads, in bold red letters, HUBBARD DIANETICS FOUNDATION. *Nor are they aware that a very different kind of service is just beginning inside, this one under the direction of Tom Davis, an ordained minister for the Church of Scientology.*

There is nothing about yourself or your life that you can't know. You can know it, with certainty." Mr. Davis's voice rises to emphasize the point. The decor of the small lecture room consists simply of four chairs, two television sets, and a white board with the Latin word "scio" and the Greek word "logos" written in blue marker. Only two of the chairs are occupied. Gesturing to the board, the minister continues. "Scientology literally means to know the word; it teaches you to know *how* to know." In contrast to the esoteric musings of most philosophical traditions, he explains, Scientology offers practical, real-world benefits for its followers. One's happiness, self-determination, and spiritual awareness can all be enhanced by upholding the teachings of this "revolutionary" religion as the standard for one's life. Deborah, a recent Scientology convert, needs little convincing. She sits attentively on the edge of her seat, murmuring words of enthusiastic assent. A struggling local musician, she is enticed by Scientology's commitment to help its parishioners lead happier, more fulfilling lives. She recently began formal pastoral counseling, known as "auditing," and thus embarked on a long journey that she is confident will lead to a more optimistic future, and ultimately to personal enlightenment.

Public lectures such as this one occur at Atlanta's Hubbard Dianetics Foundation every Sunday and Tuesday and, for many people, serve as the initial contact with the Church of Scientology. For a few, this experience will begin a lifetime commitment to the teachings of Scientology, a new and little-understood religious philosophy. This essay focuses on the theology and character of Atlanta's Church of Scientology, a growing community that has become increasingly active in the city.

HISTORY AND THEOLOGY OF SCIENTOLOGY

Scientology grew out of the work of L. Ron Hubbard, the late author of the best-selling self-help book *Dianetics: The Modern Science of Mental Health.* Originally published in 1950, *Dianetics* offers itself as an alternative to psychiatry and psychotherapy, which are dismissed by Hubbard as both inhumane and scientifically worthless. This revolutionary mental health "technology," Hubbard contends, is an empirically-based methodology for healing all manner of psychosomatic illness. Emphasis is placed on the precision of Dianetics; far from haphazard, it is an "exact science" founded upon universal "laws of nature."

The central concept behind Dianetics is Hubbard's division of the mind into two major components: the *analytical mind* and the *reactive mind.* The analytical mind is "the rational, conscious, aware mind which thinks, observes data, remembers it and resolves problems," while the reactive mind is the irrational, unconscious mind that is subject to error and negative émotion. If too much of an individual's mental processing is controlled by the reactive mind, "unwanted sensations and emotions, irrational fears and psychosomatic illnesses" can result. The driving purpose of Dianetics is to offer a technique for eliminating the reactive mind, thereby freeing the individual to live entirely within the rational realm of the analytical mind. An individual at this higher level of existence is said to be in a state designated as "Clear," unencumbered by the harmful effects of the reactive mind.

According to Hubbard, the reactive mind can be eliminated only by locating and correcting "engrams," particular bits of "false data" that have been stored in memory and integrated into an individual's mental processing. This process requires the assistance of an "auditor," a trained Dianetics technician. As a lay psychotherapist of sorts, the auditor assists the Scientologist in retracing the "time-track" of his or her existence to identify the debilitating engrams. Once an engram is located through auditing, its falseness is exposed and conscious awareness is increased.

According to the Church of Scientology, it was one year after the release of *Dianetics,* in 1951, that L. Ron Hubbard made the crucial "deduction" based on his Dianetics research that humans are unequivocal spiritual beings, or "thetans," and thus founded the religion of Scientology. The guiding purpose of the church is to employ the techniques of Dianetics to gradually free the "thetan consciousness"—the part of every human being that is "utterly incapable of error"—from the spiritually crippling effects of irrationality and falsehood. Step by step, auditing removes from an individual "those things which are not part of his inherent spiritual self," pealing away the layers of "physical existence" to uncover the "spiritual beingness" that is fundamental to humanity. While Dianetics and Scientology are closely intertwined, the Church of Scientology defines the latter as religious because it addresses questions of humankind's spiritual existence and ultimate salvation.

The religion of Scientology also added a new dimension to auditing that is absent from Dianetics. In the late 1950s, Hubbard began to experiment with what he called the *electropsychometer,* or "e-meter," a device that he claimed was capable of detecting the responses of the reactive mind. Similar to a polygraph (lie-detector) device, the e-meter sends a very low intensity electric current through the body and registers small fluctuations in an individual's electrochemical responses to stimuli. Used by a trained auditor, Hubbard claimed the e-meter facilitates the identification of harmful engrams in need of purging. The devices soon became a central part of Scientology auditing, and anxious Scientologists created an extensive market for them.

The Church of Scientology has also formalized the progression toward Clear by introducing "The Bridge," a well-defined status hierarchy corresponding to various stages of spiritual awareness. The Bridge meticulously describes each step of the Scientologist's spiritual journey and outlines the particular qualifications that merit promotion at each transition. Interestingly, the final stages of enlightenment move beyond the state of Clear into the various grades of "Operating Thetan" (OT). At these levels, an individual is said to regain many of the boundless abilities of his or her thetan consciousness. One Scientologist quoted in a church publication describes this stage as follows: "On this OT level I was able to resolve situations that had worried me for an eternity in a matter of minutes. I have become cause over any situation in my life. I can handle, resolve and accomplish what I decide to. My ability to spot the exact source of a situation and then handle it immediately is unstoppable."

For many Scientologists, the appeal of the church is its promise to improve the worldly conditions of one's life in addition to freeing the spirit. An advertisement for Scientology urged: "Go Clear—For the first time in your life you will be truly yourself. On the Clearing Course you will smoothly achieve the stable State of Clear with: Good Memory, Raised I.Q., Strong Will Power, Magnetic Personality, Amazing Vitality, Creative Imagination." The emphasis is on the benefits Scientology can bring the individual in the here-and-now, not in a distant or deferred hereafter. Further, the Scientologist alone is described as the agent bringing about these changes. Through auditing, one's inherent abilities are said to reemerge, bringing with them greater control over one's own destiny.

Scientologists describe their religion as an "applied philosophy," a set of fundamental laws that, when followed correctly, will invariably improve an individual's mental and spiritual health. Interestingly, they hasten to add, this improvement will occur regardless of an individual's faith. As one of the church's publications explains, "Scientology is not a dogmatic religion in which one is asked to believe anything on faith. An individual discovers for himself that Scientology works by applying its principles and observing or experiencing the results." One local Scientologist put it more succinctly, "It doesn't matter if you believe or not, it's a matter of workability." The church has incorporated this philosophy into its formal doctrine, emphasizing its unconditional acceptance of all religious faiths among its parishioners.

According to Scientologists, a person's advancement toward Clear is primarily an individual journey. Self-determination and control are not only the transcendent qualities for which Scientologists strive, but also "inalienable rights" guaranteed by the Scientology Creed. Members therefore insist that they are never coerced in any way to continue auditing against their will, nor are they obliged to receive these services at all. While auditing is the only way to make progress toward Clear, they explain, there are no formal means by which an individual is required or pressured to audit. It is apparent, however, that the omnipresence of the Bridge provides a strong motivation for Scientologists to continue auditing their way to enlightenment.

Partly as a result of its individualist emphasis, there are no formal periods of worship or ritualized collective practices in Scientology. While Scientologists recognize a super-individual "supreme being," the attributes of this being and its relationship to humans are left unspecified. As a result, Scientologists form a highly dispersed community whose cohesiveness stems from commitment to its religious principles and participation in individual sessions. Auditing sessions are arranged by appointment to accommodate members' schedules, and Hubbard Dianetics Foundations frequently provide services seven days a week. Further, as all discussions occurring within the auditing sessions are subject to strict confidentiality, this important aspect of religious experience is not shared collectively. The emphasis on discretion makes Scientology very different from many traditions in which the act of "testifying"—the public sharing of individual religious experience—plays a central role in group cohesion, religious reaffirmation, and conversion.

It must be mentioned that the Church of Scientology has borne persistent criticism since its inception in 1954. One of the most common allegations is that Scientology is merely a highly lucrative, profit-oriented business in the guise of a religious organization. Indeed, for four decades the Church of Scientology's claim to tax-exempt status as a religion has been repeatedly questioned by the Internal Revenue Service. In 1993, the IRS completed its most extensive investigation of the church to determine the organization's tax liability. For Scientologists, the decision involved much more than a governmental debt; Scientology's status as a bona fide religion was in the balance. Ultimately, the IRS found in favor of Scientology's claim that it is a religious organization, and the church is currently exempt from all federal taxes. Ironically, this potentially disastrous decision for the Church of Scientology now serves as its most important rhetorical claim to official legitimacy, providing a legal foundation for its religious credibility and a reassurance to its potential converts.

More recently, the Church of Scientology has been the center of a highly charged legal battle over the validity of copyright laws and the status of the First Amendment on the internet. Over the past several months, an intense debate has been raging between Scientology and an outspoken group of internet users, most of whom are contributors to the popular discussion board "alt.religion.scientology." An incident on February 13, 1995, brought the debate to a head. Several law enforcement officers executing a federal court order obtained by the Church of Scientology raided the home of Dennis Erlich, a former Scientology minister and boisterous critic of the church, and deleted a number of his computer files. The church accuses Mr. Erlich of illegally posting copyrighted materials to the internet in direct violation of the church's rights, while Mr. Erlich contends that the church has repeatedly violated his First Amendment rights in an attempt to silence his public condemnation of Scientology.

A COMMUNITY ON THE MOVE: ATLANTA'S CHURCH OF SCIENTOLOGY

Atlanta's first Scientology mission was established in 1974 by Mary Rieser, a devoted Scientologist. Under her leadership, the mission grew steadily throughout the next decade, and in 1989 it was considered for official church status by the mother church in Los Angeles. After a period of formal scrutiny, a small group of Atlantans became the newest of Scientology's 143 churches worldwide, and began delivering Scientology services to the community.

As with most churches in the organization, Atlanta's Church of Scientology is the regional hub for a broad geographical area, serving most of the southeastern United States. Scientologists come to the city from as far away as Alabama, Tennessee, South Carolina, North Carolina, Kentucky, and Mississippi for services. The Atlanta church provides them with Scientology training, auditing, and a myriad of courses on such topics as "Life Improvement," "Success Through Communication," and "Anatomy of the Human Mind." In addition, a field auditor canvasses Georgia and adjacent states as Scientology's version of a missionary, spreading the word about Dianetics and the opportunity for personal enlightenment offered by Scientology.

The Atlanta church has seen significant changes since its beginning six years ago. The number of active parishioners has grown steadily, and in 1995 reached around 3,000. To accommodate this growth, the church recently moved to its new location on West Peachtree Street at 13th. The newly-renovated office building offers much-needed space for expansion in the coming years, as well as a bookstore carrying the complete works of L. Ron Hubbard.

The increase in membership has enabled the church to expand its services into the greater Atlanta community. Public lectures introducing Atlantans to the teachings of the Scientology religion have become routine, and a few staff members and volunteer Scientologists organize and implement community action programs. Diane Stein, the Director of Community Affairs for the local church, coordinates these programs, acting as a liaison between the church and the city of Atlanta. "We are very interested in helping make Atlanta a great place to live: a clean, healthy, safe, and prosperous city," says Stein. "We live here, we work here, so we have a vested interest in that, and we aspire to accomplish it."

Recently, work has begun on a number of projects sponsored by the Church of Scientology aimed at improving Atlanta's record on crime, education, and drug abuse. One of the most successful of these programs is the Drug-Free Marshals Campaign. Responding to the increase in substance abuse among the city's youth, the local Church of Scientology, in conjunction with the mayor's office and the Public School Interfaith Community Collaborative, has undertaken the project in order to foster pride in drug-free living for hundreds of young Atlantans. The program began in Los Angeles in April 1993, and with the support of the Church of Scientology International and a number of co-sponsors, it has quickly spread across the country.

The program rewards children for remaining drug-free and gives them a role in discouraging drug abuse among their peers. "Each new Drug-Free Marshal is presented with a special `drug-free marshal' badge and signs a pledge to lead the way to a drug-free USA," Stein explains. "Kids who have been sworn-in then swear in other kids as drug-free marshals." In the summer of 1995 alone, Stein appointed over 500 drug-free marshals to kick off the program in the city. She had plans to appoint many more before the 1996 Olympics as a message to the international community that Atlanta is committed to combating drug abuse among its youth.

The Atlanta Church of Scientology has also begun a project to make L. Ron Hubbard's "Study Technology" available to students in the Atlanta area. Hubbard researched and designed the program in the 1950s, and the techniques are now used in over 150 schools worldwide, including the Lafayette Academy, a private school in Marietta, Georgia. According to Hubbard, the Study Technology overcomes the primary failures of orthodox teaching methods by emphasizing hands-on learning, matching the pace of teaching to the pace of learning, and eliminating the progressive confusion caused by misunderstood vocabulary. In March 1994, several Atlanta Scientologists, the Whitesville Missionary Baptist Church, and the Lafayette Academy combined forces to launch the Empire Project, an educational program that tutors students in language comprehension, reading, and study skills using the methodology developed by Hubbard. Using space provided by the Whitesville Missionary Baptist Church, the project began as a test to determine its feasibility and potential for growth. "The test was a complete success," recounts Stein, "and I am now working to get a model program set up through my associates in the School Interfaith Community Collaborative." The Church of Scientology hopes to expand the Empire

Project to provide educational services to more children in the Atlanta area in coming years.

Consistency of service and function is a central objective of the Church of Scientology. Individual Scientology churches are patterned on a single model that serves as the standard for all locations. As a result, when asked about the local character of the Atlanta church, Diane Stein had some difficulty answering. "The churches are very standard in how they're run and what's expected of them by international management," she explained, "but at the same time every geographical location is very different. There are different ethnic values." While Stein cites the African-American community as an important regional influence for the Atlanta church, she acknowledges that African Americans are not well-represented among the local Scientology community. There are relatively few African-American parishioners, and only one African-American staff member. But she also emphasizes that the church "is totally non-denominational. It doesn't matter what color, race, or anything; whether or not they join is totally up to them."

SCIENTOLOGY'S CONTRIBUTION TO RELIGIOUS PLURALISM IN ATLANTA

It is important to briefly consider the Church of Scientology in light of Atlanta's religious diversity and, perhaps more importantly, as it informs our understanding of what it means to be a pluralistic religious community. As a new and somewhat esoteric religious philosophy, Scientology challenges a number of traditional notions of religion. It lacks a forum for formalized worship, it emphasizes that its contributions to one's life are entirely independent of "faith," it places collective experience in a subordinate position to individual enlightenment, it upholds scientific rationality as the key to transcendence, and it suggests that humans are perfectible creatures.

In Atlanta, the Church of Scientology has begun to challenge many traditional perspectives on the meaning and function of religion. The controversy around it notwithstanding, this increasingly active church is creating space for a more pluralistic notion of religious community. By subverting popular conceptions of religion, and by asserting its difference as well as its religious authenticity, the Scientologists of Atlanta are helping to foster religious diversity and understanding. And, as one local Scientologist confidently told me, "We're used to being marginalized, but things are changing—and we're here to stay."

FOR FURTHER INFORMATION

What is Scientology? Los Angeles, Bridge Publications, Inc., 1992

The Church of Scientology: 40th Anniversary. Los Angeles, Bridge Publications, 1994

L. Ron Hubbard. *Dianetics, The Modern Science of Mental Health.* New York Paper Library, 1968 printing

Robert Kaufman. *Inside Scientology.* London, Olympia Press, 1975

Stewart Lamont. *Religion Inc.* London, Harrap,1986

Roy Wallis. *The Road to Total Freedom.* New York, Columbia University Press, 1976

CHAPTER TWENTY

RELIGION IN ATLANTA'S QUEER COMMUNITY

Angela Cotten

First Metropolitan Community Church. Photograph by Louis A. Ruprecht, Jr.

Religious communities for queers[1] *emerged from a cross-section of late-1960s and 1970s gay and lesbian liberation movements, as well as the reluctance of Protestant and Catholic churches to address this community's needs. As a result of the civil, legal, and religious oppression experienced by Atlanta's queer population during this period, the community created many organizations and institutions that dealt with its various concerns. In the late-1980s, a local chapter of Queer Nation used Dr. Martin Luther King's six principles of non-violence to protest the employment discrimination of Cracker Barrel, a restaurant chain in the region, against queer people. Another organization, Atlanta ACT UP, demonstrated against the Centers for Disease Control for what they felt was an inadequate approach to AIDS research and education. Two institutions that grew out of the 1970s movements are the Atlanta Lesbian Feminist Alliance (ALFA) and the Metropolitan Community Church (MCC). Both were founded in 1972 and continue to thrive today.*

The anthologies of autobiographical narratives by queer Jews and Christians abound with many unpleasant experiences in a variety of denominational settings. Their experiences include congregational pressures to masquerade a heterosexual appearance, to submit to pastoral and psychological counseling in order to repress their same-gender feelings, or to radi-

1 In this essay, I use the term "queer" to refer to same-gender sexuality. Before the Stonewall revolts of 1969, "queer" had been used by homophobes as an epithet to ostracize and instill shame and fear in gay men and lesbians. With the emergence of a sexual politics of pride and liberation, many gay, lesbian, and bisexual people appropriated the term and used it as a positive reference to their gender orientation and sexual preference, choices that no longer caused them shame nor a need to conceal their identities. However, some gay, lesbian, and bisexual people do not use "queer" as a self-referent since, for them, the term continues to carry negative connotations from that historical period when they endured daily harassment and brutalities. While I use "queer" in its positive, appropriated signification, I respect their reservations.

cally change their behavior or face outright expulsion. Since queer Christians found that their spirituality suffered because they could not integrate and affirm their sexuality in a traditional denominational context, they created churches and other worship communities where they could reconcile and affirm their sexuality and spirituality. MCC and other independent congregations, organizations, and spirituality groups established by queers have provided a safe place to worship without having to hide sexual orientation or fear condemnation by intolerant fellow worshipers. As longtime community activist, the Reverend Paul Turner of Abundant Grace Community Church explains, "Queer people need to know that they are a creation of God, that God doesn't make junk, and that God has looked at creation and said that that's good. So gay people need to understand that, in the eyes of God, they are good." Somewhat similar to queer Christians' experiences, queer Jews who dissociated themselves from their families' Orthodox and Conservative traditions found that their lives lacked the emotional, social, and institutional support of Jewish culture. Consequently, queer Jews began to establish synagogues and worship communities in the early 1970s.

Atlanta's queer religious community is as diverse as any other, with differences in beliefs, liturgy, and mission testifying to a wide range of interests and spiritual concerns. The congregations and organizations in this chapter are primarily Christian with two exceptions, the Jewish congregation, Bet Haverim, and an alternative spirituality group, Gay Spirit Visions. The queer religious community can be divided into six categories: Metropolitan Community Churches; independent Christian churches; heterosexual Christian churches that accept queer people; Christian organizations within mainline denominations; alternative spirituality groups; and congregations with ethnic-cultural roots. These groups share at least five social and religious characteristics. Four of these are: (1) usage of gender-inclusive language to refer to the divine; (2) blessing of same-gender unions; (3) community service, political activism, and participation in the annual Pride Parade; and (4) availability of communion (not applicable to Bet Haverim and Gay Spirit Visions) and fellowship to all persons regardless of membership status, religious background, ethnicity, sexual orientation, class, gender, age, or physical and mental ability.

The fifth characteristic, shared by the Christian community, is a commonality of theological beliefs. Whereas Christian fundamentalists believe that the Bible is the direct revelation of God and holds true for all cultures and historical ages, the queer religious community believes that scripture must be placed within its cultural and historical contexts in order to understand its messages. Less tolerant denominations cite biblical passages that prohibit same-gender sexuality, but the queer religious community argues against those interpretations and believes that same-gender sexuality is one of God's gifts to humankind. Finally, while many mainline Protestant groups concentrate on the salvific message of the gospels, queer ministers emphasize the inclusivity of Jesus' ministry. These ministers point out that the synoptic gospels record Jesus' ministry to the oppressed and mention nothing about his rejection of homosexuals.

The remainder of this chapter profiles a few congregations in each of the six categories mentioned earlier, beginning with a general discussion of the largest Christian organization, the Universal Fellowship of MCCs.

THE UNIVERSAL FELLOWSHIP OF METROPOLITAN COMMUNITY CHURCHES

MCC began in Los Angeles in 1968 when the founder, the Reverend Troy Perry, hosted twelve people in his home for an afternoon worship service. Perry had been ousted from the Church of God of Prophecy in Southern California after he refused to condemn homosexuality as sinful. Perry preached a message of Christian redemption, community, and social action, and his following increased rapidly. By 1972, thirty-five churches had been established nationwide—including First MCC of Atlanta—as branches of the Universal Fellowship of MCC (UFMCC). In 1995, UFMCC held its annual General Conference in Atlanta and hosted Mel White—the long-time closeted ghostwriter of conservative Christian leaders—who began a nationwide Christian social action campaign against the anti-queer religious rhetoric of his former employers. Today, UFMCC has a seminary, Samaritan Bible, where ministers are trained and appointed to more than 400 MCCs in eighteen countries. Although the Fellowship's congregants continue to be predominantly queer, MCC does not define itself as a "homosexual church," but as a church that welcomes everyone.

The history of the UFMCC contains tragedies, conflicts, and disappointments as well as important successes. Seventeen MCCs have burned—including one in New Orleans (in 1973) where thirty-two people were killed, and one in Atlanta (in 1982)—with arson suspected as the probable cause in many of the cases. In addition, during MCC's first three years, tensions between men and women concerning gender-inclusive references to

God and the lack of female leadership surfaced and continued to escalate, heightened by the ordination of its first woman, Freda Smith. In 1983, The National Council of Churches (NCC) refused membership status to the Universal Fellowship, and in 1994, they were denied even observer status by the same organization. In 1995, the Reverend Glenna Shepherd, a local MCC pastor, characterized the relationship between the Universal Fellowship and the NCC as "twelve years of unproductive dialogue."

First MCC, All Saints, and Christ Covenant are three Atlanta UFMCC churches. Each church has a senior pastor, choir, board of directors, and committees that are responsible for various fellowship, social, and political activities. Further, each MCC offers at least three weekly services, Bible study, a Sunday school program for children, and membership courses for adults. At this writing, First MCC is the largest of the three (with a Sunday attendance of 240), and has translators for hearing-impaired and Spanish-speaking individuals who attend. Senior pastors of Atlanta MCCs meet monthly to plan intercongregational programs and activities. All MCC services differ in preaching and hymnal style. First MCC preaches in Baptist style while All Saints favors a more Methodist orientation in sermons and hymns. Christ Covenant, on the other hand, combines low Methodist and high Episcopal styles in sermons, songs, and liturgy. An extended profile of Christ Covenant is offered here, not as representative, but as partially characteristic of Atlanta's Metropolitan Community Churches.

CHRIST COVENANT MCC

In 1992, Christ Covenant became the third MCC-affiliate in Atlanta and is now the second-largest MCC in the metro area. Like all MCCs, Christ Covenant respects the spiritual journeys of individuals and embraces those who subscribe to theologies different from their own. To become a member, individuals take a series of courses designed to instruct catechumens in the meaning and responsibility of church membership, statements of faith, sacraments and rites, and the history and polity of Christ Covenant and the Universal Fellowship. Members profess a Christian faith of liberation, asserting that all persons are created in the image of God and that through the gift of divine love and grace, individuals enter into a relationship with God as co-creators, co-sustainers, and co-redeemers. Christ Covenant celebrates the life, crucifixion, and resurrection of Jesus Christ in hymns, prayers and sermons in all worship services as an expression of their faith in God's commitment to the notion of divine-human partnership that works toward spiritual wholeness and liberation of all persons.

Christ Covenant's pastor, the Reverend Glenna Shepherd, explains that participation in the Eucharist represents the congregation's fellowship in the body of Christ and their faith in God's promise to redeem the helpless and downtrodden, a promise that was made manifest in Jesus' ministry to social outcasts. Communion is also a source for Christ Covenant's spiritual renewal and is an expression of members' ongoing commitment to fulfill their responsibilities as co-redeemers, co-creators, and co-sustainers with God in bringing about the promise of peace, equality, and harmony. Rather than reflect on the nature of the afterlife and instruct congregants on a regimen that promises entrance into heaven, Reverend Shepherd preaches about social and political problems of the present and designs outreach programs with church members to address discrimination, poverty, and homelessness.

Characterizing Christ Covenant's mission as "sacrament and social action," Reverend Shepherd explains that congregants are involved in many different social and political activities that address problems in Atlanta on both individual and institutional levels. Their mission continues the legacy of Dr. King's ministry to the poor and disadvantaged. Congregants participate in local chapters of national service organizations like Habitat for Humanity and AIDS CARE. Reverend Shepherd also encourages congregants to work against discriminatory legislation by contacting politicians and expressing their moral views on laws that exclude domestic partners from receiving occupational and federal financial benefits and that prohibit queer people from serving openly in the United States military.

In addition to Christ Covenant's participation in national and local outreach programs, the church is also involved in prison ministry work at Atlanta's women's prison, the Metro Correctional Institute. In this ministry, Reverend Shepherd emphasizes the necessity for a relational ethic—the sharing of congregants' spiritual and material resources with inmates—rather than the more traditional approach, which stresses inmates' confession of sins and subsequent profession of salvation and faith. Christ Covenant's involvement in the prison community consists of congregants' serving as pen-pals, mentors, or Big Sisters to inmates, contributing clothes and maintaining a fellowship group and choir.

INDEPENDENT CHRISTIAN CHURCHES

Queers in Atlanta have also established Christian churches that are separate from UFMCC. Among those churches are Home Free Ministries, Abundant Grace Community Church, and Circle of Grace. This section will explore the latter two congregations.

ABUNDANT GRACE COMMUNITY CHURCH

Abundant Grace Community Church is an independent Christian church of approximately sixty members that holds Sunday evening services at Virginia Highland Baptist Church. Similar to Christ Covenant's separation from All Saints MCC, Abundant Grace became an independent church in January 1995. Unlike Christ Covenant, however, Abundant Grace is not an official body of the Universal Fellowship, but a separate church with its own bylaws, statement of faith, and board of directors.

According to its pastor, the Reverend Paul Turner, queer Christians must establish their own churches and worship communities so that they will understand that spirituality does not involve the "hell and damnation" components that are often preached from pulpits in the Deep South. He explains that queer Christians should have personal relationships with God "that involve love, trust, and nurturing, and that facilitate spiritual growth." Reverend Turner also believes that queer people must take the first step in creating congregations for spiritual rebirth because, "it is similar to the same reason for the black church's emergence; if we don't do it, nobody else will." He acknowledges that "predominantly heterosexual churches are trying to address issues of homosexuality." He explains, however, "having a heterosexual deal with homosexuality, in all of its intricacies, is kind of like having a white person deal with black [people's] issues." For example, Reverend Turner requires relationship counseling for queer people who seek holy unions at Abundant Grace. While his sessions are similar in format to premarital counseling for heterosexual couples, Reverend Turner deals with issues—for example, social hostility, institutional discrimination, and family rejection—that queer people face specifically and that may be additional stress factors in their relationships.

Because Abundant Grace is a relatively new institution—still in the process of establishing a polity and finding a worship site—it has had to limit its participation in Atlanta's outreach programs. Still, Abundant Grace has found ways to contribute gifts to organizations and institutions that serve the many needs of Atlanta's queer and minority communities. At the end of each fiscal quarter, Abundant Grace contributes ten percent of its accumulated tithes to one of Atlanta's social organizations. In March 1995, the church made a donation to the half-way house of AIDS Education Services for Minorities. The church also offers fellowship, spiritual guidance, and education to student organizations at Georgia Tech, Georgia State University, and Emory University. In October 1995, Abundant Grace held its first annual revival and hosted singer and songwriter, Marcia Stephens.

Senior Deacon Sarah Hinds describes Reverend Turner as possessing a political activist fervor that is fueled by a spiritual desire to make connections with persons who are in spiritual distress. Several HIV-positive persons have come to Reverend Turner believing the rhetoric of the Reverend Charles Stanley (First Baptist Church) and other conservative Christians—rhetoric proclaiming that God has punished queer people because of their sexual orientation. "These queers are suffering from spiritual alienation from God," Reverend Turner explains, "and what they need is a personal relationship with God that is loving and nurturing." But Reverend Turner's concerns include more than pastoral counseling to spiritually troubled persons. For instance, in 1994, the Atlanta Commission for the Olympic Games (ACOG) awarded a preliminary venue for volleyball to Cobb County, whose commission had previously passed a resolution stating that "gay lifestyles" were not acceptable to Cobb's community standards. In response to the commission's and ACOG's decisions, Reverend Turner and Atlanta's queer religious community assisted other organizations and committees (Cobb Citizens Coalition, Gay and Lesbian Alliance Against Defamation, Olympics Out of Cobb) in gathering support to protest Cobb's resolution and ACOG's venue award. Reverend Turner gave an eloquent speech on inclusivity at a mass demonstration that demanded ACOG pressure Cobb's commission to rescind its resolution of intolerance or suffer the loss of the volleyball venue. Acquiescing, ACOG issued Cobb the ultimatum and, when the commission refused to revoke the resolution, ACOG moved Olympic volleyball to Athens.

CIRCLE OF GRACE

Established in 1993, Circle of Grace is a Christian community of twenty-five women who are committed to feminist principles of equality and justice. The Circle began when several women from different Protestant organizations sought to heal "spiritual brokenness" that they had experienced in mainline denominations mainly because of their gender and sexual orientations. At that time, the women witnessed one another's testimonies—including their personal triumphs and setbacks, spiritual journeys, and visions—and understood this experience as the first step toward building a community of diverse individuals who shared many commonalities. The pastor, Reverend Connie Tuttle, explains that "As feminists, there must be room for everyone's truth." She continues: "The challenge of being a part of a feminist, spiritual community, is exciting, engaging, and sometimes overwhelming." While the Circle has incorporated a variety of rituals, story-telling continues to be an important part of its process of strengthening the community and promoting the spiritual journey in fellowship because "as Christians, our spiritual tradition binds us historically and experientially in the stories and metaphors we use to talk about our common spiritual experiences of reconciliation, liberation, and empowerment."

Since congregants encountered spiritual problems in other denominations, the Circle's theology is geared toward individuals' specific needs and uses experience as one of its four pillars of faith. The pillars (the Holy Spirit, the church, the Bible, and experience) form a quadrangle that is sustained by an interactive dynamic among each. Reverend Tuttle explains that spiritual authority can be found in many sources (scriptures, doctrines, ministers, etc.) and that Circle of Grace includes experience as a source of revelation about self, God, and the world. For the Circle, "Christian feminism is a fluid exploration where we describe our spiritual experiences and relationships rather than having them prescribed by external authorities."

As reflections of congregants' spiritual histories and the Circle's theology, services are traditional in form yet non-traditional in content. Services change continually as members create new ritual and incorporate elements from other traditions that are spiritually meaningful for them. The first half of a typical service begins with meditation on an idea that has been taken from a book and progresses to a corporate call to worship, confession, and assurance of pardon. Reverend Tuttle then reads from scripture, preaches, and serves communion. Sometimes services contain special programs that minister to congregants' specific needs and wishes, such as a Litany of Tears in which the congregation asks for God's grace, comfort, and guidance during periods of mourning. Another example is Reverend Tuttle's decision, during the 1994 Advent season, to focus on female biblical figures (Tamar, Rahab, Ruth, and Bathsheba) and to ask why these women were included—since they were not "your ordinary, good `church women'"—and why others were omitted. In addition to weekly services, Circle of Grace provides opportunities for spiritual growth and community cohesion through bi-weekly prayer groups and social activities, such as potluck dinners, parties, and retreats. Like Abundant Grace, Circle of Grace also participates in Atlanta's outreach organizations such as Jerusalem House and the Council on Battered Women, volunteering their time and donating a percentage of quarterly accumulated tithes.

Because Circle of Grace emerged out of congregants' spiritual troubles, one of its future goals is to remain a safe space for healing individuals' spiritual wounds and facilitating their journeys toward wholeness in an inclusive atmosphere. Reverend Tuttle believes that "social action begins and ends with prayer," and sees the church's future as one of increasing its spiritual impact on the larger community by "standing forth as divinely empowered human beings for justice" and proclaiming the liberating message of Jesus—freedom for all peoples.

PREDOMINANTLY HETEROSEXUAL CHRISTIAN CHURCHES THAT WELCOME QUEER PEOPLE

In addition to Atlanta's MCCs and independent Christian churches, several larger mainline denominations accept queer people as fellow worshipers in their predominantly heterosexual congregations. While these churches are not part of Atlanta's queer communities, they are attentive to the concerns of the queer population. Some of these churches combine secular and religious teachings, including the Atlanta Church of Religious Science, First Existential Congregation, Fellowship of Love Christian Church, and the Mount Cavalry Lighthouse. From the Presbyterian denomination, Clifton and Oakhurst Presbyterian Churches affirm and minister to queer people, who compose about one-third of their congregations. Several Episcopal parishes welcome queers and encourage their full participation in parish life. The Catholic Shrine of the Immaculate Conception also welcomes queer persons into the fold.

Representing the Baptist tradition, Virginia Highland Baptist Church welcomes Atlanta's queer community in Christian worship and fellowship. The pastor here, the Reverend Tim Shirley, is a former Southern Baptist minister who "went through a life-long adult process of reflection, contemplation, and engagement." He believes that "I am a better Christian, more committed, and have a better understanding of the gospel than I did fifteen years earlier." Because of Reverend Shirley's developmental process and the convictions that arose from it, his relationship with the Southern Baptist

Convention (SBC) has been strained due to his belief in women's ordination, the right to abortion, and affirmation of queer people. According to Reverend Shirley, Virginia Highland Baptist accepts Atlanta's queer religious community because "We believe that was what Jesus would have done, especially when we remember that he ministered to people who were shunned by the social and political order of his time."

That Reverend Shirley also retains the original Baptist convictions of separation of church and state and the priesthood of all believers puts him at odds with the SBC which, he believes, "has abandoned its historical Baptist roots and become more mainstream and conformist with the conservative political trend that began in the early 1980s." As a "Christian community that is committed to the gospel," the church serves the Virginia Highland area in many ways. It has two day care centers, two cultural awareness programs, and functions as headquarters for John Howell Park community meetings, a rehearsal space for the Atlanta Gay Men's Chorus, and meeting space for a chemical dependency group. "Everything that we do for the community," Reverend Shirley explains, "is grounded in the gospel teachings of acceptance, love, and fellowship."

Representing the United Methodist tradition, Grant Park Aldersgate welcomes Atlanta's queer community in Christian worship, fellowship, and mission outreach. The Reverend Dr. Jean Jones, pastor, explains that Grant Park Aldersgate is a "Reconciling Congregation," a program of the United Methodist Church that conducts an investigation into human sexuality and affirms, ministers to, and blesses the unions of queer fellow worshipers. Grant Park Aldersgate is one of two congregations in the Southeastern Conference of United Methodist Churches to affirm the spiritual presence and gifts of queer people. When asked why Grant Park Aldersgate ministers to the queer community, Reverend Jones tells the following story: "One year I was staffing our church booth at the Pride Parade and a young woman with an incredulous look on her face came over. She asked me if we were a church and if she could come and be accepted. When I said 'yes,' she was speechless for a moment, and then she began to cry." Reverend Jones explains, "It is the alienation that is caused by the church's rejection of gay, lesbian, and bisexual people that is contrary to the reconciling and healing ministry of Jesus Christ. And it is because of the work of God through Christ that we are a Reconciling Congregation, providing a safe space for gay people's spiritual growth and social acceptance."

Grant Park Aldersgate has established Latina outreach and AIDS ministries, a food bank, and a multiracial summer camp. Many congregants also work as volunteers for Project Open Hand/Atlanta—a support organization that prepares and delivers meals to persons with AIDS. As Grant Park Aldersgate continues outreach programs on a local scale, Reverend Jones hopes for an act of grace on a larger level. She prays for the United Methodist Church's unconditional acceptance of queer people into its laity and polity.

In addition to the mainline churches, smaller denominations such as Atlanta's Religious Society of Friends (Quakers) and the Unitarian Universalist Church also welcome queer people in spiritual affirmation, worship, and fellowship. Unitarian Universalist was the first American church to ordain women (1841), to ordain queers (1970), and to bless same-gender unions (1984). At the Atlanta branch, 150 queer people are part of a total membership roll of 1,200. Queer congregants actively participate in the congregation's many outreach programs, and the church protests discrimination and violence against women, queers, and ethnic people. The six churches in the metro Atlanta area assisted the Cobb Citizens Coalition, Gay and Lesbian Anti-Defamation Defense, and Olympics Out of Cobb in amassing support against the county commission's anti-queer resolution and volleyball venue award.

RELIGIOUS ORGANIZATIONS WITHIN CHRISTIAN CHURCHES

Queer Atlantans have also formed religious organizations *within* several Christian churches. These groups include the Seventh-Day Adventist Kinship International, Emergence/Atlanta (Christian Scientists), Gay and Lesbian Mormons, Friends for Lesbian and Gay Concerns (Quakers), Interweave (Unitarian Universalist), Dignity (Catholic), Integrity (Episcopal), and, two that will be discussed below, Lutherans Concerned and Presbyterians for Lesbian and Gay Concerns.

Founded in 1974, Lutherans Concerned/North America (LC/NA) is a religious support organization of Lutherans who help queer persons reconcile their spirituality and sexuality in an uplifting way. Local chapters provide worship services, keynote speakers, fellowship events, and newsletters for members' spiritual growth and social support. In 1984, LC/NA initiated a dialogue with the heterosexual Lutheran faith community and started a Reconciling in Christ program to recognize congregations that welcome queer people. In initiating reconciliation, the Atlanta chapter locates and encourages Lutheran congregations and organizations engaging in inclusive ministry with queer individuals. To facilitate reconciliation, LC/Atlanta sponsors a series of educational forums with receptive congregations because, as one member explains, "hearing the experiences of gay and lesbian people and their families often creates greater understanding and insights." In its short history, LC/NA's Reconciling in Christ has succeeded in over 100 Lutheran congregations and nine synods. LC/Atlanta will continue the mission of reconciliation here and describes that future process as "affirming the God-given nature of sexual orientation, proclaiming the good news of Jesus Christ through inclusive worship and promoting positive changes in all experiences of the Lutheran Church."

Like LC/NA, Presbyterians for Lesbian and Gay Concerns (PLGC) was established in 1974 with similar goals—bridging the gap between queer Presbyterians' sexuality and spirituality, and working for inclusive ministries in Presbyterian churches and general assemblies. PLGC also works to "ensure the full membership and rights" of queer persons in society, lobbying politicians on urgent concerns of the community (for example, anti-queer violence and job discrimination) and establishing funds and organizations to improve the quality of queer people's lives. PLGC/Atlanta meets regularly for worship, support, fellowship, study, and social action. The chapter also works with local Presbyterian churches that preach the liberating and inclusive gospel of Jesus and wish to develop more inclusive ministries. Like Lutherans Concerned, PLGC fosters this process by conducting educational forums that nurture biblical, theological, confessional, spiritual, and personal development for individuals and the church. The fruit of PLGC's labors is demonstrated by the failure of a 1995 proposed amendment to the Presbyterian Church's constitution that would have prohibited the blessing of same-gender unions by ministers. Needing eighty-six votes to pass, the proposal lost by a landslide. Fueled by the liberating message of the gospel, PLGC continues to work for queer persons' civil safety, legal rights, and unqualified acceptance in the church and society.

ALTERNATIVE SPIRITUALITIES

The fifth category of worshiping communities in Atlanta's queer population relates to alternative spirituality. New Age Gays, Goddess-Oriented Spirituality, and Gay Spirit Visions combine teachings and rituals from several religious traditions and secular sources. Gay Spirit Visions will be explored as one example of a queer religious community within the diverse alternative spirituality movement.

Gay Spirit Visions (GSV) is a leaderless group of approximately 600 gay men that grew out of activist Harry Hay's Radical Fairies movement of the late 1970s. Hay had founded Radical Fairies as a safe place for men who wanted to escape momentarily "the constraining box of masculinity that society imposes on them." Throughout the 1980s, smaller Radical Fairy groups and sanctuaries appeared throughout the country where gay men celebrated holidays around annual solstices and equinoxes, and explored parts of themselves that society demanded they repress. The movement dissipated in 1988, but the Running Water Collective (Ron Lamb, Peter Kindrick, Raven Wolfdancer) in Georgia continued the tradition in GSV (1990), keeping some of the original activities and creating others.

Treewalker, a GSV member, explains that the collective retained the Radical Fairies' original purpose of maintaining a "safe space for men who love men to be men of spirit, whatever that means for them, and a space of absence for those men who have not yet come—men of color and men of different abilities." Another member, John Stowe, explains on a personal note that GSV "is my family, because it gives the gay part of me—which can never come out in society without that filter of watching people's reaction—a place to live." Al Cotton, another member, reiterates this point: "The conferences help us to heal the gay part of ourselves that has been hurt by organized religion." The group also kept Hay's philosophy of "subject-subject consciousness" and rituals like the Fire Pit and the Heart Circle, where members explore feelings and desires that society pretends men do not have. GSV member Bruce Tidwell explains that "subject-subject consciousness allows us to engage one another on equal terms rather than competing for dominance and personal agendas." "We recognize," he continues, "that there is enough spiritual energy and power for everyone and that we do not have to compete for it."

Cotton explains that "GSV added workshops, keynote speakers, and small group meetings to provide group structure and community cohesion, and to facilitate men's spiritual needs as they arise from our daily lives." The group has included a Native American Fire Circle, Silent Walk, and Gift-Giving Ritual in their activities. Around the Fire Circle, men dance to a rhythmically shifting and escalating pulse of drumming. For the Gift-Giving Ritual, members form smaller circles around objects that have had personal significance for them. When one participant chooses an object, the one who brought it tells the story of the object's significance in his life and it then becomes a gift to the recipient.

Since 1990, GSV's annual conference convenes with a keynote speaker during the autumnal equinox; it lasts for nine days, and is held at the Mountain, a Unitarian Universalist Conference Center in Highlands, North Carolina. The conference is organized around a theme and includes smaller groups that engage in workshops and rituals. The 1995 theme was aging. Treewalker explains: "As a result of AIDS, we are beginning to look at elderhood as proximity to ending life rather than accumulated years, and what that means for younger men's outlook on life." While new events add some structure to the conference, the collective continues to recognize members' individual spiritual paths and quests. Some men take a Native American environmentalist path, honoring their earth mothers and fathers. Some men work with crystals on New Age quests, while others explore the Leather Path and its meanings for a radical sexuality. Men's various spiritual paths are connected through Jungian concepts and archetypal symbology. In addition to the annual meeting, smaller, local replicas of the conference are held monthly as sources of spiritual renewal and growth for members.

FAITHS AND CONGREGATIONS WITH AN ETHNIC-CULTURAL BASE

The final category of worship in Atlanta's queer religious community includes Bet Haverim and Redefined Faith Unity Fellowship Church. Bet Haverim is affiliated with the Reconstructionist movement that Rabbi Mordecai Kaplan began in America during the 1920s. Redefined Faith is part of the historical black church tradition whose theology and worship styles differ from mainstream Protestantism and Catholicism.

CONGREGATION BET HAVERIM

The queer Jewish movement to build synagogues and worship communities began with the formation of Beth Chayim Chadashim ("House of New Life") in Los Angeles in 1972. One year later, Congregation Beth Simchat Torah was founded in New York City. Since then, queer Jews have established over twenty synagogues in major cities throughout the United States.

Congregation Bet Haverim's origins date back to 1984 when three gay men formed a *Havurah* (fellowship group) to discuss the heterosexist assumptions and innuendoes of fellow congregants that they felt were pervasive in predominantly heterosexual synagogues. Several goals emerged from their meetings: the men wanted their own synagogue and rabbi, a non-sexist and gender-neutral liturgy, and a prayerbook that would be sensitive to the lives of queer people. The following year the group established itself as a congregation, formed a steering committee that drafted by-laws, and began meeting for weekly and High Holy Day services at the Quaker Meeting House in Decatur. By 1989, with an executive board in place, Bet Haverim began to affiliate with the Reconstructionist movement (the Federation of Reconstructionist Congregations and Havurot—recently renamed the Jewish Reconstructionist Federation) and brought in student-rabbi Sharon Kleinbaum from the Reconstructionist Rabbinical College in Wyncate, Pennsylvania, for High Holy Day services. The congregation's membership surged during this period, so in 1994, Rabbi Leila Gal Berner was hired and serves as Bet Haverim's rabbi-in-residence, providing religious, educational, pastoral, and professional leadership.

Bet Haverim holds weekly Sabbath services (including one for children), celebrates all Jewish holy days, and is active in service organizations throughout Atlanta. While the congregation uses a Reconstructionist *siddur* (prayerbook) for services and celebrations, it inserts into the liturgy prayers, songs, and poems that are meaningful to queer people's lives. For instance, High Holy Days usually include sermons given by the rabbi as well as several sermons by members of the congregation that address personal spiritual and emotional issues in the context of gay, lesbian, and bisexual people's lives.

They also have linked the Passover Seder to the annual National Gay Pride celebration that commemorates Stonewall 1969—an historic event where American queers, after thirty years of abuse and oppression, refused to acquiesce any longer to police bar-raids and brutality, and rebelled in the streets of New York City for three days. Bet Haverim uses Passover rituals that include four cups of wine, four questions about gay pride and the synagogue, and ten plagues against the queer community. Congregant Richard Adler participated in the Stonewall riots and explains that, "instead of reading the passages of the Jews' exodus from Egypt, we read a special *haggadah* of the gay and lesbian riots at Stonewall that began the entire movement in 1969." Instead of the usual Passover symbols, such as bitter herbs and harosh, seder plates are filled with bricks to remember what Stonewall rioters used in defending themselves against police. Seder plates also include a pink triangle as a reminder of the queers who were interned and murdered in Holocaust concentration camps. By using the format of Passover to commemorate Stonewall, Bet Haverim draws a connection between enslavement of the Jewish people in ancient Egypt and the contemporary oppression of queer people.

The synagogue is also a programming participant with Common Ground, a weekday activities program for persons with AIDS that is sponsored by the Atlanta Interfaith AIDS Network. The congregation has also developed a religious school for children, a year-long study program for adults, and "AIDS Chaim," which offers emotional-spiritual support and practical services to congregants with AIDS or other illnesses. Members have also spoken at many *havurot* (groups) and schools throughout the city. Nationally and internationally, Bet Haverim is a member of the World Congress of Gay and Lesbian Synagogues and Atlanta's Council of Lesbian and Gay Religious Organizations. The congregation hopes to develop a social outreach program that will educate and inform the larger Atlanta community that violence and discrimination against queer people hurts everyone—queer and straight—and shatters King's dream for a just and democratic world.

Recent developments in Bet Haverim's growth have led to the congregation's becoming a more "mixed" community. Since 1994, a significant number of heterosexual Jews have begun to join Bet Haverim, and the community is now engaged in an important process of self-evaluation as the face of the congregation takes on new dimensions. For queer members, the challenge is to retain the sense of safety, validation, and intimacy Bet Haverim has offered since its inception. For heterosexual Jews, the challenge is to respectfully enter a queer Jewish community as allies and also as seekers of the deeper spirituality that this congregation offers.

REDEFINED FAITH UNITY FELLOWSHIP CHURCH

In 1995, the Reverend S. F. Mahee founded Redefined Faith Unity Fellowship Church as part of an international movement of Unity Fellowship churches—"the largest African-American gay, lesbian, bisexual, transgender organization in the world." Bishop Carl Bean started the movement in 1985 in Los Angeles, and has overseen the establishment of Unity Fellowship churches in over one hundred major cities in the United States. When asked why the Atlanta church's name is "Redefined Faith," Reverend Mahee tells the following story: "I had grown up in a fundamentalist Pentecostal church whose theology did not reflect where I was as an African-American feminist lesbian. And after embarking on a personal spiritual journey, I realized that truth comes in many forms and that I needed to rebuild my spirituality and redefine my faith to affirm my personhood." During Reverend Mahee's spiritual transformation, Unity Fellowship's liberation theology appealed to her because, "Our spirituality should be the first level of liberation that we undergo; it gives us a footing upon which to stand in the face of the daily violence that we confront as African-American gay, lesbian, bisexual, transgender people." "If we are not practicing a self-liberating theology," she continues, "we are practicing self-crucifixion."

Redefined Faith's theological foundation is in the Jewish and Christian traditions, but, Reverend Mahee qualifies, "it is not the ceiling." Her belief that truth appears in many forms and that spirituality is the first level of liberation helps to shape the church's worship services and ministries. Because congregants come from different religious backgrounds, services reflect an array of traditions, including Baptist pentecostalism, African spirituality, and the Church of God in Christ. Liturgical readings come from a variety of sources as well: "Whether it takes a reading from the Torah, the Qur'an, the gospels, or spiritual lessons from a course in miracles, our purpose is to provide spiritual nourishment and affirmation for our people."

When asked why black queers need a church for themselves, Reverend Mahee explains that "the predominantly heterosexual black church has neglected our spiritual needs because of our sexual orientation. And while the Metropolitan Community Church affirms our sexuality, it falls short in dealing with problems that black people face, and in providing the spiritedness and call-and-response nature of the black church within which we were reared." Redefined Faith builds upon the liberating theology of the black church, understanding Christ's ministry as inclusive of, and liberating to, black queer people. Reverend Mahee expounds on this point: "Jesus' ministry is very important to us right now, because conservative politicians and fundamentalists have issued a contract on certain Americans' legal and civil rights." She further clarifies, "These people would have us believe that they are doing Christ's work when, in fact, Christ's whole experience with the religious and political order of his day shows that conservative politicians and fundamentalists are the same kinds of people with whom Jesus had direct conflict while preaching God's truth of love and justice."

Congregants worked with the Rainbow Coalition to organize protests against the Cobb Commission's anti-queer resolution. The church also has an AIDS hospital ministry in which members visit local hospitals to offer spiritual support and care to patients. Redefined Faith is also forming a recording choir and working in the Interfaith Community to create prison ministries and homeless outreach services. As a member of Concerned Black Clergy/Atlanta, Reverend Mahee would like to see Dr. King's dream of an equal and free society become a reality. She hopes that "religious leaders throughout the world will unite against anti-queer and anti-ethnic violence." "They need to speak out against the train of thought that queer's and other minority peoples' lives are not of value," she explains, "because persons who commit these crimes believe that they are doing God a favor as if God needs their help."

CONCLUSION

Today queer Jews and Christians are building congregations and worshiping during a critical moment in America's history. For the past thirty years, Atlanta's queer religious communities, like others worldwide, have taken many steps in establishing their own congregations and religious organizations, and gaining support and acceptance. Some congregations have followed liturgical and organizational conventions of their traditional faith, while others have modified rituals and inserted prayers and scriptures that are more meaningful for their lives. Still others have created churches and groups that do not reflect the tenets of any specific faith, but whose practices and rituals address their own spiritual needs. While Atlanta's queer religious community has created many avenues for spiritual growth and worship, it faces a much larger task in the future. Queer Americans continue to battle religious conservative politicians for the decriminalization of their ways of living and loving, for the right to rear their children, and for legal protection from violence and discrimination, to name only a few of their primary concerns. While these rights and freedoms may seem basic and a "given" to many heterosexual Americans, they are rights and freedoms that queer people have been denied. The queer religious community could play a critical role in future struggles for human rights, freedom, and democracy. However, as the bumper sticker, "Kill A Queer for Christ" attests, the queer religious community has an enormous mountain of hatred and evil to overcome.

FOR FURTHER INFORMATION

Christie Balka and Andy Rose, eds. *Twice Blessed: On Being Lesbian, Gay, and Jewish*. Boston, Beacon Press, 1989

Evelyn Torton Beck, ed. *Nice Jewish Girls: A Lesbian Anthology*. Boston, Beacon Press, 1989

Malcolm Boyd and Nancy L. Wilson, eds. *Amazing Grace: Stories of Lesbian and Gay Faith*, Freedom, Crossing Press, 1991

Louie Crew, ed. *A Book of Revelations: Lesbian and Gay Episcopalians Tell Their Own Stories*. Washington, DC Integrity, 1991

Rosemary Curb and Nancy Manahan, eds. *Lesbian Nuns: Breaking Silence*. Tallahassee, The Naiad Press, 1985

Carter Heyward. *Speaking of Christ: A Lesbian Feminist Voice*. New York, The Pilgrim Press, 1989

Roger Lanphear. *Gay Spirituality: Experiences In Self-realization for Gay Men, Lesbians, and Elightened Heterosexuals*. San Diego, Unified Publications, 1990

John McNeill. *The Church and the Homosexual*. Boston, Beacon Press, 1988

John McNeill. *Taking a Chance on God: Liberating Theology for Gays, Lesbians, and Their Lovers, Families, and Friends*, Boston, Beacon Press, 1988

Troy Perry. *The Lord Is My Shepherd and He Knows I'm Gay*. Los Angeles, Nash Publishing, 1972

Troy Perry and Thomas L. P. Swicegood. *Don't Be Afraid Anymore*. New York, St. Martin's Press, 1990

Troy Perry and Thomas L. P. Swicegood. *Profiles In Lesbian and Gay Courage*. New York, St. Martin's Press, 1991

Moshe Shokeid. *A Gay Synagogue In New York*. New York, Columbia University Press, 1995

John S. Spong. *Living In Sin?: A Bishop Rethinks Human Sexuality*. San Francisco, Harper, 1988

John S. Spong. *Rescuing the Bible From Fundamentalism: A Bishop Rethinks the Meaning of Scripture*, San Francisco, Harper, 1991

CHAPTER TWENTY-ONE

NEW AGE IN THE NEW SOUTH: ALTERNATIVE SPIRITUALITIES IN METROPOLITAN ATLANTA

Theodore Brelsford

Unity Church of Roswell. Photograph by Louis A. Ruprecht, Jr.

Atlanta's counterculture hangs out in Little Five Points; body piercing, black leather, and ragged jeans are popular among patrons and loiterers. There is often a man with dreadlocks drumming in the small park area in front of a row of shops. Clustered with vintage clothing outlets, retro bars, and a tattoo shop, is a store called the Crystal Blue. Among the things for sale here are crystals in myriad sizes, shapes, and colors, candles and incense, Native American dream catchers, figurines of fairies and gnomes, hand made natural jewelry, T-shirts with ecological messages, meditation music, tarot cards, and books on channeling, UFOs, vegetarianism, feminism, medieval mystics, self psychology, Celtic spirituality, ecology and creation spirituality, and more. The sounds of Kitaro's gentle earthy music often wafts in the background. There is the smell of smoldering incense. A psychic is available for fifteen- or thirty-minute palm readings in a back room. Near the entryway there are piles of brochures, pamphlets, and business cards, offering a range of businesses and services, including: the Atlanta Polarity Therapy Center, numerous chiropractors, a workshop on "the metaphysical properties of Quartz Crystals and gem stones," and body-based emotional healing, as well as Reiki masters, hypnotherapy, massage therapy, rebirthing, herbs shops, and various techniques for exploring personal spirituality.

At the Unity Church, in the middle-class northern Atlanta suburb of Roswell, about 350 people gather in a bright and airy sanctuary at 11:00 on Sunday morning. The church is conveniently located in a shopping center and operates a thriving bookstore during the week. A four-piece band plays soothing, upbeat music to set the mood for this service of celebration. There is some congregational singing and guided meditational prayers aimed at, in the words of one member, "surrendering the self into universal intelligence" to attain the "higher intelligence, higher you, higher self" that lies within each individual. Congregants hear in the day's "teaching" (there are no "sermons" here) that all humans are connected to a basic unity in the universe, and that the conscious mind can connect to that unity through intentional practices of thought. As the Reverend Carol O'Connell puts it, "Spiritual psychology . . . or science of mind . . . is what we do, and what we teach here."

The Center for Health Resources is a holistic health center that allows people to make individual appointments for massage therapy, chiropractic adjustments, spiritual counseling, hypnotherapy, rebirthing, Tai Chi, and Yoga. There are also group seminars and healing sessions most evenings, including "Exploring New Paradigms," "Fundamentals of Metaphysics," "Reiki Healing Group," "Healing Shame Workshop," "Divorced and Separated Women," "Redirecting Children's Behavior," and others. Located at the end of a long drive in a wooded residential/limited commercial neighborhood in north Atlanta, a feeling of natural beauty and serenity pervades the premises even though I-285 is only a few blocks away. The center is comprised of three distinct units—a comfortably appointed office, a small gift shop, and a building that houses the center's various practitioners. A hot tub adjoins the practitioners building. In the gift shop one may buy books, herbs, incense, astrological bath oils, and, as its business card puts it, other "treasures to support your health and self discovery needs."

These vignettes depict just three of the more visible places of gathering and support in and around Atlanta for people pursuing alternative spiritual paths, sometimes labeled "New Age Spirituality." The term "New Age" is slippery and controversial because it has a broad range of meanings. For some, it denotes psychic channeling (communication from disembodied spirits), belief in the special energies and healing powers of crystals, or anticipation of the impending transformation of society into a "new age" of harmony and wholeness. For others, it simply means vegetarianism, an emphasis on holistic health, and deep concern for the environment. Nearly everyone agrees that it has something to do with a sense of the "oneness" of all that is—nature, God, humanity (mind, body, soul), good, evil are all part of the one whole.

Scholars and the popular media have commonly used the term "New Age" to talk about a rising cultural movement in American society during the 1970s and 1980s that focused on personal and social transformation (particularly the belief associated with the dawning of a new age). Adherents to this movement consider transformation possible and imminent because of the nearly limitless potential of human beings that is being progressively realized in the course of human evolution. This movement has manifested itself through, and at times been defined by, interest in trance channeling, astrology, healing with crystals, reincarnation, out-of-body experiences, altered states of consciousness, meditation techniques, UFO abductions, the intuitive powers of the brain's right hemisphere, and a spiritual connection to the earth. But many of those who have a keen interest in one or more of these alternative spiritual expressions or practices may not be particularly interested in the others. A person who uses crystals and practices astrology and yoga meditation may be disinterested in (and disbelieve reports of) UFOs and out-of-body-experiences. Others may practice yoga, hope for an out-of-body experience, and have no faith at all in crystals. Complicating things further is the reality that what is considered "alternative" or "New Age" changes over time. Some of the people who were ardent vegetarians and "into" channeling and reincarnation in the 1970s, shifted their interest to mediation and massage in the 1980s, and may now be eating meat and studying Native American shamanism. There is also significant overlap at times between "New Age" and mainstream spirituality, as exhibited most recently by the increased interest in, and popularity of, angels.

Perhaps the "New Age" movement is best characterized, if generalizations are to be made, as a spiritual avant-garde. There is a penchant for the new, the alternative, the innovative. Some of what is tried on this spiritual frontier fades away, some endures as authentic countercultural expression, and some gradually becomes part of mainstream culture. "New Age" spirituality might be defined by a willingness to innovate, to experiment with the unusual, to draw on a variety of sources (both traditional and non-traditional), and to mix and match—taking whatever works (for the individual) and discarding that which doesn't.

A prominent part of "New Age" consciousness also includes a commitment to relativism, localism, and democratic individualism. In other words, while most religious movements are defined by their dogma (their beliefs and teachings) and institutional structure, there is strong resistance among "New Agers" to these components of conventional religious organizations. Indeed, dogma and institution are precisely what these alternative spiritual paths lead away from! As Georgia State philosophy professor Mark Woodhouse puts it, what sets "New Agers" apart is not so much "what" they believe, but rather "how they come by their beliefs and promote them in public." Their beliefs tend to be intuitively based rather than derived from some external authority. Members of this diverse community tend, on the one hand, to be most comfortable with a small group of loosely formed, like-minded believers who reinforce their beliefs; on the other hand, many tend to work for practical changes in society that their beliefs inspire without overtly promoting these beliefs to the public.

The origins of the "New Age" movement are as nebulous as its definition. The publication of actress Shirley MacLaine's *Out On A Limb*, in 1983, is often credited with popularizing "New Age" spirituality and making it into a movement rather than a scattering of people engaged in unusual spiritual practices. Indeed, MacLaine's book about her own out-of-body, channeling, and reincarnation experiences and beliefs became a best seller, and the TV movie based on the book reached millions more. MacLaine brought her alternative spiritual journey into the full light of popular consciousness, providing an introduction to, and a vocabulary for, many others who would pursue similar paths. However, *The Aquarian Conspiracy,* foretelling of a "new age dawning" had already been published in 1980 and is cited by others as marking the beginning of the contemporary "New Age" movement. Even before this book, however, Carlos Casteneda's *The Teachings of Don Juan: A Yaqui Way of Knowledge,* introduced American popular culture to peyote and some Native American wisdom traditions in 1968 (with sequels in 1971 and 1974). Casteneda, whose books remain in print and ever popular, also deserves credit for initiating countercultural interest in alternative spiritual paths. The real roots of "New Age" spirituality, however, can be traced back much further, through nineteenth-century Transcendentalism and spiritualism to medieval mysticism, early Gnosticism, and ancient nature religions.

In the 1990s this movement, or "new paradigm" as some have put it, has quietly entered more and more into the mainstream and become a prominent dimension of contemporary culture. Once identified as signs of counterculture, things like vegetarianism, dissatisfaction with modern science and modern social structures, belief in auras and energies surrounding all living things, and a yearning for a closer spiritual connection to the natural world have become relatively commonplace in American society. The novel *The Celestine Prophesy,* for example, which prominently features the revelation of secret wisdom about auras and energies around humans, plants, and animals, and how to use those energy forces to achieve harmony and avoid conflict, topped the *New York Times* best seller list for several months in 1994 and 1995, and continues to sell millions of copies.

On the other hand, due perhaps to negative and sensationalist media coverage during the 1980s, few people who fit the "New Age" category based on the above criteria actually call themselves "New Age." A comment by Dan Liss, editor of the Atlanta-based *Aquarius* newspaper, illustrates the ambiguities surrounding the label for those within this community: "If asked if we are the 'New Age' newspaper for Atlanta, I would say yes. But we don't use the word 'New Age' anywhere to describe ourselves." The Reverend Carol O'Connell of the Unity Church in Roswell responds in a similar fashion: "We really are 'New Age,' but we shy away from that [term]." More often these people refer to themselves and others like them as "on an alternative spiritual path," or "non-traditional religious seekers." Some understand themselves as advocates of "New Thought"—a theological position that arose in nineteenth-century America and is characterized by a belief that human beings are partners with God (understood as non-personal collective energy) in the creation of physical and spiritual reality. The Unity churches, Religious Science churches, and several other independent churches in Atlanta, such as the Hillside Chapel and Truth Center, consider themselves a part of the New Thought tradition. Another more general term that many of these people seem comfortable with is "metaphysical." As one self-proclaimed spiritual seeker put it, "I don't know if I'm 'New Age' but I certainly am metaphysical." In this context being "metaphysical" means that one believes in realities beyond the merely physical and obvious realities of life. This may include belief in the existence of angels and other spirits, as well as an acute awareness of divine dimensions in human beings and a higher spiritual interconnectedness throughout the cosmos. "Metaphysical" in this context also implies non-allegiance with traditional western religious systems like Christianity, Judaism, or Islam. Persons who are "metaphysical" tend to reject the notion of one God "out there" in favor of multiple spiritual entities (and multiple truths) all around them. Stores like the one described at the beginning of this article are often called "metaphysical bookstores" by those who own them and frequent them.

Finding a way to talk about the "community" or the "movement" that these various alternative spiritual expressions constitute is difficult. Thus, although it is nebulous and problematic, the phrase "New Age" remains, and is used, even by those who dislike it, as an umbrella term for a range of contemporary, innovative, and alternative spiritual expressions. The phrase is used, along with "alternative spirituality," throughout this article to assert a general family resemblance among the various beliefs and practices discussed.

The growth of interest in New Age spirituality in Atlanta parallels the rising interest in such belief systems nationally, as well as the emergence of

Atlanta as a cosmopolitan city. During the turbulent 1960s, many Americans rebelled against the feeling of alienation in modern industrialized society by forming communes, using hallucinogenic drugs, dabbling in eastern religions, and rejecting established Jewish and Christian social mores along with the perceived hierarchical and authoritarian theological assumptions underpinning them. During the 1970s and into the 1980s, while a few persistent "hippies" kept their long hair and their counterculture posture, most slipped more or less comfortably into the mainstream of society. Yet their disillusionment with modern science and technology, their rebellion against hierarchical social structures and institutions, and their interest in eastern philosophies and religions did not go away. Rather, these "sixties sentiments" mellowed with age and began to find socially acceptable and sustainable expression within, or on the edges of, the structures of society, mostly in the form of books, new religious communities, and alternative health practices. This transition from anti-establishment countercultural expression to the development of New Age spirituality as an enduring and integral part of American society can be seen in the growth, since the mid-1970s, of businesses in Atlanta that cater to New Age interests.

In 1974 The Sphinx, Atlanta's oldest metaphysical book store according to some, opened its doors. By 1980 there were still only three such stores in Atlanta. Today, there are some sixteen metaphysical bookstores listed in the Yellow Pages, and the advertising section of the Aquarius newspaper lists seven more. The emergence of health food stores has a similar history—from a few in 1980 to nearly one in every shopping center today. And while many health food stores include a section devoted to herbs, there are also a dozen stores in the Yellow Pages advertising themselves explicitly as herbal shops specializing in non-medicinal remedies and cures. There are also some thirty chiropractors in the Yellow Pages (while many more advertise in other publications), and at least half a dozen alternative health centers are located around the city. Card and palm readers also proliferated in Atlanta during the 1980s, and various mediums and mystics emerged during this decade as well. Some organized religious communities also formed around the quest for personal transformation and interest in the metaphysical. Four new Unity churches were founded in the Atlanta area during the 1980s, as well as an Eckankar Center, two Religious Science churches, a Karin Kabala center, and the Hillside Chapel and Truth Center, founded by a Unity trained African-American woman.

The blossoming of non-traditional religious expressions in the Bible Belt, however, was not without incident. In the mid-1970s a couple of contemporary witchcraft practitioners opened a shop called The Boutique of the Unusual in Atlanta's Little Five Points community, offering witchcraft paraphernalia and other "unusual" items for sale. They also conducted open classes on "the Craft," and soon had students, or "novices," boarding on the premises. They formed themselves into a Wicca coven, using the name Ravenwood. Wicca is an old English term referring to magicians and/or their magical arts. In its contemporary form it is linked to a nature-based spirituality that celebrates the fertility and life cycles of plants, animals, and humans—an expression of the belief that all of nature participates in a divine cosmic process. In their rituals they honor both gods and goddesses, which they believe exist in everything and everyone, including, as one local witch put it, "trees, cats, water, every friend, everyone on the subway." Their ceremonies often involve building a fire and forming a sacred circle at an outdoor location in conjunction with certain lunar or solar phases. They use amulets, spells, and potions to protect against evil spirits and summon good ones. They also engage in astrology and read tarot cards in an effort to divine the future. Although there are both male and female witches, the religion centers around "mother earth" and at Ravenwood, as in most covens, it is a woman who serves as "high priestess."

The Ravenwood coven suffered vandalism, telephone threats, and arrests on charges of fortune telling throughout its early years. But this only increased the coven's insistence that "the Old Religion" or "the Craft," as they variously refer to Wicca, is a legitimate religion and should enjoy the same rights and privileges as any other. Several legal battles ensued, but they were finally incorporated in 1979 as a church and seminary in the state of Georgia and granted tax-exempt status. Although there would be more legal battles and public persecution, this was a significant victory for Ravenwood, representing the first time Wicca had been recognized as a legitimate religion in a United States court of law.

The local police and neighborhood association eventually came to respect the perseverance and integrity of the coven and especially its leader, known as Lady Sintana. Neighboring business leaders testified on behalf of the witches in court, and local police were said to warn would-be vandals or ill-wishers to "leave our witches alone." Nonetheless, after enduring more than a decade of vandalism, taunts, and threats, often involving students from colleges and universities around the city, the Wicca church relocated to a more secluded location in Conyers, Georgia, about forty-five miles southeast of Atlanta. Ravenwood is the oldest known coven in Georgia and one of the most public and well-known covens in the country. A book entitled *Living Witchcraft: A Contemporary American Coven* (1994), documents the history and practices of the Ravenwood coven. There may be as many as a dozen other smaller and more private covens in the Atlanta area today.

As the preceding discussion has made clear, Wicca is just one expression of the multilayered, complex, and highly diverse forms of New Age spirituality. In order to provide the reader with a spectrum of alternative spiritual expressions in the Atlanta area I will present a brief profile of six different forms, or manifestations, of New Age spirituality covering the following areas: 1) holistic health; 2) astrology, and palm and card reading; 3) spirit mediation or channeling; 4) spiritual psychology and counseling; 5) alternative churches; and 6) nature spirituality.

HOLISTIC HEALTH

Holistic health, associated with approaches to human health that refuse to separate the physical and spiritual dimensions of the human person, may be the most mainstream New Age spiritual expression. Many people who would not consider themselves part of the New Age movement frequent herb shops or health food stores, or utilize chiropractors, massage therapists, or polarity specialists. Yet the assumptions underlying these treatments are identifiably New Age. There is disillusionment with, and distrust of modern science, as well as an assumption of natural oneness, wholeness, and harmony in the human being/body. Herbs, vitamins, natural foods, chiropractic adjustments, and "body work" (such as massage, acupressure, or energy field therapy) are all aimed at restoring the body's "natural" balance. Whereas modern western medicine tends to focus on the treatment and management of disease, the focus among holistic health practitioners is the "perfect health" or natural wholeness, as it is often stated, which is believed to be the natural human state. This natural state of harmony and balance, wherein one's personal energy is flowing freely (without dis-ease), is thought to be disrupted by our various physical and emotional experiences and our unhealthy dietary practices. Thus natural foods, herbs, or body work (or most preferably a combination of these) is used to restore balance and wholeness, and free up blocked energy.

It is worth reiterating that holistic health refuses to separate the physical or chemical, from the mental, emotional, or spiritual. As chiropractor

Fred J. Blum of the Center for Health Resources in Atlanta puts it, his "Network adjustments" are "an experience of heart, mind and breath. . . . Using a precise sequence of gentle contacts, you are enabled to release deep patterns of interference locked within your nervous system (called spinal subluxations). Spinal subluxations are associated with past unhealed events in our lives of a physical, chemical or emotional nature." Body work is not just for the body—as the above chiropractor puts it, his work aims to connect the patient to the patient's own "Innate Wisdom." As one polarity therapist put it, polarity therapy (which incorporates attention to energy fields, exercise, and nutrition, along with physical massage) brings "insight and understanding into the energy that creates and sustains" each person.

One relatively new and increasingly popular holistic health practice is aromatherapy. Aromatherapy entails the use of various scents, mostly oils and essences from fruits and plants, to affect moods, or cure bodily or emotional ailments. A mixture of pine, fir, spruce, and lavender, for example, is used to relieve stress; jasmine, ylang ylang, and nutmeg is recommended for impotence; lavender and chamomile mixed with other spices is thought to cure insomnia. These oils and essences are applied most commonly by massage or used in bath water. For more intense treatment they are sometimes applied with a body wrap by a licensed aromatherapist. A few stores specialize exclusively in aromatherapy, while many metaphysical bookstores and some health food stores also carry aromatherapy products.

READING THE SIGNS

The reading of astrological signs, palms, and cards to give advice regarding one's present or future life is certainly not new. While there was a surge of interest in astrology, palm reading, and spirit mediation in the United States during the nineteenth century, there is clear evidence of such practices among the ancient Egyptians, Babylonians, and Hebrews. In the Atlanta area, however, the prevalence of "readers" is a recent phenomenon. Whereas fifty years ago a few readers may have practiced their art secretly in a back room, today astrologers are licensed by the city of Atlanta to practice their trade.

Gabriella Griffin, who calls herself "an intuitive counselor," reads palms and tarot cards, and draws on astrological wisdom and disembodied spirits to counsel patrons three evenings a week at a sidewalk table amid upscale restaurants and bars along North Highland Avenue in Virginia Highlands. Many of her patrons stop by out of curiosity or on a whim, but Griffin, a third-generation psychic, takes her "mission" quite seriously. As she recently told a local paper, she seeks to "offer my clients what they need to help them make their decisions in life." These readings are coordinated by the nearby Reader's Loft, a self-proclaimed New Age bookstore. Many other New Age or metaphysical bookstores also have readers or "counselors" available. Some astrologers, readers, and psychics also advertise via the *Aquarius* newspaper, brochures or cards, or lawn signs outside their homes, where a room may be set aside for conducting readings, seances, or intuitive counseling sessions.

MEDIUMS OR CHANNELERS

As in the case of Griffin, readers may also be channelers. But the phenomenon of channeling deserves separate consideration since many channelers are not readers, and since channeled spirits sometimes have a group of followers that form a distinct "spiritual community." Membership in these communities is quite different from the occasional ten minutes with a psychic on the way to dinner. Channeling refers to the experience of a non-bodied spirit speaking to and through some person or persons. Channelers or mediums (those who mediate the messages of a spirit to others) are considered to be clairvoyant (they see what others do not see) and/or clairaudient (they hear what others do not hear). While some mediums channel for a variety of spirits and may be continuously open to new entities, others are dedicated to giving voice to just one spirit or entity. There are a few nationally known "channeled spirits" whose teachings may be found in manuscript or video tape form in book stores across the country. These include "Seth," "Samuel," "Emmanuel," "Bartholomew," "Lazaris," "Raphael, "Alexander," and "Mission Control." "Emmanuel," and "Lazaris" seem to be the most popular in Atlanta book stores.

The Reverend Timothy L. Smith has reputedly been mediating or channeling messages in Atlanta for a "Universal Spiritual Entity" known as "TaPa" since 1969. The Alexandrian Temple of Light constitutes something of a "church" where 20 to 30 people gather regularly on Saturday evenings to experience the "Descending Light" of TaPa mediated through Smith. As an advertisement in their quarterly publication, *The Alexandrian Journal*, explains, these gatherings involve "healing, prophesy, tongues, past lives, and in-depth teachings of profound proportions." Attendees are invited to get in touch with "something Higher, Nobler." The teachings of TaPa have been recorded in written form by Smith. The King James version of the

Bible is often quoted in these writings, and in fact King James English seems to set the style of TaPa's rather dense and esoteric speech throughout. In one typical passage Smith records TaPa as saying:

> Where our strength lies, Beloved, is in the commitment of that which the spiritual in its state comes to an alignment therewith of physical expression. What care giveth then at the gift where many see the very portals themselves there before them represented? Is there not someone standing just inside that gate? Is there not someone standing right inside that door and opening thereto? For each is given. Mastery is that level that represents a touch with that with which, upon the level that we have mastered, is the exchange of communication.

There are now six different volumes of these teachings available, which may be purchased in the form of spiral-bound study manuals, each running about 400 pages.

SPIRITUAL PSYCHOLOGY AND COUNSELING

Dr. Jerry Epps considers himself a counselor who practices "body-based emotional healing" out of a "healing room" in his Marietta home. He has a master's degree in counseling and a doctorate in human relations. Epps spent some years as a counselor in both a hospital mental health ward and in private practice, but felt he "couldn't go deep enough with conventional models of therapy." In his current practice he seeks to heal emotional wounds and promote spiritual wholeness and "God consciousness" by "going deep into the DNA, energy, and cells of the body."

Underlying this practice is the assumption that everything is energy or "vibrations of energy." As bodily beings we are a gathering and unity of energies—energies that pre-existed our bodies and that continue after bodily death. As Epps puts it "In the time and space chunk of the universe where we're doing yesterdays and tomorrows, I'll buy reincarnation as a functional model [for eternal being]. . . . I assume that I was a long time ago and that I will be in the future. But all of that is just vibrations projected up out of the eternal ground of being." The ultimate goal of therapy and of life is to release the full energy potential of one's being and to be connected with the collective energy or beingness of the universe itself. Attaining such full energy potential and universal connectedness is what Epps calls achieving "God consciousness." According to Epps, "God consciousness" is widely understood among his clientele as having to do with reaching one's potential and achieving personal and universal harmony and wholeness. His assumptions about the energy basis of all physical reality and the related belief in reincarnation are also widely accepted among New Agers.

Clients typically begin their sessions with Epps sitting on a couch and talking about the life issues or concerns that have brought them in. Emotionally powerful music, such as the sound tracks from *The Last of the Mohicans* or *Schindler's List*, is often in the background. The client is soon invited to lie on some floor cushions while the music is turned up loud. Epps claims to see "spots" on peoples' bodies where energy is "blocked up." After having the client engage in deep and rapid breathing in order to "intentionally enter an altered state of consciousness," he begins to massage the identified "spots" and suggest phrases for the client to repeat—phrases that occur to him intuitively and that seem to get at the emotional experience bound up in the body. Clients then repeat "I don't want to be alone," "I hate you," "I need you," or some other phrase over and over as a way of getting to the heart of their emotional issue. Ultimately the goal is to "get the energy [in the body] moved so the person's not blocked." Emotional healing is not just about the emotions—harmony must also be sought within the body, and between the individual and the universe.

While there are others like Epps with private practices in homes or offices, many alternative health centers have similar holistic counselors on staff. Some of the larger centers have multiple counselors on staff, each with a different specialty, offering group as well as individual sessions. The group sessions tend to focus on basic life issues, such as marriage and family relations, parenting, menopause, and career planning.

ALTERNATIVE CHURCHES OR COMMUNITIES

Although there is resistance to institutions, hierarchy, and dogma among New Agers, some churches and institutes have formed in the Atlanta area that embody New Age beliefs and practices. These churches resist institutionalization and dogma by insisting upon their autonomy from any other church or denominational body (even if they are, in fact, members of a larger denomination), and insisting that they have no dogma or doctrine (even if there are some basic beliefs which bind them together). Among the most visible and successful of these churches in the Atlanta area are the Unity churches, of which there are now five.

Unity Church is a national denomination founded in 1889, with a seminary and headquarters in Kansas City, Missouri. This church considers itself to be Christian-based though not exactly in the Christian tradition. It uses the Bible, but interprets it metaphysically. As one Unity minister put it, the teachings of Jesus are taken as clues for the attainment of higher intelligence or divine consciousness of which every person is capable and that may be attained by realizing one's "connectedness to the basic unity of the universe." The declaration of Jesus' unique identity with God at the Nicene Council in 325 CE is considered to have been a grave mistake. Rather, it should be the goal and destiny of every person to identify with God in the way that Jesus did. Richard Bach's *Jonathan Livingston Seagull* (1970) and *Illusions* (1977) give popular expression to this philosophy.

Unity Church considers itself in the same New Thought family of denominations with Religious Science (of which there are two congregations in Atlanta), and Divine Science. As mentioned above, New Thought refers to a nineteenth-century American movement that sought, and still seeks, to draw upon and harmonize the wisdom and teachings of psychology, medicine, science, and religion. In 1994 a New Thought Theological Seminary was founded in Roswell by a husband and wife with PhDs from a New Thought institution in California. They offer courses through local alternative health and teaching centers and intend to be trainers of future New Thought devotees and leaders.

The Unity Church in Roswell owns and operates a metaphysical bookstore adjoining its spacious light-filled sanctuary. It sponsors workshops and lectures during the week, in addition to classes and a service of celebration and sharing on Sunday mornings. As the Reverend Carol O'Connell puts it, they are most concerned with teaching "spiritual principles and techniques for using them." Meditation is prominent among these techniques and is based on the principle that all of reality is energy vibrating at various levels. The aim of meditation is to "raise your level of vibration" or to "tune in" to the frequency of the universe (the difference between angels and humans is that "we have chosen to vibrate at a lower level"). O'Connell scoffed at the "Harmonic Convergence" that made national news in the mid-1980s when New Agers across the country sought to initiate a global shift in consciousness through joint meditation. But she does believe that a "shift in the vibration of the planet" is taking place gradually as more and more people tune in to the significance of the energies within them and around them. Eventually, according to O'Connell, a "critical mass will be reached" and we will move into a new "spiritual millennium." Each of us can contribute to this shift, and in the meantime reach our own highest potential, by constantly aspiring to bring ourselves into harmony with the universe.

O'Connell also believes that traditional Christianity may be transformed as the planet undergoes spiritual progression. She cites Robert Schuler and Norman Vincent Peale as hopeful examples of Christian leaders who focus on personal transformation instead of dogma. She is also proud that Matthew Fox, an Anglican priest and internationally renowned proponent of creation spirituality, spoke at her church in November 1995. Fox, who only recently became Anglican after being forced to relinquish his Roman Catholic priesthood, has published several books and directs the Institute in Culture and Creation Spirituality in Oakland, California, which publishes a nationally distributed magazine called *Creation Spirituality*. Fox is read and revered widely among people in the New Thought tradition, as well as among neo-pagans, Wiccans, and other New Agers. He rejects the Christian doctrine of original sin in favor of a belief in "original blessing" and promotes a worshipful reverence for all of creation, but continues to consider himself Christian—he is required reading in several courses at Emory University's Methodist-affiliated Candler School of Theology in Atlanta and at other Christian seminaries around the country. This makes evident once again the difficulty of classifying the New Age movement. Is Matthew Fox a New Age Christian? Is the Unity Church a Christian New Age denomination?

There are a number of spiritual communities or movements around the city of Atlanta that are very hard to categorize or label. Eckankar, for example, is a Minneapolis-based denomination with a center in a northeastern suburb of Atlanta. Members of this community practice soul travel, believe in the Holy Spirit, and use eastern meditation exercises. The Hillside Chapel and Truth Center, another example, is a 4,500-member church in Atlanta that combines New Thought teachings, self-help techniques, and some traditional Christian black church worship styles. More recently a new alternative spiritual community, called Four Winds, has formed just north of the city in south Gwinnett County that combines Christian, Native American, and Celtic spiritualities.

Four Winds was formed in 1994 by Jim S. Crews, a former Baptist minister who is part Cherokee Indian. The community evolved through informal meetings in people's homes and gatherings on Sunday afternoons for "celebration, worship, and community building" at open air ceremonial grounds on a privately owned farm. It has recently begun to rent space in a

Unitarian church for worship celebrations and ceremonies, which often include the use of drums and bagpipes and traditionally Christian hymns and prayers, signaling their explicit affinity with Native American, Celtic, and Christian spiritualities. Joseph Campbell (who taught that all religions are mythic expressions of deep-rooted inner truths) and Matthew Fox orient this religious community's thinking, while Native American rituals stand out in ceremonial activities. Members sometimes gather around a "sacred fire" and offer prayers to "mother earth," "the four legged ones," and "trees and rocks and stones." They honor the four directions with smoke from smoldering cedar, sweet grass, and sage near the beginning of most of their gatherings, and regularly address parts of nature as "brother," or "sister," "grandfather," or "grandmother." As Crews puts it, "we are trying to remember in a deep way who we are and who we have been . . . our connections to the earth and to God." As their mission statement declares, they are "an ecumenical faith community that embraces the Christian Tradition and the world's Wisdom Traditions . . . a pluralistic community rooted in a creation-based sense of spirituality . . . [affirming] . . . freedom of religious expression . . . autonomy of the individual . . . the sacredness and interdependence of all creation; and the common source of all reality."

The incorporation of Native American cultural traditions into alternative spiritual practices has become widespread during the 1990s. Most metaphysical book stores have a section on Native American religions and may also carry some Native American jewelry and paraphernalia, such as drums, pipes, and dream catchers. There are nationally published magazines, such as *Shaman's Drum*, which promote Native American traditions to New Agers, and Atlanta's *Aquarius* newspaper regularly features articles by or about Native American shamans, medicine men, and others utilizing Native American healing traditions.

NATURE SPIRITUALITY

While interest in a spiritual connection to the planet is present in nearly all New Age communities, there are some that are prominently and centrally nature-based. Many neo-pagan groups, for example, which include Wiccans, Druids, and others focused on Celtic spirituality, as well as various eclectic communities, orient themselves around the cycles of the moon and the seasons, and are acutely attuned to the natural ecology of the planet. Members associated with these communities engage in numerous rituals, such as a celebration of the full moon by drumming and chanting around a campfire in the woods. This has brought accusations of Satanism or devil worship—concepts that are a part of Christian theology, not neo-pagan belief systems. Neo-pagan spirituality draws from Celtic sources, which include belief in and attempts to commune with numerous nature gods and spirits, and Native American religious systems that, in some cases, include belief in a Great Spirit and the reverence for all parts of creation.

The term "pagan" was coined by medieval Christians to refer to "primitive" non-Christian, mostly nature-based religions that Christianity sought to destroy and replace. Neo-paganism seeks to recover these lost or suppressed traditions. As one self-proclaimed neo-pagan put it: "Who am I and what am I doing on this planet? . . . . Who were my ancestors? They didn't suddenly become religious when Christianity came to northern Europe. . . . They had religion before that . . . . We're trying to reclaim some of our pre-Christian heritage." While neo-pagans tend to keep their activities private, due to common misunderstandings and the threat of harassment, their numbers are growing substantially. One neo-pagan estimates that there are a half-dozen or more fairly large neo-pagan groups (not including Wiccans) in the Atlanta area, and another eight or ten smaller gatherings.

Most neo-pagans have a northern European heritage, and are at least several generations removed from those ancestors who immigrated to the United States. According to several sources in Atlanta, many neo-pagans in the South, as well as others on similar alternative spiritual paths, were raised either Roman Catholic, Baptist, or Jewish. In this sense the neo-pagan quoted earlier may be typical. He comes from a devout Irish-Catholic family in Chicago, came of age in the 1960s, and is now in his 40s. Once he was married he found the church's teaching on birth control to be "too stupid to listen to." But he still considered religion important. After his divorce he did not feel welcome in the church and was in need of some new friends, some spiritual support, and some way to make sense of his life. He attended self-development seminars and became involved in an environmentalist movement. In both the seminars and among the environmentalists he began to hear the message that "God lives everywhere and in everything . . . including in nature and in you and me." This made sense to him in ways that Christian theology never did. He also points out that choosing his own religion is "the American way." "My old religion doesn't work for me. . . . I didn't like supporting missionaries proclaiming the one true religion . . . all religions are OK. . . . I'm choosing one that makes sense for me. . . . I think we need to be connected spiritually to our environment."

SUMMARY

People connected with alternative spiritual pursuits tend to be open to new ideas and have eclectic interests. The same person may attend neo-pagan gatherings, have her palm read occasionally, and enjoy massage therapy. Others may be interested only in health food, herbs, and chiropractic treatments while retaining traditional Christian or Jewish theological beliefs. Some may attend both alternative and more traditional churches, a practice that most alternative churches seek to accommodate by scheduling at least some of their services at times other than Sunday morning.

Education, understood as learning, self-development, or personal evolution, is very important for many New Agers. They want not only to receive massage or polarity therapy, or use crystals and aromatherapy, but also to understand the theories behind the practices. They want not only to receive advice and wisdom from counselors and ministers, but also to study psychology and metaphysics for guiding their own development. A wide array of classes at alternative health centers, bookstores, and churches are offered to meet this desire for spiritual and intellectual knowledge. The monthly calendar of events available at the Inner Space bookstore in Sandy Springs, for example, lists two or three classes, workshops, or seminars nearly every night of the week, ranging from introductory levels to advanced certification and degree programs.

Demographically New Agers tend to be white and college-educated. The Hillside Chapel and Truth Center, with its 4,500 mostly African-American members, is a dramatic exception to this generalization. But all of the other alternative communities I visited were overwhelmingly white, and all the people I interviewed (including one African-American New Thought minister) agreed that New Agers are predominantly white and middle class. They also tend to be in their late 30s to early 50s—in other words, members of the Baby Boom generation. While there may be more women than men among them, this is common also in most Christian churches. Leadership as ministers, readers, channelers, and therapists is unquestionably open to both men and women.

The numbers of metaphysical book stores, health food stores, herb shops, readers, spiritual healers and therapists, alternative health centers, and alternative churches in Atlanta has grown steadily over the last decade. This reflects not only Atlanta's growing population, but also its youth and vitality as a blossoming cosmopolitan center. There is a vibrant interest here in innovation and new possibilities, a willingness to explore and experiment.

And there is money here to experiment with. As one psychic healer put it, "Atlanta is a good place to go into business . . . to open a new restaurant, or a book store, or an alternative health center. . . . There's an entrepreneurial spirit here . . . and let's face it, the people who pay me $75 an hour have some money to spend. I couldn't do this in Mobile, or even Birmingham." Alternative health practitioners, psychic readers, and metaphysical book store owners seem to agree with the Unity church minister who put it this way: "There are good vibrations in this area. . . . Atlanta and this whole southeast corridor is likely to be a spiritual hub in the next millennium."

FOR FURTHER INFORMATION

Russell Chandler. *Understanding the New Age.* Dallas, Word Publishing, 1988

Deepak Chopra. *The Seven Spiritual Laws of Success.* San Rafael, Amber-Allen Publishing, 1994

Marilyn Ferguson. *The Aquarian Conspiracy: Personal and Social Transformation in the 1980s.* J. P. Tarcher, 1980

Barbara Lewis King. *Transform Your Life.* New York, Pergee Books, 1995

Allen Scarboro, Nancy Campbell, and Shirley Stave. *Living Witchcraft: A Contemporary American Coven.* London, Praeger, 1994

Mark Woodhouse. *Paradigm Wars: Worldviews for a New Age.* Berkeley, Frog, 1995

PART IV:

UNITED IN DIVERSITY: THE SEARCH FOR COMMON GROUND

C H A P T E R   T W E N T Y - T W O

ATLANTA'S CIVIC IDENTITY: CIVIL RELIGION IN A SOUTHERN METROPOLIS

Timothy Allen Beach-Verhey

Monument to the Unknown Confederate Dead. Historic Oakland Cemetery. Photograph by Louis A. Ruprecht, Jr.

Religion plays a significant role in binding a community together by providing societal members with a common way of life and a unified set of ideals and values. A religious community's shared symbols, rituals, and memories, according to cultural anthropologist Clifford Geertz, form "the tone, character, and quality of their life, its moral and aesthetic style and mood." In 1966, Robert Bellah, a renowned sociologist, applied a similar understanding of religion to American society as a whole. He asserted that the United States has a particular identity and way of life that is promoted and preserved through "its own prophets and its own martyrs, its own sacred events and sacred places, its own solemn rituals and symbols." He claimed that, in a sense, American society has its own specific religion—what he called a civil religion—that holds its people together in a more profound way than legal citizenship or common geography.

In the years since Bellah first developed this idea, some scholars have studied different regions within the United States with civil religion in mind. They noticed that regions also have their own particular myths, heroes, symbols, and rituals that bind the people together in a special way. Many would argue that more attention should be paid to local civil religions and the diverse identities they create because they may have a more immediate impact on people's lives than the national version discussed by Bellah.

This chapter explores one specific example of a local religious identity in the South, Atlanta's civil religion, and raises a series of questions about the ties that bind the metropolitan community together. Who are Atlanta's mythic heroes and what virtues and values do they represent? Where are the sacred spaces that capture the imagination of Atlantans and represent what the city is all about? What are the rituals and symbols that preserve and promote what Atlanta was, is, and should become? This chapter answers these questions by looking at three different critical aspects of Atlanta's civic identity: first, Atlanta's southern roots and Civil War heritage; second, its "New South" identity and emergent civic spirit; and third, its African-American community and its significant contributions to the city. In addition, I will examine whether these aspects converge or diverge, and question whether Atlanta has a unified identity or many identities pulling its residents in a variety of directions. All of this will help us better understand whether there is a civil religion at work in Atlanta and if it is a source of social solidarity for its people.

ATLANTA: CITY OF THE OLD SOUTH

Margaret Mitchell's *Gone with the Wind* has indelibly burned one dimension of Atlanta's southern identity into the minds of people throughout the world. The movie version of Rhett and Scarlett's flight from Atlanta dramatically portrays the destruction wrought on the city by the Civil War. General William T. Sherman of the Union Army captured the city in September 1864, and his forces burned almost everything of value that the Confederate Army had not destroyed during its retreat. As the Union Army left Atlanta for its infamous and destructive March to the Sea, a Union soldier wrote that he looked back and saw "nothing but ruins as far as the eye could see."

The fall of this southern railroad center foreshadowed the doom of the Confederacy. Within a year, the war was over. But for many, the southern cause did not end with the war. It was kept alive through the efforts of many who continued to celebrate the South and its identity despite defeat. Oakland Cemetery is one of the places in Atlanta where the "Lost Cause" was preserved and continues to be remembered. This city cemetery, established near the heart of downtown a decade before the Civil War, became the final resting place for approximately 2,500 Confederate soldiers who died during the battle for Atlanta in 1864.

In 1894, a monument was dedicated to the unidentified Confederate soldiers who had been buried in Oakland Cemetery. It was modeled after the famous Lion of Luzerne in Switzerland and depicts a dead lion with a broken spear shaft protruding from his side. He lies among the tools of war, grasping the battle flag of the Confederacy. It is a noble but defeated beast symbolizing all the virtues of those who fought for a lost cause, conveying courage, loyalty, gallantry, pride, piety, and honor—the virtues of the chivalrous and religious society that the South believed itself to represent. Here one might expect to meet, under the magnolia trees, the ghosts of Ashley and Melanie Wilkes—characters from *Gone with the Wind* who exemplified all the virtues that southern culture valued most highly.

If this lion can be considered a solemn monument to aristocratic southern virtues, lying quietly under a canopy of magnolias and dogwoods in

Oakland Cemetery, then Stone Mountain, a granite monolith protruding from a blanket of Georgia pines, is a more populist monument. According to Dana White, who has studied Atlanta's history extensively, it was once "the Saint Peter's Basilica of the Empire of the Ku Klux Klan"; it is now a theme park on the periphery of the metro area, blending regional memories with modern entertainment. The images of the three persons whom many consider the holy trinity of the Lost Cause are carved on the side of the mountain: Robert E. Lee, Stonewall Jackson, and Jefferson Davis. Astride their horses, they sit side by side, their eyes fixed on the same distant horizon. More than six million visitors a year come to see these cultural heroes who loom larger in the imaginations of many Southerners than Abraham Lincoln, George Washington, or even Thomas Jefferson. On summer evenings, visitors can see the three brightest lights of the Confederate pantheon ride again. Through the wonders of modern laser technology, these three heroes charge across the night sky, swords held aloft. As they begin to gallop, a great whoop and cry goes up from the audience. This is an image that stirs regional pride and reawakens southern loyalties in the almost totally white crowd.

But the charge will not end in victory, as the audience and the developers of the laser show well know. The tragedy of the Lost Cause is played out nightly during the summer season with precisely focused beams of light, and the audience watches in reverent silence while the gallant and kind General Lee, the gentleman soldier, the Southern Knight, sadly surveys the wreckage of war. He watches Atlanta burn and soldiers die. Finally he draws his sword and breaks it over his knee, symbolizing the end of war, the death of the Confederate cause, and the beginning of reconciliation. The laser show ends with a tribute to the United States; the national flag is sprawled across the firmament in an explosion of sophisticated laser technology. This brings another yell from the crowd, but it is neither as loud nor as heart-felt. The crowd is proud to be American. Yet, as Southerners, their pride is still mixed with a twinge of remorse and regret.

Atlanta remembers and celebrates its southern identity at Oakland Cemetery, Stone Mountain, and other local monuments around Atlanta. But the Old South means different things to different people. It can be associated with something as simple as the regional pride that one sees at Southeastern Conference football games. It can, on the other hand, be related to the racial hatred and animosity for which the South is so well known. It can also bring to mind something as idealistic as the longing for an intimate agrarian civilization in which people valued courage, honor, piety, civility, and plain old courtesy. But, despite the multiplicity of meanings that it conjures up, the Old South remains a deeply rooted source of regional identity and collective memory for many Atlantans.

CITY OF THE NEW SOUTH

Atlanta has built monuments to the Old South and occasionally visits them to reflect on and romanticize about the city's past. But, according to Franklin Garrett, the official historian of the city, "Atlanta has never been a moonlight and magnolia, quiet southern town." It was settled by rough and ready railroad people. This gritty and bustling transportation center never had the elegant trappings, the fine manners, or the aristocratic families of some other southern cities. What it did have, from its very beginning, was a civic loyalty and energetic optimism that has come to be called the "Atlanta Spirit."

According to many Atlantans the city is far more like Rhett Butler and Scarlett O'Hara—thoughtless and opportunistic—than Ashley or Melanie Wilkes. To put Atlanta, and the heroes of *Gone with the Wind,* in a more positive light, one might say that they are aggressive, indomitable, passionate, and oriented toward the future rather than the past. Indeed Margaret Mitchell herself compares Atlanta to Scarlett in *Gone with the Wind.* She wrote that, like Scarlett, Atlanta was "crude with the crudities of youth, and as head strong and impetuous as herself." After the burning of the city and the Union victory, Atlanta, like Scarlett, would have to find a source of regeneration.

In 1887, in the aftermath of the Confederate defeat, civic leaders in Atlanta chose the symbol that would represent the city and its spirit. The city placed the Phoenix rising from the ashes on its official seal. Between its outspread wings was inscribed in Latin "resurgens" (rising again). On December 21, 1886, Henry Grady, editor of the *Atlanta Constitution* and one of the patron saints of the Atlanta Spirit, gave a short impromptu speech in New York City, trying to sell Atlanta to northern investors. He said, "from the ashes [Sherman] left us in 1864 we have raised a brave and beautiful city."

Atlanta's business and political leaders were the high-priests, prophets, and cheerleaders for the Atlanta Spirit. City leaders have given shape and substance to that spirit through the power of their personalities and the intensity of their dreams. One Atlanta historian, Lynn Watson-Powers, wrote, "the Atlanta Spirit has encompassed many different qualities over the years, from sheer manipulation, outright self-promotion, and overt optimism to genuine progress, idealism, and true vision." This is largely due to the various strengths of leading figures like Henry Grady, Ivan Allen, Robert Woodruff, William Hartsfield, Ivan Allen, Jr., Andrew Young, and Billy Payne, each of whom exemplified the Atlanta Spirit for a particular time and context—with the latter two being particularly important in selling the city as the perfect place to host the 1996 Olympics.

One facet of the Atlanta Spirit is clearly a strong tendency toward self-promotion. A monument to the great orator of the Atlanta Spirit, Henry Grady, stands downtown on Marietta Street, overlooking a business district as prosperous and flourishing as he dreamed it could be. Soon after the war, Grady used all his skills as a public speaker to convince northern audiences that Atlanta represented a New South. He helped create an image of Atlanta as a progressive city that had put the war and slavery behind it. He also helped promote a series of Cotton Expositions in the 1880s and 90s designed to focus national attention on the city's advantages as a manufacturing and transportation center. These expositions and Henry Grady's salesmanship were very successful in drawing commercial businesses to Atlanta and creating an ethos of optimism and prosperity.

Atlanta's business community has been religiously committed to industrial and economic revival in the city throughout the twentieth century. In 1925, Ivan Allen, a local businessman and civic leader, gave that commitment institutional form; he created Forward Atlanta, an advertising program focused on promoting economic expansion. The mission of Forward Atlanta was to keep the city chanting in unison the mantra "Growth, Growth, Growth," and to distribute pamphlets and tracts around the world that preached the virtues of Atlanta's wonderful business climate. Forward Atlanta has continued to be faithful to its mission, finding new and inventive ways to "sell" the city throughout the nation and the world.

A resident of Savannah once said, "If Atlanta could suck as hard as it can blow, it would be a seaport." Of course Atlantans attribute this sort of statement to jealousy and see things quite differently. One employee of Forward Atlanta said to me, "Some would call what we do propaganda. But we just want to put the exciting and attractive version of Atlanta out there for people to see." From his perspective, Atlanta is doing nothing more than putting its best foot forward.

It seems to have worked too. Atlanta has truly risen from the ashes of the Civil War and continues the ascent with the Atlanta Spirit as the wind—however blustery—beneath her wings. According to an employee at

Forward Atlanta, "We started calling Atlanta the world's Next Great International City in 1971. In 1971, there wasn't much international business going on down here except the International House of Pancakes. Now, Fortune magazine calls us the fourth best city in the world for business." Undoubtedly, Atlanta will not be content with these accomplishments. Business and civic leaders will continue to dream of a bigger and better future. And because of their abiding confidence in Atlanta, they will talk about those dreams of the future as though they had already been accomplished.

But the Atlanta Spirit cannot be depicted only as boastful optimism or swaggering salesmanship. The Atlanta Spirit has also demonstrated a more idealistic and humanitarian side. In 1916, the president of the Atlanta Chamber of Commerce defined the Atlanta Spirit as "striving for the intellectual, artistic, industrial and moral development of our people." This may seem like another case of exaggerated self-promotion, but there is some truth here. Atlanta has a reputation for civic activism. More than most American cities, Atlanta's business people are involved in helping the city. One community activist said, "You can't move up in the business community here unless you are involved in the city."

The figures who exemplified the Atlanta Spirit were not, by any stretch of the imagination, bleeding hearts. They were hard-headed businessmen. But they were also blessed with an excess of civic pride and an enlightened sense of self-interest. This can be seen most clearly in the way that Atlanta business leaders have dealt with the issue of racism. In the early twentieth century the business community publicly denounced lynching and the Chamber of Commerce promoted interracial harmony. Atlanta's civic leaders were wise enough to see that lynchings, riots, and acts of overt racism were not only morally disgraceful but also bad for business; these attitudes and activities disturbed the peace and only reinforced Northerners' negative images of Georgia and the South. The actions taken by Atlanta's business leadership were admittedly often timid and conservative, but they did have an effect on the racial climate in Atlanta.

This manner of thinking continued into the mid-1900s, when a few of Atlanta's most famous political and business leaders placed themselves, and Atlanta, on the side of the Civil Rights movement. Mayor William Hartsfield, a pro-business mayor in the 1950s who did more to turn this city into a regional metropolis than anyone, built a political coalition that included many of the region's prominent African Americans. He expressed the pro-business and anti-racism policy of Atlanta in the famous phrase, "Atlanta—The City Too Busy to Hate."

Ivan Allen, Jr., Atlanta's mayor during the 1960s, saw what was happening in southern cities like Selma, Montgomery, and Birmingham. He was convinced that it was not only wrong to oppose the Civil Rights movement, it was just plain bad for a city's reputation. Allen became the only southern mayor in favor of civil rights and through his leadership, he helped Atlanta earn national recognition as a model of racial harmony and cooperation in the South.

Robert W. Woodruff, who became president of Coca-Cola in 1923 and led the company into the 1980s, also provided important leadership during this period. This great civic leader, whose name is immortalized on many buildings throughout the city because of his legendary philanthropy, saw that it would be good for the business community to embrace the demands of the Civil Rights movement. He put his considerable political and financial weight behind the policies of these mayors.

Together, these men helped Atlanta earn a reputation for racial harmony and cooperation, which in turn has been good for the economic life of the city. At the same time, they proved that the Atlanta Spirit does have a moral and idealistic side, and succeeded in shaping Atlanta's identity as a city where all persons are welcome regardless of color, ethnicity, or religion. The Atlanta Spirit is hard to define. Part of it is as simple as a passionate love for this city and a penchant for self-promotion. But there is a more substantive side as well; there is a spirit of cooperation and civic activism, somewhat moral in nature. One person said that the Atlanta Spirit is "aspiring to something great, dreaming something big, and then making the dream a reality"—this seems to be a unifying factor whether one is talking about business growth or race relations. This is a city that, like its symbol, is always on the rise.

ATLANTA'S AFRICAN-AMERICAN COMMUNITY

Atlanta's civil religion cannot be fully understood without appreciating the contributions the African-American community has made to the city and its identity. But it would be wrong to look to *Gone with the Wind* for an accurate account of their role in Atlanta. African Americans in Atlanta have shown themselves to be nothing like the dependent, foolish, content, loyal, insignificant characters who played bit parts in this famous book and movie. They have, despite discrimination and adversity, been an independent and powerful group, producing prosperity for themselves and playing a tremendously significant role in the history of Atlanta.

African Americans have, since the Civil War, made up a substantial percentage of Atlanta's residents. Today they make up more than two-thirds of the population of the city of Atlanta. The contributions of African Americans to Atlanta, however, cannot be captured in statistics. Titles of articles in national magazines such as "Atlanta: Black Mecca of the South" and "Atlanta: Capital of Black is Bountiful," capture in a more poetic way the relationship that African Americans have had with this city.

John Wesley Dobbs, a prominent leader in the African-American community whose grandson became the first black mayor of Atlanta, often said that black people needed "the ballot, the book and the buck." This phrase is a golden thread, a constant theme, that weaves itself throughout the whole history of African American life in Atlanta. The African-American community worked hard for those three things, and that effort has had a lasting effect on the city.

Atlanta's African-American community began its quest for "the book" soon after the Civil War. In 1869, Atlanta University opened its doors. The energy and vision that had driven Atlanta's African Americans to create educational opportunities for themselves proved to be very successful; by the beginning of the twentieth century, Georgia was considered the preeminent place for black higher education, primarily because of the universities in Atlanta.

Today, the Atlanta University Center is made up of six very prestigious black educational institutions: Clark Atlanta University, Morehouse College, Spelman College, Morris Brown College, Morehouse School of Medicine, and the Interdenominational Theological Center. Together they make Atlanta one of the most important African-American intellectual and cultural centers in the country, drawing many of the best and brightest students from around the nation. Their presence in Atlanta provides the city with a large reservoir of well-educated community leaders who help promote the educational, political, and economic progress of African Americans in this city and throughout the nation. The Atlanta University Center stands as a monument to the foresight of Atlanta's African Americans, who saw that their economic and political future depended upon their commitment to education.

The success of their quest for "the book" also helped Atlanta's African-American community with "the buck." One of the effects that the Atlanta

University Center had on Atlanta was the creation of a strong and lasting black middle class. As Peter Ross Range noted in a 1974 *New York Times Magazine* article, "One generation after the colleges were founded, a black commercial elite began to develop in the city." The growth of a large and stable middle class is one of the social characteristics that makes Atlanta's African-American community unique.

In spite of a history of discrimination and exclusion from the central business districts of Atlanta, African Americans managed to build a flourishing commercial center along Auburn Avenue, just east of downtown Atlanta. Dubbed "Sweet Auburn" by John Wesley Dobbs, this street became known as one of the most prosperous places for black business in America. In 1956, Auburn Avenue, according to Fortune magazine, could "lay claim to being the richest Negro street in the world." Here, interspersed among the myriad of small businesses were some of the largest and most prestigious black-owned corporations in the country: the Atlanta Life Insurance Company, Citizens Trust Bank Company, and the Mutual Federal Savings and Loan Association of Atlanta. African Americans built a solid and proud middle-class existence for themselves along Auburn Avenue, successful in their pursuit of "the buck."

But Sweet Auburn was known as more than a business center; it was also the heart of cultural, civic, and religious life. Along this street are a number of famous churches, including Ebenezer Baptist, Wheat Street Baptist, and Big Bethel AME. These venerable institutions cast their shadows over the entire life of the community as houses of worship, promoters of culture, and supporters of civic activism. The Sweet Auburn neighborhood was also the home of the Butler Street YMCA, which was more a community center than a recreational facility. It housed the unofficial black chamber of commerce, and sponsored such activities as the "Hungry Club," a weekly luncheon forum that discussed the political needs of the African-American community.

Auburn Avenue is no longer as grand as it was in the first half of the twentieth century. Today, it is part of a depressed and poverty-stricken neighborhood. One is more likely to see a homeless person walking aimlessly down the dingy street than to see a well-dressed business person walking purposefully toward a meeting. The prosperous black middle class has moved away from Auburn Avenue, and now lives in other parts of Atlanta. Sweet Auburn, however, will always remain a potent symbol of what the African-American community has achieved and still needs to overcome.

The crypt for Martin Luther King, Jr. Martin Luther King, Jr. Center. Photograph by Louis A. Ruprecht, Jr.

Over both the University Center and Auburn Avenue hangs the memory and the legacy of Martin Luther King, Jr.—the man who led African Americans in their quest for "the ballot." King attended Morehouse College, where he learned to be a "Morehouse Man," and to live by its high standards of courtesy, strength, and morality. A statue of King stands on the campus, honoring the school's most famous graduate and reminding all students of the ideals that Dr. King embodied and the vision that he proclaimed.

Dr. King grew up on Auburn Avenue during its most prosperous days. The success of the community taught him to have confidence in himself and his race. As pastor of Ebenezer Baptist Church, Dr. King preached his vision of a just world to his congregation and to the nation. Here on Auburn Avenue the Southern Christian Leadership Conference, which King organized, had (and still has) its offices. Today, between Ebenezer Baptist and the home in which he was born, one can also find another monument to Dr. King's place in the history of America and Atlanta, his final resting place. He is entombed in a shining marble crypt, which is inscribed with the famous phrase "Free at last. Free at last. Thank God Almighty, I'm Free at last." His tomb is on the grounds of the Martin Luther King Center for Nonviolent Social Change, an institution committed to his legacy and actively engaged in promoting his agenda of non-violent social change. It is also focused on preserving his moral vision of the "Beloved Community."

Martin Luther King, Jr. is the symbolic center of Atlanta's African-American community, as well as the metro region as a whole, regardless of one's race, ethnicity, or religion. His spirit inhabits this city, and his moral vision keeps watch over Atlanta. Asked what a person should remember after having visited the King Center, one employee replied simply, "the Beloved Community." Dr. King had a dream—a dream that people would "one day live in a nation where they will not be judged by the color of their skin but by the content of their character." He had a dream that "one day, on the red hills of Georgia, the sons of former slaves and the sons of former slave owners will be able to sit down together at the table of brotherhood." He had a dream that people would realize that "the universe is so structured that things do not quite work out rightly if men are not diligent in their concern for others." This is some of what Dr. King dreamed of when he talked about a Beloved Community. And his dream had a power that is still felt in his hometown and around the world.

The African-American community in Atlanta has been a powerful force in shaping the civic spirit of this city. Its quest for "the ballot, the book, and the buck" has had a profound effect not only on one specific community but on the city as a whole. The diligence and foresight of the black community has transformed Atlanta into a leader in African-American higher education, and thus an important resource for African-American leaders. The perseverance and hard work of individuals within the community have turned Atlanta into an economic and cultural center for the black middle class, despite discrimination. Its hope and vision, embodied in the teachings of Martin Luther King, Jr., broke the bonds of segregation, and made a city that was once the "Imperial city of the Ku Klux Klan" into a city that is known for its racial harmony and cooperation.

A UNIFIED OR DIVERGENT IDENTITY?

Atlanta is a city with a rich variety of symbols, stories, sacred places, and heroes. Some are derived from the inheritance of its Civil War past, some from the legacy of its New South spirit, some from the contribution of its African-American community. The obvious diversity forces the question of whether there is truly a singular identity. Can these diverse symbols and stories converge into a unified identity? Can these different sacred places and heroes contribute to a common vision and meaning?

There is more than a little evidence that they can and they do. The Chamber of Commerce claims that the southern mystique of the city—its friendliness, courtesy, and slower pace of life—draws people and businesses here, contributing to its economic growth. On a more social level, Martin Luther King, Jr. employed some of the rhetoric of the Lost Cause, when he spoke of suffering and tragedy, and the virtues of gallantry, honor, loyalty, and pride. His vision of the Beloved Community was also unmistakably southern, drawing on, in his own words, "an intimacy of life that can be beautiful when it is transformed in race relations from a sort of lord-servant relationship to a person-to-person relationship."

Further evidence of the melding of these varied, yet distinct, images and influences can be seen literally, and symbolically, in Atlanta's mayors. Atlanta's last three mayors—Maynard Jackson, Andrew Young, and the incumbent, Bill Campbell—are African Americans who have constantly tried to represent the larger community. They have, with different emphases and differing degrees of success, tried to unite the spiritual legacies of Henry Grady, William Hartsfield, John Dobbs, and Martin Luther King, Jr. They have been representatives of a black middle class that is no longer willing to live at the margins of Atlanta's political life; they have been New South promoters of their city and protectors of its business interests; finally, they have tried, as Maynard Jackson promised in his inaugural address in 1974, "to demonstrate a new morality" that "serves the needs of the masses as well as the classes."

Another example of the way in which Atlanta combines the various streams of its past can be seen in the Atlanta Project. This organization, created and headed by Jimmy Carter, has tried to eliminate urban poverty by uniting the moral vision of Dr. King, the enlightened self-interest of Atlanta's business community, and the civic activism and pride of Atlanta's people. The Atlanta Project has succeeded in involving Atlanta's wealthy corporations in projects to help the city's poor, eliciting not only their financial contributions, but their active participation as well. The Atlanta Project hopes to "unite Atlanta as a community working to improve the quality of life in our neighborhoods."

If there is evidence that the different aspects of Atlanta's civil religious sensibility merge into a common identity with unified goals and purposes, there is also evidence that these different aspects are often in tension with one another. Atlanta's future-oriented, New South civic optimism often runs roughshod over its Old South history. There seems to be a willingness to bury its past under the new buildings and new opportunities that are springing up everywhere. Many residents admit that Atlanta is no longer really a southern city, and that it has lost its southern character in its drive toward the future. Seeing their historic inheritance disappear under skyscrapers and road projects, a few Atlantans have attempted to preserve some of the city's history. But it seems a lost cause in a city more concerned with its global future than with its regional past.

More importantly, Atlanta's swaggering self-promotion and overt optimism are often in tension with Dr. King's moral vision of the Beloved Community—enlightened self-interest is not always strong enough to hold the fraying edges of an unequal society together. The city that so proudly proclaims itself to be the fourth best city in the world for business, has also received embarrassing titles, such as being one of "America's worst cities for children." Julian Bond, an important Civil Rights leader, once said, "This is the best place (for blacks) in the United States if you're middle class and have a college degree, but if you're poor, it's just like Birmingham, Jackson or any other place." Atlanta, a city that claims it is among the most tolerant and cooperative cities in the nation, has recently been dubbed one of "America's most violent cities." The troubles that plague Atlanta are often set aside because Atlantans want to believe their own rhetoric. The Beloved Community is often ignored as Atlantans hurry toward the next project that will make Atlanta a world class city. The "city too busy to hate" could also become the city too busy to care.

All of this suggests that Atlanta's rich and diverse heritage sometimes creates tensions that place certain aspects of the city's identity in opposition to others. But there is also evidence that despite some problems, Atlantans often find creative and constructive ways to weave the various threads of the city's identity and history into a common vision and purpose. Atlanta is a city with a rich heritage that allows for creative growth coupled with often painful conflict. It is an exciting city that is both young and old, brash and thoughtful, both touched by tragedy and undaunted by it, driven by outright self-interest and tempered by true moral vision. It is a city that strides toward the future with an armful of dreams.

FOR FURTHER INFORMATION

Articles:

Andy Ambrose. "There's No Place Like Tara." *Atlanta History*, Fall, 1994

Timothy J. Crimmons and Dana F. White. "How Atlanta Grew." *Atlanta Economic Review*, January-February, 1978

Phyl Garland. "Atlanta: Black Mecca of the South." *Ebony*, August, 1971

Franklin M. Garrett. "The Phoenix Begins to Rise." *Atlanta History*, Winter, 1994

Peter Ross Range. "Making it in Atlanta: Capital of Black-is-Bountiful." *New York Times Magazine*. April 7, 1974

Lynn Watson-Powers. "The Atlanta Spirit: What Is It?" *Atlanta History*, Fall, 1993

Dana White. "The Black Side of Atlanta." *Atlanta Historical Society Journal*, Summer-Fall, 1982

Books:

Robert Bellah. *Beyond Belief*. Berkeley, University of California Press, 1970

W. Fitzhugh Brundage. *Lynching in the New South: Georgia and Virginia, 1880-1930*. Chicago, University of Illinois Press, 1993

Don H. Doyle. *New Men, New Cities, New South*. Chapel Hill, University of North Carolina Press, 1990

Webb Garrison. *The Legacy of Atlanta*. Atlanta, Peachtree Publishers, 1987

Charles Reagen Wilson. "God's Project: The Southern Civil Religion, 1920-1980." *Religion and the Life of the Nation*. Ed. Rowland Sherril, Chicago, University of Illinois Press, 1993

Charles Reagen Wilson. *Baptized in Blood: The Religion of the Lost Cause, 1865-1920*. Athens, University of Georgia Press, 1980

CHAPTER TWENTY-THREE

INTERFAITH CONVERSATION AND COOPERATION

Martha L. Moore-Keish

The Carter Presidential Center, home of the Interfaith Health Network. Photograph by Louis A. Ruprecht, Jr.

Several hundred people gather in a Christian church on a frosty January afternoon. They sing, pray, and attentively listen to a sermon. After the sermon ends, a prominent woman in the Jewish community rises to present the Martin Luther King, Sr. Minister's Community Service Award to a well-respected imam of a local mosque.

Several dozen teenagers with a number of distinct religious identities, including Muslim, Buddhist, Christian, Jewish, Bahá'í, and Hindu, gather at a camp in north Georgia for a week in the oppressive heat of July. They sing, talk, and argue about religion, politics, and sexuality. At the end of the week, they return to Atlanta with new friendships and new appreciation for the variety of religions in their city.

At the Emory School of Nursing, a group of women gather to learn how to improve the health of individuals in their religious communities through education and local activities. They talk about hypertension, cancer, teen pregnancy, child abuse, and AIDS as some of the most critical health issues for the people in their congregations. They also discuss various ways to address the problems of urban poverty. After many hours of training, they return to their own congregations with strategies for promoting good health and with new connections to members other faith communities who are facing similar challenges.

These are only a few of the many examples of interfaith conversation and cooperation that take place in metropolitan Atlanta. Some gatherings are public, some are private; some require months of preparation, others occur with little or no forethought. Many activities focus on a particular social issue or group of issues. Some grow out of the simple desire to understand each other. Regardless of the motivation behind these activities, all of them build connections among the diverse religious communities of Atlanta, so that churches, synagogues, mosques, temples, and other religious places of worship do not stand alone and isolated from one another. More and more faith groups are entering into dialogue and cooperation with each other, creating a network of religious persons who care about their common civic life and about increasing mutual understanding within Atlanta's religious communities.

HISTORICAL EXAMPLES OF INTERFAITH COOPERATION

When did Atlanta's religious communities first come together, either to talk with each other or to work toward common goals? The beginnings are difficult to pinpoint. Certainly there was ecumenical activity within the Christian community from the earliest days of the city. Indeed, the first house of worship to be built in Atlanta was a non-denominational building on Peachtree Street, used by several different congregations until they could construct separate churches. In 1847, the same year that this non-denominational building was constructed, the Atlanta Union Sabbath School was established, an organization that brought together various denominations of the city in the Sunday School movement. Through this and other ecumenical organizations, members of Christian denominations united to address issues of education, temperance, and health. The early cooperation of Roman Catholics, Methodists, Baptists, Episcopalians, and Presbyterians laid the foundation for later interaction between diverse religions in Atlanta.

While ecumenical relations among Christian churches in Atlanta began early in the city's history, the first organized interfaith interaction did not take place until well into the twentieth century. Although the presence of a strong Jewish community in Atlanta opened the door for Christian-Jewish activities as early as the 1860s, conversation and cooperation between these two religious groups did not occur on any significant scale until the 1930s and 1940s. With the rise of the Nazi Party in Germany and the eventual outbreak of World War II, many people in the Jewish community began to seek ways to promote more genuine understanding between themselves and the dominant Christian culture. At the same time, some of Atlanta's Christian leaders began to reach out to the city's Jewish community. In 1939, informal interaction found institutional expression with the establishment of a local chapter of the National Conference of Christians and Jews (NCCJ). The NCCJ focused on encouraging Christian-Jewish dialogue, but it also sponsored such interfaith programs as a cooperative effort to provide support for short-term inmates at the local jail. The establishment of this organization was followed by the founding of local chapters of the American Jewish Committee (1944) and the Anti-Defamation League (ca. 1945). Through these organizations, Atlanta's Jews entered vigorously into conversation with members of the Christian community, especially around issues of anti-Semitism and other forms of discrimination. From the creation of these organizations until the present day, Jews have been a driving force behind interfaith relations in Atlanta.

The Civil Rights movement of the late 1950s and 1960s marked a crucial turning point for interfaith activity in the Atlanta area. As Dr. Martin Luther King, Jr. gained national recognition with his vision of the Beloved Community, and as Atlanta promoted itself as "the city too busy to hate," religious people from a variety of communities came together to work for tolerance and the fair treatment of all persons. For example, in the 1960s the YMCA, the National Conference of Christians and Jews, and the Anti-Defamation League co-sponsored a program called "Operation Understanding," which brought high school students together to form friendships across racial lines. The sponsoring organizations hoped that if young people of different backgrounds learned to understand and respect one another, old prejudices and discriminatory practices might melt away. They hoped that, as these young individuals matured, Atlanta might grow into the very Beloved Community that Dr. King described.

A similar impulse inspired the television program *Sound of Youth*, which was broadcast by a local station beginning in 1966. Designed and hosted by John Allen, a Presbyterian minister, *Sound of Youth* brought together youth groups from various Christian and Jewish congregations in Atlanta to talk about racial concerns and other issues. Once a week for over a decade, this program worked to bring about greater understanding across religious and racial boundaries by giving young people a public forum for discussion.

Civic leaders in Atlanta during the Civil Rights era supported such interfaith efforts. Ivan Allen, Jr., mayor of the city from 1962 to 1970, together with business leaders such as Robert Woodruff of Coca-Cola, encouraged religious and racial cooperation because they knew that concrete examples of interaction between groups of people from diverse backgrounds could help prevent the kind of racial violence that disrupted so many other cities in the South. Sometimes publicly, sometimes behind the scenes, political and economic leaders sought to preserve Atlanta's image as "the city too busy to hate." With this encouragement, interfaith relations thrived as never before.

At the same time that religious groups were coming together to address the issue of race relations, interreligious conversation began to flourish in other areas as well. After the Second Vatican Council of 1962-1965, Roman Catholics in Atlanta as elsewhere were encouraged to interact with people of other faiths. In particular, Catholics and Jews in the city began to engage in dialogue around issues of mutual interest, including the Vatican's relationship with Israel. In the late 1960s, the American Jewish Committee and the

Atlanta Archdiocese cooperated on a study of Catholic textbooks—the first such study in the nation to include Jews. Over the years, relations between Jews and Catholics have grown in strength. Catholic-Jewish dialogue continues even today, with joint programs sponsored by the archdiocese and Jewish organizations, as well as with groups of Catholics and Jews who meet monthly to discuss topics and texts of interest and value to both groups.

In the past two decades, as the city has become an international hub of cultural and economic activity, Atlanta has witnessed a significant increase in religious diversity. People have come from all over the country and all over the globe, bringing with them their various religious practices and worldviews. This has both enriched and complicated interfaith activity. Interfaith efforts are no longer restricted to Christians and Jews; they now include Muslims, Buddhists, Hindus, Sikhs, and many, many others. Religious groups in Atlanta are no longer well-defined sets of people who gather once a week for a public act of worship led by one or more professional leaders. Rather, religious communities may be rigidly or quite loosely constituted; they may meet once a day, once a month, or once a year; they may engage in religious acts publicly or in private; and they may have a complex formal leadership structure or no specified leaders at all. As a result of this diversity, citizens of Atlanta are now having to confront their assumptions about what it means to be "religious," and they are rethinking how diverse groups can and ought to relate to one another. This kind of exploration is producing new sensitivity to the distinctiveness of each specific religious community as well as to the similar convictions or concerns that draw people of different traditions together.

The recent growth in religious pluralism has not only called into question old religious categories, it has also produced within religious communities two occasionally conflicting desires: the desire to preserve a group's particular identity and, at the same time, the desire for cooperation among religious groups. Some religious groups see interfaith involvement as either threatening or irrelevant. Others realize that an absence of interfaith cooperation would be a threat to the social cohesion of Atlanta. "If we cannot come together to discuss the social problems of our city," many wonder, "how can we adequately respond to issues such as homelessness, domestic violence, and the lack of proper health care for Atlanta's poorest citizens?"

Even with these difficulties and frustrations, however, the past two decades have seen a dramatic increase in interfaith activity in Atlanta. In a variety of settings, people are coming together to respond to particular issues and to learn more about the variety of religious communities in their city. Whether the emphasis is cooperation or conversation, the most vibrant interreligious efforts celebrate both the commonalities that unite, and the distinctive features that give texture to, Atlanta's religious landscape.

CONTEMPORARY EFFORTS

Current interfaith activities in Atlanta can be divided into two categories: 1) cooperative efforts to address particular social issues; and 2) conversations designed to deepen understanding among religious groups. Of course, these two categories are not mutually exclusive; many interfaith groups and events have a dual focus on cooperation and increased understanding. Indeed, some amount of mutual respect and understanding is clearly necessary before any interfaith work can be carried out. Willingness to learn from, and appreciate individuals with, different religious perspectives is the foundation of any interfaith work. In looking at the interreligious events and agencies in the Atlanta area, however, it is helpful to distinguish between those that are primarily oriented toward social issues and those whose central focus is religious dialogue.

Of the Atlanta organizations that emphasize interfaith cooperation, the majority focus on political and economic issues. One example of this kind of interfaith activity is the Atlanta Black/Jewish Coalition, initiated by the American Jewish Committee in 1982. It began as a group of black and Jewish leaders who lobbied in support of the Voting Rights Act of 1982, but under the leadership of founding co-chairs John R. Lewis and Cecil A. Alexander, the coalition quickly broadened its range of interests.

Since its inception, this group has lobbied for and responded to many specific issues on both a local and national scale. From 1983 to 1985, for instance, members of the coalition spoke out in support of the creation of a Martin Luther King, Jr. holiday in Georgia. Ever since the first celebration of that holiday in January 1986, the coalition has actively participated in its observance. Another issue that proved to be of vital importance to the coalition was the political struggle to end apartheid in South Africa. The group spoke out against apartheid as early as 1984, and coalition members urged Georgia's senators to support legislation limiting United States investment in South Africa. Since the release of Nelson Mandela and the ensuing political transformation of that country, the Black/Jewish Coalition has continued to hold discussions and symposia on South African democracy.

One particularly controversial topic for the coalition has been the rhetoric of Nation of Islam leader Louis Farrakhan. His anti-Semitic remarks during the 1984 presidential campaign prompted the coalition to hold a discussion and then release a statement at a press conference repudiating Farrakhan's language. In 1985 the group met with then Mayor Andrew Young to discuss Farrakhan and the future of black-Jewish relations. As recently as 1995, the coalition continued to discuss Farrakhan and the Nation of Islam, who hold out the positive message of black economic self-sufficiency and at the same time preach the destructive message of anti-Semitism. This issue, more than any other, has set the black and Jewish communities at loggerheads, and for that very reason the Atlanta Black/Jewish coalition has played a crucial role in helping to bring these communities together to discuss the Nation of Islam and formulate united responses to it.

Besides responding to particular political issues, the coalition has also planned several educational programs on black-Jewish relations. Starting in 1986, members of the coalition have held "teach-ins" on Martin Luther King, Jr. at local Jewish day schools during King Week in January. This has provided an opportunity for Jewish elementary students to learn more about King's life and teachings, as well as an opportunity for black and Jewish coalition members to work together with a team-teaching approach. The coalition has planned many joint activities for high school students from the National Association for the Advancement of Colored People (NAACP) and the B'nai B'rith Youth Organization. They have toured the King Center together, shared a Sabbath dinner, gone on weekend retreats, and had pool parties. The goal of all these activities has been to explore common ground, dissolve stereotypes, and build friendships between the two groups.

Finally, even though the primary focus of the Black/Jewish Coalition has been to respond to specific political and economic issues of concern, the group also seeks to promote mutual understanding more generally. One way the coalition has done this is by holding interfaith Passover seders. The first was held at the Temple in 1986, co-sponsored by the coalition and several other black and Jewish organizations. Rabbis Alvin Sugarman and Sam Weinstein, and Mayor Andrew Young shared leadership of the service. Since the seder celebrates the liberation of Jews from slavery in Egypt, it provides a perfect opportunity for blacks and Jews to reflect together on their similar histories. Through all of its various activities—political, educational, and liturgical—the Atlanta Black/Jewish Coalition both embodies and pursues interfaith cooperation. This is one example of vibrant interfaith activity in the Atlanta area.

Although most of the social issue-oriented Atlanta interfaith organizations focus on political and economic concerns, there are a number that specifically target health issues. One of these is Atlanta Interfaith Health (AIH) of the Carter Center. As the local focus of the center's Interfaith Health Project, AIH's mission is "to improve the health of communities through a congregation-based community approach." With an emphasis on health promotion, AIH began by forming interfaith health networks in two of the poorest neighborhoods in the city. In each network, ten to fifteen faith groups came together to form a Health Ministry Council to address the needs of their community. Each Health Ministry Council then selected a person to coordinate their efforts. These coordinators are paid by the Carter Center to oversee congregational and community health programs. In addition, each congregation in the network chose two volunteers to be trained as congregational health promoters. According to Tom Droege, the Associate Director of Interfaith Health, these health promoters have been trained by the Emory School of Nursing "to promote good health practices through programs of education and health activities, to administer a self-assessment tool for assessing health needs and priorities, to serve as advocates for persons needing health services by making appropriate referrals, and to assume primary responsibility for coordinating health programs in the congregation." Together, congregational health promoters, network coordinators, and the Health Ministry Councils are enhancing the abilities of religious communities to address chronic health problems in the most economically deprived sections of the city. Although AIH has but two networks at the moment, two more are soon to be established, thus doubling the scope of this agency's influence.

Another organization that addresses health concerns is the Atlanta Interfaith AIDS Network (AIAN). Founded in 1989, the network seeks to serve those living with and affected by HIV/AIDS. The 66 congregations that make up AIAN work within their own communities and in the greater Atlanta community to care for those living with AIDS. One example of AIAN's work is Common Ground, a comfortable day center on the first floor of a house in midtown Atlanta. Here people with HIV/AIDS who are still active but are no longer employed can gather every weekday. A typical day at Common Ground begins with meditation at 11:00. People drift into the living room from the front porch, the kitchen, the offices upstairs, and quietly take their seats in a circle. Eventually the program director settles into a chair, greets everyone by name, and updates them on those who are not present. Some of the news is sobering: "Lisa is still weak and in the hospital" or "Bob seemed very depressed and could not make it today." Other news is more hopeful: "John has turned a corner and hopes to be back with us next week." After the announcements, the director leads the group in some relaxation exercises, and then he reads from a book. The participants—volunteers, visitors, and regulars alike—reflect together on what the reading means to them. People come in and out, but the conversation continues. About noon, the director draws the discussion to a close, and everyone stands and joins hands for a prayer. Then the group moves into the next room, where members of a local congregation have prepared lunch. After the meal, some leave and everyone else goes back into the living room, to paint, draw, talk together, or write poetry.

This center provides a community and a caring place for people to visit during weekdays. But many who are affected by AIDS have other needs that Common Ground cannot address. For such needs the AIAN has established Faithful Care, a program that facilitates volunteer teams to provide nurturing and practical support for those with AIDS around the metropolitan area. Each congregation in the network may choose to establish a care team to serve those with AIDS in their area. Deb Johnson, the director of Faithful Care, organizes training events for care teams so they can learn how to respond sensitively to the needs of those with AIDS. Care teams may drive an AIDS patient to a doctor's appointment or provide company for someone at home who can neither afford a professional caretaker nor stay home alone.

Still another activity of the AIAN is the annual Interfaith Service of Hope and Healing, which draws people together to seek new vision in the midst of the AIDS epidemic. These services have been held since AIAN's inception in 1989, and they incorporate liturgical elements from a variety of religious traditions. The sounding of the shofar from the Jewish tradition, anointing with oil according to the Christian tradition, and sacred dance from African traditional religion have all been part of AIAN's interfaith services in recent years. All of the programs of the AIAN draw on the resources of a variety of religious communities to serve people from all over the Atlanta area who struggle with AIDS.

Other kinds of interfaith activity in Atlanta are focused less on social issues and more on increasing mutual understanding between various religious groups. One example of dialogue-oriented interfaith activity is Anytown, Georgia, a summer youth camp sponsored by the National Conference of Christians and Jews (NCCJ). For one week each year the NCCJ rents a camp in northern Georgia and brings about 45 teenagers from Atlanta to learn more about their own and each other's religious traditions. The campers come from Islamic, Hindu, Buddhist, Jewish, Christian, and other traditions, and many are recent immigrants to the United States. According to Jimmy Harper, the regional director of the NCCJ, Anytown has two goals: to help the youth make friends, and to help break down their stereotypes about people of other religions and cultures.

The camp tries to accomplish its goals in a variety of ways. For instance, the planners of Anytown recruit staff members who will represent all the religious traditions of the campers themselves. Thus a Muslim youth attending the camp ought to be able to speak with a Muslim staff person about religious issues. If no such staff person is available, there is at least someone who is familiar with the camper's religious background and can respond helpfully to his or her concerns.

To help campers understand their own religious traditions better, they spend part of their time at Anytown in groups with others who come from the same religious community. In these gatherings, they can explore what it means to be, for instance, a Hindu or a Sikh in the context of a religiously plural society. At the end of the week, each group has an opportunity to make a presentation about their conclusions to the camp as a whole. In this way, campers learn more about their own traditions as well as how they relate to others within these traditions.

A significant part of the time at Anytown focuses on "prejudice reduction." This begins on Monday morning, when Jimmy Harper and other staff members lead a seminar on the "nuts and bolts of prejudice." This, however, is the last such formal teaching activity of the week. Despite its imposing title, prejudice reduction at the camp consists mostly of games and role-playing activities designed to help the youth move beyond stereotypes by having fun together. In one such activity, camp staff set up a "talk show" in which four couples of different races and socioeconomic backgrounds all want to adopt a particular baby. The audience asks questions of each of the couples, prompting discussion about such issues as "Does it matter whether the race of the parents is the same as the race of the child?" and "Can wealthy parents provide better care than parents with limited income?" After many such exercises, the young participants begin to realize that their preconceived notions of certain groups may be inappropriate and that they can change their behavior toward others. At the end of the week, the participants return to their respective families, neighborhoods, and schools, with—the camp staff hopes—a broader vision of the religious and cultural diversity that is a part of daily life in Atlanta.

Another example of dialogue-oriented activity is the Interfaith Coalition of Metropolitan Atlanta. Founded in 1992 under the auspices of the Georgia Human Relations Commission, it is one of the most recently established interfaith organizations in the city. Its 44 members include representatives from most of the religious communities in Atlanta, including the Atlanta Masjid of Al-Islam, the Sikh Study Circle, the Indian American Cultural Association, The Eternal Quest, and Christians and Jews from various temples and churches. Their four-point mission statement clearly articulates their purpose as an organization:

> As a people of faith recognizing the richness of the religious diversity within our community, the Interfaith Coalition of Metropolitan Atlanta provides moral leadership
>
> —to broaden among all persons awareness and appreciation of our similarities
> —and differences
> —to promote interfaith dialogue
> —to create opportunities for consciousness raising, and
> —to advocate for peace and justice for all.

In 1994, as part of its effort to promote interfaith awareness and dialogue, the Interfaith Coalition published a booklet called *Common Threads: Faith Perspectives on Social Justice*. This collection of excerpts from the sacred writings of various traditions addresses such topics as the sacredness of life, interpersonal relations, economic justice, and religious freedom. Although the different religious writings do not agree on every point, *Common Threads* does highlight some of the places of agreement among the various traditions. As Swami Yogeshananda says in the conclusion of the booklet, "we see how the various faiths have, in their teachings, put common stress on those elements and features of human behavior that enable us to relate, one to another, in peace, justice, amity, and mutual self-interest."

CONCLUSION

The multitude of religious communities in Atlanta intersect in a variety of ways. The Black/Jewish Coalition, the Atlanta Interfaith AIDS Network, the NCCJ's Anytown, Georgia, and the Interfaith Coalition are but four examples of the interfaith efforts going on in the metropolitan area. In spite of all the cooperation and conversation that occurs, some religious leaders express frustration with the absence of substantive interreligious activity in Atlanta today. How is this possible?

Part of the answer is that Atlanta's current interfaith efforts are decentralized. Unlike the focused public network of religious leaders that was in place in earlier decades, the leadership now is more diffuse and focused on a variety of issues. For instance, the people who are on the Interfaith Coalition are not the same people as those on the board of the AIAN, and none of them may know the leadership from the Interfaith Health Project of the Carter Center. Participants in interreligious programs are even less likely than the leadership to be aware of other such activities in the city. This decentralization is perhaps inevitable in a city as large and diverse as Atlanta. Nevertheless, it can give the impression that there is not a significant amount of interfaith activity going on.

Another reason people may perceive a lack of interfaith interaction is that many of Atlanta's religious communities are new to the city, and links between religious groups have yet to be forged. This is further complicated by the fact that some of the newer religious communities in Atlanta function with different leadership structures than those of Christians and Jews. Thus, if someone from a Christian church wants to initiate a series of conversations with a representative of the Hindu community, for example, there is no public hierarchy of leaders to contact for information about possible speakers. Meanwhile, the Hindu community, for their part, may be more involved at present in building their temple and establishing their particular cultural identity than in seeking substantive relationships with other religious groups. In this way, the difference in leadership structure itself may inhibit some interaction between religious groups.

The interfaith connections among Atlanta's religious communities may indeed be limited, but they are growing. The Atlanta Interfaith AIDS Network is actively seeking Muslim involvement. The Carter Center's Interfaith Health Project is at the time of this writing about to open a new cluster in the Buford Highway corridor, which they hope will involve the religious communities of some of Atlanta's more recent Asian and Hispanic immigrants. As a result of the 1996 Olympic Games, the Atlanta Committee for the Olympic Games has sought out members from all of Atlanta's religious communities for its Interfaith Advisory Group, a committee whose mission will end with the closing ceremonies of the 1996 Games, but whose relationships will continue long after the athletes have left the city.

As the network of connections among religious communities continues to expand, interfaith activity appears in an increasing variety of forms. Sometimes it is a gathering of several hundred people at a public meeting, sometimes it is a handful of women praying together; in some places people of faith come together to address a particular political, economic, or health issue, while in other places they gather to seek mutual understanding. In all of these forms, interfaith relationships represent a movement toward the dream of one of Atlanta's favorite sons. As Bob Hudak, director of the Atlanta Interfaith AIDS Network, says, "King's vision of the `Beloved Community' is alive here. We engage in interfaith efforts with care, courage, and the conviction that we are sons and daughters of God, all one family and keepers of one another."

We do not yet live in the Beloved Community, but Dr. King's vision continues to empower people today to reach out across religious boundaries, to work with and learn from those who are different from themselves. Muslim and Jew, Buddhist and Christian, Native American and Bahá'í, Hindu and Sikh—gradually people of all religious stripes are realizing that they are not the only religious groups in Atlanta, and that none of them can build the city alone. For better or for worse, we find all of our particular communities woven together into the larger civic community that we call home. If this city, with all of its troubles and all of its hopes, does become a united community, it will happen because people of faith have summoned the courage to reach out to one another in mutual respect to work for a common dream. "If you reach out," says Sunny Stern, assistant area director of the American Jewish Committee, "there are a whole lot of hands reaching back." Across the metropolitan area today, in family rooms, temples, office buildings, and public parks, people are joining hands in interfaith cooperation and conversation, inspired by a variety of visions but pursuing a shared dream of a city in which all people can live together in safety, in comfort, and in peace.

FOR FURTHER INFORMATION

Common Threads: Faith Perspectives on Social Justice. Compiled by the Interfaith Coalition of Metropolitan Atlanta, October, 1994

CONTRIBUTORS

F. Douglas Alexander is a graduate student at Emory University, working on a doctorate in political science. His research focuses on the role of race, ethnicity, and the mass media in political behavior.

Victor Balaban is a graduate student in the Department of Psychology at Emory University. He is planning an ethnographic study of the apparition site at Conyers that also utilizes cognitive approaches to the study of religion.

Timothy Allen Beach-Verhey has a Masters of Divinity from Union Theological Seminary in Virginia. He is presently a doctoral student at Emory University studying in the Ethics and Society department of the Graduate Division of Religion.

Ajit Bhatia, a native of India, has served on the Executive Committee of the India American Cultural Association as its financial officer. He received a Masters degree in business from the University of North Carolina at Greensboro and has taught courses on marketing strategy and organizational behavior. He is presently managing product marketing initiatives for a telecommunications company in Chicago, Illinois.

Renee Bhatia received her Masters of Divinity degree from Candler School of Theology, Emory University. She has studied and participated in interfaith dialogues, especially between Hindus and Christians. She is currently a Consultant for Religious Education in the Catholic Archdiocese of Chicago, Illinois.

Helen Blier is a doctoral candidate in the Graduate Division of Religion at Emory University. Her primary area of study is religious education, with related interests in faith stories and development, diversity issues, and epistemology. She approaches her study of Catholic communities as both a researcher and an active member.

Theodore Brelsford is finishing his PhD in the Theology and Personality department in the Graduate Division of Religion at Emory University. His research interests include issues of cultural diversity in religious communities, epistemology, religious imagination, postmodern faith and identity,and religion and education.

Angela Cotten is a graduate student in the Institute of Liberal Arts at Emory University. Her areas of research and writing are poststructuralism, postmodernism, queer and women's studies, and black feminist history.

Nancy L. Eiesland is an assistant professor of Sociology of Religion at Candler School of Theology at Emory University. Her work on exurban religious change in Atlanta is forthcoming from Rutgers University Press.

Doris H. Goldstein is a free-lance writer whose special interest is historical writing about Atlanta and its Jewish community. She is the author of *From Generation to Generation*, a centennial volume of the Ahavath Achim Congregation, coauthor of *The Jews of Atlanta: 150 Years of Creating Community*, soon to be published by the Wm. Breman Jewish Heritage Center, as well as other articles on this and other subjects.

Edward R. Gray is studying the moral languages and logics of civil and religious institutions rebuilding from natural catastrophes. His other interests include religion in the public sphere, and the influence of regional subcultures and social structures, particularly in the American west, on popular and institutional forms of religious belief and practice.

Gregory S. Gray teaches in the Department of Philosophy and Religion at Morehouse College in Atlanta. He is a PhD candidate in the Institute of Liberal Arts at Emory University, and an assistant minister at Friendship Baptist Church in Atlanta.

Gary Laderman is an assistant professor in the Department of Religion and the Graduate Division of Religion at Emory University. His study of attitudes toward death in nineteenth-century America will be published by Yale University Press.

Kristin Marsh is a graduate student at Emory University working on a doctorate in Sociology.

Mike McMullen received his PhD in sociology at Emory University. He is presently assistant professor of Sociology at the University of Houston-Clear Lake, Texas. He continues to do research on the Bahá'í community as well as in organizational sociology.

Keith E. McNeal is a National Science Foundation Predoctoral Fellow and a graduate student in the Department of Anthropology at Emory University. His main interests are religion, human development, moral and gender socialization, and cognitive psychodynamics in cultural perspective. He is planning a study focused on children and their culturally constituted development.

Martha L. Moore-Keish is a graduate student in the Graduate Division of Religion at Emory University working on a doctorate in theology. She has previously studied at Harvard College, Visva-Bharati University in West Bengal, and Union Theological Seminary in Virginia.

Janice Morrill has conducted research with Atlanta's recent immigrant communities since 1988 and has produced several articles and exhibitions on the topic. She holds a Masters degree in folklore from the University of North Carolina at Chapel Hill and a Bachelors in anthropology from the University of California, Los Angeles.

Mark Padilla is a doctoral student in the Department of Anthropology at Emory University. His graduate research is funded by the National Science Foundation. His interests include Latin American ethnicity, economic development, and the Gay Civil Rights movement. He is currently undertaking a project on gay and lesbian interracial relationships in the United States.

Barbara A. B. Patterson is an assistant professor in the Department of Religion at Emory University. Her degrees are from Smith College, Harvard University, and Emory. Trained as an interdisciplinarian, she studies how categories and discourses of embodiment reflect the interplay of culture and religion. She is also particularly interested in women's spiritual practices.

Eric Riles is a graduate student in the Department of Sociology at Emory University. His areas of interest include organizations, mass media, stratification, and religion and culture.

Louis A. Ruprecht, Jr. received his doctoral degree from the Graduate Division of Religion at Emory University, where he has been teaching in the departments of Religion and Classics. His first book, *Tragic Posture and Tragic Vision: Against the Modern Failure of Nerve* (Continuum Press, 1994) received an award from the conference on Christianity and Literature at the Modern Language Association's annual meeting in 1995. His second book, *Afterwords: Hellenism, Modernism and the Myth of Decadence* (SUNY Press) has just been published.

Paige Schneider is a PhD candidate in the Department of Political Science at Emory University. She conducts research and teaches in the field of religion and politics, women and politics, and American political institutions.

Theophus H. Smith is an associate professor of Religion, Department of Religion, Emory University. He is the author of *Conjuring Culture: Biblical Formations of Black America* (Oxford University Press, 1994) and coeditor with Mark Wallace of *Curing Violence* (Polebridge, 1994). Professor Smith also directs the Atlanta chapter of the National Coalition Building Institute (Washington, DC) in presenting its celebrated "Prejudice Reduction Workshops."

Scott Lee Thumma is a doctoral candidate in the Graduate Division of Religion at Emory University. His research interests include the sociology of religion, American religious history, sociology of homosexuality, and social psychology.